SACRAMENTAL FORGIVENESS AS A GIFT OF GOD

THOMAS AQUINAS ON THE SACRAMENT OF PENANCE

Eric Luijten

SACRAMENTAL FORGIVENESS AS A GIFT OF GOD

THOMAS AQUINAS ON THE SACRAMENT OF PENANCE

PEETERS
LEUVEN
2003

© Stichting Thomasfonds - Nijmegen
ISBN 90-429-1305-3
D. 2003/0602/59

This publication is published with the financial support of (a.o.) the Stichting
Thomasfonds at Nijmegen, the Stichting Sormanifonds, the Catholic
Theological University at Utrecht, the archdiocese of Utrecht.

Table of Contents

Introduction

In the Netherlands, the practice of regular confession disappeared almost completely in the course of no more than a decade, between 1960 and 1970. Ruys explains that the first group to stay away from the confessional was the group of parents whose children were about to make their first Communion. After having had two or three children, these parents wanted to leave it at that. This led to painful situations in the confessionals on the Saturday evening before the celebration of first Communion. Within a few years, children were no longer taught to go to confession, for as Ruys puts it: "You cannot teach children what their parents have dismissed". Soon, the elderly generation stopped going to confession as well, which was strange, because they, in contrast to the younger generations, kept going to church.[1] Currently, in the majority of Dutch churches, the confessionals are used for the storage of chairs or brooms, mops and buckets.

According to Ruys, the disappearance of the practice of confession in the Netherlands was contemporaneous with the completion of the emancipation of the Catholic part of the Dutch nation, and the changed societal and ecclesial relations after the Second World War.[2] The reformation of the sacrament of penance, called for by the Second Vatican Council (1962-1965)[3], and worked out in the new *Ordo paenitentiae* (promulgated 1973), did not prevent the sacrament of reconciliation (as it is preferably called today) as an important encounter with Christ dying out for most Catholics.[4]

Many reasons have been given for this crisis in the sacrament of penance. Some blame the changing times, indicated by such terms as individualism and secularism in which people are less conscious of notions like sin, guilt and the need for forgiveness, or have difficulty in taking full responsibility for their actions. Others refer to the emancipation of lay Catholics, who no longer accept church leaders telling them what to think, what to believe and how to act.

With respect to the sacrament itself, we can distinguish between reasons regarding its form and reasons regarding its content. With respect to the content of the sacrament of penance, we can refer to the legalistic and impersonal conceptions of sin and forgiveness which dominated the theology of penance until the first half of the twentieth century. According to these conceptions, sin was primarily understood as transgression of an impersonal law, and forgiveness primarily in terms of acquittal. Most Catholics today, especially the young, fail to see the relevance to their lives of confessing a memorized 'grocery list' of sins.

---

1   Th. Ruys, "De E-8. Mijmeringen langs de snelweg", in: *Een lange adem. Opstellen over kerk en beleid in het aartsbisdom Utrecht*, 1993, pp.46-47.
2   *Idem*, pp.47-48.
3   *Sacrosanctum concilium*, nr.72.
4   G. Maloney, *Your Sins are forgiven you. Rediscovering the sacrament of reconciliation*, 1999 (1996), p.2.

In this dissertation, we will not deal with the question of the content insofar as it belongs to the field of moral theology. Instead, we will deal with sin and forgiveness from the perspective of dogmatic theology. One of the problems of the sacrament of penance today is that a genuine understanding of what is under discussion in the sacrament of penance is lacking. The aim of the new rite of the sacrament of penance was to make it more ecclesial and more personal. However, the implementation of the new rite was not followed by an effective catechesis, and consequently, many still understand notions like sin, guilt, forgiveness etc., in impersonal and legalistic terms.

Other reasons for the crisis of the sacrament of penance lie in its form. In particular, some blame the crisis on the way the sacrament of penance is celebrated. The new rite of 1973 provides for three sacramental ways in which the sacrament can be celebrated. The first form is the celebration with individual confession and absolution; the second is the communal celebration with individual confession and absolution, the third is the communal celebration with general confession and absolution. The latter, however, is only allowed under exceptional circumstances, and does not exempt one from the obligation to confess individually when possible at a later time.[5] Some hope and believe that this third form will eventually be recognized as the "ordinary" way of receiving the sacrament of reconciliation.[6] Others argue that the crisis of the sacrament of penance is, in fact, a result of there being only one form of celebrating it, i.e. the first form.[7] We will, however, not deal with the question of form insofar as it belongs to the study of liturgy. Instead, in this dissertation we will be dealing with the question of the sacramentality of the sacrament of penance. For not only is there a problem in the lack of a genuine understanding of notions like sin, guilt and forgiveness; a genuine understanding of sacramentality is also missing. How many Catholics today understand the difference between the three sacramental forms and the fourth, non-sacramental form provided for in the new *Ordo paenitentiae*?[8]

The crisis of the sacrament of penance today, and the different reasons for it which have been brought to the fore, form the background against which we will study Thomas' theology of the sacrament of penance. This subject is given

---

5   Cf. *CIC*, can. 961-963. For an examination of the third form, cf. R. Merz, *Die Generalabsolution als auserordentliche Spendeweise des Busssakramentes: Herkunft, Ortsbestimmung, Grenzen*, 1992.

6   So G. Maloney, *Your sins*, p.97.

7   So K. Koch, "Die eine Botschaft von der Versöhnung im vielfältigen Wandel des Busssakramentes", in J. Müller (hrsg), *Das ungeliebte Sakrament*, p.95: "Diese diagnose kann dabei nur lauten, dass die gegenwärtige Krise des Busssakramentes eigentlich und im tiefsten eine Krise der Einzelbeichte und damit *einer* Form des Bussakraments ist."

8   In the new *Ordo paenitentiae* of 1973, three sacramental forms are distinguished: the celebration of the sacrament of penance with individual confession and absolution (Form A), the communal celebration of penance, with individual confession and absolution (Form B), and the communal celebration with general confession and absolution (Form C). (Cf. R. Messner, *Feiern*, p.219-226) In an appendix (II) to the *Ordo paenitentiae*, the new liturgical form of communal celebrations of penance is presented, which is clearly distinguished from the celebrations of the sacrament of penance (*Idem*, p.226).

shape by the question of the role of the Holy Spirit with respect to the forgiveness of sins in the sacrament of penance in the theology of Thomas Aquinas (1224/5-1274).

With respect to the middle terms of this question: forgiveness of sins and sacrament of penance, we expect that reflection on them will yield insight into our relationship with God. In the way in which God forgives us our sins, and reconciles us with him, we expect to learn much about who God is. In fact, this is not only true of the relationship between God and man, but of all personal relationships. Where two persons fight and make up, they not only grow in understanding for each other (and for themselves), but they usually also grow in their affection for each other. Focusing on divine forgiveness provides an excellent opportunity to learn about God, and about ourselves in relation to God.[9] In Catholic tradition, nowhere does our relationship with God become more concrete, or even tangible, as it does in the sacraments. For this reason, the sacraments, and the sacrament of penance in particular, will provide an excellent field for the examination of our relationship with God.

With respect to the theology of Thomas, earlier studies have shown how theological, how biblical and how linguistic his theology in fact is. Thomas' theology is theological in the sense that it concentrates on God and all things in relation to God. Furthermore, despite the fact that in modern, and even recent times, this concentration on God has been understood in philosophical terms, nevertheless we proceed from the presupposition that at the center of Thomas' attention stands God, who has revealed himself in Scripture as Creator of all. This has profound methodological consequences, for as Creator of all, God himself is not part of the universe, and so, in a unique way, is distinguished from all there is. Since language – which is the most important instrument of any theologian – has evolved during its use within the boundaries of all there is, it consequently fails to describe God in a perfect way. Throughout his works, Thomas is constantly aware of the shortcomings of language vis-à-vis God, and in this dissertation we will see this to be also true for the sections of his works which we study.

As we will see, the emphasis on language in Thomas' theology is the direct result of the fact that we do not know God as He is in himself. However, we must not misunderstand this as opening the door to irrationality or vagueness. That we cannot know God as He is in himself does not mean that we are free to say whatever we like about him. As Sokolowksi says, Christian faith is said to be in accordance with reason, and yet to go beyond reason.[10] Both aspects are present in Thomas' theology. At times, his analyses are highly rational and his approach to the mysteries of faith very systematic. However, in Thomas' theology, system and reason are not goals in themselves. As we will show, in the more technical section on grammar in Chapter Three, for instance, his

---

9   Cf. R. Haight, "Sin and grace", in F. Schüssler Fiorenza, J. Galvin (eds), *Systematic theology. Roman Catholic perspectives*, vol. 2, pp.75-141. According to Haight, "(t)he doctrines of sin and grace define an anthropology, a Christian conception of human existence." (p.78).
10   R. Sokolowski, *The God of faith and reason. Foundations of Christian theology*, 1982, p.xi.

rationality is not aimed at subjecting the mystery of God to the demands of reason, but rather at safeguarding the mystery itself.

In this dissertation, we will concentrate on the role of the Holy Spirit. By doing so, our research joins in with recent new attention for the doctrine of the triune God. In this new attention, however, the theology of the sacraments does not play a significant role. Research into the role of the Holy Spirit in the sacrament of penance has hardly been conducted yet.[11]

Thomas' reflections on the Holy Trinity are also motivated by his concentration on the biblical God. In Scripture, God has revealed himself as Father, Son and Spirit. Consequently, the God that is at the center of Thomas' thought is the Trinitarian God. As we will see, however, this claim is not undisputed. Together with Augustine, Thomas is blamed for the loss of a theology of the Holy Trinity which is relevant for the church. Nevertheless, if the sacrament of penance provides a special moment in the relationship between God and man, then the reflection on the role of the Holy Spirit in this sacrament may yield insight into the relationship in a Trinitarian perspective. What does it mean that the One with whom we are in a relationship of love is a relationship of love himself?

We will begin this dissertation by calling attention to the hermeneutic distance that lies between Thomas and us. Thomas lived and worked more that seven centuries ago. Drawing attention to the historical distance between Thomas and us does not necessarily imply that this dissertation is going to be historical. However, it is necessary for the systematic evaluation of what Thomas says to realize that some of the questions we ask in our times Thomas asks differently, or not at all, and vice versa. As a result, it is not simple to derive answers to our questions from Thomas' theology. But investigating those questions which Thomas does ask himself, or how he asks questions, can draw attention to blind spots in our own reflections, and to the questions which we, today, have forgotten to ask.

On occasion, we will present the reader with historical reflections, which will serve to make him aware of the historical distance between the time Thomas lived and worked, and our times. In this introduction, we have called attention to the current situation concerning the sacrament of penance, the crisis it is in, and the reasons that are given for this crisis. Chapter One begins with a section in which the development of the sacrament of penance is sketched, starting from its early form as public or canonical penance, via private confession, to the sacrament of penance in the twelfth century. Since then it has, in the main, kept its structure until today. It is important to see that Thomas lived and worked at the time of the culmination of the development of the sacrament of penance (and of the notion of sacramentality in general).

---

[11] Cf. L. Lies, "Trinitätsvergessenheit gegenwärtiger Sakramententheologie?", in *Zeitschrift für katholische Theologie* 105 (1983), pp.290-314, 415-429.

Chapters Two and Four deal, respectively, with the forgiveness of sins and the sacrament of penance. We will begin both chapters by paying attention to a question that is asked in our times, and in both chapters we will see that Thomas asks the question differently. Chapter Five, which deals with the church, is motivated by the recent changes in the rite of the sacrament of penance, which aim to bring out more clearly the ecclesial character of the sacrament.

The first chapter has an introductory character. After we have examined the historical development of the sacrament of penance, we will deal with some difficulties concerning the sacrament of penance in Thomas' theology. The first difficulty is that we cannot simply refer to the treatise on the sacrament of penance in the *Summa theologiae*, Thomas most mature work, because it is unfinished. The second is that the subject of this dissertation covers a wide range of fields of theology and is consequently complex. One of the difficulties we encountered during our work was that of how to organize all the material. In the last section of Chapter One, we will deal with this question and develop a framework.

The structure of rest of this dissertation is formed by the distinction between internal and external penance. The division between internal and external, between virtue and sacrament, dominates Thomas' treatment of penance, in particular in the *Scriptum super Sententiis*. Furthermore, it characterizes the nature of the sacraments, for they are visible signs of invisible grace, and in penance the external sacrament of penance is a sign of the internal penance, the contrition or remorse for sins committed, which – as we will see – marks the beginning of the forgiveness of sins. The resulting plan for the remaining chapters consists of two chapters on what could be called the *res significata*, the 'thing' signified by the sacrament of penance, i.e. the forgiveness of sins. Of these, Chapter Two is dedicated to the forgiveness of sins as such, whereas Chapter Three is about the role of the Holy Spirit. The underlying thought is that forgiveness of sins in Thomas' theology is about the restoration of the relationship of grace, which, in the last section of Chapter Two, will be discussed with reference to his technical term, 'justification' of the godless (Chapter Two). On a more fundamental level, this restoration of the relationship of grace is understood in terms of a renewed presence or indwelling of the Holy Spirit in the hearts of men (Chapter Three).

Once we have discussed the *res significata*, we will examine the sign itself, i.e. the sacrament of penance, in Chapter Four, and its ecclesial character in Chapter Five. In these chapters we will discuss, at great length, how Thomas understands the active role of the sacrament of penance (and sacraments in the context of the church in general) in 'causing' the grace of divine forgiveness.

Within this layout, Chapter Three forms the heart and center of this dissertation. It is in this chapter that we will formulate an answer to the question of how Thomas understands the role of the Holy Spirit with respect to the forgiveness of sins. Given this answer, in the subsequent chapters we will examine the need and nature of *sacramental* forgiveness.

Chapter 1 Penance

Introduction

The main purpose of this chapter is to deal with a number of difficulties regarding the subject of this book, in order to clear the way for the following chapters. Such an introductory chapter is necessary mainly because of the complexity of the subject: Thomas' theology of the sacrament of penance. This complexity consists in several issues. First, Thomas' theology of the sacrament of penance is complex because of the many different types of language, images and metaphors he uses. This is the result of the fact that Thomas provides a digest of a period of more than a thousand years of reflection on penance, during which penance and the notion of sacrament itself underwent some considerable changes. This makes an historical overview of the development of penance from the early church up to the thirteenth century imperative. Such an overview shows how notions such as guilt and forgiveness, tariff, reward and punishment, medicine and illness, reconciliation and absolution, penitence and satisfaction function within a theology of (the sacrament of) penance, and consequently provides us with a hermeneutical background for understanding these notions in the theology of Thomas.

The second issue results from the fact that we cannot simply refer to the *Summa theologiae*, Thomas' major work, for his theology of the sacrament of penance. The reason for this is that Thomas stopped writing his treatise on the sacrament of penance after dealing with about a quarter of the number of questions that he had planned. This presents us with the questions of how to use the *Summa* and how to involve other works by Thomas. We will deal with these questions in the second section of this chapter, as part of the more general question of how the different works in which Thomas reflects on the sacrament of penance contribute to our understanding of his theology of the sacrament of penance.

Finally, the subject of this dissertation itself, i.e. forgiveness in the sacrament of penance, is complex because it concerns different fields of theology, e.g. the theology of the sacraments, the treatment of penance, and the doctrine of justification. It becomes even more complicated because the question that is central to this dissertation is about the role of the Holy Spirit with respect to sacramental forgiveness. This complexity presents us with the question of how to organize our material. For this reason, in the third section, we will try to devise a framework within which we can organize the different themes that must be dealt with in order to find an answer to our question. This framework will structure the remaining chapters of this dissertation.

1 Historical background[1]

Introduction

What was the form of the sacrament of penance on which Thomas reflected? As we will see, the sacrament of penance underwent considerable changes during the first twelve centuries.[2] The sacrament on which Thomas reflected differed in many respects from earlier forms of penance, i.e. the public penance of the early church and the penitential practice of the early Middle Ages. By the time Thomas lived and worked, the sacrament of penance had received the form it has maintained for the last seven centuries.

In this section, we will investigate how the sacrament of penance developed over the centuries. We will explain that the development of the sacrament of penance has not been linear. We will see that the sacrament of penance did not evolve from the public or canonical penance of the early church, but from the practice of private confession which originated in the monasteries of Ireland, England and Scotland. During this evolution, the sacrament of penance received its explicit sacramental character when it replaced the old canonical penance as the official ecclesial way of dealing with those among the church community who, by sinning, had separated themselves from the community and from God.

The resulting sacrament of penance is a complex phenomenon as it contains elements of both public penance and private confession. These elements determine the function of the sacrament of penance within the ecclesial structure, the way it is celebrated, and the language and metaphors with which it is described and understood. The function of the sacrament of penance within the ecclesial structure is referred to by the patristic notion of *paenitentia secunda*.[3] The *paenitentia secunda* may be defined as the official church practice or rite whereby she, under certain conditions, readmits those who have lapsed into grave sin after having been baptized.

---

[1] On the history of the sacrament of penance: C. Vogel, *Le pécheur et la pénitence dans l'église ancienne*, 1966; C. Vogel, *Le pécheur et la pénitence au Moyen-Age*, 1969; B. Poschmann, *Busse und Letzte Ölung (Handbuch der Dogmengeschichte* IV, 3), 1951; H. Vorgrimler, *Buße und Krankensalbung (Handbuch der Dogmengeschichte* IV, 3), 1978; J. Mahoney, *The making of moral theology. A study of the Roman Catholic tradition*, 1987, Ch. I "The Influence of auricular confession"; J.T. McNeill, H.M. Gamer, *Medieval handbooks of penance. A Translation of the principal* Libri Poenitentiales, 1990; R. Messner, *Feiern der Umkehr und Versöhnung (Handbuch der Liturgiewissenschaft* 7,2), 1992; G. Rouwhorst, "De viering van bekering en verzoening", in *Tijdschrift voor liturgie* 81, 1997, pp.29-42.

[2] Cf. K. Rahner, "Beichtprobleme", in *Schriften zur theologie* III, 1956, p.228: "Der hl. Joseph hat nun einmal nicht den ersten Beichtstuhl gezimmert. Es gab viele Jahrhunderte ohne Andachtsbeichte. Ein Augustinus hat nie gebeichtet."

[3] Cf. the title of chapter 26 of R. Messner's *Feiern der Umkehr*: "Paenitentia secunda" as opposed to "Paenitentia quotidiana" (ch. 25), which refers to the forgiving strength of the Eucharist, of the Word of God, of the divine office, of Lent and of the general absolution (not understood as sacrament, p.82: "Die Generalabsolution wurde als ein Mittel zur Tilgung lässlicher Sünden angesehen, das ex opere operantis, nicht aber wie das 'Busssakrament' ex opere operato wirkt").

As baptism is understood to be the first penance, the way to be reconciled again after having committed a grave sin is called the second penance.[4] The *paenitentia secunda* was, and still is, reserved for Christians, i.e. for those who are baptized.[5] The *paenitentia secunda* originated in the early Church in order to deal with grave sinners. Acts which qualify as grave or deadly sins have changed over the centuries. Formally, grave or deadly sins were, and still are, understood to be acts which separate the sinner from the church and the grace of God. Separation from the church and from the grace of God implies exclusion from participation in Holy Communion. Hence, the *paenitentia secunda* has the function, in the sacramental order, of re-admitting the sinner to the table of the Eucharist. Furthermore, in the *paenitentia secunda*, a representative of the church community is involved in accepting the penitent into the *paenitentia secunda*. He alone hears confession, determines the duration and severity of the penance, and re-admits the penitent by an act of reconciliation or absolution. The authority to do so is related to the keys of the kingdom of heaven (cf. Mt. 16, 19). Finally, the reconciliation or absolution proclaimed by the church is understood to be some sort of guarantee or announcement that God's mercy has been bestowed upon the penitent, and that the bond of grace is restored. During its evolution from private confession[6], the sacrament of penance came to replace the canonical penance precisely as *paenitentia secunda*.[7]

The sacrament of penance contains, as it did in Thomas' times and still does today, traces of both the canonical penance it replaced, and the private confession from which it evolved. For instance, the sacrament of penance shares with the old canonical penance its strong relationship with the sacrament of the Eucharist, while also sharing the emphasis on secrecy belonging to private confession. At the same time it contains new elements in comparison with the two earlier forms of penance. For instance, in the sacrament of penance, absolution follows immediately after confession, while in the

---

4   The 'paenitentia secunda' was "die zweite Bekehrung dessen, der im Glauben bzw. in der christlichen Lebensführung Schiffbruch erlitten hat, analog der Taufe als der ersten und grundlegenden Busse, eine eigentlich unverdiente, aber durch Gottes Barmherzigkeit doch noch ein einziges Mal eröffnete Möglichkeit, das Heil zu erlangen" (R. Messner, *Feiern der Umkehr und Versöhnung*, p.89). The *paenitentia secunda* was also called the second board after shipwreck (*secundum post naufragium tabulam*). Cf. Tertullian in *De Paenitentia* c. IV,2 (CCL I, p.326); cf. 1 Tim 1,19: "Some people have put conscience aside and *wrecked* their faith in consequence."

5   "Der Schwerpunkt unserer Darstellung der geschichtlichen Entwicklung der Feiern von Umkehr und Versöhnung liegt im Bereich der 'zweiten Busse', der Wiederversöhnung der schweren Sünder, welche durch ihr Vergehen die volle Kirchengliedschaft verloren haben." (R. Messner, *Feiern*, p.84.)

6   Rouwhorst, with Messner, speaks about a "process of formalization and ritualization" (G. Rouwhorst, "De viering", p.36; cf. R. Messner, *Feiern*, pp.168-175).

7   R. Messner, *Feiern der Umkehr und Versöhnung*, p.134: "Einige (vor allem euchologische) Elemente aus der kanonischen Busse sowie deren theologische Deutung wurden dabei mit dieser verbunden, so dass die Beichte aus einem Instrument der Seelenführung (und der "paenitentia quotidiana") - zumindest in der byzantinischen Kirche und im Westen – zur neuen Grundform der "paenitentia secunda" wurde."

canonical penance and the private confession, forgiveness of sins follows only after a period of penitence.

Notions from the context of the earlier forms of penance, shifted meanings, and language and metaphors that originated from earlier contexts, dominate Thomas' treatment of the sacrament of penance. This makes it nearly impossible to understand his theology of the sacrament of penance without knowledge of the history of the sacrament of penance. It explains why he sometimes uses the image of doctor to explain the role of the priest in the sacrament, while in other places he uses the image of a judge. It also explains why he speaks about forgiveness of sins with the help of language that refers first to the realm of economy, then to the realm of law, and another time to the realm of medicine. Nevertheless, one cannot explain everything by referring to the history of the sacrament of penance, because some specific forms of language do not refer to the history, but to the way Scripture speaks about forgiveness of sins. In the following chapter, we will deal more precisely with the different ways in which Thomas speaks about forgiveness of sins, and, in particular, with how he interprets them against the background of the relationship of grace. At the moment we will limit ourselves to describing more precisely how the sacrament of penance developed into the way it was celebrated at the time Thomas lived and worked.

We will divide the development of the 'sacrament' of penance up to the 13th century into two stages. The first stage is the period of the rise and fall of the canonical or public penance. The second stage is the period of the development of the practice of private confession into the sacrament of penance. At the end of the third century a consensus was reached in the churches to re-accept grave sinners insofar as they agreed to undergo an ecclesial penance. We will take the Council of Nicaea (325) as the beginning of the period of the ecclesial or canonical penance. We will take the Council of Toledo in 589, during which the church reacted for the first time to the new tariff penance, which originated in Ireland, as the moment in which the new tariff penance began to replace the old canonical penance. We will take the Fourth Lateran Council's proclamation 'Omnis utriusque sexus' (1215), containing the obligation to go to confession at least once a year, as the official moment of the birth of the sacrament of penance.

E cclesiastical or Canonical Penance, IInd to VIth century

From the beginning, the Christian community wrestled with the question of how to deal with those of its members who, after having been baptized, had lapsed into grave sin again. This became urgent during the periods of persecution in the first centuries A.D. The rigorists, in particular the Montanists, were opposed to reaccepting adulterers and apostates into the church community. The discussion was not about the question of whether grave sins could be forgiven. It was commonly acknowledged that those who lapsed into sin after baptism were not excluded from forgiveness.[8] The one text of the New Testament which seemed to suggest otherwise (Heb 6, 4-6)[9] was understood to deal with the unforgivable sin against the Holy Spirit, the sin of consciously rejecting Christ (Cf. Mt 12, 31-32).[10] For sinners who repented, forgiveness was, in principle, possible, however grave their sins were. What, then, was the discussion about?

The first problem concerned the expediency of forgiving sins. According to the Montanist movement, the Holy Spirit had said through Montanus: "The church can forgive sins, but I will do not so in order to prevent others from sinning".[11] Hence, the Montanists did not deny the power of the church to forgive sins, but were against the practicing of this power, because they thought it not to be expedient for the church to forgive sins. The main reason for this was that, according to them, forgiving grave sinners would result in others committing sins.

The second problem was more fundamental and concerned the question of which 'church' possessed the power to forgive sins. Tertullian († c.220), in his Montanist period[12], disputed that the power to bind and to loose, entrusted to St. Peter (Mt. 16, 18), was passed on to the church of the Episcopal hierarchy. According to the Montanists, the power to bind and loose was passed on to the church of the Holy Spirit and not to the hierarchical church of the bishops.[13] The denial of ecclesial reconciliation did not imply the denial of the possibility of divine forgiveness. Tertullian did not deny the possibility of accepting grave sinners in a state of penitence, but he did question the authority of the church, in particular the church officially represented by the bishops, to announce divine forgiveness in this life, and to reaccept the sinner into full community with the church. Divine forgiveness, according to Tertullian, was not in the hands of the official church, but in the hands of God. According to the Montanists, the pneumatics, i.e. those gifted with special gifts of the Holy Spirit, were the real successors of St. Peter, and bishops only insofar as they were pneumatics. Pneumatics could, on the grounds of a special divine

---

8   B. Poschmann, *Busse*, p.3; C. Vogel, *Le pécheur ... dans l'église ancienne*, p.13.

9   "As for those people who were once brought into the light, and tasted the gift from heaven, and received a share of the Holy Spirit, and tasted the goodness of God's message and the powers of the world to come, and yet in spite of this have fallen away, it is impossible for them to be brought to the freshness of repentance a second time, since they are crucifying the Son of God again for themselves, and making a public exhibition of him."

10   B. Poschmann, *Busse*, pp. 6-8. The sin against the Holy Spirit is understood in the early church to be the sin of lack of repentance

11   Cited by Tertullian in *De Pud* 21.7 C. Vogel, *Le pécheur ... dans l'église ancienne*, p.19; cf. R. Messner, *Feiern*, p.137.

12   Tertullians *De paenitentia* was written in his Catholic period, his *De exhortatione castitatis* and *De pudicitia* were written in his Montanist period.

13   C. Vogel, *Le pécheur ... dans l'église ancienne*, p.21: "La réplique de Tertullien est passionnée et contradictoire; tantôt il fait du pouvoir des clés un privilege personnel de Pierre: tantôt il reconnaît que le pouvoir de lier et délier a passé dans l'Eglise, définie dans le sens montaniste: à savoir l'Eglise de l'Esprit et non l'Eglise hiérarchique des évêques."

revelation, proclaim divine forgiveness.[14] In conclusion, the Montanist controversy was fundamentally a controversy about the vision of the church, i.e. about the relationship of ecclesial forgiveness to divine forgiveness.[15]

Despite the Montanist resistance, the Council of Nicaea (325) affirmed "a 'humane' policy of readmitting excommunicants to Communion after appropriate periods of penance, and any who had fallen away during persecution, or in any other way given up their religion."[16] Let us proceed by examining the public or canonical penance in more detail.

The public or canonical penance of the early church consisted of three stages. In the first stage the sinner was admitted to the state of penance at his own request. The sinner asked for and received the penance, which was imposed upon him by the bishop. He entered the state of penitence in an official act in the presence of the community of the faithful. This first stage was ended by a formal and liturgical act of expelling the penitent from the Church.

Though the public act of entering the state of penance involved some sort of acknowledgement of being a sinner, this may not be regarded as a public confession in the sense of an individual confession of separate sins. The nature, the proportion and the number of sins were, in principle, known only to the sinner and the minister, who was, in fact, the bishop. Insofar as a practice of public confession existed, this was exercised only by repentant sinners who were particularly zealous or exalted.[17]

Vogel stresses that, in principle, all grave sinners were admitted to the state of penance. In the early church, a distinction was made between grave sins and venial sins. Prayer and private deeds of mortification could, according to Tertullian during his Catholic period, obtain forgiveness for venial sins.[18] The

---

14   Cf. R. Messner, *Feiern*, p. 90-91, p.137.

15   J. Mahoney, *The Making*, p.2.

16   *Idem*, p.3, with referrence to *Conciliorum Oecumenicorum Decreta*, ed. G. Alberigo, et all (Bologna, 1973), nrs. 8. 11. Nr. 8 is about those who call themselves Cathars or 'the pure'. The decree states that before they can come over to the Catholic and Apostolic Church and be admitted to the clergy by an imposition of hands, they must "give a written undertaking that they will accept and follow the decrees of the Catholic Church, namely that they will be in communion with those who have entered into second marriage and with those who have lapsed in time of persecution and for whom a period [of penance] has been fixed and an occasion [for reconciliation] allotted, so as in all things to follow the decrees of the Catholic and Apostolic Church." (transl. N. Tanner s.j.).

17   C. Vogel, *Le pécheur ... dans l'église ancienne*, p.11. The exhomologesis (= confession) we find for instance in Tertullians *De Paenitentia* must not be understood to be a detailed confession of individual sins, but must be considered to be a deed of humiliation, which was part of a sum of deeds of mortification. According to Cyprian, exhomologesis stood for the whole ritual of guilty recognition in the presence of the gathered community.

18   *Idem*, p.22: "La pénitence ecclésiastique avec reconciliation par l'évêque n'est exigée que pour l'expiation des fautes graves, bien entendu; les fautes légères sont réparées par la prière et les exercices de mortification privés. Telle est l'opinion de Tertullien catholique, en conformité d'ailleurs avec les texts antérieurs. Devenu montaniste il modifiera ses conceptions à ce sujet, et prétendra que les fautes graves sont irrémissibles."

paenitentia secunda was demanded only for grave sins which cause the relationship with the Church and with God to break.[19]

The second stage was the penitential stage of expiation in which the penitent lived, as a member of the order or group of penitents (analogous to the state of the Catechumens), under the supervision of the church. The bishop determined how long the period of expiation lasted. The penitents were required to live a life of mortification, thus giving concrete evidence of the internal conversion without which reconciliation was impossible. During this stage the penitents were excluded from participating in the Eucharist. Moreover, the penitents were forbidden to join the army or to hold public offices during the period of penance, and married penitents were forbidden to live a marital life. In many ways, entering the state of penitence was much like entering the religious state.[20]

The third stage was the liturgical ritual of reconciliation in which the bishop, as representative of the church community, played an important role. The reconciliation took place through the imposition of hands, accompanied by prayer. Reconciled, the penitent was readmitted to the table of the Eucharist. R. Messner stresses the intercessional character of the canonical penance. All three stages were directed towards encouraging the church community to pray for the salvation of the penitent.[21]

Over the centuries, canonical penance became empty as a penitential regime as the Church changed from an eschatological community of saints to a Church of the people.[22] Three characteristics were immediately responsible for this. First,

---

[19] The list of grave sins was not limited to the well-known triad of adultery, idolatry and homicide, but also included fornication, false testimony, cheating, lying, and attending circus or stadium spectacles (*idem*, p.23). Also R. Messner, *Feiern der Umkehr und Versöhnung*. "Diese [Triassünden] sind natürlich als Gattungsbegriffe zu verstehen, nich als drei genau definierten Einzelsünden; Tertullian bietet in De pud. auch eine ausführlichere Liste unvergebbarer 'Sünden zum Tod' (Mord, Götzendienst, Betrug, Verleugnung, Lästerung, Ehebruch, Hurerei), für welche (nach 1 Joh 5,16) keine Fürbitte gestattet ist." (p.87-88).

[20] Cf. C. Vogel, *Le pécheur ... dans l'église ancienne*, p.38.

[21] "Es handelt sich also um einen Akt von der Gemeinde mit ihren Amtsträgern, (..) um einen Akt der Fürbitte der ganzen Gemeinde für ihre sündigen Glieder." (*Feiern*, p.90); "Sie [die Rekonziliation] ist ein gottesdienstlicher Ritus, an dem die ganze Gemeinde beteiligt ist: Während die Gläubigen beten (wodurch sie ihr priesterliches Amt als Fürbitter ausüben), legt der Bischof, der in dieser liturgischen Handlung weniger als Gottes Repräsentant als vielmehr als amtlicher Vorsteher der Gemeinde verstanden scheint, dem Pönitenten die Hände auf, um ihn wieder in die Kirche einzugliedern, die Gemeinschaf mit der Kirche wiederzuherstellen; die Handaufteilung teilt die Gemeinschaft des Heiligen Geistes mit, ist also wie die Handauflegung bei der Taufe (Firmung) verstanden." (p.95)

[22] Cf. R. Messner, *Feiern* p.116-117: "Durch die im 3.Jh. anhebende und seit der öffentlichen Anerkennung und Förderung durch Konstantin sehr rasch verlaufende Entwicklung eines sich als heilige, aus der 'Welt' herausgehobene Gemeinde der Endzeit verstehenden Christentums zur Volkskirche verlieren gerade die auf dem Gemeindebewusstsein basierende kirchlichen Lebensformen wie eben die kanonischen Busse viel von ihrem alten Sinn." R. Messner names five preconditions for the development of a new system of penance: (1) the disappearance of a sense of community due to the development of the old church into a people's church; (2) the importance of monastic life, with its sense for eschatology and its pastoral practice (monks confession), for the church of late antiquity and the early middle

the ancient penance was accessible just once in a lifetime: it was a characteristic of the canonical penance that it could not be repeated. Reconciliation, after having committed a grave sin, was possible just once in a lifetime. This non-repeatability of penance in the early church was first stated by Hermas,[23] and was justified by referring to the analogy of penance with baptism. Hermas was in accordance with those who taught that there was no remission other than that received through baptism. However, at the same time, he recognized that this was an ideal. In the eschatological perspective of the coming end of the world, Hermas offered one last chance for those who lapsed into sin after baptism. However, this remission was, and had to remain, exceptional.[24] During his catholic period, Tertullian adopted this position.[25] This principle of non-repeatability remained valid until the new system of tariff penances appeared at the end of the sixth, and the beginning of the seventh century.

A second characteristic that caused the final 'bankruptcy'[26] of the canonical penance was the fact that the ancient penance was severe in the sense that it meant, in more than one way, a social death sentence: he or she who entered the order of penitents was, aside from severe fasting, forbidden to live a normal married life, to carry arms, to hold public offices, to conduct a trade, or to enter the higher clergy (deacon, priest, bishop).[27]

The third characteristic was the fact that, once someone had entered the order of penitents, he remained marked with the penitential prohibition until the end of his days. Even though he was reconciled and re-admitted to the table of the Eucharist, his status remained one of penitent. He remained forbidden to join the army, live a marital life etc.[28]

---

ages; (3) the introduction of pagan religious conceptions (e.g. a politically understood notion of salvation, a loss of eschatological tension) by the newly converted Germans; (4) due to the loss of eschatological tension, Christian faith became more and more a system of moral teachings; (5) the new place baptism came to occupy, not at the end of a long period of conversion, but instead at its beginning. (R. Messner, *Feiern*, p.161-163)

23 Hermas *Precept* IV, Ch.1, 8. R. Messner remarks that this principle is "das erste Mal bei Hermas greifbar, dort freilich nicht auf die kanonische Busse bezogen" (R. Messner, *Feiern* p.89)

24 C. Vogel, *Le pécheur ... dans l'église ancienne*, p.17.

25 *Idem*, p.21. Vogel refers to *De Poenitentia* VII, 10: "conlocavit in vestibulo paenitentiam secundum quae pulsantibus patefaciat, sed iam semel quia iam secundo, sed amplius numquam quia proxime frustra." (CCL I, pp.333-334).

26 Cf. C. Vogel, *Le pécheur ... au Moyen-Age*, p.23: "Le désert pénitentiel était donc absolu. Une réflexion du moine Jonas, le biographe de saint Columban, illustre parfaitement la situation en Gaule – et il ne devait pas en aller différemment dans les autres pays d'Occident: «Les remèdes de la pénitence et l'amour de la mortification n'existaient plus guère dans ces regions» (Jonas, *Vie de saint Colomban*, c.11). C'est un constat de faillite."

27 C. Vogel, *Le pécheur ... dans l'église ancienne*, p.52: "Entrer en pénitence équivalait à signer un arrêt de mort civile."

28 "Même réconcilié, le pénitent gardait l'empreinte de son ancien état: interdiction de porter les armes, démission de fonctions publiques et des charges honorifiques; le commerce était fortement déconseillé." (C. Vogel, *Le pécheur ... dans l'église ancienne* p.52). According to R. Messner, *Feiern*, p.93, Origines taught "eine bleibende Folge der Sünde auch für den Rekonziliierten: Dieser darf kein Amt und kein leitende Stellung der Kirche gewählt werden. Derartige Dauerfolgen, seit dem 4.Jh. reichlich belegt, werden in der ausgehenden Antike

These characteristics lead to putting off the moment of entering the penitential order until the end of one's life. Consequently, no time remained to fulfill the penance imposed. A practice arose in which the penitent, on his or her deathbed, was reconciled immediately after the imposition of the penance. Those who lived on, however, were admitted to a stage of expiation, after which a second, solemn, reconciliation followed.

Because of the radical implications of entering the state of penitence, the bishops became extremely careful about imposing penance, even on a sick man or woman, as there was always the possibility of recovery. The radical implications also entailed that certain bishops were reluctant to impose penance on young sinners.[29] Councils even went so far as to forbid young sinners (and even married sinners without consent from their spouse) to have canonical penance imposed on them. This resulted in the paradoxical situation that theoretically the remedy of penance could cure all sins, but, at the same time, the remedy itself remained out of reach.[30]

This practice had consequences for the participation of grave sinners in the Eucharist. Vogel distinguishes between two groups of grave sinners. The first group consisted of grave sinners who were admitted into the order of penitents and who had not yet been reconciled. They were *ipso facto* excluded from participating in the Eucharist. The second group consisted of grave sinners who could not, or would not, for the reasons mentioned above, enter the order of penitents. This group formed an immense majority. In order to prevent the Eucharist from being dishonored, the church excommunicated the most unworthy. The rest were advised to temporarily abstain from Eucharistic communion.

According to Vogel it is nevertheless probable that those faithful who, under the exhortation of the pastors, repented and tried to earn the penance by doing good works, were admitted at the table of the Eucharist, without reconciliation.[31]

As the majority of sinners were excluded from official reconciliation, the canonical penance left a penitential void. Apart from the canonical penance, and before the new system of tariff penances spread throughout the continent, no other way existed for the church to offer some sort of guarantee of divine forgiveness to repentant sinners.[32]

---

zum Verfall der kanonischen Busse beitragen." Cf. also p.118: "Das bedeutet nichts anderes, als dass ein Christ, der sich dem kanonischen Bussverfahren unterzog, nie wieder ein normales Leben führen konnte; wie ein Mönch oder Kleriker war er zu lebenslänger Enthaltsamkeit verpflichtet."

[29] C. Vogel, *Le pécheur ... dans l'église ancienne*, p.53.

[30] *Idem*, p.44-45.

[31] *Idem*, p.47-48.

[32] C. Vogel, *Le pécheur ... au Moyen-Age*, p.21-23. Two others ways to obtain divine forgiveness offered no way out of the impasse, as they were no easier than the canonical penance: the monastic profession and conversion. It was believed that monastic profession or the conversion to an existence of mortification, in complete abstinence and chastity, gave the

Tariff Penance, VIth to XIIth century

The roots of the new system of private confession go back to the first centuries of Christianity.[33] Despite the introduction of the canonical penance at the end of the third century, a practice remained within the church of proclaiming divine forgiveness on the grounds of charismatic authority. From the third century, monks came to succeed the traveling prophets and apostles as bearers of this charismatic authority.

The confession of sins was the main instrument in their fight against sinfulness. The emphasis was on pastoral care, and the 'confessor' was seen, for instance by someone like Origen, as a physician. Divine forgiveness was proclaimed on the grounds of a special divine revelation to the confessor, who could consequently provide the sinner with some form of insurance with respect to his or her salvation.

The Irish tariff penance developed out of this practice of monachal confession. The Irish church dates from the fifth century. Because of the lack of towns in the sixth century, the church was organized around monasteries. As a result, church life was heavily influenced by the monachal way of life, including their way of dealing with sin and guilt. The new system, however, differed from the monachal confession in that the penance was calculated according to seemingly fixed tariffs, collected and written down in so-called Penitentials.

The oldest Penitential (*poenitentiale Vinniani*) dates from the end of the fifth century.[34] From the eighth century, the missionaries who came from the islands took their books with them to the continent. In the centuries that followed, the use of Penitentials multiplied and spread across the continent.[35]

The most striking difference between the new system and the canonical penance was the fact that one could do penance more than once in a lifetime. Each Christian, lay or cleric, could confess their sins as often as they had sinned in order to obtain forgiveness.

Furthermore, confession was made in secret to a qualified person, who was usually a priest[36], but could also be a monk (often the abbot or abbess).[37] After the sinner had given a detailed confession, the confessor imposed a penance

---

right to divine forgiveness of sins committed after baptism. The latter way was seen as a second baptism.

33 For instance, Origen (†253/254) knows the public penance as well as the practice of confessing sins. G. Rouwhorst, "De viering van bekering en verzoening", p.34-35; cf. R. Messner, *Feiern*, pp.139-140.

34 "The earliest of the extant documents belonging to the class of penitentials are probably those ascribed to Welsh synods held under the influence of St. David." The *Penitential of Finnian* (end of the fifth century) may be considered to be "the earliest of the books sufficiently comprehensive to serve the purpose of a general guide for confessors in their ministry." The Penitentials are spread throughout the continent starting from the late sixth century: Frankish lands: late sixth century; England (in which country the ancient public penance was never established): late seventh century; Italy: late eighth century; and among the Spanish Visigoths: early ninth century. (J. McNeill, *Medieval handbooks*, pp.23-26).

35 C. Vogel, *Le pécheur ... au Moyen-Age*, p.20.

36 Cf. B. Poschmann, *Busse*, p.68.

37 J. McNeill, *Medieval handbooks*, p.28; R. Messner, *Feiern* p.145.

upon him. The confession took place either spontaneously or with the help of a list of questions. The taxes were imposed with the help of a Penitential. Each sin corresponded with a certain tariff, and the total was determined by the number and gravity of the sins committed. The tariff penances consisted mostly of fasting. The whole process, including the expiation, happened in secret.

The sinner obtained forgiveness of the sins *ipso facto* when he had accomplished the penance imposed. Vogel speaks about a primitive *do ut des* in which expiation was automatically followed by forgiveness. Though there was no actual reconciliation, there are reports of penitents returning to their confessors after having accomplished the fasting, in order to obtain absolution (absolution being the term that came to replace the old term of reconciliation). If a penitent was not able to undergo the punishments, the confessor could recite the absolving prayers immediately. For those bishops and priests who were concerned with the spiritual well-being of their flock, the new system offered a valuable help.[38]

However, instead of wholeheartedly embracing this new instrument of pastoral care, the bishops' reaction was divided. First, the Council of Toledo of 589 resisted the new penitential system. Next, some sixty years later, bishops gathered at the Council of Chalon-sur-Saône (644-656) approved of the new way of doing penance. However, in the eighth century, Carolingian reformers, clerics grouped around Chrodegang of Metz (†766) and Remigius of Rouen (†772), tried to restore the religious discipline and life. The reforming Councils of 813 (Chalon-sur-Saône) and 829 (Paris) aimed, among other things, to restore the canonical penance.[39]

Since the eighth century was also the age in which the Penitentials flourished[40], the result of these reforming efforts was a dichotomy in the ways of doing penance, a dichotomy that lasted until the twelfth century. During these centuries, both penitential systems existed side by side. For those who had committed a grave public sin, the ancient form of penance offered a way to forgiveness. For others, whose grave sins were committed covertly, the system of tariff penances offered the proper way of doing penance. By the eleventh century, the church made both ways of doing penance official.[41]

With the emergence of the tariff penance, the canonical penance lost its meaning and was, as a result, seldom practiced. From the twelfth century the new term, *paenitentia solemnis,* was introduced as a counterpart to the private penance. The solemn penance was a remnant of the old canonical penance. The

[38] C. Vogel, *Le pécheur ... au Moyen Age*, p.23.
[39] *Idem*, p.15-16; H. Vorgrimler, *Busse*, p.98.
[40] B. Poschmann, *Busse*, p.66: "In derselben Zeit nun, in der die 64 Bischöfe und die 7 bischöfliche Stellvertreter ihr Verdikt über die Privatbuße aussprachen (= at the Council of Toledo 589), begann dies ihren Siegeszug auf europäischen Festland."; Cf. C. Vogel, *Le pécheur ... au Moyen Age*, p.15.
[41] C. Vogel, *Le pécheur ... au Moyen Age*, pp.24-27. Those, who by committing their grave sins, had caused a public scandal, were obliged to undergo the rite of public penance, which took more and more the character of a coercive punishment. The help of the civil authorities were invoked more and more to force the recalcitrant sinner to submit to the public penance.

term illustrates the extra-ordinary character of the public penance. Not much later, the term 'solemn penance' became used in contrast to 'public penance', which by then referred to the practice of penitential pilgrimage. In the meantime, the tariff penance had evolved into the sacrament of penance. During its evolution it had adopted properties of the old canonical penance. By the end of the twelfth century, three modalities of penance existed together: the sacrament of penance, the solemn penance, and the penitential pilgrimage. All three can, in some form, be found in the works of Thomas Aquinas (the solemn penance can for instance be found in *In IV Sent* d.14, q.1, a.5).

According to Vogel, the system of tariff penance is the direct ancestor of the sacrament of penance, which is still in use today in the Latin Church.[42] Like the tariff penance, the sacrament of penance could, and still can, be repeated as often as needed or wanted. Both have a strong private character, and both are accessible for both clerics and laymen. In contrast to the old canonical penance, the tariff penance and the sacrament of penance do not involve a special penitential order, involving prohibitions that mark even the reconciled sinner until his death.

Nevertheless, at the same time there are some significant differences between the tariff penance and the new system of the sacrament of penance. With some exceptions[43], in the system of the tariff penance the absolution was given after the sins were expiated by penance. The system of tariff penance shared this aspect with the old canonical penance. In the new sacrament of penance, the absolution follows immediately after the confession. This implied a completely new meaning for both the confession and the penance, or as it is called from now on, the satisfaction. In the system of tariff penance, confession was a means by which the confessor was able to establish the exact size and nature of the penance to be imposed, while the expiation was essential for obtaining forgiveness. In the new sacrament of penance, the confession itself constitutes a form of expiation. As a result, satisfaction received a new meaning, as it was now understood to replace the temporal punishments. Consequently, the new sacrament of penance presupposed a distinction between eternal and temporal punishments.[44]

The development from tariff penance to sacrament of penance was affirmed by the decree *Omnis utriusque sexus* (c.21) of the Fourth Lateran Council (1215).[45] The Council merely sanctioned a practice that had existed since the tenth

---

[42] C. Vogel, *Le pécheur ... au Moyen-Age*, p.27.

[43] Those penitents who were expected not to be able to fulfill the penitential obligations, for instance for reason of illness, could receive absolution before fulfilling their penances.

[44] B. Poschmann, *Busse*, p.84.

[45] "They [confession and penance] became universally obligatory in the West through a decision taken by the Lateran council of 1215. The Lateran decree on penance requires confession to a priest at least once a year, followed by faithfully performed penance, and enjoins the priest, on pain of deposition and perpetual penance, not to reveal confession by word or sign. This decision means essentially that the Celtic penance had become, with modifications, the typical penance of medieval Europe." J. McNeill, *Medieval handbooks*, p.29.

century, in which it was common to invite the faithful to confess their sins during Lent as a preparation for the Easter communion. This decree in combination with the coming into existence of the mendicant orders, heralds a new era in the pastoral care of the church.

> "All the faithful of either sex, after they have reached the age of discernment, should individually confess all their sins in a faithful manner to their own priest at least once a year, and let them take care to do what they can to perform the penance imposed on them. Let them reverently receive the sacrament of the Eucharist at least at Easter unless they think, for a good reason and on the advice of their own priest, that they should abstain from receiving it for a time. Otherwise, they shall be barred from entering a church during their lifetime and they shall be denied a Christian burial at death. Let this salutary decree be frequently published in churches, so that nobody may find the pretence of an excuse in the blindness of ignorance. If any persons wish, for good reasons, to confess their sins to another priest let them first ask and obtain the permission of their own priest; for otherwise the other priest will not have the power to absolve or to bind them. The priest shall be discerning and prudent, so that like a skilled doctor he may pour wine and oil over the wounds of the injured one. Let him carefully inquire about the circumstances of both the sinner and the sin, so that he may prudently discern what sort of advice he ought to give and what remedy to apply, using various means to heal the sick person. Let him take the utmost care, however, not to betray the sinner at all by words or sign or in any other way. If the priest needs advice, let him seek it cautiously without any mention of the person concerned. For if anyone presumes to reveal a sin disclosed to him in confession, we decree that he is not only be disposed from his priestly office but also to be confined to a strict monastery to do perpetual penance."[46]

The decree provides us with a view of the sacrament of penance as it was meant to be practiced at the beginning of the thirteenth century, just some four decades before Thomas wrote his first treatise on the sacrament of penance, when commenting upon Peter Lombard's *Sentences* between 1252 and 1256.[47]
First, the emphasis lies on confession in combination with doing penance. Second, the obligation to make confession depends on the exhortation to

---

[46] *Denz.* 437-438. Transl. N. Tanner s.j. / G. Alberigo, *Decrees of the Ecumenical Councils* Vol.I, 1990, p.245. According Rahner, theologians before Thomas taught that the annual obligation to confess also applied for those who had not committed any deadly sins ("Beichtprobleme", p.229). Cf. *CIC*, 1983, can. 989: "Omnis fidelis, postquam ad annos discretionis pervenerit, obligatione tenetur peccata sua gravia, saltem semel in anno, fideliter confitendi." This canon must be understood in combination with the previous canon that states that a member of the Christian faithful is obliged to confess in kind and number all serious sins committed after baptism: "Should one then commit a grave sin, the canon requires that he or she confess at least within a year. The failure of canon 906 of the former Code (and the earlier law [in part. Lateran IV, EL]) to make clear that the obligation of annual confession is applicable only in the case of grave sins has now been remedied." *The Code of Canon Law A text and commentary*, commissioned by the Canon Law Society of America and edited by J.A. Coriden, T.J. Green, D.E. Heintschel, 1995.

[47] In fact, on several occasions, Thomas refers explicitly to the decree: *In IV Sent* d.17, q.3, a.1 qa.3 Sc 2; co; ad 3; qa.4 Sc 1; a.4, qa.4 Sc 1.

receive the Eucharist at least once a year at Easter. Third, the (use of the) power of the keys to bind and to absolve is not simply given with ordination, but also depends on the fact of whether or not the confessor is one's own priest. The right to use the power of the keys (jurisdiction) was given either ordinarily or by delegation. Fourth, the text gives indications about how confession is to be heard. The image of the doctor dominates in this respect. Fifth, confession has the function of enabling the confessor-doctor to determine the appropriate medicine that must be applied. Sixth, the decree stresses the secrecy of the confession (seal of confession).[48]

According to Pesch, the fact that the council had to prescribe an annual confession, illustrates that one did not receive the sacrament of penance often.[49] Pesch calls the liturgy in Thomas' time a liturgy of clerics ('Klerikerliturgie'). The Eucharist was not the community worship which it is today. It was celebrated in Latin; the congregation was kept at a distance. Liturgy was something to watch, not something to participate in.[50] Furthermore, it was not the Eucharist, but rather the sacrament of penance which stood at the center of Christian life.

This was the situation by the time Thomas was appointed master *in sacra pagina*. As we will see in the next section, he wrote down his thoughts about the sacrament of penance on more than one occasion, and, in doing so, contributed to its development.

Summary

The sacrament of penance, as it was reflected upon by Thomas, evolved out of the practice of private confession known as the system of tariff penance, and, in particular, known for the use of so-called Penitentials. Simultaneously, the old public, or canonical, penance of the early church evolved into the rarely practiced solemn penance (*paenitentia solemnis*), while at the same time the term public penance came to stand for the practice of penitential pilgrimage. In the course of these related evolutions, during the process of its adoption and

---

48 It was a feature of the private confession of the tariff penance, that it was made under seal of secrecy. The first clear and unambigious authorization for secret confession and strict silence on the part of the confessor may be found in a letter written by pope Leo the Great in 459 (Ep. clxviii, 2, *PL* LIV, 1210): B. Kurtschied, *Das Biechtsiegel in seiner geschichtliche Entwickelung* 1912, pp. 28-31 (English edition: *History of the Seal of Confession* 1927, p.55).

49 O.H. Pesch, *Thomas von Aquin*, p.348.

50 The congregation was literally kept at a distance by architectural measures, for instance by a stair that blocked the view of the altar, or by a partition separating the choir from the rest of the church. Cf. O.H. Pesch, *Hinführung zu Luther*, p.137: "Schon im frühen Mittelalter entwickelt sich die Liturgie zum Klerikergottesdienst, dem das «Volk» nur von ferne und ohne Verstehen beiwohnt, abgetrennt durch die alle Sicht auf den Altar versperrende lange Treppe zum Hochchor oder später durch den Lettner. Der Sakramentsgottesdienst löst sich damit aus dem Gemeindebezug, und wen wundert es, dass in der Frühscholastik das Sakrament zum isolierten «Heilmittel» («remedium») schrumpft, was um so einleuchtender wirken muss, als für das ungebildete Volk faktisch nicht etwa die Eucharistie, sondern das inzwischen mit einer perfektionistischen seelsorglichen Systematik sondergleichen ausgestaltete Busssakrament das Hauptsakrament ist: die Ausgangssituation der Refromation bereitet sich vor."

institutionalization by the church, properties of the canonical penance were transferred to the new sacrament of penance. Consequently, the sacrament of penance can be understood as a union or combination ('Zusammenlegung') of confession and reconciliation.[51] The following diagram is presented as an illustration of the development of the sacrament of penance. The diagram is taken from C. Vogel, and is slightly adjusted:[52]

Development of the sacrament of penance

Early church	Canonical penance	Monachal confession	
High Middle Ages		Tariff penance	
Carolingian period until the 12th century	Public penance for grave public faults	Tariff penance for grave hidden faults	
Since the 13th century	Penitential pilgrimage	Private sacramental penance	Public solemn penance

The tariff penance started as a penitential system outside the official hierarchy of the church. During its development the tariff penance was incorporated by the official church, thus giving it its ecclesial and sacramental character. It evolved into the sacrament of penance while adopting the properties of the *paenitentia secunda*. As such it replaced the canonical penance in its function of ecclesial instrument for dealing with those among her members who, by grave sinning, had separated themselves from the church and from the grace of God. One of the consequences was that the church became the determiner of who could function as 'confessor'. Consequently, the church put an end to the

---

[51] B. Poschmann, *Busse*, p.83: "Mit der seit dem 11. Jahrhundert durchgeführten Zusammenlegung von Beicht und Rekonziliation hat das äußere Bußverfahren im wesentlichen die Form erreiht, in der es noch heute geübt wird, bestehend in Beichte, Bußauflegung und Lossprechung, und zwar so, daß es beliebig wiederholt werden kann und für alle pflichtmäßig ist."

[52] C. Vogel, *Le pécheur ... au Moyen-Age*, p.36. Added to the diagram is the information that the ancestor of tariff penance is the practice of monachal confession in the Early Church .

practice in which confessors were chosen for their charisma. The 'minister' of the canonical penance was the bishop, a member of the ecclesiastical hierarchy. Similarly, the minister of the sacrament of penance had to be a member of the hierarchy, the priest.[53] As a further consequence the sacrament of penance became immediately associated with the power of the keys of St. Peter (Mt. 16, 19), with the Eucharist, and with excommunication. Ultimately, the sacrament of penance received its final place and function among the seven sacraments of the church.[54]

2 Penance in the works of Thomas

A quick search with the help of R. Busa's *Index Thomisticus* shows that the sacrament of penance is treated in a limited number of works. In this section, these works will be reviewed separately. But first, we have to deal with a problem with which the *Summa theologiae* confronts us, namely that in this most mature work of Thomas the treatise on the sacrament of penance has remained unfinished.

The unfinished treatise on the sacrament of penance in the Summa theologiae

The *Summa theologiae* is Thomas' best-known and most referred to work. It is one of his three systematic works: the Commentary on Peter Lombard's *Sentences* , entitled the *Scriptum super Sententiis*, and the *Summa contra Gentiles* being the other two. As Thomas wrote the *Summa* at the end, and at the peak, of his working years the *Summa* is without any doubt his most mature work, in which he reaches the highest level of theological reflection.

In the *Summa*, the sacraments are treated *ex professo* in the third part, immediately after the section on Christ.[55] The treatment of the sacraments *in*

---

[53] The Council of Florence (1439-1443) determined that the proper minister of the sacrament of penance is the *sacerdos*, i.e. priest and bishop. Cf. the VIIIth session (from the bull on the union with the Armenians "Exsultate Deo", 22 nov, 1439): "Minister huius sacramenti est sacerdos habens auctoritatem absolvendi vel ordinariam vel ex commissione superioris." (*Denz*, 1323). The teaching on the sacraments in the bull is taken literally from Thomas' *De articulis fidei et ecclesiae sacramentis*.

[54] In Emperor Michael's confession of faith, read at the 2nd Council of Lyon, 1274, a short summary of the Western doctrine on the sacraments is given in which seven are mentioned, and among which penance is numbered: "Tenet etiam et docet eadem sancta Romana Ecclesia, septem esse ecclesiastica sacramenta, unum scilicet baptisma, de quo dictum est supra; aliud est sacramentum confirmationis, quod per manuum impositionem episcopi conferunt, chrismando renatos; aliud est paenitentia, aliud eucharistia, aliud sacramentum ordinis, aliud est matrimonium, aliud extrema unctio, quae secundum doctrinam beati Iacobi infirmantibus adhibetur." (*Denz*, 860; cf. H. Vorgrimmler *Busse*, p.121, footnote 85: "Es handelt sich um einen schon durch Clemens IV. 1267 an den byzantinischen Kaiser übersandten Text, dessen Annahme vom Papst als Vorbedingung für eine Union mit den Griechen angegeben worden war."; footnote 86: "Es handelt sich weder um einen konziliaren Text noch um eine dogmatische Definition des Papstes, aber das vom Papst vorgelegte, vom Kaiser unterschriebene und von Gregor X. entgegengenommene Glaubensbekenntniss gibt die Lehre der damaligen Kirche historisch korrekt wieder.")

[55] Part three is not the only part of the *Summa theologiae* relevant to Thomas' theology of the sacraments. The sacraments are also dealt with in the *Secunda pars*, in the sections about the old and the new Law (I-II, qq.98-114, in particular qq.101-108), and as part of the virtue of

speciali is preceded in the *Summa* by six *quaestiones* on the sacraments in general, in which many aspects are prepared that are important for understanding the sacrament of penance. In particular the structure of the sacraments, their constitution of words and things, their nature of being a sign, and their linguistic character are important for understanding how the sacraments in general give grace and are expressions of faith (*protestationes fidei*), and how the sacrament of penance, in particular, is cause of forgiveness and expression of the restoration of the relationship of grace.

Thomas deals with the particulars of the sacrament of penance in the section on the sacraments *in speciali* after he deals with, respectively, the sacraments of Baptism, Confirmation and Eucharist. In *STh* III q.84, Thomas presents his plan for dealing with the sacrament of penance. First, he intends to deal with penance as such, second, with its effect, third, with its parts, fourth, with those who receive this sacrament, fifth, with the power of its ministers, i.e. the power of the keys of St. Peter, and sixth, with the solemnity of this sacrament. However, despite his intentions, Thomas never finished his treatment of the sacrament of penance. In fact, Thomas stopped working on his *Summa theologiae* only eight *quaestiones* later, at the end of *quaestio* 90, in which *quaestio* he had just begun to deal with the parts of penance in general. The reason Thomas stopped after writing only a quarter of the treatise on penance is related to an incident that happened around 6 December 1273:

> "[W]hile he was celebrating Mass in the chapel of Saint Nicholas, Thomas underwent an astonishing transformation: 'After that Mass, he never wrote further or even dictated anything, and he even got rid of his writing material; he was working on the third part of the *Summa*, on the treatise concerning penance.' To Reginald [= Reginald of Piperno, Thomas' *socius*], who was stupefied and did not understand why Thomas was abandoning his work, the Master responded simply: 'I cannot do any more'. Returning to his charge a little

---

religion (II-II, qq.81-100), though not *ex professo* and from a different perspective. In these sections the sacraments are treated as part of the cult of God. Schillebeeckx points out that many theologians, because of the controversies with the Protestants, have neglected the aspect of worship. In these controversies, Roman Catholic theologians emphasized the aspect of the causality of the sacraments, at the expense of their role in the cult of God. As a result, many tend to overlook the fact that, in the third part of the Summa, the sacraments are also treated both as means of grace and as cultic expressions of faith. (E. Schillebeeckx, *Sacramentele Heilseconomie*, p.137) In I-II q.102, a.5 co Thomas defines the sacraments according to their place and function in the divine cult: "Sacramenta proprie dicuntur illa, quae adhibantur Dei cultoribus ad quamdam consecrationem, per quam scilicet deputabantur quodammodo ad cultum Dei". For example, Thomas gives an implicit reference to the cult-aspect of the sacraments in III q.60, a.5 co: "(I)n usu sacramentorum duo possunt considerari, scilicet cultus divinus, et sanctificatio hominis". In q.63 he is particularly clear about the two distinct aspects of the sacraments. The *quaestio* is about the sacramental character, which is defined in terms of assigning (*deputare*) men to a spiritual role in the divine cult: "(S)acramenta novae legis ad duo ordinantur; videlicet ad remedium contra peccata, et ad perficiendum animam in his, quae pertinent ad cultum Dei secundum ritum christianae vitae. (..) et ideo cum hominess per sacramenta deputentur ad aliquid spirituale pertinens ad cultum Dei, consequens est, quod per ea fideles aliquo spirituali charactere insignantur."

later, Reginald received the same response: 'I cannot do anymore. Everything I have written seems to me as straw in comparison with what I have seen.'"[56]

Two months later, at the end of January or the beginning of February, while he was with his *socius* Reginald on his way to the council of Lyon, Thomas struck his head against a branch. This accident may have led eventually to his death some weeks later, on Wednesday, March 7th, 1274.[57]

Thomas, thus, never finished the *Summa theologiae*. The sequel known as the *Supplement*[58], was composed by his disciples on the basis of his Commentary on Peter Lombard's *Sentences*.[59] Since it is not his own work, we cannot use it to gain access to Thomas' theology of the sacrament of penance. These problems mean that we cannot simply refer to the *Summa* for Thomas' theology of the sacrament of penance. The questions we need to solve here are: what place must the *Summa* occupy in our reflections of the sacrament of penance, and how do the other works add to our understanding of Thomas' theology of the sacrament of penance.

The first of these two questions we can answer here. The problem, as we sketched it above, becomes less serious when we realize that Thomas takes the major decisions regarding the structure and the efficacy of the sacrament of penance in the section on the sacraments in general. In comparison to the *Scriptum super Sententiis*, on which we will reflect below, the treatise on the sacraments in general in the *Summa* is more extensive, and, what is more important, more systematic.[60] This gave Thomas the opportunity to reflect

---

[56]   J.-P. Torrell o.p., *Saint Thomas Aquinas*. Vol. 1 *The person and his work*. Transl. by Robert Royal, 1996, p.289. With respect to Thomas' strange words, Torrell explains: "Straw is a stock expression used to distinguish, by giving it proper weight, the grain of reality within the chaff of the words; the words are not the reality, but they designate it and they lead to it. Having arrived at reality itself, Thomas had a certain right to feel himself detached with respect to the words, but this simply does not at all signify that he considers his work as without value. Simply put, he had gone beyond it." (p.293). For an elaborate account of the meaning of these strange words, cf. M. O'Rourke Boyle, "Chaff: Thomas Aquinas's repudiation of his *Opera omnia*", in *New Literary History* 28, 1997, pp.383-399. According to O'Rourke Boyle, the testimony given by Bartholomew of Capua at the process of Thomas' canonization (21 July to 18 September 1319) belongs to the literary genre of epideictic rhetoric, "a genre classically invented for the moral praise or blame of an individual". This would imply that the account of the events is less historical than it is rhetorical.

[57]   J.-P. Torrell o.p., *Saint Thomas Aquinas*, p.293: "The unlucky blow of the branch along the way may have set off a series of events whose nature we do not know, but this is not the place to expatiate on that subject."

[58]   In the *Tertiae partis supplementum*, the treatise on the sacrament of penance continues for another 28 *quaestiones*, beginning with the *quaestio* on contrition, the first of the *quaestiones* on the parts *in speciali*.

[59]   J.-P. Torrell o.p., *Saint Thomas Aquinas*, p.147. Cf. note 14: "Like Grabman and Dondaine, many people believe, with varying degrees of uncertainty, that Reginald might have been the author of the Supplement; that was already the opinion of Quétif-Echard, followed by Mandonnet, but the Leonine edition is more circumspect."

[60]   In the *Scriptum*, two questions can be regarded as dealing with the sacraments in general. D.1, q.1 deals with several questions about the sacraments in general, including the sacraments of the old law. Questions that are dealt with are: What is a sacrament (about the different definitions of *sacramentum*), what is their necessity, their constitution and their efficacy? D.2,

more fundamentally on the nature (structure) and efficacy of the sacraments, and their relation to each other and to the sacrament of the Eucharist in particular. These preliminary reflections enabled Thomas to ask questions on the sacrament of penance with more accuracy and precision. So we can refer to the *Summa theologiae* for questions that will occupy us in particular in the fourth chapter, namely on sacramental efficacy. Furthermore, we can also refer to the *Summa* without hesitation for other questions that deal, not with the sacrament of penance in itself, but with the theological notions which the sacrament presupposes, such as justification and notions from Trinitarian theology.

So, in fact, we only have to resort to Thomas' other works for questions regarding particular problems concerning the sacrament of penance itself. In the remainder of this section, we will review these works separately. We will look first at Thomas' other systematic works, his *Scriptum super Sententiis* and the *Summa contra Gentiles*. Next, we will examine his *De articulis fidei et ecclesiae sacramentis* and *De forma absolutione*. Finally, we will take a look at some scriptural commentaries and some other works in which the sacrament of penance is mentioned.

This overview will not only serve to establish in what way the different works of Thomas contribute to our understanding of his theology of the sacrament of penance. It will also provide us with a first impression of how Thomas deals with the sacrament of penance. Furthermore, insofar as one of the works mentioned is not explicitly returned to in any of the subsequent chapters, we will briefly pay attention to its content, i.e. to what the work has to say about the sacrament of penance.

Scriptum super Sententiis

The *Scriptum super Sententiis* is Thomas' commentary on Peter Lombard's *Book of Sentences*, published between 1155 and 1158.[61] Thomas began his teaching career in Paris in 1252, at the age of 27, as bachelor of the *Sentences*. Commenting on the *Sentences* was considered to be "like the chef d'oeuvre that the apprentice was required to present in order to become a master artisan."[62] Even more resolutely than many other commentators on the *Sentences*, Thomas went beyond strictly commenting on Lombard's text, introducing "new

---

q.1 deals with the sacraments of the new law in general. Questions are: How are the sacraments of the new law distinguished from each other, how are they related and whether they are instituted or not. The total number of question-units in the *Scriptum* (the number of *quaestiunculae* of both questions taken together) is 29, whereas the total number in the *Summa* (number of *articuli*) is 38.

[61] J.-P. Torrell, *Saint Thomas Aquinas*, p.40: "Alexander of Hales was the first to take it as a basic text for his teaching from 1223-1227. It was very probably this future Franciscan master who divided the work into distinctions, chapters, and articles. Initially it had been divided solely into books and chapters. The *Sentences* would remain in use – they were quickly made obligatory – in the schools for three centuries." On Thomas as Bachelor of the *Sentences*, cf. pp.39-45

[62] The structure of an academic career consisted of three steps: Baccalareus biblicus, Baccalaureus sententiarius, Magister. Cf. O.H. Pesch, *Thomas von Aquin*, p.84; J.-P. Torrell, *Saint Thomas Aquinas*, p.39.

considerations, sometimes quite distant from Lombard's. Materially, his commentary on each *distinctio* presents itself as a series – longer or shorter as the case requires – of questions that are themselves subdivided into articles and subarticles (*quaestiunculae*). The whole is framed by a *divisio textus* at the beginning, and a *expositio textus* at the end."[63]

The four books of the *Sentences* are ordered as follows: "(1) The Triune God, in His essence and His persons, with some considerations on His presence in the world and in the lives of Christians; (2) God as Creator and His work (Creation in general, creation and the fall of the angels, creation and the fall of man and woman, grace, original and personal sin); (3) The Incarnation of the Word and His redemptive work, to which are attached the analysis of the virtues and the gifts of the Holy Spirit, as well as the Ten Commandments (since they are all found within the commandment of love); (4) Teaching on the sacraments, to which is joined the teaching on our final ends."[64]

The one book we are primarily interested in for its treatise on the sacrament of penance is evidently book four. The 1947 edition of Moos, o.p (together with P. Mandonnet, who edited books I and II), only covers four of the seven sacraments of the church, including the sacrament of penance, while in fact book IV covers all seven sacraments of the church, the resurrection and eternal glory.[65] Thomas deals with penance in the distinctions 14 to 22.[66]

---

[63] J.-P. Torrell, *Saint Thomas*, p.41.

[64] *Idem*, p. 43. Cf. note 27, in which the author indicates that this Summary draws on I. Brady "Pierre Lombard", in *Dictionnaire de spiritualité* 12 (1984), 2, col. 1608. Behind this structure stand two distinctions drawn from Augustine, namely between *res et signa* and between *uti et frui*. The four books are than divided according to the division between *res fruendi, res utendi* and *res fruendi et utendi* (books I-III) and *signa* (book IV) (cf. I Sent d.1). Cf. O.H. Pesch, *Thomas von Aquin*, p.83.

According to Torrell, Thomas interprets Lombard's order as one organizing "the theological material with God as the center, and everything else around Him according to the relationships that they maintain with Him, whether they come from Him as their first cause, or return to Him as to their final end." In the prologue to the *Scriptum*, Thomas distinguishes four subjects that belong to God's wisdom: "Per sapientia enim Dei manifestantur divinorum abscondita, producuntur creaturarum opera, nec tantum producuntur, sed etiam restaurantur et perficiuntur: illa, dico, perfectione qua unumquodque perfectum dicitur, prout proprium finem attingit.". These four are the subjects that are treated respectively in the four books: I. *manifestatio divinorum*, II. *productio creaturarum*, III. *operum restauratio*, IV. *perfectio, qua res conservatur in suo fine*. (*In I Sent* pro). "Thomas sees the *ratio* in the fact that creation – the emergence of creatures from God, the first principle – finds its explanation in the fact that even in God there is an "emergence of the Principle," which is the procession of the Word from the Father. The divine efficacy that works in creation is related, thus, to the generation of the Word, just as the formal cause of the grace that will permit creatures to return to God is linked to the spiration of the Holy Spirit. More precisely and fully, we might therefore say that the divine missions *ad extra* are explained according to the order of the processions of the divine persons *ad intra*." Cf. G. Emery, "Trinité et création. Le principe trinitaire de la création dans les commentaires d'Albert le Grand, de Bonaventure en de Thomas d'Aquin sur les *Sentences*", in *Revue des Sciences philosophiques et théologiques* 79, 1995, pp.419-422.

[65] Cf. the prologue to book IV: "Sic ergo ex verbis propositis tria possumus accipere circa hunc *Quartum librum* qui prae manibus habetur, scilicet materiam; quia in eo agitur de sacramentis et de resurrectione et gloria resurgentium."

In the *divisio textus* of d. 14, Thomas presents his interpretation of the structure of Lombard's nine distinctions on penance.[67] The first division is made between what belongs to the essence of penance (dd. 14-19) and what belongs to its accidents (dd. 20-22). That which belongs to the essence of the sacrament of penance is divided into two sets of distinctions. The first is penance in general and its parts (14-17); the second concerns its minister (18-19). In this division we can recognize the distinction between the *res*, which is formed by the actions that the penitent contributes to the sacramental sign (contrition, confession and satisfaction: the *partes sacramenti*) and the *verba* that the minister adds. D.14 is about the definition (*ratio*) of penance; d.15 on its integrity; d.16 on its parts, and d.17 on the parts in comparison to each other. D.18 is about its power, which is called the keys of the church, and d.19 about those who have these keys.

Of the remaining three distinctions that concern what is accidental to the sacrament of penance, two are dedicated to the notion of time (dd.20 and 21). D. 20 is about the idea that penance should last until the end of ones life, and d.21 about some remaining questions with respect to this. The last distinction, d.22, is about what belongs to the effect of penance.

One of the problems for those commenting on Lombard's *Sentences* was that the division into distinctions hindered them in organizing the material in a suitable manner. Given the fact that most commentators commented on the *Sentences* in the early years of their careers, many chose to rewrite or edit their commentary later in their lives. It appears that Thomas began rewriting his Commentary but stopped and, instead, wrote his *Summa theologiae*.[68] In his introduction to the *Summa*, he explains his motive by referring to the problems given by some writings used until then.

> "We have observed, in effect, that, in the use of the writings of diverse authors, the newcomers to this material are hampered, sometimes by the multiplication of useless questions, articles, and proofs, sometimes because what they must

---

[66] The number of distinctions of the sacrament of penance (9) is only surpassed by the number of distinctions of the sacrament of holy matrimony (17; cf. baptism 4 d., confirmation 1 d., and Eucharist 5 d.), but the number of pages takes up more than half of the pages on the sacraments. It is an indication of how important the theme of penance (i.e. [sacramental] redemption of guilt) was for Thomas.

[67] What follows is based on the *divisiones textus* of the subsequent distinctions.

[68] O.H. Pesch, *Thomas von Aquin*, p.84. Cf. J.-P. Torrell, *Saint Thomas Aquinas*, p.144: "He tried immediately, as we have said, to reuse the commentary on the *Sentences* that he once taught at Paris for his new students. This did not appear sufficient to him, however, and he abandoned that attempt at the end of the first year (1265-66) in order to make a second effort: the composition of the *Summa theologiae*." Cf. J. Boyle, "The ordering of trinitarian teaching in Thomas Aquinas' second commentary on Lombard's *Sentences*", in E. Manning (ed), *Thomistica*, (*Recherches de théologie ancienne et médiévale*, Suppl., vol 1), 1995, p.125: "Thomas commented twice on the first book of Peter Lombard's *Sentences*. As bachelor in theology, Thomas commented on all four books at Paris (1252-56); as master, Thomas commented on book 1 a second time at Rome (1265-66). This second commentary, only recently discovered, sheds much additional light on the year immediately preceding Thomas' undertaking of the *Summa theologiae*."

learn is not treated according to the demand of the material being taught, [secundum ordinem disciplinae] but according to that which the explanation of books or the occasion of disputes requires. It may be that frequent repetition of the same thing engenders weariness and confusion in the listener's spirit."[69]

All this is particularly true for the commentaries upon the *Sentences*, including the *Scriptum*. To give an impression of the consequences of the rearrangement of questions, we have placed the list of *quaestiones* on penance in the *Scriptum* and the *Summa* side by side. For a good evaluation, it must be realized that the *quaestiones* in the *Summa* are not on the same 'level' as those in the *Scriptum*. Most *quaestiones* in the *Scriptum* are subdivided into articles and subarticles (*quaestiunculae*), while in the *Summa* the *quaestiones* are only subdivided into articles. Therefore, instead of comparing the *quaestiones*, we should compare the articles of the *Scriptum* with the *quaestiones* of the *Summa* (or even better: the *quaestiunculae* of the *Scriptum* with the *articles* of the *Summa*). However, the list of *articuli* (let alone the list of *quaestiunculae*) in the treatise on penance in *Scriptum* would be too long to handle. So despite the fact that the list of *quaestiones* in the *Summa* is longer than the one in the *Scriptum*, in fact the list of actual discussion units (*articuli* and *quaestiunculae* in the *Scriptum*, and *articuli* in the *Summa*) in the *Scriptum* is by far the longer.

The *quaestiones* on penance in the *Scriptum* and the *Summa theologiae*

Scriptum super sententiis		Summa theologiae
d.14	q.1 penance itself	q.84 penance as sacrament
	q.2 the effect of penance	q.85 penance as virtue
d.15	q.1 satisfaction	q.86 the effect of penance
	q.2 almsgiving	q.87 forgiveness of venial sins
	q.3 fasting	q.88 the recurrence of forgiven sins
	q.4 prayer	q.89 the restoration of virtues
d.16	q.1 the parts of penance	q.90 the parts in general
	q.2 forgiveness of venial sins	(q.1 contrition)
	q.3 the circumstances of sin	(q.2 the object of contrition)
	q.4 impediments of true penance	(q.3 the quantity of contrition)
d.17	q.1 justification	(q.4 the duration of contrition)
	q.2 contrition	(q.5 the effect of contrition)
	q.3 confession	(q.6 the necessity of confession)
d.18	q.1 the keys of the Church	(q.7 confession)
	q.2 excommunication	(q.8 the minister of confession)

---

[69] *STh* I, pro: "Consideravimus namque huius doctrinae novitos, in iis quae a diversis scripta sunt, plurimum impediri. Partim quidem propter multiplicationem inutilium quaestionum, articulorum, et argumentorum. Partim etiam, quia ea, quae sunt necessaria talibus ad sciendum, non traduntur secundum ordinem disciplinae, sed secundum quod requirebat librorum expositio, vel secundum quod se praebebat occasio disputandi. Partim quidem, quia eorumdem frequens repetitio et fastidium, et confusionem generabat in animis auditorum." Translation taken from J.-P. Torrell, *Saint Thomas Aquinas*, p.145.

The first thing that can be noticed is that in the *Summa* the themes that belong together are placed together, for instance the questions regarding penance in general (to which belong both d.14, q.1 and d.22, q.2 in the *Scriptum*), its effect (cf. the place of the forgiveness of venial sins and of the recurrence of sins), the parts of the sacrament of penance (which are not only placed together, but also treated in a more logical order in the *Summa*, though this order cannot exactly be called Thomas' own). Second, the treatment of the sacrament of penance, and penance as a virtue, is more balanced in the *Summa*. In the *Scriptum*, the first *quaestio* of d.14 begins with one article on penance as a sacrament, whereas Thomas continues with five articles on penance as a virtue. Third, the question on justification (d.17, q.1) was given a new place, namely in the treatise on grace (I-II q.113). In conclusion, the treatise on penance in the *Summa* is more compact and its structure is more intelligible than in the *Scriptum*.

There are two reasons why the *Scriptum* does not provide us with a suitable alternative for the unfinished treatise on the sacrament of penance. First, as has become clear from our comparison, the *Summa* is in many ways more accessible than the *Scriptum*. This is because it is easier to acquire a grasp of the coherence of the theology of the sacrament of penance from the text of the *Summa* than from the *Scriptum*. But more important than that is the fact that the *Summa*, being Thomas' most mature work, is the work in which he penetrates most deeply into the mystery of the sacraments. There are two situations, however, in which we will resort to the *Scriptum*: (a) when we are in search of specific information concerning themes belonging to the treatise on penance that are not part of the fragment in the *Summa*, or (b) when we are in search of more material information in addition to the rather formal treatment penance receives in the *Summa*.

Summa contra gentiles

The treatise on the sacrament of penance in the *Summa contra gentiles* – of which book IV, containing the treatise on the sacraments, was written in 1264-65 – is attractive as a source for Thomas' theology of the sacrament of penance for two reasons. First, it is attractive for its brevity. The treatise on the sacrament of penance covers only three chapters, which take up around five pages. It is even more succinct, considering that the first two chapters are not about the sacrament itself, but about what it presupposes, namely that it is possible for humans to sin after having received sacramental grace (in particular in the sacrament of baptism) and to repent from sin. Second, the *Summa contra gentiles* is attractive because it is not composed of *quaestiones*, but of chapters, which is more familiar to us.

Despite its brevity, the text of c.72 on the sacrament itself is particularly clear and accessible, and treats the major topics concerning the sacrament of penance in a very condensed form. The chapter can be divided into six sections. The first section is about the necessity of a sacramental forgiveness besides the forgiveness provided for in the sacrament of baptism. The second and third sections are about the 'how' of the forgiveness, which Thomas calls a spiritual curing (*spiritualis sanatio*). The second section stresses the necessity of the help of grace; the third goes into what exactly needs to be cured. The fourth, fifth and sixth sections treat the parts of the sacrament respectively, contrition, confession and satisfaction. The effect of the sacrament, and the forgiveness of eternal and temporal punishments, are dealt with within the context of contrition. The minister of the sacrament and the power of the keys are dealt with within the context of confession.

The explicit Christocentricity of the text is most striking. The necessity of the sacrament of penance is founded in the abundance of God's mercy and the grace of Christ. The degree of spiritual curing itself is defined in terms of union (*coniunctio*) with Christ. The more one is reunited with Christ the more one is spiritually cured, and the more one is freed from guilt and punishment. Sins must be confessed to the ministers of Christ and it is through the ministers that Christ passes His judgment. The keys of the church derive their efficacy from Christ who, by giving His life on the cross, has opened the gates of the heavenly kingdom. Christ is the founder of the sacraments, and only He can provide exemption from them.

Furthermore, the text is particularly clear about the nature of forgiveness, the topic that will occupy us in the second chapter of this dissertation. Thomas interprets forgiveness and the terms that surround it, i.e. guilt, punishment, sin and grace, as referring to a relationship, namely our relationship of grace or union with Christ. Nowhere in his other works is Thomas' position on this put in such clear terms.

Hence, the *Summa contra gentiles* is a valuable addition to the *Summa theologiae* and the *Scriptum super sententiis*, not only for its brevity or easy accessibility, but also for its explicit Christ-centricity and clear interpretation of words such as forgiveness and guilt in terms of union with Christ.

De articulis fidei et ecclesiae sacramentis

Thomas wrote *De articulis fidei et ecclesiae sacramentis* at the request of the archbishop of Palermo, sometime between 1261 and 1270. As the title indicates, the *opusculum* is divided into two parts. In the first part Thomas treats the twelve or fourteen articles on faith, the number of which depends on how the themes of the Christian faith are distinguished.[70] The second part is about the sacraments of the church and is, in fact, an elaboration of the fourth article on the effect of grace.[71] This second part had a considerable influence on the Council of Florence, in particular the text known as the bull of the union with the Armenians of November 22nd, 1439.[72] Thomas' text is not reproduced word for word, but the council follows Thomas' text closely (though the refutations of errors that follow the brief positive explanations in Thomas' text are left out).

The text can be divided into two series of remarks, first on the sacraments in general, and second on the individual sacraments. It is completed with a glance at the future glory which man reaches through the strength of the sacraments. First, Thomas presents Augustine's definition of sacrament: a sacrament is a sacred sign, or sign of something sacred.[73] This is followed by a brief explanation, in which the difference between the sacraments of the old and new covenant is stressed. Next, the number and place of the sacraments is explained with the help of the well-known comparison between the physical and the spiritual life. As in the physical life one is born, and grows in length and strength, and is kept alive through eating, and is healed when falling ill, so in the spiritual life one is spiritually regenerated through baptism, strengthened through confirmation, nourished by the Eucharist, healed spiritually by penance, and healed spiritually *and* physically by the anointing of the sick. The remaining two sacraments, of ordination and matrimony, are not directed at the

---

[70] Cf. *De art fid* I, (605): "Alii vero qui septem articulos circa fidem divinitatis assignant, eos sic distinguunt, ut primus sit de essentiae unitate; secundus de persona Patris; tertius de persona Filii; quartus de persona Spiritus sancti; quintus de effectu creationis; sextus de effectu iustificationis; septimus de effectu remunerationis, sub quo comprehendunt resurrectionem et vitam aeternam. Et sic dum praedictorum sex articulorum secundum dividunt in tres, quintum vero et sextum compingunt in unum, fiunt secundum eos septem articuli. Nec refert quantum ad veritatem fidei vel errorum vitationem, qualiter distinguantur.", and nr. 611: "Illi autem qui septem articulos humanitatis esse ponunt, distinguunt primum articulum in duos, ponentes scilicet sub alio articulo conceptionem Christi, et sub alio eius nativitatem."

[71] Cf. *idem*, nr. 602: "Quartus articulus pertinet ad effectum gratiae, per quam vivificatur Ecclesia a Deo, secundum illud Roman. III, v. 24: Iustificati gratis per gratiam ipsius, scilicet Dei: et sub articulo isto comprehenduntur omnia sacramenta Ecclesiae, et quaecumque pertinent ad Ecclesiae unitatem, et dona Spiritus Sancti, et iustitia hominum. Et quia de sacramentis Ecclesiae posterius est tractandum, de his interim supersedeamus, et alios errores contra hunc articulum exponamus." and nr. 612: "Nunc restat considerandum de ecclesiae sacramentis, quae tamen omnia comprehenduntur sub uno articulo, quia ad effectum gratiae pertinent. Sed quia specialem de sacramentis fecistis quaestionem, de his seorsum agendum est."

[72] "Exsultate Deo", *Denz*, nrs.1310-1328.

[73] "Sacramentum est sacrum signum, vel signum rei sacrae". More will be said on the definition of sacrament in Ch. 4.

perfection of the individual, but at the perfection and multiplication of the church as a whole.

After this explanation of the number and place of the seven sacraments, Thomas continues by listing the characteristics which the sacraments have in common, and those which are specific to each. What they have in common is that they confer grace, and are composed of words and physical things which are called 'form' and 'matter'.[74] They require that the minister's intention is to do what the church does ("cum intentione conferendi et faciendi quod facit ecclesia"). A form of guilt on the part of the recipient can impede their effect. If there is no impediment, the recipient receives the grace of the Spirit. Those who do not receive a sacrament can, nevertheless, receive its effects, namely if they have a genuine desire or longing for it. Distinguishing characteristics of the sacraments are that some impress an indelible mark, and are therefore unrepeatable, while others can be received frequently. Two of the sacraments, namely baptism and penance, are necessary for salvation, the latter for those who have sinned.

Next, Thomas proceeds with the individual sacraments, applying a similar treatment for each sacrament. First, he determines the form and matter of the sacrament. Next, he determines its minister, for whom it is stressed that he must intend to do what the church does. Finally, the effect of the sacrament is stated, after which Thomas continues with the refutation of the principal errors that are held about the sacrament.

Thomas treats the fourth sacrament, penance, in a similar fashion. First, its matter is determined. The acts of the penitent, consisting of contrition, confession and satisfaction, are its (quasi) matter. Next, Thomas determines its form as the words of the absolution 'I absolve thee'. Its minister is the priest who has the power to absolve, either ordinarily or through delegation. The effect of the sacrament of penance is the absolution from sin. Only one error is mentioned; that of the Novatians, who said that after baptism there is no possibility of receiving forgiveness for sins through penance.

Though highly condensed, the text is not without nuance, as it is particularly precisely formulated. Thomas' position on the sacrament of penance does not differ from his position in the *Summa theologiae*, though in *De articulis* we only find the outcome of the discussions in his systematic works. In conclusion, we can say that *De articulis* is a suitable source for a first acquaintance with Thomas' theology of the sacrament of penance.

De forma absolutionis

Thomas wrote *De forma absolutionis*, dated February 22nd (probably 1269), at the request of the master of the order of the Dominicans, John of Vercelli. The immediate cause was the circulation of a little book or pamphlet "whose author contests the use of the formula indicating sacramental absolution ("Ego te absolvo")".[75]

---

[74] For the precise meaning of the Aristotelian categories of 'form' and 'matter', see Ch. 4.
[75] J.-P. Torrell o.p., *Saint Thomas Aquinas*, p.353.

The question whether the absolution formula should be *per modum deprecationis*, i.e. by form of prayer, or *per modum indicativum*, was not new to Thomas, since he had already dealt with it in the *Scriptum*. Since the *Scriptum*, however, his position had developed. In the *Scriptum*, Thomas does not propose one specific absolution formula, but in general states that the words of the priest who absolves must be in the indicative mood.[76]

In *De forma absolutionis* (and consequently in the *Summa*), the question itself has developed, in that it is no longer about the formula being in the form of a prayer or the indicative mood alone, but is also about one specific indicative absolution formula, namely, "I absolve thee etc.". This development is a direct result of further reflections on the place of penance among the seven sacraments of the Church.

De forma absolutionis is divided into five chapters that cover less than ten pages. In the first chapter, Thomas expounds his position regarding the absolution formula in three steps. First, Thomas argues that, similar to the sacrament of baptism, the absolution formula should be derived from the words of Christ in instituting the sacrament (= Mt. 16,19). Second, he explains, with the help of pseudo-Dionysius, the relationship between the minister of the sacrament and God, who is first cause. Third, Thomas argues that the expression, 'I absolve thee' is not only a suitable, but even the necessary absolution formula, because penance is one of the sacraments of the new covenant, 'which effect what they signify'. In the second chapter, Thomas responds to a number (seventeen) of arguments (*rationes*) for the opposite position. In the third chapter, Thomas responds to a particular interpretation of the absolution formula, namely that the expression 'I absolve thee' means, 'I show you to be absolved'. According to Thomas, this interpretation is true, though incomplete. In the fourth and fifth chapter, Thomas deals with the question of whether the imposition of hands is necessary for the sacrament of penance.

De forma absolutionis is an illustration of how a theological position taken by Thomas develops under the influence of the discussion at that time. Furthermore, it provides insight into themes that are at stake concerning the sacrament of penance, in particular the topic of the place of penance among the sacraments of the new covenant, and – immediately connected with it – the topic of its effectiveness, in particular in the light of God, who is the first cause. Moreover, *De forma absolutionis* is important because of the background it provides for the definitive position on the absolution formula which Thomas takes in the *Summa*.

Scriptural commentaries

Two places in which the sacrament of penance is mentioned in Thomas' scriptural commentaries are of particular interest. The first is from his

---

[76] *In IV Sent*, d.22, q.2, a.2, qa.3. Thomas adds that this is about how the sacrament of penance is celebrated best, and does not belong to its essence: "Tamen non est de esse sacramenti, sed de bene esse ipsius."

commentary on the gospel according to Matthew (written 1269-70). Mt. 16,19 is the text in which Christ is said to give the power of the keys to Peter:

> "I will give you the keys of the kingdom of Heaven: whatever you bind on earth will be bound in heaven; whatever you loose on earth will be loosed in heaven"

The text provides Thomas with the opportunity to give a treatise in a nutshell on the sacrament of penance from the perspective of the power of the keys. In his explanation, much attention is given to how the power of the keys works in the sacrament of penance. Furthermore, Thomas explicitly deals with objections that deny the efficacy of the sacrament of penance. Thomas stresses that the absolution does not merely show the penitent to be absolved. Instead, the sacrament of penance, being one of the sacraments of the new covenant, confers grace.

The second text is from his commentary on Jn 20, 21-23. This text is particularly interesting because it directly touches on the subject of this dissertation, which is the relationship between the Holy Spirit and sacramental forgiveness. First, Thomas explains why Christ says a second time "Peace be with you". Next, he explains the sending of the apostles in three steps. In the first step he interprets the breathing of Christ on the disciples. In the second step he comments on words accompanying the gift of the Holy Spirit and, in the third step, he explains what he calls the fruit of this gift, the forgiveness of sins. Thomas' commentary provides us with the key to understanding the connection and coherence of themes that are treated separately in his systematic works: the missions of the divine Persons, the forgiveness of sins, the sacraments, and, in particular, the sacrament of penance. In the next section, we will return to this commentary when, at the end of this chapter, we develop a framework that will structure the remaining chapters.

Other works

In several other works of Thomas, we find additional information about Thomas' theology of the sacrament of penance. In *De veritate* (1256-59), a number of questions are dedicated to the justification of the godless, and are therefore of importance to Chapter 2, which is on the forgiveness of sins. Because of the period in which it was dictated, *De veritate* is a valuable source for any development in Thomas' theology between *Scriptum* and *Summa*.

A number of *Quaestiones Quodlibetales* (1268-72) are dedicated to subjects that are immediately related to the sacrament of penance. *Quodl* I, q.6 is about confession; IV, q.7, a.10 is about the sacrament of penance, and in particular about the question of whether guilt is forgiven through the absolution of the priests. In *Quodl* V, q.7 and XII, q.11 particular questions regarding the sacrament of penance are dealt with, some of which more immediately concern the sacrament of penance while others do so only remotely.

In his commentary on the Apostles' Creed, Thomas treats the sacrament under the tenth article of faith "[credo in] communionem sanctorum". His explanation for this is that all the faithful form one body, with Christ as its head. Within this community of saints, the good of one is communicated to the others and "the good of Christ is communicated to all Christians, as is the strength of the head to all the members; and this communication takes places through the sacraments of the church." Thomas continues the parallel between the physical body and the spiritual body that is the church when he deals with the individual sacraments. This approach is similar to his treatment of the sacraments in *De articulis fidei*, though his treatment in his *In symbolum apostolorum* is much shorter. With respect to the sacrament of penance, only its place among the seven sacraments is given, and its three parts are mentioned.

Finally, in his commentary on the Lord's Prayer (*In orationem dominicam*), a question is asked with respect to the necessity of confessing to a priest. In Chapter four, we will deal with this question (which is about the necessity of *sacramental* forgiveness) at greater length. Here, the question is asked within the context of the petition to "forgive us our trespasses, as we forgive those who trespass against us". Within this context Thomas deals with three questions, the second of which is the question of when this petition will be fulfilled. Thomas answers that remorse (contrition), involving the intention to confess and do penance, suffices to obtain divine forgiveness. Despite the fact that sins are forgiven because of remorse or contrition, it remains imperative to confess to a priest for two reasons. First, even though guilt may be forgiven, there remains the obligation to do penance (to undergo temporal punishments) in this life or in purgatory. The absolution the priest gives after confession frees the penitent from these temporal punishments. Second, as was said before, in order to suffice contrition needs to include the intention to confess at a later moment in time. Only a case of force majeure excuses the penitent from not confessing his sins. If he refrains from confessing his sins because of contempt for the sacrament, he is not liberated from guilt.[77]

Conclusion

The different works do not all have the same value and those that can contribute to our studies do not all contribute in the same way. Thomas' main and most extensive systematic works, the *Summa theologiae* and the *Scriptum super Sententiis* remain the first sources that must be consulted, and of these, the *Summa* as Thomas' most mature work, written at the end of his life, comes first. The other works are valuable for what they add to this. The combination of the *Scriptum* and *De veritate* is helpful. Together, they provide insight into the development of Thomas' theology. This development is indirectly relevant for our studies insofar as it adds to an understanding of the *Summa*. The *Scriptum* also has a relevancy of its own. Its complete, and even extensive, treatment of the sacrament of penance contrasts with both the formal approach Thomas takes in the *Summa*, and with the unfinished character of the treatise on penance in the *Summa*. The *Summa contra gentiles* is particularly interesting for its Christocentricity, especially with respect to how Thomas interprets sin and forgiveness. The relevancy of *De articulis* remains limited, insofar as it does not add new information to the extensive information provided by the other works,

---

[77] *In orat*, 5: "Unde si decederet sine confessione, non contempta tamen, sed praeventa, etc"

especially by the *Summa theologiae*. Of the texts from the scriptural commentaries, *Super evangelium Johannis* c.20, lc.4 is the most important, and it will be returned to a number of times throughout this dissertation.

The other works are relevant insofar as they contribute to particular questions concerning the sacrament of penance. *De forma absolutionis* is relevant within the context of the sacrament of penance precisely as sacrament, and some of the *Quodlibetal* questions are relevant for the subject they deal with, in particular those concerning confession.

3   A framework for the subsequent chapters

In this final section we will develop a framework within which we can organize our material, and which will determine how we will proceed in the subsequent chapters. The question of what role Thomas ascribes to the Holy Spirit in the sacrament of penance, especially regarding the forgiveness of sins, is central to this dissertation.

With respect to the first term, the sacrament of penance, we will structure our material in accordance with the structure of the sacrament itself. As in all sacraments, in the sacrament of penance we can distinguish between the sacramental sign and the signified content. In the case of the sacrament of penance, the signified content is the forgiveness of sins, including contrition, and the sacramental sign is the whole rite of confession, absolution and satisfaction. This corresponds with the two meanings of 'paenitentia' in Thomas' theology. First, *paenitentia* stands for the sacrament of penance, the ecclesial sacrament, the liturgical celebration, the means of salvation. Second, *paenitentia* stands for the virtue of repentance, the inner act of remorse, the contrition, in which – as we will see – the forgiveness of sins consists.

We will begin with the signified content, the forgiveness of sins, and then examine the sacramental expression of it in the ecclesial sacrament of penance. The subsequent chapters are structured along this division. Chapters Two and Three deal with the meaning of forgiveness of sins in Thomas' theology (Chapter Two), and the depth of the forgiveness of sins, i.e. the inhabitation and the invisible mission of the Holy Spirit (Chapter Three). Chapters Four and Five deal with the sacramental sign, first in itself and how it is the 'cause' of the forgiveness of sins (Chapter Four), and then within its ecclesial context (Chapter Five).

With respect to the second term, the Holy Spirit, the key term in this dissertation will be 'mission'. 'Mission' is a particularly suitable term because there appears to be a continuity in Thomas' theology between his teaching on the missions of the divine Persons and his teaching on the sacraments. To show this, we will take a closer look at Thomas' commentary on Jn. 20, 21-23[78]:

---

[78]   *In Ioan*, c.20, lc.4. The commentary on vs. 21 begins with "Iniungit Apostolis officium" ("He laid the office upon the Apostles") which can be understood as a summary of his interpretation of the verse.

and he said to them again, 'Peace be with you.

As the Father sent me,
so am I sending you.'

After saying this he breathed on them and said:
'Receive the Holy Spirit.
If you forgive anyone's sins,
they are forgiven;
if you retain anyone's sins,
they are retained'. [79]

Let us see how Thomas comments on this text. After some considerations concerning the peace-wish, Thomas pays attention to the parallel indicated between Christ who is sent by the Father and the Apostles who are sent by Christ. "Similarly as the Father has sent Christ diligently in the world to endure the passion for the salvation of the faithful, so Christ sends the Apostles diligently to undergo the tribulations in His name". This not only places Christ in the middle as mediator between God and men, thus underlining his authority, but also functions as a key to understanding the respective missions of Christ and the Apostles, as they are closely related. The relation between the mission of the Son and of the Apostles runs parallel to the relation between appearances of the Holy Spirit in the life of Christ and in the lives of the Apostles.

Visible signs of the Holy Spirit being given

	The mission of Christ	The mission of the Apostles
The propagation of grace in the sacraments	Christ sees the Spirit of God descending like a dove and coming down on him (Mt. 3,17)	Christ breathes on the Apostles (Jn. 20,22)
The propagation of grace through doctrine	A bright cloud covers them with shadow (Mt. 17, 5)	Tongues as of fire come to rest on the heads of the Apostles (Acts 2,3)

During the life of Christ, the Spirit appeared on two occasions in the form of a visible sign, the first time in the shape of a dove at His baptism and the second time in the shape of a cloud at the transfiguration. These two moments correspond, according to Thomas, with the two ways in which the grace of Christ is distributed among mankind through the Holy Spirit, namely "through the propagation of grace in the sacraments and through doctrine". Similarly, the

---

[79]   The text is taken from the New Jerusalem Bible, which, as all modern bibles, is a translation from the Greek. Thomas had only the Latin text of the Vulgate at his disposal, which reads: "Dixit ergo eis iterum pax vobis. Sicut misit me Pater et ego mitto vos. Hoc cum dixisset, insuflavit et dicit eis: accipite Spiritum Sanctum. Quorum remiseritis peccata remittuntur eis quorum retinueritis detenta sunt."

Holy Spirit is given to the Apostles on two occasions. As the above quote shows, it is given in order to appoint the Apostles as ministers of the sacraments, in which grace is propagated. The second occasion is Pentecost, at which time the Holy Spirit is given in order to propagate grace through doctrine.

It is striking how much the structure of each of the four events resembles the structure of the sacraments. First, both consist of something that is visible, or sensible in another way, which signifies the invisible mission of the Holy Spirit. At his baptism, Christ sees the Holy Spirit descending in the shape of a dove, which signifies the invisible mission of the Holy Spirit descending on Christ. At the scene of the transfiguration, a bright cloud signifies the mission of the Spirit descending on Christ. And in John, the coming of the Holy Spirit is signified by Christ breathing over the Apostles. Thomas emphasizes that the breathing itself is not the Spirit, but is a sign of the Spirit.[80] And at Pentecost, the coming of the Holy Spirit is signified by "a sound as of a mighty wind" and the appearance of "tongues as of fire".

Second, in three of the four events, the structure of the sign itself corresponds to the structure of the sacramental sign consisting of things and words. The things of the sacramental sign form the sensible (visible, tangible) part of the sacramental sign, while the words are added in order to complete the sacramental signification, in that its meaning is clarified. The same seems to be the case in the first three events. In the fourth event, at Pentecost, the visible sign is explained as well, namely with the words "They were all filled with the Holy Spirit and began to speak different languages as the Spirit gave them power to express themselves."

signifying event		signified content (*res significata*)
appearance	words	
Christ sees the Spirit of God descending like a dove and coming down on him (Mt. 3,17)	"This is my Son, the Beloved; my favor rests on him."	The Holy Spirit is sent over Christ.
A bright cloud covers them with shadow (Mt. 17, 5)	"This is my Son, the Beloved; he enjoys my favor. Listen to him."	The Holy Spirit is sent over Christ.
Christ breaths on the Apostles (Jn. 20,22)	"Receive the Holy Spirit ... "	The Holy Spirit is sent over the Apostles.
Tongues as of fire come to rest on the heads of the Apostles (Acts 2,3)	"They were all filled with the Holy Spirit and ... "	The Holy Spirit is sent over the Apostles.

---

[80] "Non est intelligendum quid huiusmodi flatus Christi fuerit Spiritus sanctus, sed signum eius."

This is confirmed in the text of the *Summa theologiae* on the visible mission of the Spirit (*STh* I, q.43, a.7)[81]. In his lengthy answer to the last objection, Thomas mentions the same four appearances of the Spirit, at Christ's baptism and transfiguration, at the handing over of the authority to forgive sins to the Apostles, and at Pentecost. In this article we also find more information as to the relation between the visible and invisible missions of the divine Persons. The visible missions are meant to demonstrate the invisible missions.[82] Thomas refers to a similar principle when he argues why it is necessary for sacraments to contain something sensible.[83]

This shows that sacraments are not an isolated section, but part of God's greater plan for dealing with men. More importantly, it links Thomas' reflections on the sacraments with his reflections on the divine missions. This link suggests continuity between the twofold structure of these missions and the twofold structure of the sacraments. If we can demonstrate the continuity between his theology of the Holy Trinity and of the sacraments, we can free sacramental theology from its theological isolation.[84]

On the visible level, this continuation is suggested by Jn 20, 21: "As the Father sent me, so am I sending you". Accordingly, we will deal with the question about the role of the Holy Spirit regarding the forgiveness of sins in the sacrament of penance against the background of the larger question of how the sacrament of penance in Thomas' theology can be seen as a continuation of the missions of both the Son and the Holy Spirit.

---

[81] *STh* I q,43, a.7 ad 6: "Ita tamen quod visibilis missio facta ad Christum, demonstraret missionem invisibilem non tunc, sed in principio suae conceptionis, ad eum factam. Facta autem est missio visibilis ad Christum, in baptismo quidem sub specie columbae, quod est animal fecundum, ad ostendendum in Christo auctoritatem donandi gratiam per spiritualem regenerationem, unde vox Patris intonuit, *hic est filius meus dilectus*, ut ad similitudinem unigeniti alii regenerarentur. In transfiguratione vero, sub specie nubis lucidae, ad ostendendam exuberantiam doctrinae, unde dictum est, *ipsum audite*. Ad Apostolos autem, sub specie flatus, ad ostendendam potestatem ministerii in dispensatione sacramentorum, unde dictum est eis, *quorum remiseritis peccata, remittuntur eis*. Sed sub linguis igneis, ad ostendendum officium doctrinae, unde dicitur quod coeperunt loqui variis linguis."

[82] This is confirmed in the *corpus articuli* where Thomas refers to *STh* I q.12 which is on our knowledge of God. It is said there that it is according to human nature to be led to what is invisible by what is visible: "Respondeo dicendum quod Deus providet omnibus secundum uniuscuiusque modum. Est autem modus connaturalis hominis, ut per visibilia ad invisibilia manuducatur, ut ex supra dictis patet (q.12, a.12). Et ideo, invisibilia Dei oportuit homini per visibilia manifestari."

[83] *STh* III q.60, a.4 co: "Respondeo dicendum quod sapientia divina unicuique rei providet secundum suum modum. (..) Est autem homini connaturale, ut per sensibilia perveniat in cognitionem intelligibilium." Cf. also q.61, a.1 where the necessity of sacraments as such is argued in similar terms.

[84] Cf. L. Lies, "Trinitätsvergessenheit gegenwärtiger Sakramententheologie?", in *Zeitschrift für katholische Theologie* 105, 1983, p.290: "Denn rein theoretisch könnte es ja sein, dass erst in unseren Tagen das Interesse dafür erwacht, die Sakramente aus ihrer theologischen Isolierung zu befreien und in ihrem Bereich das tiefste und eigentliche Geheimnis des christlichen Glaubens - den dreifaltigen Gott - ans Licht zu bringen, weil noch keine frühere Epoche eine ausdrückliche trinitarische Sakramententheologie geliefert hat."

Conclusion

Since Thomas defines sacraments as *signa rei sacrae*, i.e. 'signs of something sacred', in his theology of the sacrament of penance we can distinguish between the sacramental sign itself and the signified content, the 'sacred something' that is the forgiveness of sins. We will take this distinction between visible sign and invisible signified content as a structuring principle for the remaining four chapters of this dissertation. Chapters Two and Three deal with the forgiveness of sins, while Chapters Four and Five deal with the sacramental sign.

We will approach the question about the role of the Holy Spirit in the sacrament of penance from the standpoint that the visible and invisible missions are somehow continued in the (sacrament of) penance. With respect to the visible and invisible missions of the divine persons and the sacrament of penance, we will deal with two difficulties in particular in this dissertation. The first difficulty regards the role of the Spirit with respect to the *res significata*, the forgiveness of sins because Thomas relates the forgiveness of sins to the Holy Spirit by way of 'appropriation'. Consequently, without a clear understanding of appropriation, we are unable to establish the meaning of Thomas' statement that the forgiveness of sins is *per Spiritum sanctum*. For this reason, we will discuss appropriation in Thomas' theology in Chapter Three, immediately after we have examined the meaning of forgiveness itself.

The second difficulty regards the role of the Holy Spirit both with respect to the sacramental sign in itself, and with respect to the specific sacramental sign of penance. Jn. 20, 22-23 seems to suggest a relation between the gift of the Holy Spirit and the exercise of the power to forgive and retain in the sacrament of penance. We will examine what this role is, precisely, in the last section of Chapter Four. Then we will examine the relation between the Holy Spirit and the sacramental sign within the context of the church. In Chapter Five, we will examine the nature of the role played by the Holy Spirit in Thomas' ecclesiology, and how this adds to our understanding of the causality of the sacrament of penance.

Chapter 2 Forgiveness of sins

Introduction

This chapter is the first of two chapters in which we concentrate on the signified content of the sacrament of penance, i.e. the forgiveness of sins. In this chapter we will be introduced to Thomas' theology of the forgiveness of sins. We will see him at work as the careful interpreter of Scripture that he is, who is at once sensitive to the mystery of God, and not afraid to penetrate this mystery with the intellectual tools he has at his disposal.

We will deal with two questions. The first question is that of how Thomas speaks about the principal effect of the sacrament of penance, the forgiveness of sins? The second question, with which we will deal simultaneously, is that of how Thomas understands God to be the cause of the forgiveness of sins. As in all sacraments, so too in the sacrament of penance, we encounter God: in this case, God as the one who actually forgives our sins.

To direct the reader's attention to the gap that lies between the thirteenth century and ourselves, and to the problems this causes for understanding, we will not immediately dive into Thomas' theology of the forgiveness of sins. Instead, we will pay attention to the fact that, when compared to Thomas' approach, the question about forgiveness is asked differently in our times. The intention of this section is not to have Thomas answering the questions of our times, but to become aware of the difference between how we pose the questions about forgiveness of sins, and how Thomas poses them.

1 The need for divine forgiveness

In contemporary theological reflections on guilt and reconciliation, the attention seems to have shifted more and more from the relationship between God and men, toward interpersonal relationships. Words like sin, guilt and forgiveness no longer function primarily within the context of the relationship between the sinner and God. Actions are understood to be wrong insofar as they hurt others (or maybe even oneself), but not insofar as they "offend"[1] God. Similarly, the forgiveness that is sought is not primarily God's forgiveness, or divine forgiveness, but instead the forgiveness of the victim. As a result, the focus is nowadays not on God, nor on the sinner asking for divine forgiveness, but on the victim and his or her ability or inability to forgive the offender.[2]

---

[1] Cf. the definition of sin as 'offensa Dei' in the *Catechism of the Catholic Church* nr. 1850; cf. *STh* I-II, q.114, a.2 co: "peccatum sit quaedam Dei offensa excludens a vita aeterna".

[2] Take for example the special edition of *Concilium* on the theme of forgiveness ("Vergeving als cultureel, politiek en religieus gebeuren"), 1986/2. Cf. also A. Dillen, "Vergeving of 'exoneratie'? Kritische kanttekeningen vanuit en bij de theorie van Ivan-Boszormenyi-Nagy", in *Tijdschrift voor Theologie* 41, 2001, pp.61-84 (with a summary in English). Dillen compares the (religious) notion of forgiveness with the (psychological or therapeutical) notion of exoneration of Nagy. She disagrees with the assertion that forgiveness regards the offender,

This shift in attention is caused by a growing care for the victims, and a sense for the need to act on their behalf. The growing attention for the victim has been promoted by the confrontation with the experiences of traumatized soldiers who returned from the World War I, with the experiences of the survivors of concentration camps in World War II, and by the discovery in the seventies that many women suffer from violence in their relationships.[3]

The result is that, in current pastoral care and theology, the question is no longer that of how I can obtain forgiveness, but of how I can forgive, and thus be liberated from the hurts of the past. And from the position of the offender, the need to obtain divine forgiveness in the confessional is no longer felt. Instead, the forgiveness is sought of those that we have hurt through our offenses. Obtaining divine forgiveness even seems to be too easy in comparison to obtaining forgiveness from the victim himself or herself. Or, the forgiveness by the victim is felt to be a precondition for obtaining divine forgiveness.[4]

Underlying this is a sense of irrelevancy which is felt with respect to the need for divine forgiveness. Why should I seek divine forgiveness when I, with my actions, have hurt another person (or myself) in the first place? Should I not seek his or her (or my own) forgiveness, instead of God's? We seem to have come a long way from King David's utterance, "Against you, you alone, I have sinned" (Ps. 51, 3).

In this section we will deal with the question of the relevancy of divine forgiveness. First, we will examine the place of interpersonal forgiveness in the theology of Thomas. Next, we will examine how interpersonal forgiveness and divine forgiveness are related. These reflections will clear the path for examining Thomas' theology of forgiveness of sins, which we shall do in the remainder of this chapter.

---

while exoneration regards the victim: "Vergeving betekent niet alleen bevrijding voor de dader, maar kan ook zeer positief zijn voor het slachtoffer. Een situatie waarin een slachtoffer niet kan vergeven, kan voor deze zeer tragisch zijn. (..) In het verleden is maar al te vaak over vergeving gesproken door de daders (..) Het is mogelijk en zelfs belangrijk over vergeving te spreken vanuit betrokkenheid op het slachtoffer. Dit wil niet zeggen dat men het belang van de dader uit het oog mag verliezen." (p.75-76) It is clear that Dillen refers to a change in perspective.

3 Cf. A. Lascaris "Kan God vergeven als het slachtoffer niet vergeeft?" in *Tijdschrift voor Theologie* 1, 39 (1999), p.48-68 (with a summary in English). On the difference between guilt understood from the perspectives of psychoanalysis and (pastoral) theology, cf. H. Strijards, *Schuld en pastoraat. Een poimenische studie over schuld als thema voor het pastoraal groepsgesprek*, 1997, pp.19-87.

4 A. Lascaris, "Kan God vergeven", p.50: "While in Jesus' times many were convinced that only God can forgive sins (Mc. 2,7), nowadays we believe that God cannot forgive unless the victim has forgiven first." (transl. EL). I don't agree with this, and frankly I don't think, as seems to be suggested, that this is a commonly held view in current theology. As I will show below, this view follows from a misconception with respect to the relation between interpersonal and divine forgiveness.

Interpersonal forgiveness in the theology of Thomas Aquinas

One of the striking features of Thomas' theology of the sacrament of penance is the near absence of the notion of interpersonal forgiveness. As we will see in the next sections, the notion of forgiveness of sins and related notions like grace, guilt etc., are understood by Thomas in the light of the relationship of man with God. Guilt is the absence of that relationship, and forgiveness of guilt is the restoration of the relationship of grace with God. In Thomas' theology of the sacrament of penance, guilt and forgiveness do not function primarily within the context of interpersonal relationships.

In a very few places, however, Thomas does pay attention to interpersonal forgiveness. One of these places is where Thomas reflects on the fifth petition of the Our Father, in which we are summoned to forgive those who trespass against us. Thomas comments on it in his commentaries on Matthew c.6, lc.3 and on the Lord's Prayer:

"and forgive us our trespasses, as we forgive those who trespass against us"[5]

In his commentary on the Lord's Prayer[6], Thomas understands the willingness to forgive our neighbors as a precondition for our own forgiveness. We, on our side, are asked to forgive our neighbors for what they have done to us. If we do not forgive, God will not forgive us.[7] It is interesting to see that this precondition differs from the one formulated above, in which our being forgiven by the person we have harmed with our sin is a precondition for us to obtain divine forgiveness.

Thomas distinguishes between two types of willingness to forgive. Those who are perfect go and look for those who have hurt them. For others, the rule applies that whomever asks for forgiveness must be forgiven.

---

5   Mt. 6, 9-13 in the NJB reads: "And forgive us our debts, as we have forgiven those who are in debt to us." The Vulgate text on which Thomas commented reads: "Dimitte nobis debita nostra, sicut et nos dimittimus debitoribus nostris". (cf. *In Orat*, 5; *In Mat*, c.6, lc.3.) In his commentary of Matthew, Chapter 6, Thomas does not reflect on interpersonal forgiveness. Instead, all emphasis is placed on divine forgiveness, and that sinning is first and foremost something which affects our relationship with God.

6   The Holy Spirit plays a major role in Thomas' commentary on the Lord's Prayer (Cf. C. Leget, *Thomas van Aquino. Over het Onzevader en het Weesgegroet*, 2000, p.16-18). The seven petitions of the Lord's Prayer are associated with the seven gifts (*dona*) of the Holy Spirit and the seven beatitudes. This association, Thomas borrows from Augustine, though Thomas himself is responsible for the way the petitions, gifts and beatitudes are associated. The fifth petition, Thomas relates to the gift of counsel (*donum consilii*). All good counsel regarding the salvation of men, Thomas explains, comes from the Holy Spirit. When someone falls ill through sin, he must ask for counsel in order to be cured. The best counsel against sinning is to give alms and to be merciful, which is why the Holy Spirit teaches sinners to ask and pray: "forgive us our trespasses". Furthermore, our trespasses are our sins, which consist in that we deny God what He is entitled to, and for this reason the Holy Spirit's counsel is to ask God to forgive us our sins.

7   *In orat*, 5: "Circa tertium sciendum, quod ex parte nostra requiritur ut nos dimittamus proximos nostris offensa factas nobis. Unde dicitur: *sicut et nos dimittimus debitoribus nostris*: aliter Deus non dimitteret nobis. Eccli. XXXVIII, 3: "(..) Si ergo non dimittis, non dimittetur tibi."

Even though Thomas reflects on interpersonal forgiveness, the emphasis is placed on the relationship with God. Our willingness to forgive is a precondition for obtaining divine forgiveness. The only thing that is said with respect to interpersonal forgiveness is that it must be given. Nothing is said about what we may expect from those whom we forgive, except that he or she asks to be forgiven (and for those who are perfect, not even that). Should he or she not at least show some remorse, or must his or her asking for forgiveness be interpreted as a sign of repentance? And nothing is said, with respect to interpersonal forgiveness, about the need to admit what one has done wrong, or the need to pay for the hurt one has caused. This is odd, because remorse, admitting the sin and making reparation are central notions in the sacrament of penance: contrition, confession and satisfaction are what the penitent contributes to the sacramental sign.

Even though Thomas reserves the notion of forgiveness for our relationship with God, this does not imply that he does not reflect on reconciliation in interpersonal relationship. Thomas does so, even within the context of the sacrament of penance, but at a different place and in a different way. If we want to know what Thomas has to say about reconciliation between human persons, we have to look at where he reflects on satisfaction, one of the integral parts of the sacrament of penance.

In the context of satisfaction, the question is asked of how an offense to one's neighbor can be repaid.[8] Satisfaction turns out to play a role in reconciliation, that is, the restoration of the friendship with one's neighbor when this friendship has been damaged. For instance, Thomas explains that when a human person offends a neighbor, he is reconciled by showing him something of humility.[9] In another place, Thomas states that by satisfaction a man must be reconciled with God as well as with his neighbor.[10] Wissink speaks of beneficiaries of the works of satisfaction, and he distinguishes three: God, neighbor and oneself.[11] The equality of friendship, which is aimed at in satisfaction, concerns friendship with God, and also with one's neighbor, and even with oneself.

It is striking that the language with which Thomas discusses satisfaction is taken from the realm of justice. Satisfaction is aimed at removing an inequality of justice, i.e. the inequality of justice that exists in actions and passions. The equality of friendship differs from quantitative equality, or the equality in the economic or juridical sense, which is quantitative equality in the strict sense, and demands that for whatever loss is suffered, exact compensations must be

---

8   Cf. *In IV Sent* d.15, q.1, a.5.
9   *Idem*, qa.1 ad 1:"Ad primum ergo dicendum quod de offensa homo proximo non reconciliatur per hoc quod sua ei restituit, sed per hoc quod supra hoc aliquid humilitatis ei exhibet."
10   *Idem*, qa.2 co:: "Ad secundum quaestionem dicendum quod per satisfactionem oportet quod homo sicut Deo, ita proximo reconciliatur."
11   J. Wissink, "Satisfaction as part of penance. According to Thomas Aquinas." in H. Schoot (ed), *'Tibi soli peccavi.' Thomas Aquinas on guilt and forgiveness*, 1996, pp.75-95, here pp. 81-84. As Wissink points out, God cannot be taken as a beneficiary in the strict sense.

made. The equality demanded within a friendship is "milder in the sense that a friend does not demand a quantitative *aequalitas*, but considers what the other is capable of, and what his or her intention is. On the other hand, it is a more severe equality in the sense that, while in pure justice one can repay one debt and let another stand, between friends all debts are always at issue."[12]

So, though we are far from having been exhaustive on the subject of interpersonal forgiveness (or reconciliation) in the theology of Thomas, we can nevertheless say two things. First, there is the obligation of any person to forgive whomever asks for forgiveness. Second, regarding satisfaction, there is the obligation to make compensations for the offenses made to one's neighbor. Both the obligation to forgive whomever asks for forgiveness, and satisfaction, stand within the larger context of our relationship with God, and consequently within the larger context of divine forgiveness. So the question remains of how, according to Thomas, are interpersonal and divine forgiveness related?

The relation between interpersonal and divine forgiveness

Whoever has sinned against a fellow human person must seek both God's forgiveness and the forgiveness of the fellow human person he has offended. Roughly said, within the sacrament of penance, the "moment" in which the friendship with God is restored is at the beginning, namely in contrition, especially as expressed in confession to a priest, and the "place" where interpersonal forgiveness is sought is satisfaction. So in order to understand how interpersonal and divine forgiveness are related, we need to know how satisfaction is related to contrition/confession.

As we saw in the historical overview of the first chapter, when the sacrament of penance evolved out of the practice of private confession, a shift occurred: forgiveness was no longer understood to be the result of the acts of penance or satisfaction, but of the external expression of internal remorse in the confession of sins to the priest. The actual moment of divine forgiveness shifted to the earlier contrition. Consequently, the function, or meaning, of satisfaction changed, as it was no longer the place or immediate cause of divine forgiveness.[13]

Prior to making compensations for the hurt done to others, the sinner first has to regain the grace of God. The state of grace is the precondition for doing what must be done in satisfaction. In other words, divine forgiveness is the

---

[12] *Idem*, p.82, with reference to *In IV Sent* d.15, q.1, a.2 co; a.5, qa.2 co: (for the milder effect), and a.3, qa.1 co (for the totalizing effect).

[13] Satisfaction became the place in which the penitent dealt with the temporal punishments, as distinguished from eternal punishment (which distinction originated when the shift occurred). It is important to look beyond the notion of "punishment" and see what is exactly meant by it. Below, we will take an effort to investigate how Thomas reinterprets the biblical and traditional notions that function within the context of the sacrament of penance. One of them is the notion of punishment. Thomas reinterprets it in terms of the relationship of grace, as we will learn. In terms of this relationship, eternal punishment is understood to be the eternal absence of our union with God, while temporal punishment is understood as what remains to be repaired in this relationship once the relationship itself is restored.

precondition for being able to be reconciled with our fellow human persons. The grace of God is what gives the strength to actually go to the other, to ask for forgiveness, to show something of humility etc.

The theological point for Thomas is that the act of making up with others must be informed by divine grace, and thus the relationship of grace must be restored. In other words, only when we are on good terms with God are we able to restore friendship with our neighbors.

Thomas deals with the relationship of grace with God on a different level than that on which he deals with interpersonal relationships. The relationship with God must not be played off against relationships between human persons, and consequently divine and interpersonal forgiveness must not be played off against each other. Our relationship with God is not just one of many interpersonal relationships, it is not even a special one among them. The relationship with God is of a completely different order. Behind this lies the insight that God, as Creator of all there is, differs from all there is in a radical sense. We will deal with the radical otherness of God later. For now, it suffices to state the existence of this radical otherness, and to stress that consequently our relationship with God differs radically from our relationships with fellow human beings. Hence, divine forgiveness differs radically from interpersonal forgiveness, and in Thomas' theology we see that, as a result, it is treated at different places and in different ways. Playing them off against each other means missing precisely this point.

For Thomas, there is no question that everything, including the restoration of interpersonal relationships, has its beginning in God, and that consequently interpersonal forgiveness begins with turning ourselves to God, asking Him to forgive us and reaccept us in his bond of grace. The relationship of grace forms the basis for the fruitfulness of all our actions in the world, including asking those whom we have hurt with our sins for forgiveness. As we will learn below, according to Thomas, the fountain of interpersonal forgiveness is found eventually in Christ, who gave His life on the cross.

This conclusion has not yet provided an answer with respect to the question of the victim, how he or she can forgive, and thus be liberated from the hurts of the past. Based on the analysis of divine and interpersonal forgiveness, a possible answer can be found in the following direction. The current two-dimensional scheme of offender - victim differs from the three-dimensional scheme: offender - victim - God in that, in the latter, the question can be asked of whether the act of the offender, besides damaging the relationship of the offender with God, has also damaged the relationship of the victim with God. A grave sin committed with respect to a fellow human person not only breaks the relationship of the sinner with God, but can also have the "side effect" of causing anger and hate, or desperation, or the loss of faith or of trust on the side of the victim, all of which have immediate consequences for the relationship of the victim with God. Anger, hate etc., can be so intense that it causes the loss of grace in the victim. The problem is that words like sin and guilt, the traditional words with which "problems" regarding the relationship of grace are indicated, have such strong juridical and criminal connotations, that we hesitate to use them for the victim. As we will argue below, these words function in Thomas' theology first and foremost within a specific relationship. Turning our attention to the victim has the great advantage of opening our eyes to the fact that any sin not only has consequences for the sinner's relationship of grace with God, but also for the victim's relationship with God. This makes it even more important to emphasize that words like sin and guilt, when used within the context of the relationship of grace, mean something different from when they are used in normal context. Instead, as we will see below, we could focus on terms from the realm of medicine, which tradition has often used to interpret words like sin and punishment, and which can be more fittingly used to indicate the consequences a sin can have on the victim's relationship with God. God is not merely one among many with whom we have relationships. Instead He is the fountain of all of our relationships. It is because of this that both the sinner and the victim should, in their mutual (!) effort to reconcile, turn to Him to find strength.[14]

Consequently, the need for divine forgiveness is clearly given: divine forgiveness forms the basis for interpersonal forgiveness. Dealing with the question of the need for divine forgiveness has made us aware of the otherness of the relationship of grace in comparison with interpersonal relationship. A constant awareness of this otherness is a precondition for a correct understanding of Thomas' reflections on the relationship of grace.

In the remainder of this chapter, we will focus on Thomas' reflections on the notion of forgiveness of sins, and we will see how he interprets this notion, and related notions, in terms of man's relationship of grace with God (2). Next, we will examine the more technical way in which Thomas deals with the restoration of this relationship once it is broken by (mortal) sin. The technical term for the restoration of the relationship of grace is the "justification of the godless" (3). In the final section we will answer the initial question of this chapter: how does Thomas speak about forgiveness of sins, and how does he understand God to be the cause of it (4).

2 Forgiveness in the context of the sacrament of penance

In the first chapter, we saw how, in the course of the centuries, the way the church dealt with sin and forgiveness changed considerably. During this development, the language used to express the subject of guilt and forgiveness developed as well. I am not suggesting that each time had its own manner of speaking about matters concerning guilt and forgiveness. It is beyond the scope of this dissertation to investigate the history of penance on this subject, or even to formulate some sort of hypothesis with respect to such a development. The point we will be dealing with here, in this section, is that, in the works of Thomas, different types of language are present regarding the subject of guilt

---

[14] In Chapter Five, we will return to the question of sin and forgiveness with respect to interpersonal relationships.

and forgiveness. These different types of language are a result of Thomas providing a digest of reflections on the sacrament of penance by the great theologians of the first twelve and a half centuries of church history. Furthermore, it is the result of the fact that Scripture itself uses different forms of expression in order to describe the restoration of the bond with God.

These different manners of speaking are borrowed from different realms, such as those of justice, of economy and even those of beauty or purity. Sometimes sin and forgiveness are dealt with in terms of crime and punishment, of acquittal, of setting free. In other cases words like debt, equality and inequality, or payments are used. Or guilt is understood in terms of the absence of light, of brightness or beauty, and sin in terms of impurity. At other times the language for guilt and forgiveness is derived from the relational language of friendship.

The fact that Thomas uses different manners of speaking makes his theology of penance difficult to access. In this section we will, therefore, look for the framework in which Thomas interprets the different manners of speaking. It will become apparent that this framework is the relationship of grace: the friendship between God and man. In this section, we will show that Thomas reinterprets the different images and notions in relational terms, and not merely those of any sort of relationship, but in particular, in terms of the relationship of friendship. Furthermore, we will see that a special or even decisive role is given to the will of the penitent. We will see that Thomas resolves all language concerning forgiveness into restoring the relationship of grace, and subsequently into what is called the reorientation of the will to God ("reordinatio mentis ad Deum"). In the subsequent chapters, we will discover that will and Holy Spirit in Thomas' theology are related.

Furthermore, we will see that Thomas, when he reflects on the different manners of speaking, determines both their boundaries and their scope. In these reflections Thomas shows himself careful to leave God as who He is, Creator of all there is, i.e. uniquely distinct from all there is, and thus not part of all there is. The manner in which Thomas interprets the different images of divine forgiveness forms, in a way, a correction of misinterpretations of these images. His aim is to prevent the images being understood in a way that does injustice to God. As we will see in this, and in the subsequent chapters, this has consequences for our language, i.e. how we speak about God.

A acquittal from eternal and temporal punishment

One of the most dominating types of language in the field of the theology of guilt and forgiveness is taken from the juridical realm. Up until our own time this kind of language has highly colored our understanding of the sacrament of penance, giving the impression that it is a kind of tribunal for which the penitent appears to have his sins judged by the eternal judge, represented by the priest. The sin is primarily understood as a crime, as a transgression of law, for which the penitent awaits some sort of punishment. Within this type of language heaven, hell and purgatory are understood in terms of reward and punishment. Heaven is the reward for doing good deeds, while purgatory and hell are the punishments for sins: purgatory for temporal, and hell for eternal punishment.

This type of language is greatly responsible for the odor of fear that, for many older Catholics, is attached to the sacrament of penance. In our own time, many agree that the way the subject of the sacrament of penance was dealt with in juridical terms did not do justice to how our relationship to God should be understood. Though juridical language has contributed largely to the unpopularity of the sacrament of penance, it would be too easy to simply dispose of it. One of the reasons is that it has a firm basis in Scripture itself, and disposing of it would lead to great parts of the Scripture becoming incomprehensible. A better way to proceed would be to see how Thomas understands and interprets notions like guilt and punishment.

It is without any doubt that juridical language occupies a large part of Thomas' reflections on the sacrament of penance. Notions like temporal and eternal punishment, judgment, and the more complex notion of "reatus poenae", notions of confession, of condemning, of juridical power etc., are part and parcel of his dealing with sin and forgiveness. We will examine how he interprets these notions, and we will do so with the help of a text from the *Summa contra Gentiles* (VI, c.72).

In this text, juridical language is mixed with types of language borrowed from other realms, such as, for instance, that of medicine or friendship. Let us focus on Thomas' use of juridical language. The first juridical notions we come across are the notions of punishment ("poena") and "reatus poenae", which should be translated as "the state of deserving to be punished".[15] Furthermore, distinction is made between eternal and temporal punishment, and consequently between "reatus poenae temporali" and "reatus poenae aeternae". "Reatus poenae aeternae" is linked to the notion of guilt. At the heart of Thomas' dealing with confession, the scene of a tribunal is sketched. Here, the role of the priest in the sacrament of penance is understood against the background of the eternal tribunal, which is implied in the text of the *Symbolum*: "From thence He shall come to judge the living and the dead,"[16] which is more or less cited in the text fragment. The scene that is sketched is that of a tribunal in which Christ is appointed to judge the living and the dead. It is the scene of the Last Judgment known from Mt. 25, 31-46.

---

[15] R. Deferrari (*A Latin-English dictionary of St. Thomas Aquinas*, 1986) proposes "the guilty state of punishment" as translation of "reatus poenae", but this translation hardly makes thing clearer. Th. Beemer points out that "reatus poenae" must be understood against the background of the harmful effects of sinful acts. Sin harms other persons or the community as a whole. Consequently its effects remain, even when the sinful deed itself has been completed. For this harmful effect, the sinner deserves to be punished. "Reatus poenae" is the term that refers to the state of 'punishability', in which the sinner comes when he or she commits a sinful act (Th. Beemer, "Thomas on the extinction of guilt" in H. Schoot (ed), *'Tibi soli peccavi'. Thomas Aquinas on guilt and forgiveness*, 1996, pp. 47-58; here p. 49).

[16] Thomas' reference to Christ as "iudex vivorum et mortuorum" seems to refer to the "inde venturus est iudicare vivos et mortuos" in the *Symbolum apostolorum*.

Christ is presented as the eternal judge, in whose place the priest acts in the sacrament of penance. The penitent is the defendant. Explicit attention is given to the power on the basis of which the priest passes judgment with respect to punishment for the guilt. This power is known as the keys of St. Peter: the *potestas absolvendi et condemnandi* and the *potestas jurisdictionis* (see below). It is the power to investigate the guilt and to pass judgment. Forgiveness of sins within this type of language is understood as the acquittal of punishment.

Though not explicitly mentioned in this text, sin itself is, within this type of language, understood in terms of transgression of divine and ecclesial laws or rules. This transgression results in guilt, which is understood in terms of being in a state of deserving to be punished. The distinction between eternal and temporal punishment follows from the fact that the tribunal is not of this world, but instead extends beyond this life into the hereafter. Temporal and eternal punishments correspond in the hereafter with the notions of purgatory and hell. The main difference between purgatory and hell, regardless of any differences between the severities of the punishments, is that purgatory, despite the fact that it is a place that can best be avoided, at least holds out the prospect of being admitted into heaven eventually.

To understand how Thomas interprets this way of speaking of guilt and forgiveness in juridical terms, we must see how he understands the notion of forgiveness itself in this text. The passage immediately preceding the scene of the eternal tribunal: the text on the power of the keys and Christ being appointed judge over the living and the dead, is crucial in this respect.

"In the later spiritual healing we are conjoined to Christ in accord with our own operation informed by divine grace. Hence, we do not always entirely, nor do we all equally, achieve the effect of remission by this conjunction. For there can be a turning of the mind toward God, and to the hatred of sin which is so vehement that a man perfectly achieves the remission of sin, not only with regard to wiping out the fault, but even with regard to remission of the entire punishment. But this does not always happen. Hence, after the fault is taken away by contrition and the guilt of eternal punishment is relieved (as was said), there sometimes persists an obligation to some punishment to maintain the justice of God which requires that fault be ordered by punishment."[17]

This text gives the ground for the necessity of a confession: the appearance before the tribunal. Forgiveness of sin (*remissio peccati*) is put in terms of

[17] ScG IV, c.72: "In hac vero spirituali sanatione Christo coniungimur secundum operationem nostram divina gratia informatam; unde non semper totaliter nec omnes aequaliter remissionis effectum per hanc coniunctionem consequuntur. Potest enim esse conversio mentis in Deum et in detestationem peccati tam vehemens quod perfecte remissionem peccati homo consequitur, non solum quantum ad purgationem culpae, sed etiam ad remissionem totius poenae. Hoc autem non semper contingit. Unde quandoque per contritionem amota culpa et reatu poenae aeternae soluto, ut dictum est, remanet obligatio ad aliquam peonam temporalem, ut iustitia Dei salvetur, secundum quam culpa ordinatur per poenam." (Transl. according to C. O'Neil, *St. Thomas Aquinas. On the truth of the catholic faith. Summa contra Gentiles*, Book four: Salvation, 1957).

conversion of the mind to God, the conjunction of the penitent with Christ. It is possible, Thomas says, that the conversion and the resulting reunion happen with such force (vehemently), that there remains no guilt to be purged, and subsequently no punishment unforgiven. The meaning of words like guilt, and consequently "reatus poena" are given in the context of a relationship which is primarily the relationship (or conjunction) between man (sinner, penitent) and Christ. The amount of punishment that remains after conversion is inversely proportional to the vehemence of the conversion to God. The notion of "reatus poenae" becomes a notion that, first and foremost, says something about how the penitent is or is not united with Christ. "Reatus poenae aeternae" (or the corresponding notion of guilt) says that the union is completely absent, while "reatus poenae temporali" says that the union may be restored, but is incomplete. Punishment itself becomes a term that functions less within the context of vindictive justice, in which "an eye is demanded for an eye and a tooth for a tooth". Instead, it receives its meaning in being aimed at deepening the friendship by removing the attachments to this world that keep the penitent from growing in his union with Christ.

The beginning of the restoration of friendship with Christ consists in what Thomas calls the reorientation of the mind to God (*reordinatio mentis ad Deum*), which is the core of contrition. Contrition is one of the three integral parts (*partes integrales*) of the sacrament of penance, the other two being confession and satisfaction. In this text confession receives the primary meaning of instrument for the priest to establish the punishment that remains. In other texts, confession is primarily understood as the expression of internal contrition. In these texts, confession is part of the external penance which is a sign of internal penance which primarily consists in contrition. In Chapter Four we will deal with internal and external penance, and with confession as the main expression of internal contrition.

The interpretation confession receives in the text of the *Summa contra gentiles* reminds one of the early medieval practice of private confession, or tariff penance, which we came across in the historical overview in the first chapter. In this practice, confession was necessary for the confessor to be able to calculate which "tariff" should be imposed on the penitent. At the same time, Thomas' interpretation of contrition, and his explicit mentioning of the possibility of the contrition being so vehement that there remains no "reatus poenae temporali", is a clear illustration of the shift from the old practice to the new sacrament of penance, in which sins are not primarily forgiven by doing penance, but in the act of contrition.

Setting free (absolution)

Juridical language is immediately connected with the type of language in which sin and forgiveness is spoken about in terms of imprisonment, or being set free (absolved). The central text from Scripture that must be associated with this type of language is Mt. 16, 19:

"I will give you the keys of the kingdom of Heaven: whatever you bind on earth
will be bound in heaven; whatever you loose on earth will be loosed in heaven."

On one hand, the central terms are the keys of the kingdom of heaven (*claves
regni caelorum*) and, on the other hand, the binding (*ligare*) and loosing (*solvere*) on
earth and in heaven.

In the *Scriptum*, Thomas devotes two *distinctiones* to the keys of the church, in
the context of the sacrament of penance. In the *Summa theologiae*, the keys of the
church are mentioned in the context of the sacrament of baptism, when the
difference between penance and baptism is at stake, and in the context of the
sacrament of penance. The following is a paraphrase of what is found there.[18]

Within the metaphor referred to by notions such as keys, and binding and
loosing, forgiveness of sins has to do with the opening of the door to the
kingdom of heaven, which door was closed by sin. Insofar as the door was
closed by original sin, the sacrament of baptism re-opens the door. This is why
baptism is called the door to all other sacraments. Once opened by baptism, the
door to the kingdom of heaven can be closed again by actual (mortal) sin, and
be opened again by the sacrament of penance. Sin closes the door, because it
causes both the stain of guilt (*macula culpae*) and the state of deserving to be
punished (*reatus poenae*). Actual sins are forgiven through the sacrament of
penance. The minister of this sacrament must have the keys of the church, i.e.
the power to bind or loose. And this power is called the power of the keys of
the church, or the keys of St. Peter. The keys of the church, then, are the means
by which actual sins are forgiven. The forgiveness regards both the stain of
guilt and the punishable state. This is done by binding the penitent to the works
of satisfaction and loosing him from his sins.[19] Through this, the doors to the
kingdom of heaven are opened again.

Furthermore, the keys of the church are the link between the passion of Christ
on one hand, and the penitent on the other. The penitent benefits from the
saving effect of the passion of Christ by subjecting himself to the power of the
keys of the church in confession.[20]

The interesting thing is that, in fact, these keys not only admit or exclude from
the kingdom of heaven, but also admit and exclude from participation in
communion in the sacrament of the Eucharist. The metaphor of the keys of the
church, and of the binding and loosing, refer to both the admittance to, and the
exclusion from, the final goal of men that is metaphorically called the kingdom
of heaven, and the admittance to, or exclusion from, the Eucharist.

Thomas' discussion of "*claves ecclesiae*" in the *Scriptum* and the *Summa contra
Gentiles* shows that the power of the keys of the church is twofold. It consists in
the actual power to absolve or condemn, and in the authority to know the guilt
of the penitent.[21] The first is given when one is ordained priest, and is, in fact,

---

18   *STh* III, q.68, a.6 co; q.69, a.1 ad 2; q.84, a.3 ad 3 and ad 5,; q.84, a.7 co, and ad 2,; q.86, a.6
     co, and ad 3; q.88, a.2 co; q.89, a.1 ad 2 and a.3 ad 2.
19   *STh* III q.68 a.6 co.
20   See also Chapter Four.
21   *In IV Sent* d.18, q.1, a.1, qa.3 co; *ScG* IV c.72.

equal in substance with the power of consecrating bread and wine. Nevertheless, the power to consecrate and the power to absolve or condemn (both powers of ordination) differ *ratione*, because they are put to different use.[22]

The second belongs to the same authority given in the ordination, but at the same time differs from the act of absolving. In fact it is the authority to judge whether one is worthy, or not, to receive absolution. This judgment is passed based on (acquired or infused) knowledge of the law. The authority is the exercise of the act of knowing. One also needs to have jurisdiction in order to use the keys of the church legitimately. To illustrate this: one can have the power to absolve, including the authority to judge whether one is worthy of absolution, because one is ordained a priest, but nevertheless one can be prevented from using this power.[23]

In some respects, the metaphor of opening and closing a door can be misleading, for instance in how we understand the accessibility of heaven. According to Rv. 4, 1, the door of the kingdom of heaven is always open, since it was opened by the passion of Christ. Thomas stresses that the door is called "closed" because of something blocking its entrance, not on the part of God but on our part. It is not God who keeps the door of heaven closed, but it is we who keep it closed by sinning and not wanting to repent.

Furthermore, the metaphors of the keys can suggest that heaven and hell are related to each other as opening and closing, or as keys of heaven and keys of hell. The latter can even suggest heaven and hell to be equal alternatives or alternatives on the same level. Hell and heaven can be understood as two sides of the same coin. However, Thomas does not understand heaven and hell as equal alternatives, or as being on the same level. When Thomas distinguishes between the keys of heaven and the keys of hell, one would immediately think of the keys of hell as the counterparts of the keys of heaven. As the keys of heaven are those that allow someone into the kingdom of heaven, so the keys of hell would be the keys that let someone enter hell. Thomas however, interprets the keys of hell unexpectedly in a completely different way. The keys of hell are not understood as the power to condemn someone, but as the power to confer grace through which one is either led out of sin, or kept from more sinning. In other words, they have the same "positive" meaning as the keys of heaven.[24]

This asymmetry between heaven and hell, and more fundamentally, between good and evil (as is most explicitly expressed by the definition of evil as *privatio boni*), is present throughout all of Thomas' works. This asymmetry determines his understanding of the power of the keys of the church as well. Here, the same danger exists of misunderstanding the two sides of the power of the keys: the power to accept and to exclude. What is not meant is that the priest, by excluding, is impeding someone's entrance into the kingdom of heaven. What

---

[22] *In IV Sent* d.18, q.1, a.1, qa.2 ad 1.
[23] *Idem*, ad 2.
[24] *Idem*, ad 3.

is meant, according to Thomas, is that, in excluding, the priest is not removing that which impedes someone's entrance the kingdom of heaven.[25] We must keep in mind that when Thomas speaks of heaven and hell, of keys, of binding and loosing, he is using metaphors. Thomas explains what heaven and hell are in terms of being or not being with God, i.e. in terms of relationship.

Spiritual healing

The text of the *Summa contra Gentiles*, parts of which we read above, is also rich in language borrowed from the medical realm. This type of language dominates the immediate beginning of the chapter on the sacrament of penance, where penance is understood as being similar to a spiritual healing, and as a remedy against sin committed after having been baptized. Thomas' theology of the sacraments is famous for the parallel he draws between the physical and spiritual life (e.g. in *De articulis fidei at ecclesiae sacramentis*, treated in ch. 1). Parallel to birth, growth in length and strength, nourishment and healing in the physical life, one is regenerated spiritually in the sacrament of baptism, strengthened by the sacrament of confirmation, nourished by the Eucharist, healed spiritually by the sacrament of penance, and healed spiritually *and* physically by the anointment of the sick.

What does the mental illness that is healed in the sacrament of penance consist of? Thomas distinguishes between three "injuries" (*incommoda*) that must be cured. The first is the disorientation of the mind, in that it is averted from God and converted to sin. The second is the "reatus poenae". The third is what Thomas calls the weakening of the natural good ("debilitatio naturalis boni"). Notice that different types of language are mixed in these descriptions of the three "injuries" caused by sin. While "weakening of the natural good" can, with a little good will, be taken to have its origins in the medical realm, this is clearly not the case with the psychological, or better, moral notion of mental orientation, and the juridical "reatus poena" we came across earlier.

Furthermore, within the context of confession, Christ was presented as "judge over the living and the dead" (*iudex vivorum et mortuorum*). Here, within the context of contrition, Christ is presented as "the physician of our souls" (*medicus animarum nostrarum*). As we saw earlier, spiritual healing is understood in terms of our conjunction with Christ, i.e. in terms of relationship.

The use of medical language in our reflections on guilt and forgiveness does not have the same negative connotations of fear etc. as language from the juridical realm. For that reason, some prefer this type of language to juridical language. But speaking of sacraments in terms of medicine has its own difficulties. When we think of medicines, we often think of a pill or a mixture. These kinds of medicines work in a rather mechanical way, without any contribution from the patient himself. He or she takes the medicine, and with the help of this medicine the body restores its health. Such an interpretation of the effectiveness of the sacrament of penance is problematic on four points.

---

[25] *Idem*, ad 4.

1. The freedom of God. When the sacraments are understood as medicines, and they are given to the church in order to be distributed among those who need them, God tends to disappear from the stage. The sacraments, like medicines, may seem to have their healing strength in themselves, distinct from the original provider of the sacraments, Christ.
2. The role of the Church. Medicines have their effectiveness apart from the surrounding community. But sacraments are first and foremost communal celebrations. As we will see in the fifth chapter, the church as the community of the faithful plays an important role with respect to how sacraments "work".
3. The freedom of the penitent. Medicines heal the body in a rather mechanical way. However, forgiveness of sins is not some sort of physiological process: applying the sacrament of penance does not "do the trick". Forgiveness of sins, as we will see below, has to do with free choices, the choice of a free will for freedom.
4. The role of the will. In the case of natural life, there is a certain distance between the disease and the cure on the one hand, and, on the other, the one who is sick and is cured. Because of this distance, the one who is sick does not coincide with his sickness. Therefore, there can be a free choice by the one who is sick to take medicines. In the case of sin, however, it is the will itself that is sick. This means that, in a way, the will to take the medicine forms itself the beginning of the process of healing.

The nature of the forgiveness of sins consists, according to Thomas, in the fact that the sinner is reunited with Christ. The sinner receives the forgiveness of his sins in the measure in which he is united with Christ. At this point the language with which the curing of the soul is described shifts from medical to relational. In physical life, recovery has nothing to do with being re-united with someone, but has to do with the regulation of physical processes in the body according to their proper rules. Here, however, the healing of the soul has to do with the (re-)orientation of the mind.

One could argue that the reorientation of the mind is a psychological process, which justifies the use of medical language. The disorientation of the mind away from God is then understood as a mental illness. The notion of "the weakening of the natural good" (*debilitatio naturalis boni*) could be understood in similar terms. But the point is not that whoever sins suffers from some form of mental illness. The notions of disorientation of the mind and weakening of the natural good are not of a psychological order but of the moral order, which is understood in terms of the relationship of the sinner to God. There is nothing psychologically wrong with the one who sins, though his actions must be said, on a different level, to "miss the point", i.e. to fail to accomplish what they are after. Sinning does not mean that someone is mentally ill. On the contrary, mental illness excuses the sinner of any consequences of his deed. To put it in a different way: sinning presupposes being in control over one's actions, being free to choose otherwise, being responsible for the consequences of one's deeds. At the same time, what makes the act a sin can be put in terms of failure to take control, to make use of this freedom to act otherwise, to take responsibility. More on the nature of sin will be said below. For now it will suffice to see that the notion of forgiveness of sins goes beyond the field of medical language, and that consequently, medical terms are used metaphorically when they are applied to the theological field of sin and forgiveness.[26]

Crushing the heart

We saw above that Thomas ascribes a central role with respect to forgiveness of sins to contrition, in which the reorientation of the mind to God consists. To understand better the nature of this reorientation of the mind, and consequently of sin, we will investigate Thomas' etymological analysis of "contritio".

The Latin noun "contritio" means "crushing" or "grinding".[27] In the *Scriptum*, Thomas explains what contrition, or "remorse" in ordinary language, has to do with crushing or grinding. His explanation of this metaphor sheds further light on how he understands sin and forgiveness:

> "The beginning of all sin is pride (Qo. 10, 15), through which man clings to the sensitive part of his soul, and withdraws from divine commands. And therefore it is necessary that what destroys sin causes man to depart from the sensitive part of the soul. He, however, who clings to the sensitive part of his soul, is called rigid and hard by comparison, and is called broken when he has been torn away from the sensitive part of the soul. But, as has been said in Book IV Meteor (6 9, 386ª, 12-14), there is a difference between breaking and crushing in material things, from which these names are transferred to the realm of spirituality. Something is called broken when it is divided into large parts; but is called crushed when something solid is reduced to small parts. And because remission of sin requires that a man completely relinquishes the effects of sin, through which he had a certain continuity and solidity in the sensitive part of his soul, this act by which sin is forgiven is, by comparison, called contrition."[28]

---

[26] The use of the medical analogy by Thomas is not limited to the field of the theology of the sacrament of penance, but can be found as well in his theology of sin. For a brief evaluation of the analogy of disease for sin in Thomas' theology, see M. Jordan, "Error, failure and sin in Thomas' *peccatum*" in *Jaarboek van het Thomas Instituut te Utrecht*, 1996, p.26-27.

[27] R. Deferrari, *A Latin-English dictionary*.

[28] *In IV Sent* d.17, q.2, a.1, qa.1 co: "Respondeo dicendum ad primam quaestionem, quod initium omnis peccati est superbia, per quam homo sensui suo inhaerens, a mandatis divinis recedit; et ideo oportet quod illud quod destruit peccatum, hominem a sensu suo discedere faciat. Ille autem qui in sensu suo perseverat, rigidus et durus per similitudinem vocatur; unde et frangi aliquis dicitur, quando a sensu suo divellitur. Sed inter fractionem et comminutionem, sive contritionem, in rebus materialibus, unde haec nomina ad spiritualia transferuntur, hoc interest, ut dicitur in 4 meteor., quod frangi dicuntur aliqua quando in magnas partes dividuntur; sed comminui vel conteri, quando ad partes minimas reducitur hoc quod in se solidum erat. Et quia ad dimissionem peccati requiritur quod homo totaliter affectum peccati dimittat, per quem quamdam continuitatem et soliditatem in sensu suo habebat; ideo actus ille quo peccatum remittitur, contritio dicitur per similitudinem." For a biblical reference for "contrition", cf. Ps. 51 (50), 16-17: "Sacrifice gives you no pleasure,

It is revealing to see that Thomas understands *contritio cordis*, which is at the center of the forgiveness of sins, as the crushing of the heart. It is revealing, because it draws the attention to the nature of sin, or better, to the effect of sin, which consist in some sort of hardness, rigidity, or solidity of the soul, or heart, of man. Thomas understands this solidity in terms of an excessive adherence of the will to the sensitive part of the soul.[29] This excessive adherence must be broken in order to make the sinner free for relationship with God. Forgiveness implies, in this respect, a liberation from the captivity of sin.

This liberation does not take place without pain (*dolor*). For this reason, contrition is also defined in terms of pain: "pain from the sins committed, with the intention to confess and give satisfaction".[30] But here, pain is a figure of speech, for Thomas does not have actual physical pain in mind, when he agrees with the definition of contrition in terms of pain.[31] Thomas distinguishes explicitly between *dolor in voluntate* and *dolor in parte sensitiva*. The latter is not contrition *essentialiter*, but is more an effect of contrition. Thomas interprets it as a discomfort over some sort of evil, according to which the effect in the will is named by names of passion.[32]

It is important to liberate the concept of contrition from all physical connotations. Contrition, as a virtuous act, belongs to the will. Even though the crushing of adherence to the sensitive part of the soul can be painful, and cause actual physical grief, tears, etc, these tears, this physically felt remorse, is not what is essential to contrition. The essence of contrition is that the will itself is being torn away from the changeable good that holds it in its grasp.

The notion of "the weakening of the natural good" (*debilitatio naturalis boni*) points to the possibility that at the same time in which the will is converted away from sin towards God, traces remain of the attachment to the changeable good. In other words, though the will can be freed from its former rigidity, there can still remain traces of this rigidity in the person. This is the consequence of the fact that sinning is habit forming, because of which "man by sinning is rendered more prone toward sinning and more reluctant toward doing well."[33] With regard to this, acts of satisfaction must be understood as exercises, by which the person "learns" to do well.

That the will becomes excessively attached to changeable goods, and that sinning is habit-forming in that it becomes more difficult to do good (and as a

---

burnt offering you do not desire. Sacrifice to God is a broken spirit, a broken, contrite heart you never scorn."

29 Following Aristotle's *De Anima*, Thomas distinguishes between three parts of the soul: the *pars vegetativa*, the *pars sensitiva* and the *pars intellectiva*. The first is the lowest part, and it is occupied with nutrition, production and growth, the second comprises the apprehensive and appetitive functions, while the last and highest part contains the intellect and the will.

30 *In IV Sent* d.17, q.2, a.1, qa.1: "dolor pro peccatis assumptus cum propostito confitendi et satisfaciendi"

31 *Ibidem.*

32 *Idem,* qa.2 ad 1.

33 *ScG* IV c.72: "Tertium [detrimentum] est quaedam debilitatio naturalis boni, secundum quod homo peccando redditur pronior ad peccandum et tardior ad bene agendum."

consequence more easy to sin again), points to the fact that sinning is not an abstract act of a person rejecting God before His face, but instead has to do with concrete and particular choices of the will. It shows something of the tragedy of sin, as something that is never chosen but is instead a consequence of poor choices for things that, in themselves, are good.[34]

Removing the stain of guilt

From what we have seen above, we can conclude that, with respect to forgiveness of sins, two moments must be distinguished. The first moment is the reorientation of the will, the reordering of the mind away from sin toward God (*reordinatio mentis ad Deum*), with the help of grace. This moment corresponds to the notion of eternal punishment and the forgiveness of guilt. The second moment is the strengthening of the natural good, and this corresponds to the notion of temporal punishment.

The notion of the stain of guilt (*macula culpae*) is an almost technical term, with which Thomas, throughout his theological work, refers to the absence of grace. It consists in the disordering of the mind, in that the mind is turned away from God, and turned toward sin. We find the notion of the stain of guilt in different places in different works of Thomas, but he speaks most extensively about it in the *Scriptum* (*In IV Sent* d.18, q.1, a.2, i.e. in the context of the sacrament of penance) and in the *Summa theologiae* (*STh* I-II q.86). We will take a look at both places, to see how the notion functions in Thomas' theology. First we will look at the *Scriptum*, second, at the text of the *Summa*.

In the *Scriptum*, Thomas understands the stain of guilt on the soul from the use of the word "stain" in ordinary language. Under normal circumstances, something is called stained when it is deprived of a beauty that is supposed to be there (*debita pulchritudo*).[35] Or, comparatively, something is called stained, when something else is placed between it and the source of the light that shines upon it, so that that which is placed in between casts a shadow upon it. "Stain" is then understood as darkness (*tenebra*), i.e. the deprivation of light.

From this, St. Thomas understands the stain of guilt on the soul to be the deprivation of the beauty (*pulchritudo*) of the soul, which consists in the assimilation of the soul to God. The soul is assimilated to God by the clarity of grace that shines upon the soul.[36] Sin has as its effect that it prohibits the light of grace from falling upon the soul; consequently it causes the stain of guilt upon the soul.

Thomas uses this analysis to argue that the stain of guilt is not something positive, but is instead the absence of something positive, namely the grace of God. At the same time, he holds that God is not the immediate cause of the

---

[34] For an analysis of Thomas' category of *peccatum*, see M. Jordan "Error". Below, we will deal with the notion of sinning more extensively.

[35] *In IV Sent* d.18, q.1, a.2, qa.1 co: "Dicendum ad primam quaestionem quod ex hoc aliquid maculatum dicitur, quia debitae pulchritudinis patitur detrimentum."

[36] *Ibidem*: "Pulchritudo autem animae consistit in assimilatione ipsius ad Deum, ad quam formari debet per claritatem gratiae ab eo susceptam."

absence. It is not God who withholds His grace from shining upon man, but man, who by sinning, blocks the light of God's grace.

In comparison with the *Scriptum*, Thomas makes this picture even more "physical" in the *Summa theologiae*. In the *Summa*, the notion of stain is also explained from its use in the physical realm (*in corporalibus*). The examples he uses are bodies made of silver or gold that have the property of shining brightly. When these bodies come in contact with something they can become stained.[37] In the *Summa*, Thomas uses a different word for beauty: *nitor* (in the *Scriptum: pulchritudo*). *Nitor* has a slightly different meaning to *pulchritude*, as, besides "beauty", it also means "brightness", "luster", "sheen".[38] I suppose that it can best be understood as the ability to reflect light. It is the ability to reflect light that makes gold and silver beautiful.[39]

According to Thomas, the brightness or beauty of the human soul is twofold: (1) through the reflected luster of the light of natural reason; (2) through the reflected luster of divine light, i.e. wisdom and grace. When this brightness of the soul is harmed or lost by sin, this deprivation of brightness is metaphorically called "stain". Note that the notion of the stain of guilt, as Thomas interprets it, refers less to the biblical notion of ritual or liturgical impurity[40], and more to the doctrine of divine illumination.

In his later works, especially in the *Summa*, *macula* has become the standard or technical term for the privation of grace, distinguished from the punishable state and the corruption of the natural good, which, according to Thomas in the *Summa*, are the three effects of sin.[41]

Now that we know how Thomas interprets the notion of the stain of guilt, we can ask how he understands forgiveness of sins in terms of the removal of the stain. The removal of the deprivation of light consists in the removal of that which prohibits the light of grace from falling upon (*Scriptum*) or being reflected by (*Summa theologiae*) the human soul.

This does not simply consist in the removal of sins. Deeds from the past cannot be made undone, and thus a sin cannot be removed as it has already glided into the past. But what remains is the effect of sin, namely that it prohibits grace from shining upon the soul. The effect is that, in sinning, the mind turns away from God. Though the sin glides into the past, the aversion from God remains. And not only the aversion from God remains, but also the

---

[37] *STh* I-II q.86, a.1.

[38] Cf. R. Deferrari, *A Latin-English Dictionary*.

[39] It seems that Thomas derives the term 'nitor' from the gloss on Ps. 103,15 'ut exhilaret faciem in oleo': 'gratia est nitor animae, sanctum concilians amorem' (*STh* I-II q.110, a.2 Sc).

[40] For instance Ps. 51 (50) speaks about the iniquities or sins being washed off, a clean heart, cleansing of sins, etc. The sacrament of baptism itself is rooted in the notion of sin or guilt as some sort of impurity being washed off by water and the Holy Spirit. Besides water, scripture also speaks of purification by fire. Especially in the Old Testament one can find numerous places where sin and guilt are understood in terms of impurity.

[41] *STh* I-II, q.86. However, as early as the *Scriptum* (*In IV Sent* d.17, q.2, a.1, qa.1 ad 1) Thomas uses *macula* in combination with *reatus* as the two main effects of sin.

weakening of the natural good, as we already saw earlier, which has to do with the habit-forming property of sinning.

It is the aversion from God that deprives the soul of the light of grace, because it hinders the light of grace from being reflected by the soul. It turns out then that Thomas eventually interprets the notion of the stain of guilt, and the removal thereof, in terms of aversion and conversion of the free will.

The restoration of friendship

Finally, there is a type of language in which forgiveness of sins is primarily understood in terms of the restoration of a just relationship. This type of language is borrowed from the realm of justice, not, however, that of criminal justice, as is the case when guilt and forgiveness is understood in terms of (acquittal from) punishment. It is also a type of language which differs from that borrowed from the realm of justice which we dealt with above.

When Thomas deals with just relationships, they are understood in terms of equality and inequality. Sin, in this type of language, is understood as offense against God, incurring an inequality in the relationship between the sinner and God. In a just relationship, this inequality must be understood as being incurred through one of the partners in the relationship depriving the other of something he owes. As such, it is a type of language that suits the economic realm as well. The restoration of the just relationship consists in restoring the inequality to an equality by some form of compensation. One must "pay" for the damage one has caused either with money, by "doing jail time", or maybe even with one's life, or one must return what one has taken unlawfully.

In the case of sin, the sinner must compensate for the offense. However, in sinning, there is something infinite about what is stolen from God. According to Thomas, though the inequality incurred in the conversion to some changeable good is finite, in the aversion from God the inequality is infinite. This places man before an insoluble problem. How can he ever cross this infinite distance between God and man which he caused himself by sinning? The solution is that God himself crosses this distance. In fact, He has already crossed this distance through Christ, in particular through Christ's passion. The infinite distance is crossed by grace, which informs the act of repentance of the penitent. Through this "information" the act of repentance receives the power of the passion of Christ, which is sufficient for crossing the infinite inequality sin has caused. In order to compensate for the offense, the penitent only needs to offer his contrite heart to God (cf. Ps 51 (50), 17: "Sacrifice to God is a broken spirit, a broken, contrite heart you never scorn."[42]).

The way in which "equality/inequality" is used, means that it no longer refers to the realm of justice. Instead is begins to refer to that of friendship. For this, Thomas refers to Aristotle, stating that both justice and friendship consist in an equality. However, on two points the roads of justice and friendship differ. First, the relationship between the offender and the one who was offended may, through some sort of punishment of the offender, be restored with regard

---

42   "Sacrificium Deo spiritus contribulatus", cited in *In IV Sent* d.14, q.2, a.1, qa.1 ob 1.

to justice, but they may nevertheless not have become friends. Second, the relationship between the offender and the one who was offended may be restored with regard to friendship by a verbal reconciliation between the two, but the relationship may nevertheless remain in need of some sort of compensation with regard to justice.

When this is applied to the relationship between God and man, it can be said that by sinning we violate both God's friendship and His justice. Because sinning involves the unordered conversion to some changeable good, and aversion from God, God's friendship is violated, because He was deprived of the love we owe Him. At the same time, we withhold honor from Him by disobedience to his divine Law. Through the first we send away grace, and through the second we deserve punishment. This state of deserving punishment is called a state of guilt, which corresponds to the absence of grace. We saw that Thomas uses the technical terms of *macula animae* or *macula culpae* for this absence of grace.

Forgiveness of sins, understood as the restoration of equality between God and man, i.e. the restoration of the relationships of justice and friendship between God and man, consists therefore in both the forgiveness of guilt, and forgiveness of the *reatus poenae* (both *temporalis* and *aeternae*). Penance, in the narrow sense of contrition and confession, involves the forgiveness of guilt and of *reatus poenae aeternae* and part of the *reatus poenae temporali*. Through works of satisfaction the forgiveness of the rest of the *reatus poenae temporali* is "merited" with the help of grace, which light reflects on the soul now that the friendship with God is restored. Consequently, the remaining inequality of justice is restored to equality.

It is important to notice two things. First, the relationship of justice between God and man, according to Thomas, only describes half of the relationship between God and man. The equality that establishes the relationship between God and man is not only an equality of justice but also one of friendship. Consequently, the relationship between God and man goes beyond a mere relationship of justice.

Second, the rules regarding the relationship of friendship differ from the rules that regard the relationship of justice. In the relationship of justice an equality of justice is required, while in a relationship of friendship an equality of friendship is demanded. Between God and man the relationship of friendship is decisive, not the equality of justice. In fact, the reestablishing of the equality of justice is an act of friendship on the part of God. With this act of friendship, the reestablishing of the equality of justice begins, and it is the restoration of friendship offered by God which makes it possible for the penitent to restore the equality of justice.

Conclusion

We began this section with the observation that, in Thomas' theology of penance, different types of language are used, partly as a result of the fact that Thomas provides a digest of the theological reflections on sins and forgiveness from the centuries before him, and partly because Scripture itself uses different types of language to describe it. The different designations of forgiveness of sins we have found in Thomas' theology are: acquittal from eternal and temporal punishment, setting free (absolution), spiritual healing, crushing of the heart, removal of the stain of guilt, and restoration of friendship. The different designations refer to different types of language.

The first thing that we have seen is that Thomas is sensitive to the boundaries of each designation. For instance, when he discusses the biblical notion of keys of the kingdom of heaven, he stresses that the doors to heaven are not closed by God, but by us. The designations are metaphors or analogies, and as such are only partly capable of describing what is at issue in the forgiveness of sins.

Second, we have seen that Thomas sometimes uses different metaphors in one and the same text. Where this is the case, as for instance in the text of the *Summa contra gentiles*, we can see that he interprets the different types of language in terms of relationship, of union with Christ. Notions like sin, guilt, grace, forgiveness, punishment are understood in terms of what they express with respect to this relationship. Furthermore, in Thomas' theology this relationship appears to be primarily a relationship of friendship, i.e. a relationship of love.

As we saw when we dealt with the designation "crushing" the heart, and as will be seen below and in the following chapters, the will is decisive with respect to this relationship of friendship. In the anthropology of Thomas, will and love are strongly connected. A relationship of love is determined by a knowing and willing. Forgiveness of sins, in Thomas' theology, has to do with the removal of that which hinders the sinner/penitent from loving God, i.e. to will God as the highest Good. It is also precisely the will which has the most important place in Thomas' doctrine of justification.

3 Justification of the godless[43]

In this section, we will proceed with our examination of the notion of forgiveness of sins in Thomas' theology. Here, though, we will deal with the more technical notion of the justification of the godless (*iustificatio impii*), which regards the forgiveness of mortal sins, the removal of guilt (*macula culpae*), the restoration of the friendship with God insofar as it was broken by sin.[44]

First, we will examine how forgiveness of sins and justification of the godless are related. Once we have found that out, and how justification of the godless is about forgiveness of sins, we will deal with the possibility of sinning, insofar

[43] On the doctrine of the justification of the godless in Thomas Aquinas, see: O.H. Pesch, *Die Theologie der Rechtfertigung bei Martin Luther und Thomas von Aquin :Versuch eines systematisch-theologischen Dialogs*, 1967 (Serie: Walberberger Studien der Albertus-Magnus-Akademie. Theologische Reihe Bd. 4), O. H. Pesch, A. Peters, *Einführung in die Lehre von Gnade und Rechtfertigung*, 1989: pp.64-107 "Die Gnadenlehre bei Thomas von Aquin", O. H. Pesch, *Thomas von Aquin. Grenze und Größe mittelalterliche Theologie*, 1995³: Ch. 8 "Rechtfertigung des Sünders oder: Das Gottesbild".

[44] The Latin *iustificatio impii* is translated in this dissertation as 'justification of the godless', for it regards the justification of those who through an act of sin have 'lost' the presence of God as known and loved (cf. Ch. 3).

as it concerns the metaphorical justice that is intended in justification. Third, we will examine justification as part of Thomas' doctrine of grace, and here we will examine how Thomas deals with the Pelagian position that the beginning of conversion is man's, in response to which God bestows grace. Fourth, we will deal with the preparation for justification, and we will discover that Thomas ascribes the *instinctus divinus*, which marks the beginning of the preparation for justification, to the Holy Spirit. Finally, we will deal with the actual justification, and the required elements that together form the so-called *processus iustificationis*.

Forgiveness of sin and justification of the godless.

How are forgiveness of sins and justification of the godless related? In the first *articulus* of *STh* I-II q.113, and of *De Veritate* q.28, the question is asked of to what forgiveness of sins must be ascribed. In the objections, a number of candidates pass review: justice, grace[45], faith, charity, mercy[46]. In the *corpus articuli* of q.113 of the *Prima Secundae*, Thomas explains that justification means making just, i.e. importing a straight order (*rectitudo ordinis*), either into the way a man acts, or into the inner dispositions of a man. The first is called justice *proprie dictum*, for *iustitia* is *ad alterum*, i.e. is about proper relations between people, either between individuals or between an individual and the common good. But when we speak about justification of the godless, we have the second justice in mind, which is a metaphorical justice (*iustitia metaphorice dicta*). The justice meant in justification is about the proper ordering of the inner dispositions of man, so that what is highest in man is subjected to God, and the lower powers are subjected to what is highest, namely reason. Justification of the godless means a transmutation from the state of injustice (equally metaphorically used) to the state of justice, which transmutation is through forgiveness of sins. The reason why it is called justification is because as most motions or changes, the transmutation from injustice to justice derives its name from its *terminus ad quem*. An example of a different *motus*, which derives its name from its *terminus ad quem* as well, is *calefaction* (heating; *motus ad calorem*).[47]

For two reasons, ascribing forgiveness of sin to justice is more precise than ascribing it to faith or charity. First, faith and charity name a special ordering of the human mind to God, namely through intellect or love. Justice, however, refers to a more general right order. Second, though charity is said to be the cause of the forgiveness of sins, insofar as it is through charity that he who was averted from God by sin is reunited with God, and though faith is essential to spiritual life, in that, in the act of faith, spiritual life is manifested, nevertheless not all sins are opposed to charity or faith directly and immediately. But all sins are directly against the justice that is meant by justification.[48]

---

[45] *De Ver* q.28, a.1, ob. 2: "Ergo peccatorum remissio non debet dici iustificatio, sed magis gratificatio."
[46] *Idem*, ob. 9.
[47] Cf. the very beginning of the *corpus articuli* of *STh* I-II q.113, a.1.
[48] *De Ver* q.28, a.1 ad 3 et ad 4.

In the sixth *articulus* of *STh* I-II q.113, Thomas deals with the question of whether or not forgiveness of sins is one of the four elements that are required for justification (see below). The result of the first *articulus* is brought in as the first objection to the thesis that forgiveness of sins should be enumerated among the things that are required for the justification of the godless. As justification of the godless itself is forgiveness of sins (as is argued there), it should not be enumerated among the elements that are required for the justification of the godless. The *Sed contra* argument already gives a firm hint of the direction in which the answer should be found: being the end in the justification of the godless, and thus being the highest, forgiveness of sins must be enumerated among the things that are required for the justification of the godless. Forgiveness of sins is the end (the *terminus ad quem*) of the whole motion from the state of injustice or guilt to the state of justice. And because each motion receives its species from its end, justification of the godless is said to be the same as forgiveness of sins, even though more is required to reach this end than forgiveness of sins alone, namely the infusion of grace and the motion of the will.[49] While in the first *articulus* Thomas argued that forgiveness of sins (the transmutation from the state of injustice to the state of justice) is the same as justification of the godless because this transmutation is named from its *terminus ad quem*: the state of justice, here, he argues that justification of the godless (the motion in which the soul is moved by God from the state of guilt to the state of justice) is the same as forgiveness of sins, because this motion is named from its *terminus ad quem*: the forgiveness of sins.

The possibility of sin

Next, we will pay some special attention to what is said about the lower powers of the soul being subjected to reason. A proper understanding of this aspect of justification sheds light on the nature of sin, or more specifically: on the causality of *peccatum*. More importantly, it adds to our understanding of the metaphorical justice that is intended in justification.

A first set of remarks concerns the relation of reason to the lower powers of the soul, the *passiones animae*. Jordan[50] points out that Thomas, when he is in

---

49 *STh* I-II q.113, a.6 ad 1.
50 For what follows, I lean heavily on M. Jordan "Error, failure and sin in Thomas' *peccatum*", pp. 22-33. Jordan begins his article with some remarks on the translation of 'peccatum' with 'sin': "Because I am concerned in this paper just with the way that *peccatum* combines several meanings that modern European languages are accustomed to distinguish, I will begin by not translating the term. By the end of the paper, I hope I have shown that the term cannot be responsibly translated by the English 'sin' or most of its modern European equivalents, so far as I understand them. This is in part because Thomas' category of *peccatum* is much wider than the modern category of 'sin'. What is more important, and I hope more interesting, the category of *peccatum* bridges the distinction between philosophy and theology in a way that most modern writers, not least most neo-Thomists, would find disconcerting. Thomas means to do with the term *peccatum* exactly the opposite of what most modern writers mean to do with words like 'sin'. They mean to mark off a separate realm of Christian ethics; Thomas means to show that the theological consideration of human acts is anything but separate." (pp.12-13). Cf. also. J. Pieper, *Über den Begriff der Sünde*, 1977, pp.28-30.

dispute with the Stoics (*STh* I-II q.73 a.1) and with Socrates (*STh* I-II q.77 a.2) on the causality of sin, discovers a tendency to isolate reason, and, as a consequence, to exaggerate its role in moral decisions. In contrast, Thomas understands reason in relation to the *passiones animae*, to which reason has a relation, which is similar to the relation a ruler has to his people. In themselves, "the passions are neither morally good nor morally bad. It is only so far as they "lie under the rule (*imperium*) of reason and will" that moral qualities can be ascribed to them (*STh* I-II q.24, a.1 *corpus*)." According to Jordan,

> "Thomas uses words with political resonances, as well as images of the limiting, ordering, and regulating done by reason. These words, these images, are meant to suggest that reason should govern the passions politically, despotically. Reason engages the passions. It reasons with them. It cannot simply dominate them or dictate them. Nor can reason refuse to engage the passions if they do not obey slavishly."[51]

This corresponds with the fact that Thomas, when speaking of metaphorical justice, does not speak of the subjection of an isolated reason to God, but of subjection to God of reason, to which in turn the lower powers of the soul must be subjected as well. Justification is not merely about an isolated reason that needs to be converted away from sin and towards God. It is also about the diminishing of the weakness of the natural good by bringing the passions under the proper rule of reason.

A second set of remarks has to do with the proper cause of sin, or what Jordan calls the rationality of *peccatum*. By insisting that reason is an interlocutor with other powers in the soul, Thomas moves "beyond the philosophical disputes into a nuanced account of how reason is in play with forces at least as complicated as those that are combined in the body's physiology."[52] This provides a better environment to deal with the question of the cause of sin. But there is a second step necessary in order to deal with the question of the cause of sin, without making it into either an insoluble puzzle or a pure contradiction, and avoid what Jordan calls the melodrama of sin. This step consists in a shift to the concrete level of individual acts. It is only when stated abstractly that the question of why someone chooses to act while at the same time refusing to accept its consequences, is puzzling. It is only on the abstract level that the fact that most of us commit *peccatum* from certain malice seems to contradict the given rule that the will can only want what is good. And it is only when we fail to see that all human acts take place on the concrete level of particular deeds, that the act of sin seems to involve the confrontation of a bodiless sinner who, eye in eye with a fully apprehended God says, "I reject you".

On the concrete level of individual acts, however, it becomes understandable why the will can actually refuse to think of the consequence of an act, which consists in the loss of beatitude. For "(t)he soul *in via* can always shift attention away from thoughts about the highest good, precisely because the act of

---

51 M. Jordan, "Error", pp.25-26.
52 *Idem*, p.28.

thinking about the highest good is itself a particular and imperfect act that can be compared with other particular and imperfect acts."[53] Were our understanding of the unchangeable good perfect, we would not be able to want anything else than the unchangeable good, and consequently be unable to sin![54] The possibility of sin stems, thus, from the fact that the act of thinking of the highest good is itself particular and imperfect. Consequently, when confronted with the choice between some pleasure and upholding divine teaching, the will can still choose pleasure at the expense of loosing eternal bliss. For even when confronted with the consequences, "(t)he will could still choose to shift attention elsewhere. Or it could minimize the threatened pains in comparison with the delicious pleasure. Or it could drown itself in the rush of its passions. Or it could choose to get drunk."[55] The answer to the question of the cause of sin lies in liberating it from abstractness and reducing it to particularities. "At that level, many puzzles dissolve, many objections disappear."[56]

A ctual and habitual operative grace.[57]

According to Thomas, justification is the effect of operating grace.[58] Operating grace is distinguished from cooperating grace. The distinction between operating and cooperating grace goes back to Augustine. Lonergan sketches the history of the distinction up to Thomas' time as follows.[59]

Augustine introduced the distinction between divine operation and divine cooperation in his *De gratia et libero arbitrio*, when dealing with the Pelagians, who argued "that the grace that causes good deeds is meted out according to the previous merit of good will".[60] The distinction underlying the argument is between good will and good performance. Augustine countered the argument saying: "God cooperates with the good will to give it good performance; but He alone operates on bad will to make it good".[61] Operative grace brings us into the spiritual life, and once reborn into the spiritual life, cooperative grace helps us to bring this life to perfection. Operative grace, thus, causes the transition from the state of guilt to the state of grace: God "operates in the good will itself, when he removes the heart of stone and inserts a heart of flesh." So both good performance and good will are to be attributed to grace.

Augustine never meant the distinction between operative and cooperative grace as a technical distinction. Thomas brought the distinction to its technical

---

53   *Idem*, p.31.
54   Which is precisely how things will be *in patria*.
55   *Idem*, p.31.
56   *Ibidem.*
57   On Thomas' doctrine of grace, cf. S. Duffy, "Friar Thomas d'Aquino: Grace perfecting nature", in id., *The dynamics of grace. Perspectives in theological anthropology*, 1993, pp.121-170.
58   *STh* I-II q.113, pro: "Deinde considerandum est de effectibus gratiae. Et primo de iustificatione impii, quae est effectus gratiae operantis; secundo de merito, quod est effectus gratiae cooperantis."
59   B. Lonergan, *Grace and freedom. Operative grace in the thought of St. Thomas Aquinas*, (Collected works of Bernard Lonergan, vol. 1), 2000.
60   *Idem*, p.4.
61   *Idem*, p.5.

precision.[62] Thomas' position on grace and justification must be understood against the background of a developing teaching on grace, between his *Commentary of the Sentences* and the *Summa theologiae*. Since Lombard's *Sentences* had become the primary textbook, the teaching on the sacrament of penance had become the classical place for a more or less expanded treatise on the justification of the godless.[63] So in the *Scriptum*, we find the treatise on justification in book four, within the context of the sacrament of penance. In the *Summa*, when no longer bound to the organization of material in the *Sentences*, Thomas treats justification as part of a separate teaching on grace. According to Pesch, the general teaching on grace enables Thomas to deal with the question of the justification of the godless without restrictions.[64]

In q.110 of the *Prima Secundae*, *articulus* 2, Thomas deals with the question of whether or not grace is suitably distinguished between operative and cooperative. The *Sed contra*-argument refers to the text of Augustine in *De gratia et libero arbitrio*: "By cooperating God makes perfect in us that which, by operating, God has begun." The first distinction that Thomas makes in the corpus is between *motus* and *habitus*. Grace can be understood as divine aid, which moves us to good will and good performance, and it can be understood as habitual gift. In both ways, grace can be distinguished between operative and cooperative.

Lonergan points out that, in comparison with divisions of grace in previous works of Thomas, it is new that that, here, actual grace is both operative and cooperative.[65] He relates this to Thomas' growing awareness of the need for actual grace in the preparation for justification (see below):

> "Now if we examine St Thomas' successive treatments of the preparation for justification, we find the following development. In the commentary on the

---

62 O.H. Pesch, *Thomas von Aquin. Grenze und Grösse mittelalterlicher Theologie*, 1995³ (1988), p.170; cf. *STh*. I-II q.111, a.2.

63 O.H. Pesch, *Thomas von Aquin*, p. 167-168. According to Pesch, the teaching on justification was no theme in medieval theology until the thirteenth century. Hugo of St. Victor in his *De sacramentis christianae fidei* not even dedicated one chapter to the theme of justification. In his *Sentences*, Peter Lombard used the word justification (*iustificatio*) once within the context of the sacrament of penance (book IV, dist. 17 c.1), in a citation of Ambrose (*De Paradiso* 14,71). "Diese kleine Bemerkung führt dazu, dass man im Rahmen der Abhandlung über das Busssakrament und zunächst auch beschränkt auf diesen Zusammenhang auf das Thema "Rechtfertigung des Sünders" als eigenes theologisches Thema wieder aufmerksam wird."

64 *Idem*, p.169: "Die allgemeine Gnadenlehre schafft die Voraussetzungen, die Frage nach der Rechtfertigung des Sünders einwandfrei zu beantworten." The replacement of the treatise on justification presupposed the existence of a genuine and substantive teaching on grace. According to Lonergan, such a teaching required that first the notion of the supernatural was developed theoretically (cf. B. Lonergan, *Grace and Freedom*, p.15: "without the idea of the supernatural there can be no satisfactory definition of grace."). According to him, the final steps resulting in the theory of the two orders, one natural and one supernatural, were taken by Philip the Chancellor (first half of the thirteenth century; B. Lonergan, *Grace and Freedom*, p.17).

65 B. Lonergan, *Grace and Freedom*, p.41. McGrath is not overdoing it when he says that it is clear that Thomas' changing views on the nature and divisions of grace are complex and difficult to follow (A. McGrath, *Iustitia Dei*, p.107).

Sentences this preparation is ascribed to providence working through such external causes as admonitions or loss of health. In the *De veritate* the period of transition has begun: alternatively to external causes there is mentioned a [*divinus*] *instinctus secundum quod Deus in mentibus hominum operatur*. Finally, in the *Quodlibetum primum*, which belongs to the second Paris period, the beginning of conversion is attributed exclusively to such an internal operation, and any other view is branded as Pelagian. Since this internal operation is prior to justification, it must be an actual grace. It is difficult to doubt that such is the origin of St Thomas' idea of actual grace as operative."[66]

The resulting scheme is then as follows. Previous to justification, actual grace moves the will, in order to prepare it for justification (actual operative grace). Habitual grace is both operating on the will, reordering it away from sin and towards God, and cooperating with the reordered will as principle of meritorious acts. Habitual operative grace is the formal principle of justification, as we will see below. Habitual cooperative grace is the formal principle of merit. Once justified, man requires assistance from actual cooperative grace in order to actualize good intentions in the form of external actions:

> "No matter how perfect the habit may be, man is sufficiently frail that he requires the continual assistance of further divine graces functioning as *gratia cooperans* – i.e., acting on man who already is in a state of habitual grace. No habit or set of habits is sufficiently efficacious to make man's operation truly good, as God alone is capable of perfect action. Thomas makes it clear that he now regards man as requiring actual grace before and after his conversion: the internal change wrought within him by the habit of created grace requires further supplementation by external graces."[67]

The change of position is historically linked with the rediscovery of two works of Augustine: *De praedestinatione sanctorum* and *De dono perseverantia*. In these works, Augustine takes a position against the (semi-) Pelagian thought that the beginning of conversion is man's, in response to which God bestows grace.

---

[66] B. Lonergan, *Grace and Freedom*, p.41-42. McGrath, though following Lonergan in his analysis of Thomas' changing view on the nature and divisions of grace, comes to a slightly different evaluation as to the underlying factors explaining the leading features of these changes (A. McGrath, *Iustitia Dei. A history of the Christian doctrine of justification*, 1998, p.107): "The decisive alternation which appears to underlie Thomas' changing views on the nature and divisions of grace appears to be his growing pessimism concerning man's natural faculties, which we noted earlier in relation to Thomas' teaching on the nature and necessity of man's preparation for justification." I doubt whether it is a growing pessimism. I suspect it is rather a growing insight into the mystery of salvation through Christ, and in particular in the fullness of salvation brought about by Christ on the cross (cf. Ch. 4 regarding Thomas' changing position with respect to the causality of the sacraments). A growing awareness that Christ at the cross accomplishes all, has as its counterpart a growing awareness of man's dependence on Christ (God) at all stages of becoming justified. But such a growing awareness of man's dependence on God, however, need not necessarily be qualified as pessimism concerning his natural faculties.

[67] A. McGrath, *Iustitia Dei*, p.108.

According to Bouillard[68], these works of Augustine both motivated and enabled Thomas to formulate more precisely his position on the role of God in the preparation for the reception of justifying grace. In his early works, esp. the *Scriptum* and *De veritate*, Thomas discusses the preparation for justification as "the preparation of matter for the reception of form: the form of grace (habitual grace) is finally infused when the "matter" into which grace is to be infused is adequately prepared, or disposed, for this form."[69] In the background is Thomas' understanding of justification in the Aristotelian terms of generation and corruption of form, i.e. the generation of the form of grace and the corruption of the form of guilt.

The sinner prepares himself for the reception of justifying grace by doing morally good deeds. These human acts constitute the ultimate disposition for the reception of grace. This understanding of the preparation for justification does not make Thomas a semi-Pelagian, even though, when he had read the above-mentioned works of Augustine, he realized that such a formulation could easily be mistaken for the semi-Pelagian views Augustine attacks.[70] The view itself is not semi-Pelagian because Thomas emphasizes the role of God prior to justification, as we saw above.[71] In the *Scriptum*, Thomas explains God's involvement in the preparation for justification with the notion of divine providence:

> "To the first it must be said that justification, of which we speak now, is always with the cooperation of the will, which is called preparation. But this preparation, as is said, sometimes begins even before grace is infused; sometimes, however, when it is perfect, it is accompanied by immediate justification. Hence it can occur that when someone has the purpose and the intention to commit a sin, his will is at once converted to God, either by

---

[68] H. Bouillard, *Conversion et grâce chez S. Thomas d'Aquin*, 1944. The main question Bouillard discusses is under what conditions conversion is possible, and what is its relation to grace and divine initiative? (p.1). Cf. the discussion of Bouillard's work by J. Wawrykov, *God's grace and human action*, 1995, pp.34-42.

[69] J. Wawrykov, *God's grace*, p. 36. Cf. H. Bouillard, *Conversion*, p.26: "Cependent, pour que le sujet puisse recevoir une nouvelle forme, il faut qu'il y soit préalablement «disposé». La generation ne peut avoir lieu sans alteration. Et celle-ci s'étire dans le temps. Pour que l'air puisse devenir du feu, il faut d'abord qua la chaleur en chasse l'élément humide et le dispose ainsi à recevoir la forme du feu. Cette operation est progressive. Quand la chaleur est au maximum (*consummatus*), la forme du feu est introduite."

[70] Cf. J. Wawrykov, *God's grace*, p.37.

[71] Wawrykov is not fully convinced that Thomas in his early works is not guilty of semi-Pelagianism: "Bouillard does not believe that Thomas was guilty of "semi-Pelagianism" in the early work. Rather, Thomas is at most guilty of a looseness of language, due to his ignorance of the heresy of semi-Pelagianism. This is a rather common conclusion of students of Thomas – Pesch, for example, argues similarly – but it is hard to see how the discussion of free works which serve as the material cause of the infusion of justifying grace and, in general, the affirmation of the *facere quod in se est* in the early works does not in substance equal the semi-Pelagian position attacked by Augustine and unequivocally rejected by Thomas from the middle period on." (*God's grace*, p.38, n.84).

receiving an opportunity from something external, as was the case with Paul; or from an internal instinct, through which the heart of a man is moved by God."[72]

So Thomas knows of a divine intervention preceding the actual infusion of justifying grace, either externally or internally.[73] But such intervention is not understood as the normal way of things. Therefore, the emphasis still lies on God bestowing grace on the one "who does what he can" (*faciente quod in se est*). This could easily be mistaken for affirming that the beginning of faith and conversion comes from human effort.

To avoid this, it is necessary to insist that the free acts that prepare for justification are themselves (necessarily) caused by grace. To argue this, Thomas refers to Aristotle, who explains in *Liber de bona fortuna* that God stands at the beginning of any period of deliberation and initiates the chain of taking counsel:

> "The beginning of the will is choice, and the beginning of choice is deliberation. Were one to ask how deliberating begins, one could not say that deliberating stems from deliberation, for this would proceed infinitely. Hence, there must be some external principle that moves the human mind to deliberate on what must be done. This must be something better than the human mind. This then, is not a celestial body, which is inferior to the intellectual strength, but God, as the Philosopher concludes in the same place [*Liber de bona fortuna*]. Just as the motion of heaven is the principle of all motions of inferior bodies, which are not always moved, so the principle of all motions of inferior minds is God who moves. So then, no one can prepare himself for grace, nor do anything good, unless by divine help."[74]

---

[72]   *In IV Sent* d.17, q.1, a.2, qa.1 ad 1: "Ad primum ergo dicendum, quod iustificatio, de qua nunc loquimur, semper est cum cooperatione voluntatis, quae praeparatio dicitur. Sed haec cooperatio, ut dictum est, quandoque diu ante incipit quam gratia infundatur; quandoque autem, quia perfecta est, statim iustificationem adjunctam habet; unde potest contingere quod aliquis dum est in proposito et intentione peccandi, subito eius voluntas convertatur ad Deum, vel ex aliquo exteriori occasionem accipiens, sicut fuit in Paulo; vel etiam ex aliquo interiori instinctu, quo cor hominis movetur a Deo."

[73]   Cf. S. Duffy, *The dynamics of grace*, p160: "If one is not yet regenerated by habitual grace, the positive response to the divine movement or actual grace is one of remotely or imperfectly preparing oneself for that rebirth."

[74]   *Quodl.* I, a.7 co: "(V)oluntatis autem principium est electio, et electionis consilium. Si autem quaeratur qualiter consiliari incipiat, non potest dici quod ex consilio consiliari inceperit, quia sic esset in infinitum procedere. Unde oportet aliquod exterius principium esse quod moveat mentem humanem ad consiliandum de agendis. Hoc autem oportet esse aliquod melius humana mente. Non ergo est corpus caeleste, quod est infra intellectualem virtutem, sed Deus, ut Philosophus, ibidem [*Liber de bona fortunae*], concludit. Sicut ergo omnis motus inferiorum corporum, quae non semper moventur, principium est motus caeli, ita omnium motuum inferiorum mentium principium est a Deo movente. Sic ergo nullus potest se ad gratiam praeparare, nec aliquid boni facere, nisi per divinum auxilium." (transl. EL). Cf. Bouillard, *Conversion*, p.124. With respect to the reference to *Liber de bona fortuna*, Bouillard notices "Il renvoie à certain chapitre *De bona fortuna*. Alléguant ailleurs le même texte, il l'attribue à l'*Ethica Eudemica*. C'est en effet un fragment appartenant au chapitre XIV du VIIe livre de l'*Ethica Eudémienne*." According to E. Schillebeeckx, Thomas' source was not Aristotle's *Ethica Eudemica* directly, but the *Liber de bona fortuna* that contained parts of the *Ethica Eudemica*, which he came to know in Italy (1259-1260). ("Het niet-begrippelijke

Here, Thomas argues, with the help of Aristotle, for the need of external help from God to initiate deliberation preparing for justification.[75] In other words, God, even before (habitual) grace is infused in the act of justification, acts immediately and interiorly in the soul of the one who is preparing (or being prepared) for the reception of justifying grace.

Consequently, in the *Summa theologiae* we see that Thomas affirms the necessity of a material disposition for the infusion of grace, but subsequently ascribes the required preparation itself completely to God: no other preparation for the infusion of grace is required than that which God himself makes.[76] So in the *Summa*, Thomas understands the ultimate disposition for the infusion of grace itself as a gift of God. The result is that human activity is no longer understood as material cause of grace.[77]

The "instinct" of the Holy Spirit and the conversion of the sinner

What is the precise meaning of this "divine instinct" (*instinctus divina*), to which the beginning of conversion is ascribed? First of all, although we shall translate "instinctus" as "instinct", it should be remembered that it is a technical term which includes, but is not limited to, the usual meaning of the English word 'instinct' as innate behavior. We will be helped by the work of J. Walgrave, who made an analysis of the term *instinctus* in Thomas' works, proceeding from the observation that Thomas, in his later works, gives a theological meaning to "instinctus", which is absent in his earlier works.[78]

---

kenmoment in de geloofsdaad: een probleemstelling", in id., *Openbaring en theologie*, 1964, p.238)

[75] J. Wawrykov, *God's grace*, p.38: "the actual taking counsel or process of doing so must be set off by a divine initiative or instinct."

[76] *STh* I-II q.112, a.2 ad 3: "Ad hoc quod Deus gratiam infundat animae, nulla praeparatio exigitur, quam ipse non faciat." Cf. H. Bouillard, *Conversion*, p.148.

[77] Cf. J. Wawrykov, *God's grace*, p.39. Above, we saw that according to Lonergan, the main result of the development Thomas underwent with regard to the teaching of grace is the discovery of an actual operating grace. Bouillard, who must be credited for his research on the historical factors, which have played an important role in this development, asserts that Thomas does not know of an actual grace (*auxilium*). He has been criticized for this by Lonergan. According to Wawrykov, Bouillard's principal argument for this assertion "hinges on what he says is Thomas' insistence that human action on the supernatural level is possible only when human potencies are perfected by supernatural habits: Since the acts which are required in justification are supernatural, the *auxilium* by which God causes these acts must itself be habitual grace, which not only moves the sinner to repentance but infuses the habits which elevate the individual to the level of God." According to Lonergan, the assumption is incorrect. Thomas does know of "instances in which supernatural acts arise from faculties which lack supernatural habits. In these cases, God simply causes acts of *sentire*, *intelligere*, or *velle* to be received in their respective faculties." (J. Wawrykov, *God's grace*, p.41; cf. H. Bouillard, *Conversion*, p.196)

[78] J. Walgrave, "Instinctus Spiritus Sancti. Een proeve tot Thomas-interpretatie" in J. Walgrave *Selected Writings*, 1982, pp. 126-140. Walgrave shows how Thomas under the influence of Aristotle starts using the term *instinctus* as a technical term for such biblical notions as divine vocation, attraction, invitation and inspiration: "the highest and most intimate way in which God moves the soul in the supernatural order: the originating act of this order in the genesis of faith and the perfecting acts in the same order through the gifts of the Holy Spirit." (cf.

Walgrave's analysis corresponds with what we have said above about the need for a divine instinct, which starts the process of deliberation which eventually leads up to the reception of justifying grace. The (Aristotelian) principle we encountered above (in the *Quodlibetum*-text) is that the beginning of deliberation cannot be itself the result of deliberation, for then the question would be what began this first deliberation. The same line of thought returns in the analysis of *instinctus* in Walgrave's article, though in more general terms. To prevent an infinite regression (*non procedere ad infinitum*), it is necessary to affirm that the first movement of the will originates from the instinct of an external mover.[79]

The pivoting point is that the will can only be moved out of itself to its goal when it recognizes its goal as such. In the case of the ultimate good, this can only be recognized as such by the will when it is liberated, i.e. when it is aimed at it as its goal. Therefore, even though, in contrast to irrational beings, rational beings are capable of moving themselves, *ex imperio voluntatis*, they cannot move themselves to the ultimate goal as long as they do not know it as such. At this point, the notion of instinctive motion appears as the motion towards a goal that is not recognized as such.[80]

Walgrave draws a parallel between animals and human beings, with respect to how they are capable of estimating what they observe as useful or dangerous, as good or bad. The animal is moved by the many things it observes. This specifies its different observations. The instinct causes the animal to recognize and evaluate that which is of value to life in and through the multitude of what is being observed. This recognition surpasses the observation as such. Similarly, someone is brought to faith by what he sees and hears. These clarify his faith in many points of doctrine. The divine instinct causes him to recognize and appreciate, in the multitude of articulated points of doctrine, the self-revealing First Truth as the highest good.[81] So one is brought to faith in a twofold way, namely externally by what one sees and hears in liturgy and preaching, and internally by the instinct of the Holy Spirit:

> "The first in which predestination begins to be fulfilled is the vocation of man, which is twofold, one exterior, which happens through the mouth of the preacher. (..) The other vocation is interior, which is nothing else than a certain instinct of the mind, through which the heart of man is moved by God to assent to the things that belong to faith or to virtue. (..) And this vocation is necessary

---

the English summary on p.140). Cf. M. Seckler, *Instinkt und Glaubenswille nach Thomas von Aquin*, 1962. Seckler had noticed that the introduction of references to *pelagiani* in Thomas' works (for the first time in *ScG* III, cc.89, 147) concurs with the introduction of the notion of *instinctus* in relation to the act of faith (p.88; cf. E. Schillebeeckx, "Het niet-begrippelijke kenmoment", pp.233-261).

79 J. Walgrave, "Instinctus", p.131. Walgrave cites from the *Prima secunda* (q.9, a.4 co), where Thomas refers not to Aristotle's *Liber de bona fortuna*, but to his *Ethica Eudemica*. (cf. footnote 74).
80 *Idem*, p.130-131.
81 *Idem*, p.134-135.

because our heart would not convert itself to God if God Himself would not draw us to Him."[82]

Commenting on John 6, 44: "No one can come to me unless *drawn* by the father who sent me", Thomas explains:

> "Not only the exterior revelation or object has the strength to attract, but also the interior instinct which persuades and moves to believing. Therefore the Father draws many to the Son through an instinct of divine operation which moves the interior heart of man to believing."[83]

Each time something objective (a revelation or preaching) is opposed to something subjective. The Aristotelian notion of "instinct" helps Thomas to understand the biblical notions of vocation, attraction and invitation as actual divine impulses bringing man to (justifying) faith.[84]

Thomas' use of the notion of the instinct of the Holy Spirit is not limited to the beginning of life in faith, the life of the Holy Spirit as children of God. Even though, once we are initiated into the new life of freedom, we can, to a certain extent, control our lives, we nevertheless stay in need of divine inspiration. In fact, Thomas' teaching on the gifts of the Holy Spirit means to explain precisely how, in the life of grace, man is adapted to God in such a way that he can be moved by the *instinctus divinus*:

> "(T)he gifts are certain perfections of man, by which he is disposed to follow well the instinct of the Holy Spirit. It is clear, however, from what has been said above, that moral virtues perfect the appetitive power insofar as it somehow participates in reason; insofar namely as it is brought into subjection to the rule (*imperium*) of reason. In this way the gifts of the Holy Spirit affect humans in relation to the Holy Spirit, as moral virtues affect the appetitive power in relation to reason. Moral virtues are habits, by which appetitive powers are disposed to promptly obey reason. Hence, the gifts of the Holy Spirit are habits as well, by which man is made perfect in order to promptly obey the Holy Spirit."[85]

---

[82] *In Rom* c.8, lc.6: "Primum autem in quo incipit praedestinatio impleri, est vocatio hominis, quae quidem est duplex, una exterior, quae fit ore praedicatoris. Prov. 9, 3 : *Misit ancillas suas, ut vocarent ad arcem.* Hoc modo Deus vocavit Petrum et Andream, ut dicitur Matth. 4, 18. Alia vero vocatio est interior, quae nihil aliud est quam quidam mentis instinctus, quo cor hominis moventur a Deo assentiendum his quae sunt fidei vel virtutis. Is. 41, 2: *Quis suscitavit ab oriente iustum, et vocavit eum ut sequeretur se?* Et haec vocatio necessaria est, quia cor nostrum non se ad Deum converteret, nisi ipse Deus nos ad se traheret."

[83] *In Ioan* c.6, lc.5: "Sed quia non solum revelatio exterior vel objectum virtutem attrahendi habet, sed etiam interior instinctus impellens et movens ad credendum; ideo trahit multos Pater ad Filium per instinctus divinae operationis moventis interius cor hominis ad credendum; Phil 2, 13: *Deus est qui operatur in nobis velle et perficere*; Ho 2, 4: *In funiculis Adam traham eos in vinculis caritatis*; Prov. 21, 1: *Cor regis in manu Domini: quocumque voluerit inclinabit illud.*"

[84] Cf. Walgrave, "Instinctus", p.134.

[85] *STh* I-II q.68, a.3 co.

It turns out that, according to Thomas, man is moved by two leading principles: internally, man is moved by reason, and externally, man is moved by God.[86] In contrast to virtues, which perfect man so that he can act meritoriously according to reason, the gifts of the Holy Spirit adapt man so that he can be moved by God. Even if it is made perfect by the virtues, reason remains only capable of operating within its natural domain. With respect to the domain of the supernatural, the motion of reason only suffices when it is being assisted by the instinct of the Holy Spirit. The gifts of the Holy Spirit make us receptive to this instinct:

> "In the order of the supernatural final end, to which reason moves, insofar as it is somehow and imperfectly informed by theological virtues, this motion of reason does not suffice, without the addition of the instinct and the motion of the Holy Spirit from above."[87]

Since there are two principles of how we live our life in the Holy Spirit, what we do proceeds from our own reasoning, or from the impulse of the Holy Spirit. The more we grow in perfection, the more we decide and act immediately as out of divine instinct. Furthermore, though the divine instinct is external in its origin, it is nevertheless interior in how it works. The more perfect we become, the more the instinct of the Holy Spirit is interiorized and the more our will and the Holy Spirit come to work as if one and the same principle.[88]

---

[86] *STh* I-II q.68, a.1 co: "Est enim considerandum, quod in homine est duplex principium movens: unum quidem interius, quod est ratio; aliud autem exterius, quod est Deus, ut supra dictum est (*q.9, a.4 et 6*), et etiam Philosophus dicit hoc in cap. *De Bona Fortuna*. Manifestum est autem, quod omne quod movetur, necesse est proportinatum esse motori."

[87] *STh* I-II q.68, a.2 co: "Sed in ordine ad finem ultimum supernaturalem, ad quem ratio movet, secundum quod est aliqualiter, et imperfecte informata per virtutes theologicas, non sufficit ipsa motio rationis, nisi desuper adsit instinctus, et motio Spiritus Sancti, secundum illud Roman. 8 : *Qui spiritu Dei aguntur, hi filii Dei sunt, et haeredes,* et in Psal. 142 dicitur : *Spiritus tuus bonus deducet me in terram rectam,* quia scilicet in haereditatem illius terrae beatorum nullus potest pervenire, nisi moveatur, et deducatur a Spiritu Sancto; et ideo ad illum finem consequendum necessarium est homini habere donum Spiritum Sancti."

[88] J. Walgrave, "Instinctus", p.139: "The growth of being moved by the Spirit does not diminish the self-movement of the freedom. For under the New Law, the instinct of the Holy Spirit becomes our own instinct" Cf. *In Gal.* c.5, lc.5 (318): "(E)t sic iusti non sunt sub lege, quia motus et instinctus Spiritus sancti, qui est in eis, est proprius eorum instinctus, nam charitas inclinat ad illud idem quod lex praecipit. Quia ergo iusti habent legem interiorem, sponte faciunt quod lex mandat, ab ipsa non coacti." According to Walgrave (*ibidem*), "The instinct of the Holy Spirit itself operates the movement of the free will", cf. *In Rom* c.8, lc.3 (635): "Illa enim agi dicuntur, quae quodam superiori instinctu moventur. Unde de brutis dicimus quod non agunt sed aguntur, quia a natura moventur et non ex proprio motu ad suas actiones agendas. Similiter autem homo spiritualis non quasi ex motu propriae voluntatis principaliter sed ex instinctu Spiritus sancti inclinatur ad aliquid agendum, sicut illud Is. lix, 19: *Cum venerit quasi fluvius violentus quem spiritus Dei cogit*; et Lc. iv, 1, quod Christus agebatur a spiritu in deserto. Non tamen per hoc excluditur quin viri spirituales per voluntatem et liberum arbitrium operentur, quia ipsum motum voluntatis et liberi arbitrii Spiritus sanctus in eis causat, secundum illud Phil. ii, 13: *Deus est qui operatur in nobis velle et perficere.*"

The result of this analysis of *instinctus divinus* is a first glance at the major role Thomas ascribes to the Holy Spirit with respect to conversion of the sinner and life with God. In Chapter Three, we will continue with our examination of the role of the Spirit with respect to divine forgiveness.

The processus iustificationis

According to Thomas, in whatever motion in which something is moved by something or someone else, three elements are required: the motion of the one who moves, the motion of the one who is moved, and the completion of the motion: the arrival at its end. With respect to justification of the godless, what is required is that God infuses grace, that the free will is moved, and the completion of the motion in the forgiveness of sins. Because the motion of the free will (being moved by God through the infusion of grace) implies both the removal from a term and the motion towards a term, we must distinguish between the motion of the free will away from sin and the motion of the free will towards God. This is how Thomas understands the process of justification, and how he arrives at the following four requirements: the *infusio gratiae*, the *motus liberi arbitrii in Deum* through faith, the *motus liberi arbitrii in peccatum* (contrition) and the *remissio culpae*.[89]

From the beginning of the twelfth century different formulations of the *processus iustificationis*, determining the inner structure of justification, are discussed.[90] According to McGrath, the discussion of the *processus iustificationis* is an important development in the history of the doctrine of justification, as it marks an attempt to correlate the process of justification with the developing sacramental system of the church. In the process of justification which Thomas presents, it turns out that one of the requirements of justification, namely the *motus liberi arbitrii in peccatum* or contrition, is, at the same time, one of the (integral) parts of the sacrament of penance.[91] The threefold structure of the process of justification, with the infusion of grace as first requirement and the forgiveness of sin as its end term, was soon set aside for a fourfold structure, in which the previous single notion of *liberum arbitrium* subsequently came to be divided into two components: the motion of the free will towards God and away from sin.

> "The infusion of grace thus initiates a chain of events which eventually leads to justification: if any of these may be shown to have taken place, the remaining three may also be concluded to have taken place."[92]

Such is also the case with Thomas' formulation of the process of justification. Therefore, Thomas' definition of justification as *remissio peccatorum* expressly includes the three remaining elements.[93]

---

[89]   *STh* I-II q.113, a.6 co.
[90]   A. McGrath, *Iustitia Dei*, p.4ff.
[91]   Cf. *Idem*, p.42-5.
[92]   *Idem*, p.44.

The use of the notion of *motus* to explain the process of justification reveals the influence of Aristotelian physics, and is characteristic for Thomas. But the use of *motus* can also be misunderstood to imply that the process of justification takes place in the course of time. To make it clear that the *motus* implied in justification happens in an instant, we have to focus on justification as the transmutation from the state of guilt to the state of grace.

According to Thomas, grace and guilt are forms of the soul, which exclude each other. Where there is guilt, there can be no grace, and where there is grace, there can be no guilt. Guilt and grace oppose each other as darkness and light (cf. the notion of *macula*). Where there is light, there is no darkness and vice versa.

Thomas understands the transmutation of the state of guilt to the state of grace as the *generatio* of grace and the *corruptio* of the state of guilt. Both imply each other: the removal of guilt implies the introduction of grace, and, with an exception we will encounter shortly, vice versa. As the removal of guilt implies the introduction of grace, this could easily mislead us into thinking that the infusion of grace and the remission of guilt are the same. But this is not so. To show this, Thomas argues that motions which have different ends differ.[94] Since the end of the infusion of grace is that there is grace, and since the end of remission of guilt is that there is no guilt, both motions differ insofar as the presence of grace (*gratia inesse*) and the absence of guilt (*culpa non esse*) differ.

Thomas proceeds by saying that though it may seem that the presence of grace and the absence of guilt are the same *secundum rem*, and that therefore *secundum rem* the generation of grace seems the same as the corruption of guilt, nevertheless the presence of grace and the absence of guilt do differ *secundum modum intelligendi*. For though the denial of something may not be a real thing, it is a rational reality, and therefore the denial of the denial of grace differs *secundum modum intelligendi* from the affirmation grace. Thus *secundum modum intelligendi* the corruption of guilt and the generation of grace are different. Remission of guilt and infusion of grace may be the same *secundum rem*, but they differ *secundum rationem*.[95]

Taking it one step further, Thomas argues that guilt is more than the mere absence of grace.

> "The absence of grace considered in itself only has the note of punishment and not that of guilt except insofar as the guilt is left from a preceding voluntary act."[96]

---

93 *Idem*, p.45: "Some commentators have misunderstood Thomas' occasional definition of justification solely in terms of the remission of sin, representing him as approaching a forensic concept of justification. It will be clear that this is a serious misunderstanding."

94 *De Ver* q.28, a.6 co.

95 *Ibidem.* "Patet igitur quod, si culpa omnino non est aliquid positive, idem est infusio gratiae et remissio culpae secundum rem; secundum rationem vero non idem."

96 *Ibidem.* "Absentia enim gratiae secundum se considerata habet tantum rationem poenae, non autem rationem culpae, nisi secundum quod relinquitur ex actu voluntario praecedente"

The culpability of the absence of grace depends on whether or not there has been a preceding act of the will. Thomas illustrates this with the image of light: the absence of light, the mere darkness, must be distinguished from shadow, which implies a body that is blocking the light. The body in question here is the will, blocking the light of grace. Forgiveness of guilt does not involve the removal of the darkness alone, but also the removal of that which blocks the light, namely the fact that the will has averted itself from God. Thus, Thomas can conclude that not only according to reason but also *secundum rem* remission of guilt and infusion of grace are not the same.

Being forms of the soul, grace and guilt exclude each other, and at the same time they imply each other, for when there is no guilt there is grace, and when there is no grace, there is guilt. This is true but for the exception in which there is absence of grace without guilt, i.e. without a preceding voluntary act. But in the case of the justification of the godless, which Thomas is considering here, this exception can be left aside:

> "After a man has fallen into sin there cannot be any mean between grace and guilt, because guilt is not taken away except through grace, as is evident from what has said above [arts. 2 & 6-8]. Nor is grace destroyed except through guilt, though before guilt there would be a mean between grace and guilt in the opinion of some."[97]

Once guilt has entered the scene, only two possibilities are left, namely either guilt or grace.

The fact that there is neither a situation possible in which guilt and grace are in the soul at the same time (*culpa et gratia non sunt simul in anima*), nor a situation in which there is neither grace nor guilt in the soul (*postquam homo in culpam incidit, non potest esse medium inter gratiam et culpam*) forces us to understand the justification of the godless as something that happens in an instant. There can neither be a period of time in between the remission of guilt and the infusion of grace, nor can there be a transient phase in which guilt is lessening and grace is growing until the moment in which the guilt is fully remitted and grace is fully infused.

Because of the instantaneousness of the process of justification, a sharp distinction must be made between the justification itself, and the *via in justificationem*, the preparation for justification.[98] The first happens in an instant, and the second normally happens over a period of time. Thus, the deliberation that precedes the consent does not belong to the substance of justification, but belongs to the *via in iustificationem*. An exception to this is the conversion of St. Paul.[99] But normally, the preparation for justification takes some time, and this

---

[97] *De Ver* q.28, a. 9 ad 13: "Ad decimumtertium dicendum, quod postquam homo in culpam incidit, non potest esse medium inter gratiam et culpam, quia culpa non aufertur nisi per gratiam, ut ex supradictis patet: nec gratia perditur nisi per culpmam; quamvis ante culpam esset status medius inter gratiam et culpam, secundum quorumdam opinionem." (transl. Schmidt, 1954).

[98] Cf. *De Ver* q.28, a.2 ad 10.

[99] Cf. *In IV Sent* d.17, q.1, a.2, qa.1 ad 1.

preparation should be distinguished from the actual justification itself. Thomas explains:

> "Since the infusion of grace takes place in an instant, it is the end of a continuous movement, such as a meditation by which the will is disposed for the reception of grace; and the end of the same movement is the forgiveness of guilt, for guilt is forgiven by the very fact that grace is infused. In that first instant, then, there is the end of the forgiveness of guilt, that is, the absence of guilt, and the end of the infusion of grace, that is, the possession of grace. Then in the whole preceding time that ends at this instant, by which the movement of the meditation just mentioned was measured, the sinner had guilt and not grace, except only at the last instant, as we have said. But before the last instant of this time we cannot pick out another immediately next to it, because, if any instant at all other than the last is taken, between it and the last there will be an infinite number of intervening instants."[100]

The idea then is that we must not distinguish between two instants of which in the first there is guilt, and in the second, grace, but we should distinguish between the end of the period of time in which the one being justified has guilt, and the instant in which grace is infused. Since Aristotelian logic teaches that between two different instants in time, there are infinite instants, we cannot distinguish between two subsequent instants, one in which there is guilt, and the following in which there is grace. Instead, distinction must be made between the end of the period of guilt, and the instant at which the new situation of grace begins.

In the remainder of this section, we will make some remarks concerning the role of the free will in the process of justification. We already saw that Thomas distinguishes a twofold motion of the free will (the *motio mobilis*: the motion of what is mobile). It can be understood as the motion towards a term, and a motion away from a term. Let us see how they relate to each other. First, the two motions are ultimately one motion, because the will is moved to God and, at the same time, hates sin because it is against God.[101] One could compare the motion of the will to the motion of the needle of a compass. The needle turning toward the North Pole can be understood as a motion towards the North Pole, and as a motion away from "not being pointed towards the north

---

[100] *Ibidem.* "Nam infusio gratiae, cum sit in instanti, est terminus cuiusdam continui utpote actus meditationis, per quam affectus disponitur ad gratiae susceptionem; et eiusdem motus terminus est remissio culpae, quia ex hoc ipso culpa remittitur quod gratia infunditur. In illo ergo instanti est primo terminus remissionis culpae, scilicet non habere culpam, et infusionis gratiae, scilicet habere gratiam. In toto ergo tempore praecedenti quod terminatur ad hoc instans, quo tempore mensurabatur motus meditationis praedictae, fuit peccator habens culpam et non habens gratiam, nisi tantummodo in ultimo instanti, ut dictum est. Sed ante ultimum instans huius temporis non est accipere aliud immediate proximum: quia quodcumque instans accipiatur aliud ab ultimo, inter ipsum et ultimum erunt infinita instantia media." (transl Schmidt *On Truth* 1954)

[101] *De Ver* q.28, a.9 ad 1. Thomas takes great pain to discuss whether or not both motions are of one potentia.

pole". Furthermore, the motion towards God is the cause of the motion away from sin. Consequently, the motion of the free will towards God precedes naturally (not temporally!) the motion of the free will away from sin.[102]

Thomas identifies the motion of the free will towards God with the motion of faith (*motio fidei*), through which, according to Paul, man is justified; cf. Rom 5,1: "So then, now that we have been justified by faith, we are at peace with God etc."[103] According to Pesch, this was an important innovation by Thomas:

> "The most important innovation: Thomas identifies this act of conversion to God, which God himself operates in the freedom of man through the infusion of grace, with *faith*, through which, according to Paul, justification takes place. Thomas understands this faith, following Hebr. 11,6, as prime conversion (*prima conversio*), and fruit of the converting act of God; everything else belonging to justification, is submitted to this faith."[104]

The identification of the motion of the free will towards God with the act of faith in Rom 5,1 implies that justification is through *fides informata* (faith informed by charity), not through *fides informis*.[105] This follows from the fact that the motion of the free will towards God, being a requirement of justification, implies all other requirements, including the infusion of grace. The faith that justifies, according to Thomas' interpretation, not only involves a cognitive orientation to God, but also an affective orientation. The justification of the godless involves the conversion of the whole human mind.[106]

The motion of the free will towards God (faith informed by charity) implies that one detests what is against God[107]. Consequently, as we saw above, the motion of the free will can be called the cause of the motion of the free will away from sin. The motion of the free will away from sin is called the detestation of sin. In the *Scriptum*, Thomas explicitly identifies this motion of the free will with contrition, being one of the three *partes integrales* of penance.[108]

---

[102] *STh* I-II q.113, a.8 co.

[103] "Iustificati igitur ex fide, pacem habeamus ad Deum", cited in *STh* I-II q.113, a.4 Sc.

[104] "Die wichtigste Neuheit des Überlegungsganges: Thomas identifiziert nun diesen Akt der Hinkehr zu Gott, den Gott selbst durch die Eingießung der Gnade in der Freiheit des Menschen erwirkt, mit dem *Glauben*, durch den nach Paulus die Rechtfertigung geschieht. Diesen Glauben versteht Thomas hier im Anschluß an Hebr 11,6 als Urbekehrung (*prima conversio*) und Frucht des bekehrenden Handeln Gottes, und alles andere, was zur Rechtfertigung gehört, ist diesem Glauben subsumiert." O.H. Pesch, *Thomas*, p.175.

[105] *STh* I-II q.113, a.4 ad 1: "motus fidei non est perfectus nisi sit caritate informatus: unde simul in iustificatione impii cum motu fidei, est etiam motus caritatis. Movetur autem liberum arbitrium in Deum ad hoc quod ei se subiiciat: unde etiam concurrit actus timoris filialis, et actus humilitatis."

[106] *Idem*, co.

[107] *Idem*, a.5 ad 1: "Et ideo sicut ad caritatem pertinet diligere Deum, ita etiam detestari peccata, per quae anima separatur a Deo."

[108] Cf. *In IV Sent* d.17, q.1, a.3, qa.4, though the term 'contrition' only appears in the question at the top of *quaestiuncula* 4, and not in the *corpus*. However, in the follow up of this question, it becomes clear that for Thomas in the *Scriptum* the *motus liberi arbitrii in peccatum* is the same as the *motus contritionis* (Cf. *In IV Sent* d.17, q.1, a.4, qa.2).

In *De Veritate*, the identification is more or less implied.[109] In the *Prima Secundae*, "contritio" is mentioned only once, namely in the sixth article of the *quaestio* on the justification of the godless, where an implicit identification is made between *motus liberi arbitrii in peccatum* and *contritio*.[110] In the *Tertia Pars*, however, the motion of the free will away from sin is explicitly called an act of penance[111], while contrition is called the first act of penance or of the penitent.[112]

The will of the penitent is the point of application of justifying grace. What consequence does this have for the freedom of the penitent? According to Thomas, God moves the penitent to justice according to the condition of the penitent's human nature:

> The justification of the godless is caused by God who moves man to justice. For according to Rom. 4, 5, *it is He who justifies the godless*. Now God moves all things according to their own manner, just as we see that in natural things, what is heavy and what is light are moved differently, on account of their diverse natures. Hence He moves man to justice according to the condition of his human nature. But it is man's proper nature to have free will. Hence in him who has the use of reason, God's motion to justice does not take place without a movement of the free will; but He so infuses the gift of justifying grace that at the same time He moves the free will to accept the gift of grace, in those who are capable of being moved thus.[113]

By emphasizing that justification is in accordance with human nature, Thomas means to say that God does not force his grace upon us, but that He, when He justifies man according to his human nature, leaves the freedom of his free will intact.[114] However, even though God justifies man according to his human

---

109 *De Ver* q.28, a.5 Sc 2: "ad iustificationem impii contritio requiritur, quae est prima poenitentiae pars, per quam peccata tolluntur. Sed contritio est dolor de peccato. Ergo motus liberi arbitrii in peccatum requiritur in iustificatione impii."

110 *STh* I-II q.113, a.6 ob 3: 'remissio peccatorum consequitur ad motum liberi arbitrii in Deum et in peccatum sicut effectus ad causam: per fidem enim et contritionem remittuntur peccata. Etc.''

111 *STh* III q.85, a.6 co: "Sicut in 2. habitum est in iustificatione impii simul est motus liberi arbitrii in Deum, qui est actus fidei per charitatem infomatus, et motus liberi arbitrii in peccatum, qui est actus poenitentiae"

112 *Contritio* is the *actus primus poenitentis* or the *primus actus poenitentiae*. (Cf. *STh* III q.89, a.1 ad 2 and ad 3)

113 "(I)ustificatio impii fit Deo movente hominem ad iustitiam; ipse enim est qui iustifcat impium, ut dicitur Rom. 4,5. Deus autem movet omnia secundum modum uniuscuiusque: sicut in naturalibus videmus quod aliter moventur ab ipso gravia et aliter levia, propter diversam naturam utriusque. Unde et homines ad iustitiam movet secundum conditionem naturae humanae. Homo autem secundum propriam naturam habet quid sit liberi arbitrii. Et ideo in eo qui habet usum liberi arbitrii, non fit motio a Deo ad iustitiam absque motu liberi arbitrii; sed ita infundit donum gratiae iustificantis, quod etiam simul cum hoc movet liberum arbitrium ad donum gratiae acceptandum, in his qui sunt huius motionis capaces." (*STh* I-II q.113, a.3 co).

114 In the *Scriptum*, Thomas is even more explicit about the incompatibility of the free will and violence: "(G)ratia quae datur ad recte vivendum et peccatorum remissionem, per prius respicit voluntatem quam alias potentias: per eam enim peccatur et recte vivitur; et ideo oportet quod infusio gratiae iustificantis sit secundum talem modum qui voluntati competat; et propter hoc oportet quod a tali infusione omnis ratio violentiae excludatur, quia violentiae

nature, leaving his freedom of will intact, this does not mean that the whole process of being prepared for being justified is a painless operation. As we saw earlier, the term contrition refers to a crushing of the hardness of the will. This crushing, as Thomas points out, can be a painful event, and involve tears. But the end of this process is a will that is truly free.

4 Conclusion

We began this chapter with the question of how Thomas speaks about the forgiveness of sins, the principal effect of the sacrament of penance, and how he understands God to be the cause of it. It turns out that forgiveness of sins primarily concerns the relationship of grace. Thomas interprets all the different manners of speaking, with which the forgiveness of sins is put into words, against the background of man's lost, or at least damaged, friendship with God, which he has incurred through committing sin.

The loss of, or damage to, friendship with God does not consist in something in God. The image of God being hurt by the sin of man, and consequently withholding his grace from man, is corrected by Thomas when he stresses that that which blocks the light of grace must not be attributed to God, but to man. Though the cause of forgiveness of sins must be ascribed to God, it does not mean that something must be changed in God. Instead, it means that a change needs to occur in the sinner, the cause of which is subsequently ascribed to God. This change in man, his sins being forgiven him, does not consist in the sin itself being undone. This would be impossible, for what has glided into the past cannot be undone in the present. What can be undone, however, is the effect of sin, and in particular insofar as this effect consists in something blocking the light of grace from falling onto the soul of the sinner. Again, it is not God who withholds his grace, and who must be turned. Instead, it is the will of the sinner, which, being averted from God, blocks the light of grace, and which must be converted to God.

At this point, a distinction must be made between the forgiveness of mortal sin and forgiveness of venial sins. In the case of mortal sins, the friendship with God has been lost, and a situation occurs in which God is no longer within reach to help the sinner to restore the friendship. Forgiveness of sins, in this situation, is referred to by the technical term of justification of the godless. It means the transition from the state of guilt, in which the will of the sinner is

---

capax non est. Ad hoc autem quod violentia ab actione tollatur, oportet quod patiens cooperetur agenti secundum modum suum; unde in illis quae nata sunt agere, requiritur quod active cooperentur; in illis autem quae sunt nata recipere tantum, sicut materia prima, sufficit ad violentiam tollendam naturalis inclinatio ad formam; et ex hoc dicitur generatio naturalis. Sed quantum est ibi de contrarietate, tantum est ibi de violentia; unde quando voluntas non habet actum contrarium, sicut est in pueris, sine violentia voluntatis potest infundi gratia per sacramentum, sicut pueris baptizatis; et sine sacramento, sicut patet in sanctificatis in utero. Sed quando voluntas habet suum actum, sicut est in adultis, requiritur actus voluntatis ad gratiam suscipiendam, animam ad datorem ordinans; et ideo ad iustificationem, quae per infusionem gratiae fit, requiritur motus liberi arbitrii in Deum." (*In IV Sent* d.17, q.1, a.3, qa.2 co).

averted from God, toward some changeable good, to the state of grace, which is metaphorically called a state of justice. This *iustitia metaphorice dicta* consists in reason being placed under the rule (*imperium*) of God, and the lower parts of the soul, i.e. the passions, under the rule of reason.

This double "alignment" corresponds with the notions of forgiveness of mortal sins, and forgiveness of venial sins. In the case of venial sins, the grace of God is not actually lost, and God is within reach in the form of grace. In particular, virtues, which perfect the rational soul, enable it to undertake meritorious acts. Reason is still subjected to the rule of God, though the *imperium* of reason over the lower parts of the soul is weakened. In this case, Thomas speaks of a *debilitatio*, a weakening of the natural good. Forgiveness of sins in this case consists of strengthening the *imperium* of reason over the lower parts of the soul, which is obtained by doing good deeds (cf. the *opera satisfactionis*: almsgiving, prayer, fasting). In the case of mortal sins, the subjection of reason to God and the *imperium* of reason over the lower parts of the soul are both lost. Forgiveness of sins regards both subjecting reason to the rule of God and bringing the lower parts of the soul under the *imperium* of reason.

The justification of the sinner, the transition from the state of guilt to that of grace, is caused by God in that He infuses his grace, which infusion results "in an instant" in the conversion of the will to God in the act of faith, the aversion away from sin in the act of penance, and consequently in the forgiveness of sins.

Finally, God is cause, as well, of the period of deliberation preparing the sinner for the reception of justifying grace. To indicate this, Thomas develops, in the course of his working years, the notion of actual operating grace (*auxilium*), as opposed to the habitual grace of justification, by which distinction he is able to refer to God's activity operating interiorly on the soul prior to the infusion of justifying grace. The Aristotelian notion of "instinct" helps Thomas to understand the scriptural notions of vocation, attraction and invitation as actual divine impulses (*instinctus divinus* or *instinctus Spiritus Sancti*) bringing man into the supernatural order of grace.

In the next chapter, we will once again focus on the forgiveness of sins, i.e. the restoration of the relationship of grace, and on how God is understood to be cause of it. But this time, we will concentrate on the role of the Holy Spirit. We will see that, in the theology of Thomas, the indwelling of the Holy Spirit turns out to be constitutive of the relationship of grace, and we will see what it means to ascribe the restoration of friendship with God to the Holy Spirit.

Chapter 3 The Holy Spirit

Introduction

In the previous chapter, we have established that, according to Thomas, forgiveness of sins consists primarily in the restoration of the relationship of grace between God and man. In this chapter, we will reflect on (the restoration of) the relationship of grace from the perspective of the theology of the Holy Trinity. In particular we will examine the role of the Holy Spirit with respect to the forgiveness of sins. We will discover that, according to Thomas, the indwelling of the Spirit is constitutive for the relationship of grace. In addition, we will discover that this indwelling is said of Father, Son and Spirit alike, and said of the Holy Spirit in particular, and we will find out how Thomas deals with this.

The reason why we focus on the role of the Holy Spirit in the forgiveness of sins is that Scripture suggests a special relationship between forgiveness and the Holy Spirit. In Jn 20, 21-23 the power to forgive sins is explicitly connected with the gift of the Holy Spirit.[1] And in Rm 5,5 it is said that "the love of God has been poured into our hearts by the Holy Spirit which has been given to us."[2] These and other texts[3] seem to suggest a special role for the Spirit with respect to our relationship with God in general, and forgiveness of sins in particular. Thomas adopts this view when, in several places, he states that sins are forgiven *per Spiritum sanctum*[4] By focusing on the role of the Holy Spirit, we expect to join in with the current theological interest in trinitarian theology.[5]

We will begin by examining a central text that will help us to understand how Thomas sees the involvement of God, Father, Son and Spirit, in salvation history, and especially, how He is related to his creatures and restores this relationship in so far as it is damaged or broken by sin. This text, *STh* I q.43 (at the end of the doctrine of God in the *Summa*, in particular the end of the section on the Trinity of the divine Persons), is about the missions of the divine

---

1   Cf. *In Ioan* c.20, lc. 4. See also Chapters One and Four.

2   For instance *STh* I, q.43, a.3 ad 2.

3   Cf. Acts 2, 37: "You must repent, and every one of you and your children must be baptized in the name of Jesus Christ for the forgiveness of your sins, and you will receive the gift of the Holy Spirit."

4   Cf. *In IV Sent* d.5, q.1, a.1 Sc 2; a.2 Sc; d.18, q.1, a.3, qa.1 Sc 2; *STh* III q.3, a.8 ad 3. In *STh* III q.22, a.3 Sc, Hebr. 9, 14 is quoted, in which the Holy Spirit is named as the one through whom the blood of Christ has purified our conscience. In III q.32, a.1 co it is said that we are sanctified through the Holy Spirit; in III q.38, a.2 ad 1 it is said that we are baptized through the Holy Spirit.

5   Cf. C. LaCugna, "The trinitarian mystery of God", in F. Schüssler Fiorenza, J. Galvin (eds), *Systematic theology. Roman Catholic perspectives*, vol. 1, 1991, p.153: "Today trinitarian theology is being recovered as a fruitful and intelligible way to articulate what it means to be 'saved by God through Christ in the power of the Holy Spirit.' In the past few years virtually every theological journal, and many others oriented to pastoral, liturgical, and spiritual questions, have begun to include significant scholarly articles on issues related to the Trinity."

Persons. Reading this text will help us to gain insight into our relationship with God who is Father, Son and Holy Spirit, and especially how the Holy Spirit is involved in this relationship.

While reading these texts, we will encounter a number of difficulties, which have to do with how our language functions *in trinitate*. God-talk has to take in account that all human language used *in divinis* must be cleared of those connotations that do not fit God, who is Creator of all. All language that somehow may suggest that God is not beyond time, that there are sequential 'moments' in God, that there is change in God, etc., must either be corrected or be removed from our God-talk. These rules also apply when we speak of God the Father, God the Son and God the Spirit, because when we speak about Father, Son and Holy Spirit, we speak about God. At the same time, an extra set of rules must be introduced, which safeguard both God's unity and the Trinity of divine Persons. In the second section of the chapter, we will examine this set of rules, and we will especially examine the rule of appropriation.

This investigation of our language *in trinitate* will ultimately provide us with the instruments to investigate what it is that, according to Thomas, Scripture and tradition are saying when they suggest such a close relationship between grace and Spirit, and especially between the Holy Spirit and forgiveness of sins.

1   The invisible mission of the Holy Spirit

Quaestio 43, on the missions of the divine Persons, is the last of the *quaestiones* on how the divine Persons are distinguished from each other (qq.27-43). Much is written about how we should interpret the division Thomas makes between this section and the section which deals with the essence of God (qq.3-26). This division is held responsible for the unsound practice of dividing the doctrine on God into two parts, one about the one God (*De Deo uno*) and one about the triune God (*De Deo trino*).[6]

Rahner has criticized Thomas (and Augustine[7]), for putting the Trinity aside in such a way that it became detached from the rest of theology. As a result the theology of the Trinity became irrelevant for salvation and the life of the

---

6   "This separation corresponded with the way Augustine in his *On the Trinity* began with the one essence of God, in which he sketched the Trinity. The first treatise dealt with the part of our faith, which we have in common with Jews, Moslems and many philosophers. The second dealt with what is specifically Christian. The first treatise is blamed for having become more and more philosophical." (J. Wissink, *Thomas van Aquino. De actuele betekenis van zijn theologie. Een inleiding*, 1998, p.109; transl. EL) For a brief overview of the debate, cf. G. Emery, "Essentialism or personalism in the treatise on God in Saint Thomas Aquinas", in *The Thomist* 64, 2000, pp.521-563.

7   E. Hill, who published a "translation for the 21st century" of Augustine's *De Trinitate* (*The Trinity. Introduction, translation, notes*, 1991) has defended Augustine against the criticisms in an article entitled "Karl Rahner's Remarks on the dogmatic treatise *De Trinitate* and St Augustine", in *Augustinian Studies* vol. 2, 1971, pp. 67-80. Unfortunately, regarding Rahner's criticisms he fails to give the same amount of credit to Thomas as he does to Augustine. Cf. also E. Hill, "St. Augustine's *De Trinitate*. The doctrinal significance of its structure", in *Revue des Etudes Augustiniennes* 19, 1973, pp.277-286, esp. pp.284-286.

faithful.[8] Since then, many have either followed Rahner in his criticisms, or tried to refute the argument.[9] Those who argue against the criticisms argue that these may be valid for the *Wirkungsgeschichte* but not for the *Summa theologiae*.[10] They point out that the whole section from q.3 to q.43 is about the triune God, and that the divine Persons are already mentioned in the section on the divine essence. The section on the divine essence is not about the essence as abstracted from the divine Persons, but about the divine essence as shared by the divine Persons.

I concur with this latter position. One does injustice to Thomas when one does not acknowledge how Trinitarian his view on the divine essence, in fact, is. Thomas himself is clear about the relation between the trinity of divine Persons and divine essence: "In God, the relations [between the divine Persons] are the divine essence itself".[11] Hence, *quaestio* 43 must be read as the last *quaestio* of the

---

8   K. Rahner, "Der dreifaltige Gott als transzendenter Urgrund der Heilsgeschichte", in: *Mysterium Salutis*, Bd. 2, p. 319: "All das wird indes nicht darüber hinwegtäuschen dürfen, dass die Christen bei all ihrem orthodoxen Bekenntnis zur Dreifaltigkeit in ihrem religiösen Daseinsvollzug beinahe nur «Monotheisten» sind." One of the reasons Rahner gives is the separation between the treatise "De Deo uno" and "De Deo trino", for which he primarily blames the replacement of Peter Lombard's *Sentences* by Thomas' *Summa theologiae*. (p.323).

9   Cunningham refers to this practice of blaming the decline of trinitarian theology on one theologian or theological movement as 'historical scapegoating' (D. Cunningham, *These three are one. The practice of trinitarian theology*, 1998, p.31. For further references, see: H. Rikhof, "Trinity in Thomas, Reading the *Summa theologiae* against the background of modern problems" in *Jaarboek 1999 van het Thomas Instituut*, pp.83-85.

10 Cf. Y. Congar, *I believe in the Holy Spirit* vol. III (1997), pp.116-117: "Any attempt to present him [Thomas] as an 'essentialist', that is, as being conscious of and as affirming first and foremost the common divine essence, and only secondarily the Persons in that essence, would be to betray the balance of his theology. Such an interpretation should no longer be possible since the appearance of the studies by A. Malet, H.F. Dondaine, E. Bailleux, M.-J. Le Guillou and others. This interpretation has all too frequently been based on the fact that Thomas' study of the Trinity of Persons in the *Summa* is preceded by a study of the divine essence. Surely, however, it is hardly possible not to proceed in this way from the point of view of teaching? Is this procedure not justified by the economy of revelation itself? Did John of Damascene not begin with the unity of 'God'?" Cf. also D. Cunningham, *These three are one*, p.32-33: "So, for example, Karl Rahner worries that Thomas Aquinas, by turning first to the doctrine of the one God (*de Deo uno*), and only later to the doctrine of the triune God (*de Deo trino*), sets in motion the process of decline away from a fully-articulated doctrine of the Trinity. But Thomas knew that, among the members of the audience to which *he* was speaking (in the *Summa Theologiae*, at any rate), it *would not even have crossed their minds* to imagine God in anything *other* than trinitarian categories. Centuries later, audiences may no longer operate with this assumption; we need to take this into account, but it can hardly be blamed on Thomas."

11 Cf. *STh* I q.39, a.1 co: "Sed, sicut supra ostensum est, sicut relationes in rebus creatis accidentaliter insunt, ita in Deo sunt ipsa essentia divina." G. Emery observes that "(i)n the *Summa Theologiae*, Thomas announces a treatise on God divided into three sections (*consideratio autem de Deo tripartita erit*): (1) concerning the divine essence, (2) concerning the distinction of persons, and (3) concerning the procession of creatures *ab ipso* (*STh* I, q.2 pro; q.27 pro). It is essential to note that the treatise on God, the *consideratio de Deo*, does not consist of two but rather of three sections. (..) The study of God as principle [of creation] is not determined by the aspect of unity or of Trinity, but rather is determined by the unique and entire reality of God (the three persons of one and the same essence) which is posed here in a theological

whole doctrine of God, and not just as the last *quaestio* of the doctrine of the Trinity of divine Persons. The question on the divine missions "opens the great movement of the Trinitarian economy of grace which attaches the *Secunda* and the *Tertia pars* to the Trinitarian treatise".[12]

In *quaestio* 43, Thomas deals with the missions of the Son and the Spirit. It is the question "in which Thomas, in very general and abstract terms, sketches the pattern of God's dealing with humanity. It contains, therefore, the key to understanding those *quaestiones* in which he concentrates upon aspects of the *oikonomia* such as the theology of grace or the theology of the sacraments."[13] More particularly, it contains the key to understanding indwelling, the way in which God is present in the hearts of men. This indwelling, as we will see, is grace formulated in terms of the triune God. Indwelling is said of God with respect to us when we are sanctified by grace. Grace and indwelling are two sides of the one 'coin' that is constitutive for the relationship of grace with God.

In this section, we will read this important *quaestio* closely, in order to acquire an understanding of how Thomas sees indwelling, and how he relates it to the missions of Son and Spirit, and to gain insight into the relation between indwelling on the one hand and grace and the sacraments on the other. The latter brings us to the focal point of this and the previous chapter, namely the forgiveness of sins, which is the restoration of the relationship of grace.

Quaestio 43 is about the involvement of Father, Son and Spirit in salvation history. The *quaestio* is interesting precisely because it deals with God's involvement in salvation history, and it is also interesting because it deals with how the divine Persons are related to each other in the context of their involvement in salvation history.

This involvement is both visible and invisible. The distinction visible/invisible, together with the distinction between Son and Spirit, structures the whole *quaestio*. After a conceptual analysis of the notion of 'missio' in the first two *articuli*, Thomas discusses the invisible mission of the divine Persons in four *articuli*. These four *articuli* carry the burden of the *quaestio*. In the seventh *articulus*, Thomas deals with the visible missions of the divine Persons. The eighth and last *articulus* deals with a specific problem, namely how temporal mission and eternal procession are related.

The most attention is given to the invisible missions of the Son and, in particular, of the Holy Spirit. This does not mean that the visible missions are less important: the theological notion of the 'visible mission of the Son' refers

---

synthesis resulting from the first two sections of the treatise. Regarding the first two sections, there is no question of a "one God" or of a "tri-God", but of God considered *under the aspect* of the essence and *under the aspect* of the distinction" ("Essentialism and personalism", p.532). Cf. also p.553: "The essence that is in question in the first section of the treatise on God is not a source of the plurality of persons. It is, from one end to the other of the treatise, "the unique essence of three persons," numerically one, subsisting in each of the persons, never outside of the pesons among which it does not number."

12   *Idem*, p.536.
13   H. Rikhof, "Trinity in Thomas", p.87.

to the incarnation of the Son, the life of Jesus of Nazareth from his conception to his death and resurrection, his ascension to heaven and his sitting at the right hand of the Father. The fact that Thomas pays most attention to the invisible missions has to do with the fact that there are some difficulties regarding being sent invisibly which he wants to clarify here. These difficulties concern the depth of the invisible mission (art. 3), the question of who is sent and how the distinct invisible missions relate (art. 4 and 5), and the *terminus ad quem* of the invisible mission (art. 6). With respect to the visible mission, the attention is primarily focused on the visible mission of the Holy Spirit (art. 7).

In the following section we will read the eight articles of question 43 closely. With respect to each article, we will present the objections and the argument *Sed contra* which, together with the question asked, form the formulation of the problem of the article. Next we will present, explain and evaluate the position Thomas takes in the *responsio*, and finally, if relevant, we will present his answers to the objections.

Being sent

Thomas begins the *quaestio* on the missions of the divine Persons with a conceptual analysis of the term 'missio'. The reason for this is that the use of the term 'missio', in describing the involvement of the triune God in salvation history, may lead to some misunderstandings if the term is not cleared from connotations that do not fit God. Some of these unfitting connotations are presented in the objections: being sent could be understood to suggest that the One being sent is less (*minor*) that the One who sends (cf. ob 1). Or to send may suggest a separation between Sender and the divine Person being sent (cf. ob. 2), or it may suggest that the divine Person being sent becomes present where He was not present before, which would contradict the omnipresence of the divine Persons.

The argument *Sed contra* of the first article is taken from the gospel of St. John 8, 16: "(..) because I am not alone: the one who sent me is with me."[14] It is important to see that the use of 'missio' is a biblical one. In the New Testament, 'to send' or 'sending' is used in three different contexts. First, it is used for Jesus, though in a specific way. Secondly, the Spirit is sent. Thirdly, Jesus refers to the Father as the One who sends him.[15] Later in this *quaestio*, we will see that the divine missions correspond with the eternal relationships between Father and Son, and between Father (and Son) and Spirit.

In the *corpus articuli*, Thomas argues that the verb 'to send' imports a relationship of the one being sent to the one who sends, and a relationship of the one being sent to the one he is being sent to. In both relationships, some connotations that the verb 'to send' might introduce must be avoided.

---

[14] *STh* I q.43, a.1 Sc: "Sed contra est, quod dicitur Ioan. 8: 'Non sum ego solus, et qui misit me, Pater.'"

[15] H. Rikhof, "Trinity", pp. 88-90. A fourth mentioned context, the disciples, remains undiscussed; "they are sent as part of Jesus' ministry (Mt 10,5; Mk 3,14; 6,7) or as a continuation of his ministry (John 17,18; 20,21; cf. Mt 28,19-20)." (footnote 13, p.89-90)

With respect to the relation with the one who sends, Thomas distinguishes
three different types of relation. The relation between sender and the one being
sent can be one of lord and servant. Or it can be one of counselor who by
counseling can be said 'to send' someone to something, for instance a king to
war. Neither type of relationship fits the relationship between the Father who
sends and the Son or the Spirit being sent, because both relationships imply an
inequality in essence between sender and the one being sent, between Father
and Son, or between Father (and Son) and Holy Spirit. And this is contrary to
what we believe, namely that Father, Son and Spirit are of one essence.
However, if 'to send' is understood as a relationship of origin, like blossom that
originates from a tree, the connotation of inequality is avoided. So Thomas
determines that 'being sent',' when said of Son and Spirit, must be understood
in terms of a relationship of origin.

With respect to the relationship to the addressee, Thomas explains that being
sent somewhere implies that one begins to be there somehow. And this can be
in two different ways: one can begin to be somewhere where before one was
not, or one can begin to be somewhere in a certain way in which one was not
there at an earlier time. Only this second way fits the way in which divine
Persons are sent somewhere, since only this second way does not imply some
sort of spatial movement.[16]

In his answer to the first objection, Thomas explains that a procession of origin
does not introduce an inequality between the divine Persons.[17] Both the second
and the third *objectiones* are refuted by what is said in the *corpus articuli*, because
there is only a question of separation between sender and the one being sent,
when 'to send' is understood in terms of locomotion. But this is not the case
with the missions of divine Persons, because they do not begin to be present
where they were not before.[18] For the same reason, if 'to be sent' is understood
properly, there is no contradiction between being sent and being omnipresent.

As an illustration of what is meant, one can think of the following. Take for
example the situation of a new colleague who has come to work with you, and
compare this with the situation of falling in love with a colleague you have
known and worked with for a period of time. In the first situation, the
colleague is present where before he or she was not. In the second situation,
the presence of the object of your affection receives a whole new dimension
from the moment of falling in love. The example of falling in love is chosen in
order to make clear that the 'newness' of the way a divine Person is present is

---

[16] *STh* I q.43, a.1 co: "Missio igitur divinae personae convenire potest, secundum quod importat
ex una parte processionem originis a mittente, et secundum quod importat ex alia parte
novum modum existendi in aliquo: sicut Filius dicitur esse missus a Patre in mundum,
secundum quod incoepit esse in mundo visibiliter per carnem assumptam; et tamen ante *in
mundo era*, ut dicitur Joan. 1."

[17] *Idem*, ad 1: "Sed in divinis non importat, nisi processionem originis, quae est secundum
aequalitatem, ut supra dictum est."

[18] *Idem*, ad 2: "persona divina missa, sicut non incipit esse, ubi prius not fuerat, ita nec desinit
esse, ubi fuerat. Unde talis missio est sine separatione sed habet solam distinctionem
originis."

with respect to us, and not with respect to the divine Person.[19] The change is on our side; there is no suggestion of a change in the one being sent, while at the same time it is clear that the change in presence itself is not 'caused' by the one falling in love, but by the object of affection.[20]

In the second article, the question is asked of how the eternal processions of the Son from the Father, and the Spirit from the Father and the Son, relate to the temporal missions of Son and Spirit (cf. ob. 3). How does the mission of the Son relate to His generation, i.e. His procession from the Father (cf. ob. 1)? What can be said with respect to mission about time/change and eternity/unchangeability (ob. 2)? The text quoted in the argument *Sed contra* is taken from Paul, Gal. 4, 4: "(..) but when the completion of time came, God sent his Son".[21] As we saw earlier, the verb 'to send' in the New Testament is used either for the Son and the Spirit, saying that they are sent, or it is used for the Father, saying that He is the One who sends. We said that 'to send' is one of the biblical terms used to denote God's involvement in salvation history. The question is, how is the eternal God involved in time?

What follows in the *corpus articuli* is an analysis of language being used to name the relationships of origin of the divine Persons. These relationships of origin can be named with respect to their principle, and in that case words like 'processio' or 'exitus' are used. They can be named with respect to their eternal end, and then we use words like 'generatio:', and 'spiratio'. And they can be named with respect to the end in time, and then words like 'missio' and 'datio' are used. Thomas explains further that 'to be sent' means that someone is present in someone, while 'to be given' means that someone is held by someone. And to say that a divine person is held by a certain creature, or is present in him or her in a new way, is to say that something occurs in time. Expressions like 'begotten' (*generatus*) or 'breathed' (*spiratus*) have eternal connotations, while expressions like 'to come forth' or 'to proceed' have either eternal or temporal connotations, depending on the end term of the procession. So words like 'proceed', 'being begotten' and 'being sent', all said of the Son, do not indicate different relationships between the Son and the Father, but all

---

[19] *Idem*, a.2 ad 2: "Ad secundum dicendum, quod divinam personam esse novo modo in aliquo, vel ab aliquo haberi temporaliter, non est propter mutationem divinae personae, sed propter mutationem creaturae: sicut et Deus temporaliter dicitur Dominus propter mutationem creaturae."

[20] I have adapted the illustration given by J. Wissink, *Thomas van Aquino*, p.116. In his illustration, the presence of a policemen who is visiting me, receives a whole new dimension when, by telephone, he is given the order to arrest me. In this illustration, however, the change may still be understood to occur in the one being sent. This has the danger of suggesting that there are different moments in the divine Person, one in which He was just visiting me, and the next in which He receives a new order. As we will see later, the change is on our side, and is not unlike falling in love.

[21] *Idem*, a.2 Sc: "Sed contra est quod dicitur Gal. 4: *Cum venit plenitudo temporis, misit Deus Filium suum.*"

indicate the one relationship between Father and Son; however they differ depending on what aspect of this relationship is being expressed.

The article draws attention to a question which dominates Trinitarian theology at the moment, and which concerns the distinction and relationship between what, since Rahner, is known as immanent and economic Trinity. The two sets of words which we meet in this article, 'missio:' and 'datio' on the one hand and 'processio' and 'exitus' on the other, correspond with the notions of economic Trinity and immanent Trinity respectively. In order to give a new impulse to Trinitarian theology, Rahner formulated the axiom "the immanent Trinity is the economic Trinity and vice versa".[22] The intention of the formula is correct, in as far as it helps us to realize that we do not know any other triune God than the one we meet in the economic order. It corrects any suggestion that there are two sets of revelations, one about the economic Trinity and one about how the triune God is in Himself. We meet God in the economy of salvation. Nevertheless, the formula, particularly the 'vice versa', obscures the point that salvation history, and the reflection upon salvation history, are on two different levels. The one revelation of God in salvation history can be reflected upon on different levels. We can ask about how God acts in salvation history, and we can ask who the God is who acts in salvation history. The first results in a reflection on the missions, while the second results in a reflection on the eternal processions.

First, it is important to notice that Thomas does not imply that there are different processions of one divine Person, some eternal, and others temporal. On the contrary, the one procession of a divine Person can be understood from different perspectives, and our language corresponds with how the procession is understood. If the procession is understood with respect to its effect in time, we speak of mission or gift.

Second, mission relates to procession like the salvation history in which God reveals Himself, relates to the theological reflection upon this revelation. And since the reflection is always later than that which is reflected upon, the encounter with Son and Spirit in salvation history precedes the reflections upon this encounter, that result in statements on how Father, Son and Spirit relate. The reflections are not simply aimed at discovering how God is in himself (even though in every relationship of friendship there should be a healthy curiosity as to who the friend is), but at making sense of what is revealed about God at different stages in salvation history.

Third, with respect to this, a remark must be made about the *ordo disciplinae*[23] of the *Summa Theologiae*, because the current order of the *quaestiones* in the Summa can mislead us into thinking that the subjects brought into relationship by Scriptural texts are the result of a deduction from (philosophical) axioms about God. But on the contrary, the more abstract *quaestiones* are the result of reflection upon Scripture, and it is only due to the *ordo disciplinae* that Thomas

---

22   Cf. K. Rahner, "Der dreifaltige Gott", pp.318-347.
23   Cf. *STh* I prologue.

presents the reflections first, which subsequently help us to explain what is said in Scripture. Hence, *quaestio* 43 can be seen as the *quaestio* in which Thomas, after a long sequence of reflections, finally comes to the point he was aiming at from the beginning: explaining how the biblical statements about the missions of Son and Spirit, and about the actual involvement of God in salvation history, and in his church, must be understood.

Indwelling: the invisible mission of the Spirit

Some of the phrases in the third *articulus* which have the function of explaining indwelling have already been met in the previous *articulus*. These phrases are 'to be present in someone in a new way', and 'to be held by someone', and are counterparts of 'to be sent' and 'to be given'. In the third article on the invisible mission, Thomas explains that 'to be present in someone in a new way' or 'to be held by someone' is always according to sanctifying grace.

Rikhof argues that the question of the *articulus* is about the depth or impact of the *missio*. In the *articulus* the question concerns the basis on which a divine Person is sent. In his analysis of the *articulus*, Rikhof distinguishes three different candidates being presented in the *objectiones*: the charismatic gifts (*gratia gratis data*, cf. obj. 3 and 4), sanctifying grace (cf. *Sed contra*) and the divine Persons themselves (obj. 1 and 2). The argument *Sed contra* is taken from Augustine's *De Trinitate* XV,27, in which it is said that the Holy Spirit proceeds temporally in order to sanctify creatures. The text links the (invisible) mission of the Spirit with sanctifying grace. Thus the question of the *articulus* is: "Does the *missio* mean that the creature on the receiving end becomes someone who is an instrument of grace, edifying and helping others? Does the *missio* mean that the creature on the receiving end becomes a graceful and holy person? Or does the *missio* mean that the divine Person is given?"[24]

In the *corpus articuli*, only the last two candidates, sanctifying grace and the divine Person, return; the charismatic gifts, however, return in the answer to the fourth objection (see below).

Thomas takes the position that the invisible mission involves both the gift of the divine Person and the gift of sanctifying grace. He begins by distinguishing between different ways in which God is present in his creation. First, He is present in all things "per essentiam, potentiam et praesentiam", like a cause is present in its effects which are participating in the good of the cause. Beyond this presence in all creatures, there is a special presence of God that is only fitting for rational creatures, for they alone are capable of knowing and loving God. Through knowing and loving God, God is present in the knower and the lover as the one who is known and loved. Hence, by knowing and loving God, the rational creature 'reaches' God himself (*attingere*). And because of the special way in which God is present when known and loved, we do not merely speak of presence, but of indwelling, or abiding: of God residing in us as in his

---

[24] H. Rikhof, "Trinity", p.95.

temple. So only sanctifying grace can be the reason why a divine Person is present in a new way in the rational creature.[25]

It is clear that, according to Thomas, the invisible mission not only means that we are sanctified or given charismatic gifts, but also means that the divine Person is really present in our hearts. At the same time, he does not say anything about what this presence of the divine Persons means with respect to the divine Persons, with respect to God. On the contrary, Thomas speaks only about what this divine presence is for us. For us, the presence of God consists in our knowing and loving God. For us, the way the divine Persons are present is through knowing and loving them, which – again on our side – corresponds with sanctifying grace. Therefore, apart from emphasizing that the divine Persons really become present, Thomas refrains from saying anything about what this presence means for God.

A similar line of thought can be detected when Thomas deals next with *habere* and *datur*. 'Having' and 'being given' are words that Scripture particularly applies to the Holy Spirit. They are different words used, in a similar way, to name the intimate presence of the Holy Spirit in our hearts. This time Thomas expresses this intimacy by the use of the word 'to enjoy' (*frui*). Thomas explains that when we are given something (or someone) it means that we can either freely use (*uti*) or enjoy (*frui*) what is given. That we can enjoy a divine Person is, however, only according to sanctifying grace. But in this gift of sanctifying grace, the Spirit is possessed.[26] Again we see how Thomas on the one hand explains what this 'having' or 'possessing" a divine Person means with respect to us. On our side there is sanctifying grace through which we are able to enjoy the divine Person. On the other hand, Thomas stresses that, in this gift of sanctifying grace, the Spirit is actually possessed. The emphasis on what the Holy Spirit being given means for us must not be understood to say that the divine Person is not actually possessed. The fact that we can only say what the gift of the Spirit means for us, and not what it means for the Spirit, does not mean that the depth of the mission is limited to the second candidate, i.e. the sanctification of the person to whom the divine Person is sent .

This last reflection returns in Thomas' answer to the first objection: sanctifying grace makes the rational creature perfect so that he is free, not only to use the gift of grace, but also to enjoy the divine Person himself. The answer to the second *objectio* specifies the relationship between the gift of the Holy Spirit and

---

[25] *STh* I q.43, a.3 co: "Est enim unus communis modus, quo Deus est in omnibus rebus per essentiam, potentiam et praesentiam, sicut causa in effectibus participantibus bonitatem ipsius. Super istum modum autem communem est unus specialis qui convenit creaturae rationali, in qua Deus dicitur esse, sicut cognitum in cognoscente, et amatum in amante. Et quia cognoscendo et amando creatura rationalis sua operatione attingit ad ipsum Deum, secundum istum specialem modum Deus non solum dicitur esse in creatura rationali, sed etiam habitare in ea, sicut in templo suo. Sic igitur nullus alius effectus potest esse ratio, quod divina persona sit novo modo in rationali creatura, nisi gratia gratum faciens."

[26] *Ibidem* "Similiter illud solum habere dicimur, quo libere possumus uti, vel frui. Habere autem potestatem fruendi divina persona est solum secundum gratiam gratum facientem. Sed tamen in ipso dono gratiae gratum facientis Spiritus Sanctus habetur, et inhabitat hominem."

the gift of grace. In the *objectio* it was stated that the phrase 'according to the gift of sanctifying grace" seems to imply that the gift of grace is cause of the gift of the Holy Spirit, which would be contrary to what is said in Rom 5,5: "the love of God has been poured out into our hearts by the Holy Spirit which has been given to us".[27] Thomas answers that it means that the gift of grace itself is from the Holy Spirit (*a Spiritu sancto*). Since sanctifying grace prepares the soul for having the divine Person, it is true to say that the gift of the Spirit is according to the gift of grace.

In Thomas' answer to the fourth objection, the first candidate, the grace of charismatic gifts, returns. Thomas explains that any gratuitous grace (*gratia gratis data*), whether it is the gift of prophecy or of conducting miracles, is a manifestation of the Holy Spirit, and of the gift of sanctifying grace. But it is possible for someone to be given a gratuitous grace without sanctifying grace, i.e. without the Spirit dwelling in the soul. In that case we speak of specific spiritual gifts, such as the gift of the spirit of prophecy, or the gift of the spirit of miracles, which means that the Spirit has given someone the power to prophesy or to conduct miracles. In this case the Holy Spirit is not given *simpliciter*[28]. So the Holy Spirit can said to be sent according to the charismatic gifts, but then 'to be sent' is understood differently, namely not in terms of a renewed presence as known and loved, nor as possessed to be enjoyed.[29]

From Thomas' answers we can conclude that the (invisible) mission, or gift, of the Spirit means that the Spirit begins to be present in a new and intimate way in our hearts, and that this presence of the Spirit means that we are sanctified, and consequently made suitable for this presence. At the same time the notion of gift, or mission, of the Spirit leaves room for a different presence of the Spirit, not as 'known and loved' or "possessed to be enjoyed', but in the sense of spiritual powers that can be ascribed to the Spirit.

As a final reflection regarding this *articulus*, we will introduce the notion of actual operating grace as we have developed it in Chapter Two. How does this notion of grace, associated with the *instinctus Spiritus Sancti*, relate to the candidates presented as a basis for the invisible mission of the Holy Spirit? Since we are dealing with an actual operating grace, which precedes the actual justification, that is, the actual infusion of (sanctifying) grace, we can rule out the second candidate: sanctifying grace. With respect to the third candidate, the Holy Spirit himself, we must conclude that the instinct of the Spirit does not

---

[27] *STh* I q.43 a.3 ad 2: "*charitas Dei diffunditur est in cordibus nostris per Spiritum sanctum.*".

[28] *Idem*, ad 4: "Ad quartum dicendum, quod operatio miraculorum est manifestiva gratiae gratum facientis, sicut et donum prophetiae, et quaelibet gratia gratis data. Unde I ad Cor. 12 gratia gratis data nominatur manifestatio Spiritus. Sic igitur Apostolus dicitur datus Spiritus sanctus ad operationem miraculorum, quia data est eis gratia gratum faciens cum signo manifestante. Si autem daretur solum signum gratiae gratum facientis sine gratia, non diceretur dari simpliciter Spiritus sanctus: nisi forte cum aliqua determinatione, secundum quod dicitur, quod alicui datur spiritus propheticus, vel miraculorum, inquantum a Spiritu sancto habet virtutem prophetandi, vel miracula faciendi."

[29] We will return to this third candidate in Chapter Four, when we deal with the gift of the Spirit accompanying the mission of the apostles in Jn 20, 21-23.

refer to a presence of the Spirit as known and loved, as indwelling, for this could, according to Thomas, only be according to sanctifying grace. It could, however, refer to a different, hidden (in the sense of unknown) presence of the Spirit.

Does it correspond with candidate number one, the grace of charismatic gifts? The answer must be that is does not, because, according to Thomas, charismatic gifts are given to human persons in order to bring others to justifying faith, while the instinct of the Holy Spirit is given to help a human person in the preparation for his or her justification.[30]

Therefore, the conclusion is that the notion of the instinct of the Holy Spirit does not fit into what Thomas says here with respect to the invisible mission of the Holy Spirit. For our study on the role of the Spirit in the forgiveness of sins, it is important to see that the notion of *instinctus Spiritus sancti* appears to refer to a different kind of mission from the mission of the Holy Spirit as understood by Thomas in this article. We shall return to the instinct of the Holy Spirit at the end of Chapter Four when we examine the role of the Spirit in the sacrament of penance.

Indwelling of Father, Son and Spirit

In the previously discussed *articulus*, the emphasis lies on the Holy Spirit. The Spirit is mentioned explicitly in three of the four *obiectiones*, in the argument *Sed contra*, and in the *corpus*. Furthermore, besides 'being sent', which in Scripture is used for both the Son and the Spirit, the verb 'being given' is discussed, which in Scripture is associated with the Holy Spirit.[31]

Nevertheless, as the mention of the Son in the third *obiectio* indicates, we need to realize that indwelling is not exclusively said of the Holy Spirit, cf. Jn 14, 23:

"Anyone who loves me will keep my word,
and my Father will love him,
and we shall come to him,
and make our home in him."[32]

In the fourth and fifth *articuli*, the question is concerned with how the Father and the Son are part of the invisible mission, and their indwelling in the hearts of man. The question, however, is asked in different ways in both *articuli*. First, in *articulus* 4, the question is asked of whether or not it is fitting to say that the Father is sent (visibly or invisibly), while in *articulus* 5, the question is of whether or not it is fitting to say that the Son is sent invisibly.

---

30 *STh* I-II q.111, a.1 co: "Secundum hoc igitur duplex est gratia: una quidem, per quam ipse homo Deo coniungitur, quae vocatur gratia gratum faciens; alia vero, per quam unus homo cooperatur alteri ad hoc, quod ad Deum reducatur. Huiusmodi autem donum vocatur gratia gratis data: quia supra facultatem naturae, et supra meritum personae homini conceditur. Sed quia non datur ad hoc, ut homo ipse per eam iustificetur, sed potius ut ad iustificationem alterius cooperatur, ideo non vocatur gratum faciens. Et de hac dicit Apostolus I ad Cor 12: Unicuique datur manifestatio Spiritus ad utilitatem, scilicet aliorum."

31 H. Rikhof, "Trinity", p.96.

32 Cf. *STh* I q.43, a.4 ob 2, and esp. a.5 co: "Ad eum veniemus, et mansionem apud eum faciemus."

The discussion in the fourth *articulus* is a fine example of a discussion about grammar *in trinitate*, which, as we will see in the next section, is about being sensitive to unwanted connotations while speaking about Father, Son and Spirit. Thomas' answer to the question, "Is it fitting to say that the Father is sent?" is negative: it is not fitting, because 'to be sent' connotes that the Father is *ab alio*, and this is contrary to who the Father is. However, since the Son and the Spirit proceed from the Father, 'to be sent' can be said of both. However, the fact that the answer is negative does not imply that the Father does not dwell in one who loves him. To say that the Father dwells in a person (or: 'makes a home in him') does not import any connotation of 'being *ab alio*'. In the second *obiectio* Thomas explains that the Father dwells in a person in as far as He is known in time.[33]

It is even possible to say that the Father is given, as long as it is understood in terms of free self-communication. In his reply to the first *obiectio*, Thomas answers that the Father gives Himself in as far as He communicates Himself freely to his creatures in order to be enjoyed. However, when 'to give' is understood as referring to a giving authority apart from the Father, it is not fittingly said of the Father.[34] The third *obiectio*, and its answer, involve a rule for speaking *in trinitate* and will therefore be treated in section two.

Summarizing: there are three sets of words that are used to denote the presence of the divine Persons in the rational creature: (1) indwelling, abiding making a home etc.; (2) being given, being possessed; (3) being sent. Those words that do not import any connotation of being *ab alio*, such as indwelling or gift, if explicitly understood as self-giving, can be said of all three divine Persons. Those words, however, which, like mission (to be sent) or gift in the sense of being given by another, imply an *esse ab alio* can only be said of the Son and the Spirit, and not of the Father. From the way Thomas treats the missions of the divine Persons in previous articles and in this article, it becomes clear how linguistic his approach is, and, in particular, how sensitive he is to language vis-à-vis Father, Son and Spirit.

In the fifth *articulus*, the invisible mission of the Son is questioned. The question is of whether or not it is fitting to say that the Son is sent invisibly. Though the *articulus* deals with the indwelling of the Son, the discussion in the *articulus* goes deeper than that since it deals with the relationship between the two invisible missions of the Son and the Spirit. The first two *obiectiones* connect the gifts of grace exclusively with the invisible mission of the Spirit, leaving no room for any association between a gift of grace and the invisible mission of the Son. The third *obiectio* brings the tension between the coherence of, and distinction between, both invisible missions to a head.

The text quoted in the *Sed Contra*-argument is taken from Wisdom (9,10):

---

33 *Idem*, a.4 ob 2 and ad 2.
34 *Idem*, ad 1.

"Dispatch her [Wisdom] from the holy heavens,
send her forth from your throne of glory
to help me and to toil with me
and teach me what is pleasing to you;"[35]

Thomas has probably chosen the text for the use of the verb 'to send'. The text makes it clear that the article is about the relationship of the invisible mission of the Son ('Wisdom') to the invisible mission of the Holy Spirit.

In the *corpus articuli*, Thomas begins by stating that the whole Trinity is the subject of indwelling. Thomas refers to Jn. 14, 23, as he did in the second *objectio* of the previous *articulus*. Next, he retrieves the conclusion of the third *articulus*, which said that to send a divine Person to someone means that the divine Person is present in someone in a new way. Since both the Son and the Spirit can be said to be *ab alio*, both can be said to be sent (invisibly). Thomas repeats the conclusion of the previous *articulus*, arguing that for the same reason the Father cannot be said to be sent, though He can be said to abide through grace. Conclusion: it is not only the Holy Spirit who is sent invisibly, but also the Son.

The argument presented in the corpus is completely formal: no substantial new information is given. The real discussion takes place in the answers to the objections. There, Thomas balances carefully between two extremes, i.e. between not losing the distinction between the (invisible) missions of Son and Spirit while at the same time keeping them together. The language he uses to indicate the relationship is prudent: relationships are formulated in terms of attribution, appropriation, and assimilation, and these are terms that suggest associations rather than connections. As a result, the connection between the gifts of grace and the Holy Spirit is made less exclusive, making room for the mission of the Son to be associated with these gifts as well.

The first step in doing this is taken in the answer to the first *obiectio*. The answer begins with the statement that all gifts, in as far as they are gifts, are attributed to the Holy Spirit. The reason for this is that the Spirit holds the notion of first gift. This argument has been prepared in q.38, where Thomas treats one of the biblical names of the Holy Spirit, namely Gift. The biblical name 'Gift' for the Holy Spirit is associated with the notion of gift of grace. The grounds for this association are a certain correspondence of likeness (*similitudo* is the term Thomas uses, as we will see in the next section) between the gift of grace, and the Spirit being the first Gift, which functions as grounds for attributing all gifts of grace *inquantum dona sunt* to the Holy Spirit. This explanation does justice to the text from Corinthians, quoted in the first *obiectio*: "But at work in all these is

---

[35] Cf. *STh* I q.43 a.5 Sc: "Sed contra est quod Sapientia 9 dicitur de divina sapientia: "Mitte illam de coelis sanctis tuis, et a sede magnitudinis tuae." The identification of the (invisible) mission of the Son with biblical testimonies about the presence of the divine Wisdom in creation dates from the first centuries, and can for instance be found in Augustine's *De Trinitate*. "Verbum enim Patris est Filius, quod et sapientia eius dicitur. Quid ergo mirum si mittitur non quia inaequalis est Patri sed quia est *manatio quaedam claritatis omnipotentis Dei sinceris* (Wisd. 7,25)?" (*De Trin.* IV, 20).

one and the same Spirit, distributing them at will to each individual." (1 Cor. 12, 11).

At the same time it opens up the possibility for another attribution of gifts of grace, this time not in so far as they are 'gifts' and on different grounds. Thomas does not specify these grounds, but instead states that "for proper reasons" the gifts that belong to the intellect are attributed to the Son. We can fill in the grounds for this attribution ourselves: the Son, being the Word, proceeds from the Father *per modum intellectus*, and the association between this and the gifts that belong to the intellect is clearly sufficient for their attribution to the Son. Thomas introduces a special name for this attribution, calling it an attribution through a certain appropriation (*per quamdam appropriationem*).[36] In the following section, we will deal with appropriation at great length.

Now that there is room for the invisible mission of the Son in the relationship between the gifts and the Holy Spirit, the question can be asked of how both invisible missions relate and how they correspond with distinct gifts of grace. The answer can be inferred from the answers to the *obiectiones* two and three. First, the most prominent gift of grace, the gift of charity, without which sanctifying grace cannot be possessed, corresponds with the invisible mission of the Holy Spirit. The formulation Thomas chooses is somewhat stronger than the associative language of his answer to the first *obiectio*. The soul, he says, is assimilated to God through grace. So, through the gift of charity, the soul is assimilated to the Spirit, who is love. In a similar fashion, the soul is assimilated to the Son, who is the Word.[37]

This clear distinction between different gifts of grace, which result in different assimilations of the soul to the Spirit and the Son respectively, contains the risk of implying too much of a separation between the invisible missions. This risk is made even greater by the Spirit being connected with the one gift of grace which is decisive with respect to the indwelling itself, i.e. the gift of sanctifying grace, of charity. As a consequence, the invisible mission of the Son could become somewhat superfluous (the latter being exactly the point of the third *obiectio*).

Being aware of this risk, Thomas begins by stressing the interconnectedness between the Holy Spirit and the way the Son proceeds from the Father before he distinguishes the way in which the soul is assimilated to the Son. The Son is the Word, he says, however, he is not just any word, but the Word that breathes love (*spirans amorem*). Correspondingly, the Son is not sent according to just any

---

36 *STh* I q.43, a.5 ad 1: "(L)icet omnia doni, inquantum dona sunt, attribuantur Spiritui Sancto, quia habet rationem primi doni, secundum quod est amor, ut supra dictum est (q.38, a.2), aliqua tamen dona secundum proprias rationes attribuuntur per quamdam appropriationem Filio, scilicet illa, quae pertinent ad intellectum."

37 *Idem*, ad 2: "(A)nima per gratiam conformatur Deo. Unde ad hoc, quod aliqua persona divina mittatur ad aliquam per gratiam, oportet, quod fiat assimilatio illius ad divinam personam, quae mittitur per aliquod gratiae donum. Et quia Spiritus Sanctus est amor, per donum charitatis anima Spiritui Sancto assimilatur. Unde secundum donum charitatis attenditur missio Spiritus Sancti."

perfection of the intellect (= the corresponding gift of grace), but according to an instruction of the intellect, which bursts out in an affection of love.[38]

The gift of wisdom, which is associated with the invisible mission of the Son, is thus a 'warm' and not a 'cold' instruction of the intellect. It is a knowing which comes together with love (a 'willing').[39] So, basically, the two highly coherent invisible missions of the Son and the Spirit correspond with two highly coherent effects of grace, namely the illumination of the intellect and the enkindling of the affections.

In the answer to the third *objectio*, Thomas again undertakes an attempt to keep both missions and their corresponding effects together, and again his approach is linguistic. When we speak (cf. "si *loquamur* de missione etc.") of missions with respect to their origin, they must be distinguished, just as the processions of the Son and the Spirit from the Father, the *generatio* and the *processio*, are distinguished. With respect to the effect of grace, the missions convene in the root of grace but are distinguished in the effects of grace, i.e. the illumination of the intellect and the enkindling of the affections. Notice how Thomas does not indicate immediate relationships between both effects and the two missions. First, he stresses that both missions result in a shared effect, which is the root of grace. Second, the illumination of the intellect and the enkindling of the affections are called effects of grace, and not immediate effects of respectively the mission of the Son and the mission of the Spirit. To remove any doubt regarding the inseparability of the two missions, Thomas adds that one cannot be without the other since neither can be without sanctifying grace, nor is one Person separated from the other.[40]

From what we have read above, we are now able to make some remarks regarding the initial question of this section: what is constitutive of the relationship of grace? First, Thomas gives an interpretation of indwelling in terms of grace: Indwelling is the presence of Father, Son and Spirit as known and loved in our hearts. In this knowing and loving, we 'reach' God. Such is the

---

[38] *Ibidem.* "Filius autem est Verbum, non quaelumque, sed spirans amorem. Unde August. dicit in 9. lib. de Trinit. (cap. 10 circa fin): *Verbum, quod insinuare intendimus, cum amore notitia est.* Non igitur secundum quamlibet perfectionem intellectus mittitur Filius, sed secundum talem instructionem intellectus, qua prorumpat in affectum amoris.

[39] *Ibidem.* Thomas refers to different passages of Augustine's *De trinitate.* The notion of a 'loved knowledge' (*amata notitia*) is particularly developed in book 9 of the *De trinitate*, chapter 10; cf: "Verbum est igitur quod nunc discernere et insinuare volumus, cum amore notitia. Cum itaque se mens novit et amat, iungitur ei amore verbum eius. Et quoniam amat notitiam et novit amorem, et verbum in amore est et amor in verbo et utrumque in amante atque dicente."

[40] *Idem,* ad 3: "cum missio importet originem personae missae, et inhabitationem per gratiam, ut supra dictum est (aa.1 et 3), si loquamur de missione quantum ad originem, sic missio Filii distinguitur a missione Spiritus Sancti, sicut et generatio a processione. Si autem quantum ad effectum gratiae, sic communicant duae missiones in radice gratiae, sed distinguuntur in effectibus gratiae, qui sunt illuminatio intellectus, et inflammatio affectus. Et sic manifestum est, quod una non potest esse sine alia: quia neutra est sine gratia gratum faciente, nec una persona separatur ab alia."

intimacy of the relationship of grace, of which indwelling, as well as grace itself, are constitutive. Thomas shows himself to be a negative theologian, for the arrow of his attention is pointed toward us and the interpretation he gives is with respect to us: the indwelling of God consists in our knowing and loving Him. On the subject of indwelling with respect to God, no further information is given.

Second, the inseparability of the divine Persons implies that indwelling is always with respect to all three divine Persons. One of the implications of this is that indwelling and Holy Spirit must not be identified too quickly. Though it becomes apparent from Thomas' texts that there is a special relation between indwelling and the Holy Spirit, the conclusion cannot be drawn that only the Holy Spirit dwells in the sanctified man. Similar connections are made between Son and incarnation, and between Father and creation. The identification is of course suggested by the creed, in which faith is confessed in the Father, who is creator of all visible and invisible things, in Jesus Christ, who is born from the virgin Mary by the Holy Spirit, God from God, Light from Light, and in the Holy Spirit, Lord and Giver of life. Thomas teaches us that these identifications are too simple, and need to be considered in more detail. With respect to the identification of Son and incarnation, this consists in first drawing attention to the dominant role the Holy Spirit plays in the life of Christ. Second, we must consider Thomas' claim that, though the second Person of the Holy Trinity is the end term of the incarnation, the whole Trinity is *auctor incarnationis*. This does not diminish the fact that, with respect to incarnation, only the Son of God can be said to have become man. However, the same is not true for the identification of the Holy Spirit and indwelling. Though there are many expressions in both Scripture and tradition that suggest a special involvement of the Holy Spirit in indwelling, we cannot say that only the Spirit dwells in us, or that the Holy Spirit dwells in us more than the Father or the Son.

Third, we have seen that, in a very subtle way, Thomas associates certain effects of grace with the distinct invisible missions of Son and Holy Spirit. The invisible mission of the Spirit is associated with the gifts of grace precisely as gifts, and with the gift of charity, which is constitutive of the relationship of grace. Some effects of grace, especially those that regard the intellect, can be appropriated to the Son. It is tempting to make this into a schema in which all effects of grace are divided into those regarding the will and those regarding the intellect, and to subsequently ascribe them respectively to the Holy Spirit and to the Son. But Thomas takes great pains to make clear that the missions cannot be separated from each other, but only distinguished, that they convene in the one root of grace before they can be distinguished according to their distinct effects, and that the intimate connectedness of both missions reflects how the procession of the Son from the Father is not without the procession of the Spirit.

At all times Thomas seems concerned to safeguard the identity of the triune God: Creator of all there is, and therefore not part of all there is. This has, at least at two points, immediate consequences for the way he reflects on indwelling.

First, there is a continuous negative-theological ring to his reflections. When individual effects of grace are associated with individual divine Persons, we must constantly realize that, in the first place, these associations say something about how we know God, Father Son and Spirit. Note that Thomas defines the presence of God in our hearts in terms of our knowing and loving Him. The 'newness' of the presence of God in the case of indwelling is with respect to us: the renewal concerns our knowing and loving. So when Scripture says "the love of God has been poured into our hearts by the Holy Spirit who has been given us", we must realize that this is said with respect to our knowing and loving God, and less with respect to alleged individual and subsequent actions of the Holy Spirit. Once we realize this, many of the tensions that seem to be present in the text of *articulus* five are resolved.

The second consequence is immediately related to this first concern, and is that, in his reflections, Thomas shows a great sensitivity with respect to language. He is particularly aware of the failure of language to describe God perfectly. This shortcoming of our language concerns both language about God and language about the divine Persons and their interrelatedness. Understanding how language behaves when we deal with the triune God is important to our understanding of formulations regarding a special role of the divine Persons with respect to the forgiveness of sins. That is why we will discuss the use of language *in trinitate* extensively below.

Missions and the sacraments

Reading the first five *articuli* of *quaestio* 43 has yielded an understanding of what is meant by a divine Person being sent somewhere: being where the divine Person was before, but this time in a new way, and this newness is with respect to our knowing and loving.

This notion of 'to be sent' applies to both the invisible missions (which dominate the first five *articuli*) and the visible missions, as we will see in the next section. Second, we have acquired an understanding of the meaning of being sent somewhere invisibly, and we have come to see how being sent invisibly and indwelling relate to each other. We have learned that 'to be sent' can only be said of Son and Spirit, and that 'to dwell in' the hearts of men (to make a home) can be said of all three divine Persons. We have seen that to be given can be said of the Father, as long as it is understood in terms of self-giving. Third, we have learned how Father, Son and Spirit are simultaneously distinguished and kept together. Moreover we have come to understand Thomas' negative theological approach and the linguistic character of how he deals with the question concerning the missions of divine Persons. With these results in mind, we can turn to the *articulus* that deals with the *terminus ad quem* of the invisible mission(s).

The question asked in *articulus* 6 is whether or not the invisible mission happens to all who share grace, i.e. who possess sanctifying grace. The question asked corresponds more or less with the question asked in *articulus* 3, but its intention differs. In a.3 the question was about the depth or impact of the invisible mission. Here, it is about the addressee or the *terminus ad quem* of the mission. Four different addressees are discussed, which correspond with different 'moments' in the history of salvation[41]: the period of the Old Law (ob. 1), the Christian life of grace (ob. 2), the life in the fullness of grace with God (ob. 3). The fourth objection regards the question of whether the sacraments are the end term of the invisible mission. The text of the *Sed contra*-argument is taken from Augustine's *De Trinitate* III, 4, XV, 27: the invisible mission happens in order to sanctify creatures. And since all sanctified creatures posses grace, it appears that the invisible mission happens to all creatures who have grace.

In the *corpus articuli*, Thomas recapitulates the position he took in the third *articulus*, that is, that to be sent means that a divine Person begins to be somewhere where He was before, but in a new way. We have already seen that this new way involves a knowing and loving, which implies grace. In other words, the new way of being present involves an innovation in the soul through grace. Thomas stresses that the coming of the Holy Spirit does not happen without the internal reshaping of men[42], turning their souls towards God; in other words it does not happen without their justification and sanctification (cf. Ch. 2).

One may take notice of the formulation Thomas uses: the divine Person "begins to be where He was before, but in a new way, according to which the mission *is attributed to the divine persons*".[43] Again he uses the verb 'to attribute' to relate certain effects to a mission. In this case, 'to attribute' is used for relating the mission itself to a divine Person. The intention is, however, not to identify too immediately a new way of being present (which is a knowing and a loving on our part) with an individual divine Person. As we have indicated before, it is part of a careful way of speaking about Father, Son and Spirit.

In the first *objectio*, the question is asked of whether the invisible mission of the Spirit happens to the fathers of the Old Testament. In the next chapter, we will deal with the relationship between salvation under the Old and under the New Covenant from the perspective of the theology of the sacraments. Here, it will suffice to say that according to the tradition of the church in which Thomas stood, there was, and is, no question about the fact that salvation was possible for those who lived before the coming of the Redeemer. This tradition can refer to the letters of Paul, in particular his letters to the Galatians and to the Romans, where Abraham is presented as an example of those who are justified

---

[41] Cf. J. Wissink *Thomas van Aquino*, p.120; p.130.

[42] *STh* I q.43, a.6 co: "(I)n eo, ad quem fit missio, oportet duo considerare, scilicet inhabitationem gratiae, et innovationem quandam per gratiam. Ad omnes ergo fit missio invisibilis, in quibus haec duo inveniuntur."; cf. J. Wissink, *Thomas van Aquino. De actuele betekenis van zijn theologie*, 1998, p.123

[43] *Ibidem* "(I)ncipiat esse, ubi prius fuit, sed quodam modo novo, secundum quod missio attribuitur divinis personis."

through faith (Rm 4:3; Gal. 3:6; cf. Gn 15:6c). In the *obiectio*, however, this tradition is confronted by Jn 7:39:

> "He [Jesus] was speaking of the Spirit which those who believed in him were to receive, for there was no Spirit as yet because Jesus had not yet been glorified."

This text seems to suggest that there was no invisible mission of the Spirit (or of the Son) to the fathers of the Old Testament, and that the Spirit was first sent after the glorification of Christ. In his answer, Thomas begins by quoting from Augustine's *De Trinitate* (IV, 20), in which he says that the Son has been sent invisibly to the patriarchs and the prophets. From this he concludes that the text from the gospel of John must be interpreted otherwise: "for there was no Spirit as yet" must be interpreted to mean that the Spirit was not yet given together with visible signs, as on the day of Pentecost. His answer is surprisingly short, especially when taking into account that what we are dealing with here is the transition from the old law to the new law. In the next chapter we will see that one of the most important consequences of this transition is the fact that the sacraments come to play the decisive role regarding the infusion of the Spirit in the hearts of the faithful.

In the second objection, the notion of invisible mission is confronted with the experience from the Christian life that our love for God can both grow and fade. The point is that the notion of mission seems to imply a discontinuity, whereas the growth in love for God seems to import continuity. Thomas begins with a statement from Augustine's *De Trinitate* (IV, 20), which supports the notion of a continuous mission of the Spirit.[44] The first matter of importance for Thomas is to make clear that there is no growth in love for God without an invisible mission. This disqualifies the idea that, once the Spirit is given, the effects of this gift can grow through their own strength. But if there is no growth without mission, how can continuous growth be explained in terms of mission, which has the connotation of discontinuity? Thomas resolves this by distinguishing between 'to be sent' and 'to dwell' or 'to make a home'. Though 'to be sent' may seem to suggest a discontinuity, 'to dwell' or 'to make a home', being the other words Scripture uses to refer to the presence of the divine Persons in the hearts of men, do not. These latter terms have, more than 'to be sent', the connotation of continuity, which corresponds with the notion of continuous growth of love for God. So expressions such as 'mission' or 'to be sent' are, because of their connotation of discontinuity, used more for moments in which something new happens, when someone reaches a new state of grace, for instance in the case of miracles, prophecies, or in the case of risking ones life for the love of God. Thus, Thomas resolves the seemingly incompatibility of mission and continuous growth of grace, by focusing on how language functions.

---

[44] *STh* I q.43 a.6 ad 2: "(E)tiam secundum profectum virtutis, aut augmentum gratiae fit missio invisibilis. Unde August. dicit 4 de Trinit., quod *tunc aliquam mittitur Filius, cum a quoquam cognoscitur, atque percipitur, quantum cognosci, et percipi potest pro captu vel proficientis in Deum, vel perfectae in Deo animae rationalis.*"

The next *obiectio* draws our attention to special cases of having grace. Christ and the *beati* have the fullness of grace. As such, both Christ, insofar as He is man, and the blessed, are fully united with God. Is it possible to say that a divine Person is also sent to Christ, or to the blessed? This would not seem to be consistent with the fact that 'to be sent' implies a distance between sender and addressee. Thomas responds by stating that an invisible mission to the blessed takes place at the beginning of the beatitude itself. But an invisible mission takes place even after that, though not according to grace, but according to new mysteries that are revealed to them until the end of time. Hence, the growth of love concerns not the love itself, but its applicability to a greater number of particulars. Grace grows not in intensiveness, but in extent.[45] For Christ, however, things are different. Only on the day of his conception did an invisible mission to Christ take place, from which moment He possessed the plenitude of all wisdom and grace.[46]

The fourth and final objection has the most immediate relevance to our study, because it treats the relationship between mission and the sacraments. In the objection it is argued that the sacraments of the New Covenant are said to contain grace. Since the invisible mission always happens to one who (or to what) contains grace, one should expect that the invisible mission happens to the sacraments as well. However, this is not the case. In the answer Thomas gives, elements from his theology of the sacraments in the *tertia pars* of the *Summa* are present, in particular the difference between principal and instrumental cause (cf. *STh* III q.62, a.1 co). The sacraments of the New Covenant are said to contain grace in the sense that they contain a certain instrumental strength to cause grace instrumentally (*STh* III q.62, a.3 co).[47] Hence, Thomas answers that grace is instrumentally in the sacraments of the New Covenant. As such, they are not the goal of the mission. The goal of the mission is the one who receives grace through the sacraments.

This analysis gives us a framework for how things 'work' in the sacrament of penance at its deepest level. The relationship of grace, which is restored, or repaired, in the sacrament of penance, consists, at its deepest level, in the indwelling of Father, Son and Spirit.

Through sin, the bond of knowing and loving is broken, and grace is lost. Faith is not necessarily lost, but charity is. Subsequently, the intimate presence of Father, Son and Spirit as loved and known is lost, and God is not said to dwell in the heart of the sinner anymore. This loss of indwelling does not consist in a change in God. It is not as if God is no longer present where He was before, due to an act of sinning. The change occurs in us. It is the sinner who, through

---

[45]   J. Wissink, *Thomas*, p.128.

[46]   For Thomas, growth in knowledge, wisdom and grace points to an initial lack of perfection, which is why he thinks that an invisible mission to Christ could only be possible at the time of His conception. Cf. J. Wissink, *Thomas*, p.128.

[47]   For instrumental causality, see Ch. 4, final section.

a sinful deed, blocks the light of grace, stopping it from shining upon his soul, and so cutting off the gift of loving and knowing God.

The sacrament of penance restores the grace of God in the heart of the sinner, because the sacrament consists in the Father, Son and Spirit coming to dwell in the soul of the penitent. The notion of discontinuity, introduced by the notion of forgiveness, corresponds with the notion of 'to be sent'. So in sacramental forgiveness, God becomes present again as known and loved, which renewed presence is understood in terms of the invisible mission of Son and Spirit by the Father (and, in the case of the Holy Spirit, by the Son).

We have seen that both the missions of the Son and of the Spirit are in some way related to particular gifts of grace. We have also seen that, in particular, the gift of charity, without which sanctifying grace cannot be possessed, is associated with the mission of the Holy Spirit. It is on the grounds of these associations, that the forgiveness of sins is related to the gift of the Holy Spirit, and said to be *per Spiritum sanctum*. The precise meaning of relating certain gifts of grace to individual missions of Son or Spirit, and the grounds on which the gift of charity is particularly associated with the Holy Spirit, still need to be investigated in the next section. In particular the notion of appropriation will be examined, which provides the *ratio* based on which effects are ascribed to distinct invisible missions, and the term will be placed within the wider context of grammar *in trinitate*.

But before we come to that, we will read the last two *articuli* of this *quaestio* on the missions of the divine Persons. In the next *articulus*, more is said about the relationship between Son and Spirit from the perspective of their respective visible missions. In the last *articulus*, the relation between eternal processions and temporal missions is looked at.

The visible missions of the Son and the Spirit

We have said above that the distinction visible/invisible, together with the distinction between Son and Spirit, structures the *quaestio*. After two *articuli*, in which the notion of 'to be sent' is analyzed conceptually, and, after four *articuli* that deal with the invisible missions, in the seventh article Thomas turns to dealing with the visible missions. Moreover, even though the visible mission of the Son is mentioned, the article deals primarily with the visible mission of the Holy Spirit. The question is asked of whether or not it is fitting for the Spirit to be sent visibly. Thomas pays no further attention to the visible mission of the Son, except for making comparisons with the visible mission of the Spirit. This is probably because the whole first half of the *Tertia pars* of the *Summa theologiae* deals, in fact, with the visible mission of the Son.

In the objections one and four the visible missions of the Spirit are compared with the visible mission of the Son. In the second objection the visible missions of the Spirit are compared with the sacraments. In the third and fifth objections the question is asked of whether the visible creature according to which the Holy Spirit is visibly sent refers to the Spirit or to the Trinity as a whole (ob. 3) or to the angels (ob. 5). The sixth and final objection asks about the opportunity of the visible missions of the Holy Spirit: why is there no visible mission corresponding to each invisible mission of the Holy Spirit?

The *Sed contra*-argument refers to the scene of the baptism of Jesus, its being one of four different occasions which Thomas identifies as visible missions of the Holy Spirit (cf. Chapter one). The other three comprise Christ's breathing on the apostles (Jn. 20, 21-23), the Holy Spirit appearing in the shape of a cloud at the transfiguration, and the appearance of the Holy Spirit in the shape of tongues of fire at Pentecost. In this article, Thomas mentions all four in his answer to the sixth objection.

In Chapter One, we indicated the striking correspondence between the sacraments and the missions in Thomas' theology. As sacraments consist of things and words, so do the visible missions, and as sacraments are given to men in order to bring them, through what is visible, to what is invisible, so the divine Persons are sent visibly, since it is connatural to men to be led by what is visible to what is invisible. In the *corpus articuli* this same general insight, developed in the twelfth *quaestio* of the *Prima pars*, which deals with our knowledge of God, is presented.[48]

However, this article is not only interesting because of the parallel between missions and sacraments. It also provides us with important insights regarding the nature of the missions of the Spirit, and especially the relation between the mission of the Spirit and of the Son. In the *corpus articuli*, it appears that the difference between the eternal processions of Son and Spirit is responsible for the difference between how both are sent visibly. Thomas explains that it is fitting for the Son, being the *principium* of the Spirit, to be the one who sanctifies (*auctor sanctificationis*). Consequently, the Son is sent visibly as *auctor sanctificationis*. Since the Spirit proceeds from the Father as love, it is therefore fitting for the Spirit to be the gift of the sanctification. Consequently, the Spirit is sent visibly as sign of the sanctification (*sanctificationis indicium*).[49]

The two relationships between visible and invisible and between Son and Spirit, which together structure the whole question, can be placed into the following schema:

	Son	Holy Spirit
Visible missions	*auctor sanctificationis*	*indicium sanctificationis*
Invisible missions	*auctor sanctificationis*	*donum sanctificationis*
Eternal processions	*principium Spiritus sancti*	*processio ut amor*

---

[48] *STh* I q.43, a.7 co: "Deus providet omnibus secundum uniuscuiusque modum. Est autem modus connaturalis hominis, ut per visibilia ad invisibilia manuducatur, ut ex supra dictis patet (q. 12 art. 12). Et ideo invisibilia Dei oportuit homini per visibilia manifestari. Sicut igitur seipsum Deus, et processiones aeternas personarum per creaturas visibiles secundum aliqua indicia hominibus quodammodo demonstravit: ita conveniens fuit, ut etiam invisibiles missiones divinarum personarum secundum aliquas visibiles creaturas manifestarentur."

[49] *Ibidem*: "Nam Spiritui Sancto, inquantum procedit ut amor, competit esse sanctificationis donum: Filio autem, inquantum est Spiritus Sancti principium, competit esse sanctificationis huius auctorem."

It appears that Thomas approaches the six objections with this, or a similar, schema in the back of his mind. Before we continue with his answers to the objections, we must first make some remarks with respect to the schema. First, the Holy Spirit is sent visibly in order reveal the invisible gift of sanctification, which in turn is associated with the invisible mission of the Spirit. In contrast, the visible mission of the Son refers to the incarnate Word, the hypostatic union of God and man in Jesus Christ. As we will see in the following chapter, the human and divine nature of Christ relate to each other as instrument to principal agent. In other words, the revelation in Jesus goes further than merely making something visible, as seems to be the point of the visible missions of the Spirit. Thomas uses the same designation for the visible and invisible mission: the Son is *auctor sanctificationis*, both as man and as God. Second, the relationship between Son and Spirit, as *auctor sanctificationis* and *donum sanctificationis*, makes it clear that Christ, and not the Holy Spirit, is the cause of the sanctification of man, and that consequently, the role of the Holy Spirit with respect to the forgiveness of sins must be interpreted accordingly.

In his answer to the first objection, Thomas stresses the special character of the visible mission of the Son, which consists in the special way in which the second Person of the Trinity is united to "the visible creature, in whom He appears". A consequence of this hypostatic union is that what is said of this creature can also be said of the Son of God. Because of His assumed human nature, the Son is said to be less than the Father is. However, the Spirit is not united in the same way with the creature in which He appears, and is therefore not said to be less than the Father. The difference between the missions of the Son and the Spirit is the subject of both the fourth objection, and Thomas' answer to it. In the fourth objection, the question is asked of whether or not the Spirit should have been sent as a rational creature, similarly to the Son. The difference between Son and Spirit, and between their respective roles indicated in the *corpus articuli*, finds its expression in their respective visible missions. In other words: the Son must be shown to be the one who sanctifies. Therefore, the Son must be sent according to rational nature, for only a rational nature can act in such a way that it can be sanctified. However, since any other creature can be a sign of sanctification, it is, therefore, not necessary that the Spirit takes to himself self a personal union with a visible creature because, as a visible creature, He only indicates, and is not the one who acts. That the Spirit is sent visibly only as a sign also explains why the sign only lasts as long as its presence is required.

The second objection points to a similarity we have already noticed between the visible missions of the Holy Spirit and the sacraments. Both are signs, i.e. visible aids meant to lead men to the invisible realm of spiritual things. However, the difference between both is that, in the case of the sacraments, something that already exists becomes a sign, while in the case of visible missions of the Holy Spirit, the dove and the fire appear with the sole purpose of signifying the presence of the Spirit.[50] In his answer to the third objection, Thomas adds that the dove and the fire are especially brought into being for the purpose of signifying one Person in particular, namely the Spirit. As created, they are signs of the whole Trinity. However, as created with the special purpose of signifying the Holy Spirit, they are especially signs of the Holy Spirit. From his answer to the fifth objection, we learn that that these visible creatures, such as the dove or the tongues of flames, are formed by the ministry of the angels. However, we must not conclude from this that the angels are sent visibly instead of the Holy Spirit, as the objection argues. Thomas acknowledges that the formation of the dove and the fire is achieved by the ministry of angels, however, not in order to signify the person of the angel, but to signify the Person of the Holy Spirit.

In the sixth and last objection, the question is asked of how the visible and the invisible missions of the Holy Spirit relate. Why is there not a visible mission on each occasion on which the Spirit is sent invisibly? Thomas explains that the (visible) manifestation of the invisible mission of the Spirit is only given when it benefits the church[51], namely when, through these visible signs, the faith is confirmed or spread. Since faith is primarily confirmed or spread by Christ and the apostles, the visible mission of the Spirit had to occur especially to Christ and the apostles, and to some of the early Saints, on whom, in a sense, the church was founded. Subsequently, Thomas explains the four passages of the Scripture that we mentioned earlier, and in which a visible mission of the Spirit is mentioned. The way in which Thomas explains these visible missions reveals a resemblance between the visible missions and the sacraments, as we have pointed out in Chapter One.

At the end of his explanation of the four texts, Thomas adds that the Spirit could not have been sent visibly to the fathers of the Old Testament, because first, the visible mission of the Son had to be fulfilled before the Spirit could be sent visibly, since the Spirit reveals the Son, as the Son reveals the Father. In as far as visible apparitions of the divine Persons were given to the fathers of the Old Testament, they must not be called visible missions, for they were not given to indicate the indwelling of a divine Person by grace, but to reveal something else.[52]

---

[50] *Idem*, ad 2. Also at stake is the difference between signs that anyone can see (visible missions of the Spirit, the sacraments) and signs that are only visible to prophetic vision.

[51] Cf. 1 Cor 12, 7: "The particular manifestation of the Spirit granted to each one is to be used for the general good."

[52] *Idem*, ad 6: "Ad sextum dicendum quod non est de necessitate invisibilis missionis, ut semper manifestetur per aliquod signum visibile exterius, sed, sicut dicitur I Cor. xii, *Manifestatio spiritus datur alicui ad utilitatem*, scilicet Ecclesiae. Quae quidem utilitas est, ut per huiusmodi visibilia signa fides confirmetur et propagetur. Quod quidem principaliter factum est per Christum et per Apostolos, secundum illud Hebr. ii, *cum initium accepisset enarrari per Dominum, ab eis qui audierunt in nos confirmata est*. Et ideo specialiter debuit fieri missio visibilis Spiritus sancti ad Christum et ad Apostolos, et ad aliquos primitivos Sanctos, in quibus quodammodo

Mission and procession

The eighth and last *articulus* of the question remains to be discussed. It deals with, on one hand, the missions in relation to the processions, and on the other, the effects of the mission. The question is that of whether what is true for the processions concerning how the divine Persons relate, is also true for the missions. Since the Son proceeds from the Father, and the Spirit from the Father and the Son, it would seem that only the Father can send the Son, that only Father and Son can send the Spirit, and that the Spirit cannot send either the Father or the Son. How, then, must we interpret texts from Scripture which seem to suggest that the Spirit sends the Son, as in the text from Isaiah 48, 16, quoted in the *Sed contra*-argument:

"And now Lord Yahweh has sent me with his spirit."[53]

Thomas begins by stating two positions. The first says that when the Spirit is said to send the Son, what is meant is that when the Son preaches according to his human nature, He preaches by the Holy Spirit (*a Spiritu Sancto*). In other words, when the Spirit sends the Son, it is according to His assumed human nature. The defenders of this position keep to the principle that a divine Person can only be sent by the one from whom He proceeds eternally. For the second position, Thomas refers to Augustine (*De Trinitate* II,5). Augustine says that the Son is sent both by Himself and by the Holy Spirit, and that the Holy Spirit is sent both by Himself and by the Son. According to this second position, there is no necessary correspondence implied between, on the one hand, relations of procession and, on the other hand, relations of mission. That the Son proceeds from the Father, and the Spirit from the Father and the Son and not vice versa, does not compel us to deny that the Son is sent by the Spirit.

Thomas takes a position that is between these two alternatives. Both positions contain elements of the truth, he says, because the one mission can be

---

Ecclesia fundabatur. Ita tamen quod visibilis missio facta ad Christum, demonstraret missionem invisibilem non tunc, sed in principio suae conceptionis, ad eum factam. Facta autem est missio visibilis ad Christum, in baptismo quidem sub specie columbae, quod est animal fecundum, ad ostendendum in Christo auctoritatem donandi gratiam per spiritualem regenerationem, unde vox Patris intonuit, *hic est filius meus dilectus*, ut ad similitudinem unigeniti alii regenerarentur. In transfiguratione vero, sub specie nubis lucidae, ad ostendendam exuberantiam doctrinae, unde dictum est, *ipsum audite*. Ad Apostolos autem, sub specie flatus, ad ostendendam potestatem ministerii in dispensatione sacramentorum, unde dictum est eis, *quorum remiseritis peccata, remittuntur eis*. Sed sub linguis igneis, ad ostendendum officium doctrinae, unde dicitur quod coeperunt loqui variis linguis. Ad Patres autem Veteris Testamenti, missio visibilis Spiritus sancti fieri non debuit quia prius debuit perfici missio visibilis filii quam Spiritus sancti, cum Spiritus sanctus manifestet Filium, sicut Filius Patrem. Fuerunt tamen factae visibiles apparitiones divinarum personarum Patribus Veteris Testamenti. Quae quidem missiones visibiles dici non possunt, quia non fuerunt factae, secundum Augustinum, ad designandum inhabitationem divinae personae per gratiam, sed ad aliquid aliud manifestandum."

53   *Idem*, a.8, Sc: "Sed contra est quod Filius mittitur a Spiritu Sancto, secundum illud Isa. 48, 16: *Nunc misit me Dominus, et Spiritus eius*. Filius autem non est a Spiritu sancto; ergo persona divina mittitur ab ea, a qua non est."

approached both from the perspective of origin, and from the perspective of its visible or invisible effect, depending on according to which the mission is perceived. Looked at from the perspective of origin, it is not fitting to say that a divine Person is sent by any other divine Person than the one from whom He proceeds. From this perspective, the Son is sent by the Father, and the Spirit by the Father and the Son. But when we understand the Person being sent to be principle of the effect of the mission, the whole Trinity can be said to send the divine Person.

Again the tension, which seems to be in Thomas' explanation, is resolved once we realize the negative theological character of his approach. Once we deal with the effects of the missions, we are bound by the limitations of how we know God to be at once one and three. To say that a divine Person is sent denotes the presence of the divine Person as known and loved in our hearts, and denotes how we have come to know the divine Person to proceed from the Father, or from the Father and the Son. At the same time the heartwarming effect of this presence must be ascribed to the whole Trinity, or can, through appropriation, be ascribed to the divine Person being sent.[54]

Conclusion

The close reading of *quaestio* 43 about the missions of the divine Persons has yielded a number of results for our investigation of the sacrament of penance. First, it has shown that the indwelling of Father, Son and Spirit is constitutive of the relationship of grace that is restored or repaired in the sacrament of penance. God Himself comes to dwell again, or with renewed fervor, in the heart of the man or woman whose sins are forgiven.

Second, with respect to the Son and the Holy Spirit, this indwelling is understood in terms of being sent. The discussion about the visible missions has shown that the difference between the visible missions of Son and Holy Spirit corresponds with different roles of Son and Spirit with respect to sanctification: it is fitting that the Holy Spirit is the gift of sanctification, while it is fitting that the Son is *auctor sanctificationis*. Thomas finds the reasons why these ascriptions are fitting in the eternal processions of the Son and the Spirit.

Third, the fact that the gift of sanctification is associated with the Holy Spirit corresponds with other ascriptions of effects of grace to the Holy Spirit. The fundamental gift of charity is ascribed to the mission of the Spirit, as are all gifts of grace insofar as they are gift. The fundamental gift clearly suggests a special role for the Spirit with respect to sanctification in general and forgiveness of sins in particular. Thomas explains this each time by referring to how the Holy

---

[54] The answer Thomas gives corresponds with the position he has taken in the previous articles. In the first article, a similar distinction is made within the notion of mission: it can be understood with respect to the *terminus a quo* and with respect to the *terminus ad quem.* In the subsequent articles, we have seen how careful Thomas is not to make the relationships between divine Persons and certain effects in salvation history too immediate. The same concern appears to be present in this *articulus.* The guiding rule here is the axiom that all actions of the Trinity *ad extra* are of all three divine Persons together. What this rule aims to protect is the unity and trinity of God.

Spirit proceeds from the Father and the Son as love, which justifies why the Spirit is called 'first gift'. But even though the most fundamental gift of charity, and the gifts of grace in so far as they are gifts, are ascribed to the Spirit, some gifts can nevertheless be ascribed to the Son as well.

Fourth, being sent means that Son and Spirit become present as known and loved in the hearts of the one to whom they are sent. By defining mission in terms of being present as known or loved, Thomas focuses on our side of the relationship, on our knowledge. With respect to God, Thomas' theology remains negative. The ascriptions of distinct effects to distinct missions of Son and Spirit are, for Thomas, always through a certain appropriation. Thomas's remark that the missions are only distinguished with respect to their origin, while as to their effects they convene in the root of grace, is crucial to this view. Finally, the close reading of the *quaestio* has yielded how profoundly linguistic Thomas' approach is to the question of the missions of the divine Persons. To miss the linguistic character of his treatment would be to miss the point of the *quaestio* altogether. To be able to fully appreciate this we will now turn to what we have come to call 'grammar *in trinitate*', which is about how we should use language when we speak about Father, Son and Holy Spirit.

2   Grammar in trinitate

In this section we will deal with language in general vis-à-vis God who is Father, Son and Spirit.[55] The main focus, however, will be on appropriation. In the current debate on the theology of the Holy Trinity, appropriation is evaluated rather negatively. The current debate, – as we saw at the beginning of this chapter, – is largely dominated by the remarks of K. Rahner in *Mysterium Salutis*, in which he has set the agenda for the discussion about the theology of the Trinity in our day.[56] In *Mysterium Salutis*, K. Rahner begins by observing that for current theology, and the life of the faithful, the doctrine of the Trinity has failed to prove itself relevant. This is due to the fact that the doctrines of *De Deo uno* and *De Deo trino* have become separated. In the theological handbooks on which Rahner reflected, once the doctrine of the Trinity had been dealt with, it disappeared from reflections on other areas of theology. Consequently, the doctrine of grace, for instance, has become practically unitarian instead of Trinitarian. According to the critics, the rule that all works of the Trinity *ad extra* are of the three divine Persons together is blamed for making it almost impossible to relate certain actions of God in salvation history to distinct divine Persons. Hence, all that is left is ascribing moments or actions in salvation history to divine Persons by 'mere appropriation'.[57]

---

55   On language in Thomas' theology of the Holy Trinity, cf. G. Hibbert, "Mystery and metaphysics in the trinitarian theology of Saint Thomas", in *Irish Theological Quarterly* 31, 1964, 187-213.

56   K. Rahner, "Der dreifaltige Gott", 1967.

57   *Idem*, pp.369-385. Cf. H.C. Schmidbaur, *Personarum Trinitas. Die trinitarische Gotteslehre des heiligen Thomas von Aquin*, 1995, pp. 497: "Karl Rahner hat in seinem vielbeachteten Versuch einer heilsökonomischen Neubegründung der Trinitätslehre die (neu)scholastische Appropriationlehre heftig kritisiert." Schmidbauer agrees with Rahner's intentions, and with

In this section we will investigate whether this negative evaluation of appropriation is justified, i.e. based upon a correct understanding of Thomas' theory of appropriation, an understanding in which justice is done to the linguistic character of appropriation.[58] For this we will focus on the two *articuli* where Thomas explicitly deals with appropriation in the *Summa theologiae*. We will read these *articuli* against the background of the *quaestio* at the end of which they are found. In particular we will show the profoundly linguistic character of appropriation. We will relate appropriation to analogy and show that appropriation is a special case of analogy, and that appropriation is, with respect to language *in trinitate*, what analogy is with respect to our language *in divinis* in general.[59]

General remarks on medieval language theories[60]

a. Language, Thought, and Reality

We will begin by presenting a number of distinctions. The first distinction is between language, thought and reality. We find this distinction in Thomas'

---

the criticisms insofar as they regard the neoscholastic understanding of appropriation. Insofar as they regard Thomas, he rejects Rahner's criticisms, however on the wrong grounds. Whereas Rahner appears to make them into 'mere appropriations', it seems that Schmidbaur places appropriations almost on the same ontological level as properties (cf. pp.494-495, 498). However, neither of them appears to acknowledge the linguistic character of Thomas' theory of appropriations, and consequently, both seem to confuse the logical and the real order, as many have done with respect to Thomas' 'doctrine' of analogy.

[58] On Thomas' theory of appropriation see A. Chollet, "Appropriation aux personnes de la sainte Trinité", in *Dictionnaire de théologie catholique* I,2, 1931, pp.1708-1717; C. Sträter "Het begrip 'appropriatie' bij S. Thomas" in: *Bijdragen* 9 (1948), pp.1-41; pp.144-186, J. Châtillon "Unitas, aequalitas, concordia vel connexia. Recherches sur les origines de la théorie thomiste des appropriations." In: *Thomas Aquinas 1274-1974. Commemoratiue Studies*, 1974, pp.337-380, H.C. Schmidbaur, *Personarum Trinitas. Die trinitarische Gotteslehre des heiligen Thomas von Aquin*, 1995, pp. 488-501; T. Smith "The context and character of Thomas' theory of appropriations" in *The Thomist* 63, 1999, pp. 579-612. Only the latter truly acknowledges the linguistic nature of Thomas' theory of appropriations. Cf. also H. Rikhof, "Lumen Cordium", Katholieke Theologische Universiteit te Utrecht, 1993.

[59] Cf. A. Chollet, "Appropriation aux personnes de la sainte Trinité", in *Dictionnaire de théologie catholique* I,2, 1931, p.1708: "L'appropriation (..) est un procédé de langage théologique employé pour traiter des trois personnes divines. L'esprit humain est très pauvre en concepts propres concernant la Trinité, et la parole n'a que peu de termes pour exprimer les relations mutuelles et le caractère personel du Père, du Fils et du Saint-Esprit. Pour obvier à cette indigence, la théologie a recours à des concepts et à des mots par lesquels sont traduits d'autres objets, elle les applique par analogie ou par appropriation aux personnes de la sainte Trinité."

[60] On medieval logic and language theories, cf. Ph. Boehner o.f.m., *Medieval Logic. An Outline of its Development from 1250 to c1400*, 1966 (1952); F. Manthey, *Die Sprachphilosophie des hl. Thomas von Aquin und ihre Anwendung auf Probleme der Theologie*, 1937; J. Pinborg, *Die Entwicklung der Sprachtheorie im Mittelalter*, 1967; J. Pinborg, *Logik und Semantik im Mittelalter. Ein Überblick*, 1972; L. de Rijk, *Logica Modernorum. A Contribution to the History of early terminist logic*, 1962 (2 vols); L. de Rijk, *Middeleeuwse wijsbegeerte. Traditie en vernieuwing*, 1977; L. de Rijk, "The origin of the theory of the properties of terms", in: Kretzmann, Kenny, Pinborg (Ed.) *The Cambridge History of Later Medieval Philosophy*, 1982, pp. 161-173; E. Ashworth, "Logic, medieval", in E. Graig (ed.), *Routledge Encyclopedia of Philosophy*, vol. 5, 1998, pp.746-759.

theology in the beginning of *quaestio* 13 on the names of God, where he cites Aristotle saying that words are signs of the things understood and the things understood are likenesses of things as they exist in reality.[61] It appears that, according to Thomas, there are three levels to be distinguished: the level of the things as they exist in themselves, the level of the things as they are known and the level of the words. Each of these levels can be reflected upon. We can reflect upon the way things exist in reality, i.e. on the *modus essendi*. We can reflect on the way things are known or understood by the human intellect, i.e. upon the *modus intelligendi*. And we can reflect upon the way things are signified by our language, i.e. upon the *modus significandi*.[62]

The relation between language and reality is mediated, and not immediate. Words do not signify the things as they exist in reality immediately. Instead, they signify the things as we know them. Words signify the things mediated by our knowledge. Our language follows our knowledge, or as Thomas often puts it: we name as we know.[63] This insight plays an important role in Thomas' theology.

Furthermore, our use of words to signify a notion is conventional, and due to human institution. It is according to different conventions whether we use the word 'human', the word 'homo' or the word 'anthropos' to signify a human being. The relation between the notion and the thing in reality, however, is not conventional. Thomas, together with Aristotle, calls this relation a relation of similitude. This means that there is a certain resemblance, though not a complete equality, between the thing as it exists in reality, and the thing as it is known to us.

The distinction between reality on the one hand, and thought and language on the other hand, is important if we are to avoid rather fundamental mistakes, as McInerny has pointed out.

> "When the different modes of existence which nature has in reality and in the mind are not distinguished, we have the Platonic confusion. Aristotle's criticism of Plato is that he confused the logical and real orders, that he wanted something real to respond *as such* to the intentions which the mind forms in knowing. This issued in a reification of the logical universal so that not only was there to be a concept of man representing a nature common to many individuals, but there would also be an Idea, Man in himself, which exists apart and by participation in which particular men are. That the World of Ideas arose from the reification of logical entities seems obvious. The Platonist saw that in universals there is something one which is common to many, and it was this one

---

61 *STh* I q.13, a.1: "Respondeo dicendum quod, secundum Philosophum, voces sunt signa intellectum, et intellectus sunt rerum similitudines."

62 On the relation between language, thought, and reality cf. De Rijk "The origins of the Theory of the Properties of terms".

63 For instance: *STh* I q.13, pro: "Consideratis his quae ad divinam cognitionem pertinent, procedendum est ad considerationem divinorum nominum: unumquodque enim nominatur a nobis, secundum quod ipsum cognoscimus."; a.1 co: "Secundum igitur quod aliquid a nobis intellectu cognosci potest, sic a nobis potest nominari."; q.32, a.2 co: "Quia secundum quod intelligimus, sic nominamus."

thing which was postulated as enjoying separate existence. Logically, they would be forced to maintain that there must be separate genera as well and the World of Ideas soon becomes more densely populated than the world of singulars it is meant to explain."[64]

In the language-theories Thomas uses, his sensitiveness for what Burrell calls the distinction between surface grammar and depth grammar appears.[65] On the surface there is difference in form, in the depths there is a connection of meaning. He who only has an eye for the different forms connects a difference in reality too easily and too quickly with this superficial difference. He loses an eye for the activity of human knowing and speaking. He who only has an eye for unity on the level of reality, risks dismissing the difference in form as being mere language. He loses the chance to acquire insight into reality. Thomas uses language-theories, and his sensitiveness for surface and depth grammar, in his analyses of our language about God.[66]

b. Res significata, Modus significandi[67]

The second distinction is between *res significata* and *modus significandi*. The latter is a term that was originally used (for instance by Boëthius in his commentary on Aristotle's *Perihermeneias*) to denote, in a grammatical sense, the different forms and declensions of words like 'he walks', 'she walked', 'walking' and 'to walk', which are declensions of the verb 'o walk'. At a later stage, the term *modus significandi* was used (also by Boëthius) to denote the variety of ways in which a word signifies on a semantic level. One can say that words like 'he walks', 'she walked', 'walking' and 'walk' signify the same content 'walking', while at the same time signifying it all in a different way.[68]

Hence, the distinction between the thing signified (*res significata*) and the mode of signifying (*modus significandi*) can be helpful to explain, for example, the difference between the words 'good' and 'goodness'. Both words signify the same content, but they differ in the way they signify it, since the *modus significandi* of 'good' is concrete, while the *modus significandi* of 'goodness' is abstract. As we will see below, the difference between *modus significandi* and *res significata* plays an important role with respect to the doctrine of analogy.

c. Signification and Supposition

The third distinction is between signification and supposition. Signification has to do with the meaning of a word, while supposition has to do with the use of a

[64] R. McInerny, *The Logic of Analogy. An interpretation of St. Thomas*, 1961, p.47. McInerny refers to *In I Metaphys* lc.14 n.209.
[65] D. Burrell, *Aquinas. God and Action*, 1979, p.4.
[66] H. Rikhof, *Over God spreken. Een tekst van Thomas van Aquino uit de Summa theologiae. Vertaald, ingeleid en van aantekeningen voorzien door dr. H.W.M. Rikhof*, 1988, pp.139-140.
[67] On the history of the distinction between *res significata* and *modus significandi*, and their use in Thomas, esp. regarding the analogical nature of divine predication, cf. G. Rocca, "The distinction between *res significata* and *modus significandi* in Aquinas's theological epistemology", in *The Thomist* 55, 1991, pp.173-197.
[68] Cf. H. Rikhof, *Over God spreken* pp.138-140; H. Schoot, *Christ the 'name' of God. Thomas Thomas on naming Christ*, 1993, p.45.

word for something. Given its meaning, or signification, a word 'stands for' (*supponere pro*) or refers to something. For instance, the signification of 'tree' is 'a perennial plant with a single self-supporting trunk of wood, usually with no branches for some distance above the ground'. In contrast, the supposition of 'tree' can be, for instance, "this particular oak in the garden behind my house". A word can have different meanings, and, given one of its meanings, it can stand for different things. On the other hand, different words with different meanings can stand for the same thing. An often-used example of the latter is the sentence "the morning-star is the evening-star". 'Morning-star' signifies something other than 'evening-star'. However, both stand for the same celestial body: Venus.

De Rijk describes the development of the doctrine of the property of terms, especially of *suppositio* as a growing interest in the linguistic context of the words. He has labeled this concentration of attention the 'contextual approach'

> "The sound basis of the contextual approach seems to be undermined (..) by the implicit presupposition of the natural priority of signification. (..) They (the medieval logicians) would have done a better job, if instead of rejecting such notions as natural or simple supposition, they had abandoned their notion of signification itself."[69]

According to De Rijk, the medieval logicians held to the notion of signification of a term that is, in the end, independent of any context, i.e. of the actual use of the term in a proposition, instead of holding to the notion of natural supposition. "Natural supposition is unlike signification in that there is a context, an actual linguistic framework, which is left out of account for a moment." If they had amputated the right leg (in the vocabulary of De Rijk), they would have cut off signification instead of natural supposition. For the modern observer, it is apparent that the medieval logicians realized that the context was important but nevertheless, at the same time, held to the signification of a word. For us moderns, to have the notion of signification in addition to a notion like natural supposition is superfluous, from the viewpoint of both logic and semantics.[70]

d. Univocity, equivocity

The fourth distinction, between the univocity or equivocity of words, is related to the previous notion of signification. Univocity and equivocity is a matter of signification and not of supposition. With univocity and equivocity, the question is not whether a word refers to one or more things, but whether a word has one or more notions (*rationes*). For instance, the word 'human' can stand for more than one person, without becoming equivocal.[71] On the other hand, the meaning of the word 'light' in "Can you give me a light" differs from the meaning of the same word in "He is a light eater", and, consequently, there

[69] L. de Rijk, "The origins of the Theory of the Properties of terms".
[70] L. de Rijk, *Middeleeuwse wijsbegeerte*, 1977, p.244.
[71] H. Rikhof, *Over God spreken*, p.141.

is a clear case of equivocity with respect to the use of the word 'light' in these two sentences.

e. Analogy and Metaphor

The fifth and final distinction is between speaking analogously or metaphorically. Speaking analogously or metaphorically about God can be explained in terms of signification and supposition, and univocity and equivocity. For instance, when we call God a lion or a rock, we name God metaphorically. The signification of the word lion or rock is the same when said of God and of this animal, or of this big lump of stone, and thus the term is used univocally. However the supposition differs, depending whether the word 'lion' stands for God or for the animal. Speaking metaphorically is, in other words, a matter of supposition.

However, when we call God 'good', we name God analogously. The signification of 'good' said of God differs from the signification of 'good' said of creatures: there is no univocity. However, neither is there complete equivocity. We will explain in which way the signification differs in these cases in the next section.

Analogy[72]

When Thomas explains how analogy 'works', his favorite example is the use of the term 'healthy'. When we say "the dog is healthy", "the medicine is healthy" and "the urine is healthy", the word 'healthy' is used neither completely equivocally, nor simply univocally. Instead the word 'healthy' is used analogously. This means that one can discern certain comparative relations (*proportiones*) between the different occasions in which something is called healthy. In this example we can distinguish between two types of comparative relations. First, when we call medicine and urine healthy, both are called healthy in comparison with a third. In this case there is a comparative relation of many to one (*multa ad unum*). Second, when we call medicine and the dog healthy, the medicine is called healthy in comparison with healthy as said of the dog. In this case there is a comparative relation of one to another (*unum ad alterum*). These comparative relations can be determined. In the case of healthy as said of medicine, this comparative relation is one of cause. Medicine is called healthy because it causes health, for instance in the dog. Urine is called healthy when it is a sign of the health of the dog, for instance. The dog is called healthy when it is the subject of health.[73]

---

[72] On 'analogy' in Thomas, cf. R. McInerny, *The logic of analogy*, 1961; "The analogy of names is a logical doctrine", in *Atti del congresso internazionale (Roma-Napoli-17/24 aprile 1974) Tommaso d'Aquino nel suo settimo centenario, VI: l'Essere*, 1978; S.-C. Park, *Die Rezeption der mittelalterlichen Sprachphilosophie in der Theologie des Thomas von Aquin. Mit besonderer Berücksichtigung der Analogie*, 1999. According to Park, analogy is not *the* instrument of thomistic theology as Thomists often say. It is even questionable whether a *doctrine of analogy* can be found in Thomas (cf. p.452ff).

[73] *STh* I q.13, a.5 co.

In all three cases something is called healthy with respect to another thing. This is peculiar to analogy.[74] In this example medicine and urine are called healthy with respect to healthy as said of the dog. Healthy as said of the dog is placed in the definition of healthy as said of urine and as said of medicine. So that which is signified by healthy as said of the dog is first (*per prius*) in healthy as said of the dog, and next (*per posterius*) in healthy as said of medicine and urine. In other words, healthy is said *per prius* of dog and *per posterius* of medicine and of urine.[75] In the case in which the meaning is held *per prius* one can find the proper notion (*ratio propria*) of the term. In this example the *ratio propria* is found in healthy as said of the dog. The *per prius*-meaning of healthy is 'one who has health' or 'one who is the subject of health'. The *per posterius* meanings of healthy are "is cause of health in the subject of health" and "is a sign of health in the subject of health". The common notion (*ratio communis*) 'health', i.e. the meaning that is held in all three cases, is called the *res significata*. In all three cases the term 'healthy' signifies the same *res significata* ('health'), but in each case the way the term signifies (*modus significandi*) differs. In the case of the dog the *modus significandi* is 'having health', in the case of the medicine the *modus significandi* is 'causing health', and in the case of urine the *modus significandi* is 'signifying health'.

It is important to notice that this naming of dog, medicine and urine as healthy depends on the way we know a dog, medicine or urine to be healthy. In other words, we name a dog healthy because we know it to have health; and we name a medicine healthy because we know it to cause health. Furthermore, we name urine healthy when we know it to be a sign of health. Therefore, to understand analogy we have to distinguish between the thing as it exists, the thing as known, the word that signifies the thing as known immediately, and the thing as it exists as mediated.[76]

Now let us take a look at how Thomas applies this to our speaking about God. *Quaestio* 13 of the *prima pars* of the *Summa Theologiae* is about the names of God, about the possibility of speaking truthfully about God. In the fifth and sixth articles, Thomas deals with words that are used analogously.

---

[74] *Idem*, a.6 co: "(I)n omnibus nominibus quae de pluribus analogice dicuntur, necesse est quod omnia dicantur per respectum ad unum".

[75] *Ibidem.*

[76] Cf. R. McInerny, "The Analogy of names", p.650: "When Thomas introduces analogy, he places it between univocality and equivocality. Similarly to univocality and equivocality, analogy is something that has to do with the way words are used, and not with the way things are in themselves." For McInerny this implies that, like univocality and equivocality, analogy is a logical doctrine (on the level of the *modus significandi* and *modus intelligendi*), instead of a metaphysical one (on the level of the *modus essendi*). McInerny blames Cajetan (*De nominum analogia et de conceptu entis*, 1498) for having obscured the concept by confusing the logical order and real order. An overview of recent studies in Thomas' 'doctrine' of analogy shows that his account of analogy has nothing to do with the conceptualistic version of Cajetan; cf. C. Leget, *Living with God. Thomas Aquinas on the relation between life on earth and 'life' after death*, 1997, p.36, footnote 78.

Q.13 contains twelve articles. After an opening article, six articles are devoted to our naming God. The articles 8 to 11 deal with one special name for God: the name 'God' itself. The twelfth article is about propositions about God.

In the opening article, Thomas deals with the question of whether or not it is possible for us to speak about God at all (cf. *nominabilis*). The answer is that we can speak about God, though because we name as we know, and because our knowledge of God is from creatures, and because the mode of being of creatures differs from the mode of being of the Creator, therefore our names for God do not express God's essence as it is in itself.[77]

In the second *articulus*, Thomas distinguishes between words that are said absolutely and confirmatively of God, like *bonus* and *sapiens*, words which are only said negatively, and words that signify a relation with creatures. Only the first category of words signifies the divine substance, and can be predicated of God *substantialiter*. Because we know God through His creatures and because creatures represent God only in an imperfect way, our knowledge of God is imperfect. Therefore, our naming of God is imperfect. Here, imperfect does not mean wrong, but something like 'incomplete' or 'limited'. We can speak truthfully about God, but because we have no perfect knowledge about God, what we say truthfully about Him remains nevertheless imperfect.[78]

For instance, we know about God's goodness from His creatures. However, creatures represent God's goodness in an imperfect way, because creatures posses goodness only in a limited way. In creatures, goodness does not belong essentially to human nature - otherwise we would all be good simply through being born. Instead a person acquires human goodness gradually over a long period of time. Besides, human goodness is something that must be distinguished from other 'perfections', like human wisdom, etc. In God, however, goodness exists in a sublime way, namely in such a way that it cannot be divided from the divine essence itself. And in reality, God's goodness does not differ from other 'perfections', such as His wisdom, His justice etc.[79]

---

[77] *STh* I q.13, a.1 co: "Ostensum est autem supra, quod Deus in hac vita non potest a nobis videri per suam essentiam, sed cognoscitur a nobis ex creaturis secundum habitudinem principii, et per modum excellentiae, et remotionis. Sic igitur nominari a nobis ex creaturis. Non tamen ita, quod nomen significans ipsum exprimat divinam essentiam secundum quod est."

[78] *Idem*, a.2 co.

[79] This has been expounded excellently by H. Goris, *Free Creatures of an Eternal God. Thomas on God's infallible foreknowledge and irresistible will*, 1996, Ch. 1 "God-talk in Thomas" pp.6-33, especially pp.16-17. Goris distinguishes between imperfection on a grammatical-syntactic level, and imperfection on a logical-semantic level. What we have been describing here are the imperfections on the logical-semantic level. On the grammatical-syntactic level we encounter imperfection in using words like wise and wisdom, good and goodness for God. "Terms like 'good' and 'wise' signify in a concrete way, signifying the inherence of a form in a subject and not the absolute identity of subject and form. Therefore, when we say 'God is wise', we do speak the truth and we do speak properly, but imperfectly. We have to complement it by using an abstract term, saying 'and God is wisdom itself' which again falls short in its mode of signifying because it signifies something as non-subsistent. Such an ineluctable deficiency in the mode of signifying, i.e. in the grammatical structure of language

We can clarify this further by distinguishing between what is signified (*res significata*) and the way it is signified (*modus significandi*). When a word like 'good' is used of God and of creatures it shares, in both cases, the same *res significata* ('goodness'). However, the *modus significandi* of 'good' said of God is taken from goodness found in creation. When used of creatures the *res significata* is signified as being distinct from human nature, and as being distinct from other 'perfections'. But when used of God the *res significata* is signified as being the divine essence itself, and as being identical with other perfections.

We said above that perfection-words, when used of God, take their way of signifying (*modus significandi*) from creatures. For that reason they are only used properly according to what they signify (the *res significata*), and not according to the way they signify (the *modus significandi*). Moreover, perfection-words are not only said properly of God according to what they signify, they are even said more properly of God than of creatures. Perfection-words like 'good' and 'wise" are said *per prius* of God and *per posterius* of the creatures.[80]

As we have seen, perfection-words are said of God in such a way that they are not distinct from God's essence, and are not distinct from each other. In other words, all perfection-words when said of God signify the same thing (*res*). Does this mean that these perfection-words are synonyms, or not? This question is asked in the fourth *articulus*. In his reply Thomas stresses that all perfections pre-exist in God in a united and simple way (*unite et simpliciter*). However, because, in creatures, these perfections are many and varied (*divise et multipliciter*), and because the perfection-words take their *modus significandi* from the creatures, they are not synonyms. This is because synonyms share the same *res significata* and the same *modus significandi*.[81]

The distinction between the *modus essendi*, *modi intelligendi* and the *modi significandi* dominates this analysis. On the level of the *modus essendi* of God, all perfections are one and the same and equal to God's essence. However, since we only know God from his creatures, and since we name God as we know Him, our knowledge and naming is dependent on the way we know God's perfections from his creatures, i.e. as being distinct from each other. We know God to be wise, good, powerful, just, etc. However, though on the level of the *modus essendi* there is no distinction between God's wisdom, goodness, etc., nevertheless on the level of the *modi intelligendi* there is, and consequently on the level of the *modi significandi*. Words differ from each other, as do their meanings, and our knowledge of God's perfections. However in God they are all one and the same divine essence.

Up until now we have only been reflecting on the first four *articuli* of *quaestio* 13. It is clear that Thomas has gathered the necessary elements for the position

---

itself, goes for all human God-talk: concrete and abstract nouns and adjectives, but also pronouns and tensed verbs." (p.16). Goris refers to *STh* I q.13, a.1 ad 3.
[80] *STh* I q.13, a.3 co.
[81] *STh* I q.13, a.4 co: "Et ideo nomina Deo attributa, licet significent unam rem, tamen, quia significanet eam sub rationibus multis et diversis, non sunt synonyma."

taken in *articuli* five and six: that proper God-talk is by means of analogy. The first element is the distinction between *res significata* and *modus significandi*. When we use the same term for creatures and for God, for instance the term 'good', it signifies the same content (goodness), though there is difference in the way it is signified. This corresponds with what was said about analogy. There is something that is equal and there is something that differs. There is equality in the *res significata*, but difference in the *modus significandi*. The second element is the remark that perfection-words are said *per prius* of God and *per posterius* of creatures. We had seen that, in the case of analogy, it is necessary that the words used analogously are said with respect to one thing in particular. This is expressed by the expression *per prius et posterius*. Perfection-words are said most properly of God. This means that when we say "God is wise" and "Socrates is wise" we use the term 'wise' in the latter case with respect to the use of the term for God. This is what we mean when we say that a term like 'wise', when applied to God, is used analogously. In the fifth *articulus*, Thomas explains that when words are used analogously, there is no univocity between them. Words used analogously are equivocal, but not completely equivocal. In the sixth *articulus* analogy is contrasted with speaking metaphorically about God.

Now there is one final remark to be made. Normally when the use of a term in a new situation differs in the way it signifies, it is used analogously with respect to the use of the term in the old situation. In the old situation the word is used *per prius*, and in the new situation *per posterius*. However when we make the shift from the natural setting to the Christian setting, the new setting is acknowledged as the setting that should provide the norms for everything else. When we encounter God and learn about His wisdom, we realize that God's wisdom is the wisdom to which we should compare our wisdom. There is a reversal of the *per prius* and the *per posterius* when we use terms analogously for God and for creatures. Thomas expresses this when he says "all that is said about God and creatures, is said according to an ordering of the creatures to God, as to their principle and cause, in which all perfections of things pre-exist excellently".[82] This reversal of the *per prius et posterius* is why some say that the term 'analogy' itself is used analogously when said of proper God-talk.

Our knowledge of God Father, Son and Spirit

Our main focus will be on the way Thomas uses language-theories in q.39, the *quaestio* at the end of which Thomas comes to reflect on appropriation. However in the previous section we have seen that our language follows our knowledge. Therefore to understand how we name the trinity of Persons, we should first see how we know the trinity of Persons. This is confirmed in the corpus of *articulus* seven where Thomas begins by referring to q.32 on the knowledge of the divine Persons. Therefore, before we examine q.39, we will

---

[82] *STh* I q.13, a.5 co: "Et sic, quidquid dicitur de Deo et creaturis, dicitur secundum quod est aliquis ordo creaturae ad Deum, ut ad principium et causam, in qua praeexistunt excellenter omnes rerum perfectiones."

first say something about our knowledge of the essence of God and of the trinity of divine Persons.[83]

The created intellect, Thomas concludes at the end of the *corpus* of the fourth *articulus* of *quaestio* 12 about the way God is known to us, cannot see (*videre*) God *per essentiam*, though there is an intimate knowledge possible by grace.[84] Nevertheless we can know God by created similarities, though we do not know God's essence through these.[85]

> "It was shown above that one cannot attain knowledge of God by natural reason except from creatures. Creatures lead us to knowledge of God the way effects lead to their cause. Therefore, by natural reason we can know of God only that which necessarily fits Him insofar as He is principle of all beings, and we have used this fundamental principle above when considering God (12, 12). The creative power is common to the whole Trinity; hence, it belongs to the unity of essence, and not to the distinction of Persons. Therefore, through natural reason only what belongs to the unity of God's essence can be known, not, however, what belongs to the distinction of Persons.[86]

How should we interpret this text? Does it mean that we can know God's unity, but not His Trinity? This is the usual interpretation, which has the danger of leading to a division of the treatise on God in *De Deo uno* and *De Deo trino*, parallel to a division in natural knowledge of God and revealed knowledge of God.[87] But how does this interpretation relate to what was said earlier, namely that the created intellect cannot know God *per essentiam*? In other words, how do Thomas' remarks about what we cannot know about God, relate to his remarks about what we can know about God?

Let us take a closer look at what Thomas says in the beginning of the fourth *articulus* of *quaestio* 12 on how we know God. The main point is that it is impossible for the created intellect to know God's essence, because the way the created intellect knows (*modus intelligendi*) does not correspond to the way God

[83] Cf. G. Hibbert, "Mystery and metaphysics", p.192.

[84] *STh* I q.12 a.4 co: "Non igitur potest intellectus creatus Deum per essentiam videre, nisi inquantum Deus per suam gratiam se intellectui creato coniungit, ut intelligibile ab ipso."

[85] *STh* I q.12 a.4 ad 1: "Sed cognoscere Deum per similitudinem creatam, non est cognoscere essentiam Dei"; cf. a.2.

[86] *STh* I q.32, a.1 co: "Ostensum est enim supra (q.12 a.4.11.12) quod homo per rationem naturalem in cognitionem Dei pervenire non potest nisi ex creaturis. Creaturae autem ducunt in Dei cognitionem, sicut effectus in causam. Hoc igitur solum ratione naturali de Deo cognosci potest, quod competere ei necesse est secundum quod est omnium entium principium: et hoc fundamento usi sumus supra in consideratione Dei (cf. q.12 a.12). Virtus autem creativa Dei est communis toti Trinitati; unde pertinet ad unitatem essentiae, non ad distinctionem Personarum. Per rationem igitur naturalem cognosci possunt de Deo ea quae pertinent ad unitatem essentiae, non autem ea quae pertinent ad distinctionem Personarum."

[87] Cf. Sträter's article on appropriation. Sträter even goes so far as to distinguish between two analogous notions of appropriation, one philosphical (the appropriation of essential names, known from natural reason) and one theological (the appropriation of revealed realities). C. Sträter, "Het begrip appropriatie", p.3.

exists (*modus essendi*).[88] The *modus intelligendi* of the created intellect corresponds with the *modus essendi* of created things. Therefore it is possible for the created intellect to have knowledge about created things. Insofar as created things, as effects, refer to their cause, the Creator, we can have knowledge about the Creator, i.e. about the things that belong to the unity of God's essence. But this doesn't imply that we have knowledge about God's essence. Only God knows His essence, because only God's *modus intelligendi* corresponds with his *modus essendi*.[89]

So the conclusion is that we neither know God's unity, nor His trinity *per essentiam*. What is meant then by the statement that we can know the things that belong to the unity of the divine essence, though we can't know the things that belong to the distinction of the Persons? A more subtle interpretation than the usual one is required.

First of all we should realize that, according to Thomas, both the oneness and the trinity of God are beyond our grasp, for both together constitute the way God exists (his *modus essendi*). God's essence is both one and three and this *modus essendi* exceeds the *modus essendi* of creatures. Because both His oneness and His trinity are beyond our grasp, our language isn't able to speak adequately either with respect to God's oneness or with respect to God's trinity. Only when we realize this can we subsequently ask what is meant by the statement that through natural reason we can only know what belongs to the unity of God's essence, not what belongs to the distinction of the divine Persons. The point is not that we can have perfect knowledge of the unity of God's essence and not of the trinity of God's essence. Both our knowledge of the unity and of the trinity of God's essence is imperfect. The point is that in the case of the unity of God's essence, this imperfect knowledge can be inferred from creation by natural reason, while the imperfect knowledge of the trinity of God's essence, is through revelation alone.

So the imperfection of our knowledge of God's essence is with respect to both the unity of God's essence and the trinity of divine Persons, as both the unity and trinity together are God's essence. God is triune, and his relationships are his essence. Since we cannot reflect on God's unity and trinity at the same time, we are bound first to reflect on his unity and then on his trinity, or vice versa. When reflecting on his unity, the imperfection of our knowledge of God's essence results in God-talk that is at the same time true and imperfect. Hence, the need for analogy. But since analogy only regulates the use of perfection

---

[88] *STh* I q.12, a.4 co: "Respondeo dicendum quod impossibile est quod aliquis intellectus creatus per sua naturalia essentiam Dei videat. Cognitio enim contingit secundum quod cognitum est in cognoscente. Cogitum autem est in cognoscente secundum modum cognoscentis. Unde cuiuslibet cognoscentis cognitio est secundum modum suae naturae. Si igitur modus essendi alicuius rei cognitae excedat modum naturae cognoscentis, oportet quod cognitio illius rei sit supra naturam illius cognoscentis."

[89] *Ibidem*: "Solius autem Dei proprius modus essendi est, ut sit suum esse subsistens. (..) Relinquitur ergo quod cognoscere ipsum esse subsistens, sit connaturale soli intellectui divino, et quod sit supra facultatem naturalem cuiuslibet intellectus creati (including that of the angels, EL): quia nulla creatura est suum esse, sed habet esse participatum."

words, i.e. words that signify the divine essence in its oneness, it is not sufficient for our reflections on the trinity of divine persons, which, on top of analogy, requires another linguistic rule. This second rule for proper God-talk is, as we will show next, called appropriation.

Appropriation

Thomas treats appropriation *ex professo* in the last two *articuli* of *STh* I *quaestio* 39 on the relationships between the divine Persons and the divine essence. Q.39 is placed in the middle of the treatise on the trinity of Persons (qq.27-43), and at the beginning of the part on the Persons in comparison with each other (qq.39-43). *Quaestio* 39 can be divided into three parts. The first two *articuli* are dedicated to the way the three main terms in this *quaestio*: 'essence', 'relationship' and 'person' relate to each other. The principal decisions are made in these *articuli*. Next, Thomas examines in four *articuli* some statements that circle around the two basic maxims of Trinitarian theology, namely that the three Persons are God and that (the one) God is three Persons. In the last two *articuli* Thomas examines appropriation. In our treatise of Q.39 we will follow this division.

a. Essence, Relation, Person

The basic question of q.39 concerns the relation between the divine Persons and the divine essence. In the first *articulus* of the *quaestio*, the question is asked of whether the divine essence is the same as Person. This question is concerned with statements like "the Father is God", "the Son is God" or "the Holy Spirit is God". From the first objection, notions are used that refer to language-theories. In the first objection 'person' (*persona*) is identified with the *suppositum essentiae*, i.e. that which stands for the essence. An example may clarify this. We can, for instance, say that 'Socrates' is a *suppositum* of human nature, when, within a certain context, 'Socrates' stands for a human nature. The point of the first objection is that when *persona* and *essentia* are the same, there is only one *suppositum essentiae*. When, in our example, Socrates and human nature coincide, there is only one *suppositum* of human nature, namely Socrates. In the case of the divine essence and Person, this would imply that there is only one divine Person.

In his reply, Thomas begins by referring to God's simplicity. God's simplicity implies that, in God, essence and *suppositum essentiae* are the same, while in intellectual substances, the suppositum is nothing other than the person. Irrespective of the multitude of persons in God, the essence retains its unity. How is that conceivable? Thomas escapes from this paradox by introducing the term 'relation'. In Aristotelian philosophy, the category of relationship is the weakest of the ten categories. Moreover, when said of creatures, relationship is an accident. But when said of God, relationship is not accidental, but the divine essence itself.[90] So Thomas derives the notion of relationship from Aristotle, but when he introduces it in his theology, his God-talk, he reverses it from

---

[90]   *STh* I q.39, a.1; cf. q.28. Cf. G. Hibbert, "Mystery and metaphysics", p.200.

something accidental to something essential. With this reversal something happens that makes it possible for Thomas to say something very intriguing:

> "Compared to essence there is no difference between relationship and essence in reality, but only conceptually. However, compared to an opposite relationship, the relationship has, in virtue of the opposition, a real distinction.[91]

Now here some interesting qualifications are made: *re* (opposed to *ratione tantum*), and *real*. Both qualifications indicate that something is said about the *esse* of God, about His *modus essendi*.[92]

According to Thomas the term '*persona*' signifies a relationship. When we say 'person', we name the relationship that does not differ *realiter* from essence, but at the same time does differ *realiter* from opposite relationships. Therefore we can say that in God there is no other essence than Person *secundum rem*, while, nevertheless, the Persons are *realiter* distinguished from each other. The *modus essendi* of God is that He is both one essence and three Persons, because He is at once relationship and opposite relationships. Irrespective of the fact that we can't conceive this mystery, we can reflect on our language when we speak about the relationship between the divine essence and the divine Persons. The term 'Person' signifies at once the relationship as it subsists in the divine nature, and the relationship as being distinct from other relationships.[93]

According to Hill, compared with Augustine, in this argument Thomas moves beyond psychology to ontology. "Augustine was simply seeking in man's psyche something that might serve to illumine what was believed of God." The trinity of *mens*, *verbum* and *amor* served as a simile for the tri-unity of God. As in all similes, it doesn't include proper or true talk about God's being.

> "Thomas deliberately attempts a transition beyond the psychological processes of the soul to its very beingness. The resultant rationality is an ontological one, grounded in being itself as a dynamism and not merely a self-referencing achieved by way of the soul's activity. The knowing and naming of God moves in the same direction as it did for Augustine, namely, from revelation about God to the perceiving of analogies in the soul. But behind the notion of God as Trinity lies the notion of God as the Pure Act of Being, wherein "to be", "to know" and "to love" coincide in absolute self-identity. This opens up for Thomas the possibility that the use of analogy can take upon itself an intrinsic character, enabling it to serve as an instrument of speech in making assertions

---

91   *Idem*, co: "Relatio autem ad essentiam comparata non differt re, sed ratione tantum. Comparata autem ad oppositam relationem habet virtute oppositionis realem distinctionem." For an explanation of how Thomas understands the real relations in God, with the help of the analogy of a pregnancy, cf. D. Cunningham, *These three are one*, pp.58-65.

92   On the notion of 're', 'realis' as opposed to 'ratione', 'rationis tantum', cf. H. Schoot, *Christ the 'name' of God*, p.50; H. Rikhof, *Over God spreken*, p.89; F. de Grijs, "Spreken over God en Thomasinterpretatie" in: *Jaarboek 1984 van het Thomas Instituut Utrecht*, pp.7-38.

93   Cf. Y. Congar, *I believe* vol. III, p.118: "What constitutes the Person, then, according to Thomas, is his relationship of origin. Through that relationship, the Person is *really* distinguished from the Person who is correlative to him. But in God, these relationships are *really* identical with the sovereignly simple essence and this means that they have that quality of 'subsistent relationships' that Thomas defines and employs in his triadology."

about the intrinsic beingness of God himself. At the same time such manner of "saying" retains its strictly analogical character whereby, in the case of predication about the divine, it is no more than a human naming of the Unknown. It remains a designating from the perspective of a creaturely concept of what cannot be represented in the determinateness of any concept."[94]

Analogy enables Thomas to speak properly and truly though imperfectly about God's beingness, i.e. about God's three-unity, while retaining its mystery.

> "The import of ontologizing relation should not be missed. It draws the attention to the startling insight that at the very heart of being as such, of all being, there resides a mysterious *respectus ad alterum*. A certain inner-relationality is revealed in the depths of reality that is not merely incidental. And, what is more, the inner-relationality is not reduced to mere essential otherness."[95]

These insights provide the starting-point of Thomas' examination of Augustine's translation of '*homoousios*' as: the three Persons are of one essence (*Tres Personas sunt unius essentiae*).[96] Again Thomas reminds us that we name the divine things, not in the way they exist in themselves, but in the way they are found in created things, and consequently not according to the *modus essendi* of God, but according to the *modus essendi* of the created things.[97] So when we try to speak about God's oneness and trinity, we use the way we speak about created things.

With respect to created things, we speak about nature and individuals as *forma* and *supposita formae*. For instance, we can say that Socrates is a *suppositum* of human nature. Consequently, when we say "Socrates is a human being", human nature is the form of Socrates. However, when we say this person has a certain substantial or accidental *forma*, we add some qualification concerning the way he "has this *forma*". We cannot say "Socrates has human nature", except when we add an adjective, for instance "Socrates has a virtuous human nature". "This is a mode of being of created things that is reflected in our mode of signifying: the subject-term is signified as the thing having a form, and the predicate as the form that is had."[98]

In the same way in which we speak about nature and individuals as *forma* and *supposita formae*, we speak *in divinis* about the essence as the *forma* of the three Persons, and about the Persons as the *supposita formae*. This is not a description of the way things are organized in God's essence, but a regulation of our language. '*In divinis*' does not mean 'in God', but 'in our language about God'.

---

[94] W. Hill, *The Three-Personed God. The Trinity as a Mystery of Salvation*, 1982, p.70.

[95] *Idem*, p.73.

[96] *STh* I q.39, a.2 Sc: "Sed contra est quod Augustinus dicit, in libro II *Contra Maximinum*, quod hoc nomen *homousion*, quod in Concilio Nicaeno adversus Arianos firmatum est, idem significat quod tres Personas esse unius essentiae." On the misleadingness of the concept of 'person' as translation of the Greek '*hypostasis*', cf. N. Lash, *Believing three ways in one God. A reading of the Apostles' creed*, 1994[2], pp.30-33.

[97] *STh* I q.39, a.2, co: "Sicut supra dictum est (q.13 a.1 ad2; a.3), intellectus noster res divinas nominat, non secundum modum earum, quia sic eas cognoscere non potest; sed secundum modum in rebus creatis inventum."

[98] H. Schoot, *Christ the 'name' of God*, p.52.

Thomas stresses this by adding *quantum ad modum significandi*: according to the mode of signifying.[99]

We speak about the divine Persons as *supposita* of the divine essence, in the same way as we speak about the way a person relates to a certain nature as *suppositum* to *forma*. And since *in divinis* the fact that there is more than one Person does not multiply the essence, and since our language follows the way we know God from creation, therefore we do not say "Three persons are of essence", but "Three Persons are of *one* essence".[100]

b. Three persons are God and God is three Persons[101]

Now that he has determined the relation between 'essence' and 'person', Thomas examines some other statements about the holy Trinity. In four articles he moves from the examination of the statement "Three Persons are God" to the examination of the statement "God is three Persons". Notice that behind these statements stands the basic Trinitarian insight "that the one God is a trinity and the three Persons are a unity."[102] We will examine these *articuli*, because they show the linguistic nature of Thomas' approach in this *quaestio*.

First, Thomas examines the statement that "Three Persons are God".[103] How can we predicate an essential name like 'God' *singulariter* of three Persons? Shouldn't we say that three Persons are Gods (*pluraliter*)? To be able to explain what we do (what Scripture does) when we say that three Persons are God, Thomas distinguishes between substantive and adjectival essential names. 'God' is a substantial essential name, and therefore the name derives its number from the signified *forma*. And because God's essence is *simplex et maxime una*, 'God' is said *singulariter* of the three Persons. An adjective essential name like '*habens deitatem*' derives its number from the signified *supposita formae*. Therefore we say, "Three Persons are three *habentes deitatem*". This is how Scripture can say that God is one, while He is three Persons (cf. Dt 6,4).[104]

Next, Thomas distinguishes between abstract and concrete essential names, using the distinction between *res significata* and *modus significandi* in combination with the theory of supposition.[105] While signifying the same content, concrete and abstract essential names nevertheless differ in the mode of signifying. A concrete essential name signifies in a concrete way, an abstract essential name signifies in an abstract way. A concrete essential name like 'God' can, because of its mode of signifying, stand for (*supponere*) both the divine essence and the divine Persons. When we say, "God creates", 'God' stands for the divine

---

99 *STh* I q.39, a.2 co: "(P)ropter hoc etiam in divinis, quantum ad modum significandi, essentia significatur ut forma trium Personarum."

100 *Ibidem*.

101 For a more elaborate explanation of the following articles, with extensive attention to their linguistic character, see T. Smith, "The context and character of Thomas' theory of appropriations", in *The Thomist* 63 (1999), pp. 579-612.

102 Cf. E. Hill, "Karl Rahner's remarks", p.70.

103 *STh* I q.39, a.3.

104 *Idem*, a.3 sc: "Sed contra est quod dicitur Deut. 6,4: *Audi Israel, Dominus Deus, Deus unus est.*"

105 *Idem*, a.4 and a.5.

essence. However when we say, "God generates", 'God' stands for 'God the
Father'. And when we say "God spirates", 'God' stands for both 'God the
Father' and 'God the Son'. This is what makes it possible to say "God of God",
because the first use of the term 'God' stands for the 'Son', and the second use
of the term 'God' stands for the 'Father'.[106]

An abstract essential name like 'essence', because of its mode of signifying,
cannot stand for a divine Person. For though 'essence' and 'God' both signify
the same divine essence, and thus share the same *res significata*, they differ in the
mode of signifying. Therefore we cannot say, "Essence generates essence".[107]

In the same *articulus* Thomas distinguishes adjectival personal or notional
names. For instance, a name like '*generans*' refers only to God the Father. So
besides the fact that it is an adjectival (as opposed to a substantive) name, it is
also personal or notional. The use of such a name is limited. One cannot say
for instance "*essentia est generans*", because personal adjectives, like *generans*
cannot be predicated of *essentia*, unless with an added substantive. Hence, we
can add, for instance, *res* or 'God': "*essentia est Deus generans*", wherein 'Deus'
stands for a divine person.[108]

Thomas also uses the concept of 'identitas rei' in the sixth *articulus*. Between
substantive personal names like 'Father', 'Son' and 'Spirit', and 'essence' there is
an *identitas rei*. Therefore we can say, "Essence is Father, Son and Spirit". And
because 'God' can stand for (*supponere*) 'essence', we can say, "God is three
Persons". This is how we can understand Augustine to say, "We believe that
one God is one divinely named Trinity."[109]

c. Appropriation and Analogy

Now let us compare analogy, as we have learned to understand it as a logical,
instead of a metaphysical doctrine, to appropriation, as Thomas understands it
in the last two *articuli* of Q.39.

In a.7 Thomas speaks formally about appropriation. In a.8 Thomas examines
some known examples of appropriation in works by Hilary and Augustine, and
some forms of appropriation found in Scripture.[110] It is important to realize
that Thomas does not invent a way of speaking about the holy Trinity, rather

---

106 *Idem*, Sc: "Sed contra est quod in Symbolo (Nicaeno) dicitur *Deum de Deo*."
107 *Idem*, a.5 Sc: "Sed contra est quod Augustinus dicit, in I *De Trin*, quod *nulla res generat seipsam*.
   Sed si essentia generat essentiam, non generat nisi seipsam: cum nihil sit in Deo, quod
   distinguatur a divina essentia. Ergo essentia non generat essentia."
108 *Idem*, ad 5.
109 *Idem*, a.6 Sc: "Sed contra est quod Augustinus dicit: *Credimus unum Deum unam esse divini nominis
   Trinitatem.*"
110 Hillary appropriates *aequalitas* to the Father, *species* to the Son and *usus* to the Spirit; Augustine
   appropriates *unitas* to the Father, *aequalitas* to the Son and *unitatis aequalitatisque concordia vel
   connexio* to the Spirit, as well as power to the Father, wisdom to the Son and goodness to the
   Spirit, and *ex ipso* to the Father, *per ipsum* to the Son en *in ipso* to the Spirit (cf. Rm 11:36);
   finally, Thomas finds the appropriation of truth, book of life, and *Qui est* to the Son in
   Scripture.

he encounters, in Scripture[111] and in Tradition, a manner of speaking about Father, Son and Spirit which he tries to understand. Actually, we should read articles seven and eight in reversed order to find out what Thomas is after (as is so often the case in the *Summa*). In order to explain what is being done in the appropriations of *articulus* eight, Thomas needs the instrument which he develops in *articulus* seven. The order is determined by the *ordo disciplinae*.

Thomas defines appropriation as the manifestation[112] of the Persons through essential attributes.[113] He distinguishes between two ways of appropriating essential attributes. First, essential attributes are appropriated when there is a similarity (*per viam similitudinis*) between the *appropriatum* and a *proprium* of a divine Person,[114] and secondly, when there is dissimilarity (*per viam dissimilitudinis*) between the *appropriatum* and the *proprium personae*.

To understand what a *proprium* is we have to return to the analysis of *persona*, *essentia* and *relatio* at the beginning of the *quaestio*. The conclusion of the analysis was that *persona* signifies *relatio*, that *relatio* does not differ in reality from essence but only according to reason, and that *relatio* does differ in reality from other relationships. In other words, the distinction between the divine Persons is only with respect to each other, and not with respect to the divine essence, and certainly not with respect to something in creation. What is proper to a divine Person is therefore always proper with respect to other Persons. So what is proper to a divine Person is nothing other than that which distinguishes Him from the other Persons, and is consequently stated in relational terms: the Father being the principle that is not from any principle (*principium non de principio*), the Son being principle (of the Spirit) who is himself from a principle (*principium de principio*) and the Spirit being he who proceeds from both (*processio de duobus*). Other properties (*proprietates*) of the divine Persons, like *paternitas* and *innascibilitas* for the Father, and *filiatio* for the Son, or proper names like Word or *processio per modum intellectum* for the Son, or Gift or Love or *processio per modum*

---

111 Cf. A. Chollet, "Appropriation", p.1709: "(I)l était donc d'une suprême utilité d'enrichir le langage théologique concernant la sainte Trinité. La tradition autorisée par la sainte Écriture elle-même l'a fait par les vestiges et par l'appropriation." Cf. also p.1713ff.

112 Cf. T. Smith, "Thomas' theory of appropriations", p.584: "Manifestation" means beginning with the revealed doctrine and then providing reasons for the congruence of this doctrine with those things that can be more easily known." Moreover, "[u]sing appropriated attributes to manifest these Persons demands that one already has knowledge of these Persons." (p.606)

113 *STh* I q.39, a.7 co: "Et haec manifestatio Personarum per essentialia attributa, appropriatio nominatur." Another definition is found in *De Ver* q.7, a.3 co: "(A)ppropriare nihil est aliud, quam commune trahere ad proprium."

114 Though Thomas isn't explicit in *quaestio* 39 about what it is that the *appropriatum* is similar with, this can be deduced from other texts: *In I Sent* d.31, q.1 a.2 co: "Quamvis enim attributa essentialia communia sint tribus, tamen unum secundum rationem suam magis habet similitudinem ad proprium unius personae quam alterius, unde illi personae appropriari potest convenienter."; also: *In I Sent* d.3, q.2 a.1 ad 3: "Appropriata autem sunt essentialia, quamvis similitudinem habeant cum propriis personarum." ; *De Ver* q.7, a.3 co: "(A)ppropriare nihil est aliud, quam commune trahere ad proprium."

voluntatis for the Spirit, are simply other words for their relation to other relationships.[115]

Consequently, a divine Person can be manifested by drawing attention to what is proper to the divine Person, i.e. how the divine Person is related to other divine Persons. A *proprium* of a divine Person can, according to the definition of appropriation, be manifested by associating an essential name with a *proprium*. This association is based on a similarity or dissimilarity between the *appropriatum* and the *proprium*. For instance, wisdom is appropriated to the Son, because the Son, insofar as He is the Word, is nothing but the conception of wisdom. In the same way power is appropriated to the Father because of a similarity between power and what is proper to the Father, and because the notion of principle can be found in both power and in "being the principle that is not from any principle" (*principium non de principio*). Power is not appropriated to the Father as though He has more power than the Son. There is no more power in the Father than in the Son, but there is more similarity between power and what is proper to the Father, than between power and what is proper to the Son.[116]

Furthermore, essential attributes are appropriated when there is dissimilarity between the *appropriatum* and the *proprium personarum*. Thus power is appropriated to the Father, because, among mankind fathers are, because of their old age, usually weak.[117]

Since the text of the *Summa* is rather short on the point of appropriating an essential attribute on the grounds of dissimilarity, we will have to see what Thomas says in the *Scriptum*. It seems, however, that this second way of appropriating can't be found in the parallel-text in the *Scriptum*. Nevertheless, Thomas does distinguish in the *Scriptum* between the appropriateness of the appropriation seen from our point of view and seen from the thing itself.[118] When he explains his favorite example of appropriation, namely the appropriation of power to the Father, wisdom to the Son and goodness to the Spirit, he distinguishes between "*appropriatio per contrarium, ut modus creaturae a Creatore excludatur*" and "*appropriatio per similitudinem ad proprium*".[119] This distinction, found in the *Scriptum*, corresponds with the duplex way in which essential names are appropriated in the *Summa*. From this we can derive that the

---

[115] Cf. *STh* I q.39, a.8 co.

[116] This is precisely what Thomas says in *In I Sent* d.20, q.1, a.2 ad 1: "(P)otentia appropriatur Patri, non quia magis sibi conveniat quam Filio, sed quia maiorem similitudinem habet cum proprietate Patris quam cum proprietate Filii: potentia enim habet rationem principii et Pater est principium non de principio."

[117] *STh* I q.39, a.7 co: "Alio modo, per modum dissimilitudinis: sicut potentia appropriatur Patri, ut Augustinus dicit, quia apud nos patres solent esse propter senectutem infirmi; ne tale aliquid suscipimur in Deo."

[118] *In I Sent* d.31, q.1, a.2 co: "Respondeo dicendum quod de appropriatione dupliciter convenit loqui: aut ex parte nostra, aut ex parte ipsius rei; et utrobique invenitur convenientia."

[119] *In I Sent* d.34, q.2, co.

second way of appropriating is based on Thomas' concern to remove from God that which belongs to the *modus essendi* of creatures.[120]

The distinction between the two modes of appropriating in the *Scriptum* goes back to the way we use the names of Persons *in divinis* and *in creaturis*. Though Thomas doesn't use the term 'analogy' it is obvious that this is what he means. The names are not used univocally, but *per prius et posterius*.[121] They are said first of one instant, and next of other instants. This is the case when we use a name analogously. So when the terms 'fatherhood' (*paternitas*) and 'sonship' (*filiatio*) are used of the divine Persons, it is used according to a mode (*secundum alium modum*) other than that used for creatures. The twofold way in which a name is appropriated is based on this difference in modes, according to which a term is used *in divinis* and *in creaturis*.

So what can be concluded about the relation between analogy and appropriation? When we appropriate for instance wisdom to the Son (I Cor 1, 24: "Christ the power of God and the wisdom of God"), wisdom is used analogously. Therefore there is something similar and there is something dissimilar. The similarity is between the *appropriatum* and the *proprium* (the Son, insofar He is the Word, is nothing but the conception of wisdom). The dissimilarity is between the modes of signifying wisdom said of creatures and wisdom said of the Son. This shows that appropriation is a form of analogy.

d. Conclusion

What is, according to Thomas, the significance of Scripture or Tradition appropriating qualities or actions to divine Persons individually? We know who God is from what He has revealed about Himself to us. God is Father, Son and Holy Spirit. The Father is not the Son, the Son is not the Spirit and the Spirit is not the Father. The Father is God, the Son is God and the Holy Spirit is God, and yet they are not three Gods but one God. So in God there is a mysterious oneness and trinity at the same time. As we have seen, both His oneness and His trinity are beyond the grasp of our knowledge and hence beyond the grasp of our language.

Because we are creatures we can arrive at certain knowledge of essential attributes of the Creator. These essential attributes can have a twofold relationship of similitude[122] with the mode of being of God. First, there is a relationship of similitude with the divine essence. This makes it possible to

---

120 Cf. G. Hibbert, "Mystery and metaphysics", p.194: "We hold on to and affirm with all our power that which truly links us to God, that which is truly signified in the words we use (i.e. the *res significata*, e.g. the goodness, the love or the Fatherhood, etc. of God), and at the same time deny and reject every creaturely manner of signifying (*modus significandi*) that those words would normally have or could be made to have, for this is precisely what would bring the spirit prematurely to rest, or in other words to close its openness and cease its movement towards God."

121 *Ibidem.* "Respondeo dicendum quod nomina personarum dicuntur et de divinis et de rebus creatis, non quidem univoce, sed per prius et posterius".

122 Note Aristotle's saying that "voces sunt signa intellectum, et intellectus sunt rerum *similitudines*."

speak about God's essence properly and truly, however imperfectly, because of the difference in the mode of signifying. Second, there is a relationship of similitude with what is proper to the divine Persons. Both relationships of similitude are, in another respect, relationships of dissimilitude.

Take, for example, the essential name 'wisdom'. We can say "God is wisdom", because there is a relationship of similitude between what we know to be wisdom from creation and the wisdom that belongs to the divine essence. And we can say "The Son is wisdom", because there is a relationship of similitude between what we know to be wisdom from creation and what is proper of the Son (namely that He proceeds from the Father as His Word, and consequently is the conception of divine wisdom). So one essential name can at the same time signify God's essence and what is proper to one of the Persons, i.e. that which distinguishes them from each other[123]: the Father being *principium non de principio*, the Son being *principium de principio*, the Spirit being *processio a duobus*.

Not all statements about God's trinity are appropriations. For example, when we say, "God is a trinity", 'trinity' is said analogously of God. We speak properly and truly, though imperfectly, because when we say that something is three, it implies that a division in the something 'three' is spoken about. However, the trinity said of God retains the unity and simplicity of God's essence. However imperfect the expression, saying "God is three" is proper and true. Saying for instance "God is four", or "God is two" would be false. So we speak the truth about God when we say "God is three", though we fail to grasp what we say in the end.

The same is true of other statements concerning God's trinity, like "God is Father, Son and Holy Spirit"; "The Father is not the Son, the Son is not the Spirit and the Spirit is not the Father"; "The Father is God, the Son is God and the Holy Spirit is God and yet they are not three Gods but one God". These statements are true and proper, though in the end we fail to grasp what is being said (cf. Thomas' examinations of statements concerning the relationship between essence and Persons in the *articuli* 2 to 6).[124] In all these statements, which are not appropriations, words like Father, etc are being used analogously. In those statements that Thomas does consider to be appropriations, the appropriated terms have a double relationship to the divine essence, because, in the sentence, "Christ the power of God and the wisdom of God", 'wisdom'

---

[123] *De Ver* q.10 a.13 co: "Propria autem personarum sunt relationes, quibus personae non ad creaturas, sed ad invicem referentur." In book I of the *Scriptum* Thomas speaks in dd.26-32 about the properties through which the persons are distinguished. Dd.26-30 are about the properties that are proper to the Persons; dd. 31-32 about what is appropriated to the Persons (*In I Sent* d.26, *divisio textus*: "Postquam determinavit Magister de essentia et personis, hic determinat de proprietatibus quibus personae distinguuntur. Dividitur autem in partes duas: in prima determinat de proprietatibus propriis personarum; in secunda de appropriatis personis, XXXI dist., ibi etc"). From this we can derive that the *propria* and the *appropriata* together are the properties (*proprietates*) that distinguish the divine Persons.

[124] It has been pointed out by Newman that though each of the statements concerning the Holy Trinity are simple and concrete, taken all together they express a mystery beyond the grasp of our understanding (J. Newman, *An Essay in Aid of a Grammar of Assent*, 1992⁴ p.115).

signifies at once the divine essence and that which is proper of the Son, namely that He proceeds from the Father as his Word, i.e. *per modum intellectum*. Compare this to how all relationships in God are said to be the essence of God in reality, while they must be distinguished from each other in reality as well. So, similarly, a word like 'wisdom' can signify God's essence, and consequently be said of all three Persons alike, and also be said of one of the three Persons in particular insofar as 'wisdom' signifies that which distinguishes the Person from both other Persons.

Triads of essential names, for instance power, wisdom and goodness, clarify further how appropriation 'works'. Each of those words individually signifies God's essence, simplicity and unity. But at the same time all three together signify the distinctions between the three divine Persons. With respect to God's essence, power, wisdom and goodness exist in God in such a way that they are nothing but the divine essence itself. With respect to the distinction of the divine Persons, the fact that for us (*ratione*) the essential names are distinct from each other makes it possible to use the essential names to express the distinctness of the three divine Persons.[125]

So when power is appropriated to the Father, wisdom to the Son, and goodness to the Spirit with respect to God's essence, the three essential names signify the unity of the one simple divine essence, while, with respect to the divine Persons, the distinctness these three essential names have for us enables them, as *appropriata*, to signify at the same time the distinctness of the divine Persons in relation to each other.

3   Forgiven per Spiritum Sanctum

In this final section, we will synthesize the points which we have analyzed above, and formulate an answer to the initial question of what is meant by the statement that our sins are forgiven us *per Spiritum Sanctum*. We will recapitulate what has been said with respect to indwelling and incarnation, and we will add some remarks regarding creation as well. We will do this with the question in mind of whether or not something proper is said with respect to one of the divine Persons especially, because, as we said before, the division found in the *Symbolum* between creation, incarnation and indwelling does not correspond simply with the distinction between Father, Son and Spirit. Nevertheless a

---

[125] *De Ver* q.1 a.1 ad 5: "Ad quintum dicendum, quod ratio illa deficit in tribus. Primo, quia quamvis personae divinae re distinguantur, appropriata tamen personis non differunt re, sed tantum ratione. Secundo, quia etsi personae realiter ad invicem distinguantur, non tamen realiter ab essentia distinguuntur; unde nec verum quod appropriatur personae Filii, ab ente quod se tenet ex parte essentiae. Tertio, quia, etsi ens, unum, verum et bonum magis uniantur in Deo quam in rebus creatis, non tamen oportet, quod ex quo distinguuntur in Deo, quod in rebus creatis etiam distinguantur realiter. Hoc enim contingit de illis quae non habent ex ratione sua quod sint unum secundum rem, sicut sapientia et potentia, quae, cum in Deo sint unum secundum rem, in creaturis realiter distinguuntur: sed ens, unum, verum et bonum secundum rationem suam habent quod sint unum secundum rem; unde ubicumque inveniantur, realiter unum sunt, quamvis sit perfectior unitas illius rei secundum quam uniuntur in Deo, quam illius rei secundum quam uniuntur in creaturis."

special relationship is, at least, suggested between creation and the Father, incarnation and the Son, and indwelling and the Holy Spirit. The first two are of lesser importance for the present discussion. However, the special relation between indwelling and the Holy Spirit is important. But to understand the meaning of this special relationship, we have to compare it with the way the Son is specially related to incarnation, and the Father related to creation.

Indwelling

One of the results of our analysis of *quaestio* 43 on the missions of the divine Persons is that we learned that the indwelling of the divine Persons in the heart of man, as in their temple, is constitutive for the relationship of grace. Our analysis has shown that according to Thomas the depth of this relationship consists not only in the gift of sanctifying grace, which makes the human person acceptable for God, but also in the gift of God himself. God Himself, Father, Son and Spirit, comes to live in the heart of man as in His temple, and He is present as known and loved in the one who is sanctified. The depth of this union with God is so intimate that Thomas does not hesitate to speak of man "reaching God Himself" (*attingere ad ipsum Deum*).

A second result of our analysis is that we have learned to understand the restoration of the relationship of grace in terms of the invisible mission of divine Persons. When Thomas explains how the discontinuous notion of mission relates to the experience of Christian life that love and grace can grow, he explains first that there is no growth in union with God without the invisible missions of the Spirit and the Son, and second that we best apply terms like 'indwelling', 'making a home' etc. to the continuous presence of God in our hearts, which is responsible for the continuous growth in union, while reserving the term 'mission' or 'gift' for those particular moments in man's life where we can speak of discontinuity in growth. One of those moments of discontinuity is clearly the moment of justification, in which the presence of God as known and loved, which has been lost by sin, is restored again.

It is clear that, in the texts that we have read, a special role is ascribed to the Holy Spirit. First, when Thomas discusses the invisible mission of a divine Person in terms of renewed presence as known and loved, the Holy Spirit is mentioned explicitly a number of times, even though at one moment the invisible mission is discussed in terms of temporal knowledge of the Son. Second, when discussing the gifts of grace and how they are related to singular divine missions, not only the gifts of grace as gifts are ascribed to the Holy Spirit, but also the most decisive gift with respect to indwelling: the gift of charity. This is explicitly ascribed to the Holy Spirit, even though Thomas emphasizes time and again how both missions of the Son and the Spirit must be held together.

But it is also clear that the way the Holy Spirit is especially related to indwelling is always through appropriation. Now we have learned something about how Thomas understands appropriation in the previous section, and it is time to use those insights in explaining what is meant by ascribing a divine operation to a divine Person through appropriation.

First, attention must be given to a difficulty regarding the applicability of the analysis of Thomas' doctrine of appropriation to actual appropriations of divine operations. The point is that the two articles on appropriation, discussed above, do not deal with the appropriation of divine operations, such as making us into a temple of God[126] or indwelling through a certain gift[127], such as the gift of grace[128], the power to create[129], the forgiveness of sins[130], the adoption of men [and women] as sons [and daughters] of God[131], and the judgment at the end of time[132], but with the appropriation of essential attributes, like power, wisdom and goodness. As far as I can tell, this difficulty is only apparent from the fact that, when examined closely, Thomas does not really develop a doctrine on appropriation in article 7. He merely gives some considerations needed for the reflection in the next article on a number of actual appropriations of essential attributes known from Tradition or Scripture. These considerations are developed as he goes along. And because, here, he needs them within the context of his reflections on the relation of the distinct divine Persons to the one divine essence, his focus is on the appropriation of essential attributes, and not on the appropriation of divine operations. But nothing prohibits us from

---

126 *In I Sent* d.14, q.2, a.2 sc 2: "Spiritus sanctus non procedit in aliquem nisi quem inhabitat Deus, sicut in templo suo: quia per Spiritum sanctum efficitur quis templum Dei, I Cor. VI. Sed in nullo dicitur habitare Deus nisi per gratiam gratum facientem. Ergo secundum hoc donum tantum temporalis processio Spiritus sancti attenditur."

127 Cf. *De ver* q.27, a.2 ad 3: "Ad tertium dicendum quod tota Trinitas in nobis inhabitat per gratiam; sed specialiter alicui personae appropriari potest inhabitatio per aliquod aliud speciale donum, quod habet similitudinem cum ipsa persona, ratione cuius persona mitti dicitur."

128 *STh* I q.43, a.5 ad 1; II-II q.1, a.8 ad 5 ("[S]anctificatio creaturae per gratiam, et consummatio per gloriam fit etiam per donum charitatis, quod appropriatur Spiritui sancto, et per donum sapientiae, quod appropriatur Filio; et ideo utrumque opus pertinet ad Filium et ad Spiritum sanctum per appropriationem secundum rationes diversas." N.B.: in the *obiectio* it is said that, in the articles of faith, an *opus* is appropriated to the Father, namely the work of creation, an *opus* is appropriated to the Spirit, namely *who has spoken through the Prophets*, and consequently an *opus* must be appropriated to the Son.)

129 *STh* III q.3, a.8 ob 3: "sed potentia creandi appropriatur Patri".

130 *Idem*, ob 3: "remissio autem peccatorum attribuitur Spiritui sancto, secundum illud Joan. 20: *Accipite Spiritum sanctum quorum remiseritis peccata, remittuntur eis.*" Thomas replies: "Ad tertium dicendum quod Spiritui sancto proprium est, quod sit donum Patris, et Filii; remissio autem peccatorum fit per Spiritum sanctum, tanquam per donum Dei; et ideo convenientius fuit ad iustificationem hominum quod incarnaretur Filius, cuius Spiritus sanctus est donum."

131 *STh* III q.23, a.2 ad 3: "Assimilatur autem homo splendori aeterni Filii per gratiae claritatem, quae attribuitur Spiritui sancto; et ideo adoptatio licet sit communis toti Trinitati, appropriatur tamen Patri ut auctori, Filio ut exemplari, Spiritui sancto ut imprimenti in nobis huius similitudinem exemplaris."

132 *STh* III q.59, a.1 ad 1: "Ad primum ergo dicendum quod ex illa ratione probatur, quod iudiciaria potestas sit communis toti Trinitati: quod verum est. Sed tamen per quandam appropriationem iudiciaria potestas attribuitur Filio, ut dictum est. (in corpore articuli)." In the corpus Thomas explains: "et quia Filius est sapientia genita, et veritas a Patre procedens, et ipsum perfecte repraesentans, ideo proprie iudiciaria potestas attribuitur Filio Dei"

applying the definition of appropriation developed for essential attributes to the appropriation of divine operations.[133]

So what is meant, exactly, by the appropriation of the forgiveness of sins to the Holy Spirit? First, we require a more differentiated examination of the special relationship between indwelling and the Holy Spirit, because, not only does the whole Trinity abide in a person, the indwelling itself can be ascribed to either the Spirit or to the Son, based on which gift of grace, according to which the Trinity abides, is accentuated. When the gifts as gifts, or the gift of charity are emphasized, the indwelling is appropriated to the Spirit. But the indwelling based on the gift of wisdom is appropriated to the Son.

Second, we have to apply the rule that appropriations are aimed at manifesting what revelation has taught us to be *propria* of the divine Persons. Note that appropriation does not mean that we can deduce an operation of a divine Person in salvation history from one of its *propria*. Rather, one of God's operations is used to manifest what revelation has taught us to be a *proprium* of a divine Person. The indwelling based on the gift of sanctifying grace, or based on the gift of charity, seems, then, to be appropriated to the Holy Spirit to manifest primarily that the Spirit is the love of the Father and the Son. The indwelling based on the gifts of grace, precisely as gifts, is appropriated to the Spirit to manifest that the Spirit is the gift of both the Father and the Son. And finally, the indwelling based on the gift of wisdom is appropriated to the Son in order to manifest that the Son proceeds from the Father *per modum intellectus*, as his Word.

Third, according to St. Paul any perfection of the intellect, whether it is the gift of prophecy, of knowing miracles, of having knowledge, or having enough faith to move mountains, is worthless if it is without the gift of love.[134] The fact that Thomas, in his reply, emphasizes the union between the invisible missions of the Spirit and the Son (emphasizing that the Son is only the Word insofar as He breathes love (*spirans amorem*), and that consequently we must say that the Son is sent, not according to any perfection of the intellect, but according to an instruction of the intellect such that it bursts out in the affection of love)[135], does not diminish but even strengthen the dominance of love with respect to

---

[133] Cf. G. Müller, "Die Trinitätstheologie des hl. Thomas von Aquin", in idem, *Katholische Dogmatik für Studium und Praxis der Theologie*, Freiburg i. Br. 2000⁴, p.457: "Obwohl alle Werke in der Trinität gemeinsam sind (gemäss dem vom Vater ausgehenden ordo processionis), gibt es eine gewisse Zuordnung der absoluten Eigenschaften (z.B. Macht, Barmherzigkeit, Güte) oder der Werke Gottes in Schöpfung, Erlösung und Heiligung oder der göttlichen Namen (Gott als 'Vater Jesu Christi', der Sohn als 'Retter und Heiland' sowie der Geist als 'Herr und Lebensspender') an die drei göttlichen Personen (Appropriationen)". That we can distinguish between appropriations of essential names and of divine operations does not justify qualifying the first as philosophical and the only second as theological, as Sträter does. Both appropriations are theological in the sense that they are part of our reflections on revelation. Cf. footnote 87. Cf. also A. Chollet, "Appropriation", pp.1710-1712.

[134] Cf. I Cor 13, quoted in *STh* I q.43, a.5 ob 2.

[135] *STh* I q.43, a.5 ad 2.

salvation.[136] This corresponds with the dominance of the will in Thomas' teaching on the justification of the godless. And it corresponds with the fact that there can be faith (and hope) without love, i.e. not informed by grace, but there can be no love (charity) without being informed by grace.

So fourth, the special emphasis on the Holy Spirit, the dominance of the invisible mission of the Spirit regarding indwelling, and the fact that often the gift of the Holy Spirit is mentioned as *pars pro toto* for the gift of the whole Trinity, is based on the fact that the two dominating notions regarding indwelling, love and gift, correspond with the two proper names of the Holy Spirit: Love (q.37) and Gift (q.38). Based on this correspondence, or likeness (*similitudo*) in the terms of Thomas, appropriating indwelling to the Spirit functions as a means to manifest what revelation teaches us about the Spirit being the gift and the love of the Father and the Son.

It would be a mistake to misread this special attribution of indwelling, and in particular the forgiveness of sins *per Spiritum sanctum*, as saying that the Holy Spirit is the exclusive cause of the indwelling of Father Son and Spirit, or that the Holy Spirit is the exclusive cause of the forgiveness of sins, i.e. cause of the justification and sanctification of the human person.

Let me recall the reflections on the visible missions of the Son and the Spirit where Thomas explains the difference between how the Son is sent visibly and how the Holy Spirit is sent visibly. He finds the reason for this difference in the fact that it suits the Holy Spirit, insofar as He proceeds as love, to be the gift of sanctification, and consequently to be sent visibly as sign of sanctification, in the shape of a dove, or of tongues of fire. It suits the Son, however, being the principium of the Holy Spirit to be the cause (*auctor*) of the sanctification, and consequently to be sent visibly as *auctor sanctificationis*.[137]

When it comes to determining who the cause is of indwelling, it has already been made clear that though, in certain terms, indwelling can even be ascribed causally to the Spirit when the Spirit is said to make (*efficere*) us into a temple of God, nevertheless the whole Trinity must be said to be the cause of indwelling.[138] Consequently, any attempt to make the Holy Spirit into a second cause of salvation apart from the saving work of Christ on the cross must be considered false.[139]

---

[136] Cf. *In I Sent* d.14, q.2, a.2 ad 3: "Ad tertium dicendum quod non qualiscumque cognitio sufficit ad rationem missionis, sed solum illa quae accipitur ex aliquo dono appropriato personae, per quod efficitur in nobis coniunctio ad Deum, secundum modum proprium illius personae, scilicet per amorem, quando Spiritus sanctus datur. Unde cognitio ista est quasi experimentalis."

[137] *STh* I q.43, a.7 co.

[138] The whole Trinity comes to dwell in a person, and is consequently the cause of the indwelling, as the whole Trinity must be said to be the cause of the incarnation (and is even said to assume human nature, even though only the Son assumes human nature to himself. Cf. H. Schoot, *Christ the 'Name' of God*, pp.93-4).

[139] A good example of how cause can be formulated in terms of Father, Son and Spirit is found where Thomas reflects on the cause of our adoptive sonship (*In III Sent* d.10, q.2, a.1, qa.3 co): "Ad tertiam quaestionem dicendum, quod haec praepositio *per* potest denotare duplicem causam: scilicet agentem mediam; et sic sumus adoptati a Deo Patre per Filium, ut

So how must we understand the ascription of the forgiveness of sin *per Spiritum sanctum*, if it does not mean that the Holy Spirit is the cause of the forgiveness of sins? The ascription *per Spiritum sanctum* indicates the gifts of (sanctifying) grace according to which the Trinity dwells in a person, the gifts that makes us suitable for indwelling, the gifts that sanctify us, the gifts by which we are united with God. The ascription *per Spiritum sanctum* indicates that God dwells in us in a way that is proper to the Holy Spirit, i.e. God inhabits us *per amorem*.[140]

Incarnation

Since indwelling is only ascribed to the Holy Spirit through a certain appropriation, this means that indwelling, even though closely associated with the Holy Spirit, is not a *proprium* of the Spirit.

First, let me make clear that the notion of *proprium*, used to suggest a special relation of indwelling to the Spirit, is not the same as the notion of *proprium* in the sense of the technical term, indicating that which is revealed with respect to how the divine Persons are related to each other, the Father being *principium non de principio*, the Son being *principium de principio*, and the Spirit being *processio a duobus*. When *proprium* is mentioned with respect to indwelling, what is meant is the question of whether, similarly to the fact that incarnation seems to be something proper to the Son, indwelling is something proper to the Spirit.[141]

---

appropriate loquamur: quia per eum Deus Pater multos filios in gloriam adduxit, ut dicitur Ad Hebr. 2, secundum quod eum misit in mundum Salvatorem. Potest etiam notare formalem causam; et hoc dupliciter; vel inhaerentem, vel exemplarem. Si inhaerentem, sic adoptati sumus per Spiritum sanctum, cui appropriatur caritas, secundum quam formaliter meremur. Ideo dicitur Ephes. 1, 13: *Signati estis Spiritu promissionis sancto, qui est pignus hereditatis nostrae.* Si vero designat causam exemplarem formalem, sic sumus adoptati per Filium; unde Rom. 8, 29: *Quos praescivit conformes fieri imaginis filii sui, ut sit ipse primogenitus in multis fratribus."* Note that the actual cause of the adoption, i.e. the one who adopts, is God the Father.

140 Cf. *In I Sent* d.14, q.2, a.2 ad 3. Note that *amor* here must not be taken as *proprium* of the Spirit, but as *appropriatum*. On the difference between *amor* as *proprium* and *amor* as *appropriatum*, cf. *In I Sent* d.10, q.1, a.1 ad 4: "Ad quartum dicendum, quod amor in divinis tripliciter sumitur. Quandoque enim sumitur essentialiter, quandoque personaliter, quandoque notionaliter. Quando sumitur essentialiter, non dicit aliquam processionem vel relationem realem, sed tantum rationis, sicut etiam cum de Deo dicimus intelligens et intellectum: eadem enim persona potest esse intelligens et intellecta. Quando autem dicitur personaliter, tunc importatur processio et relatio realis, et significatur ipsa persona, sive res procedens, sicut amor est quoddam procedens. Quando autem dicitur notionaliter, significat ipsam rationem processionis personae: quia amor non tantum est procedens, sed etiam dicit rationem sub qua alia procedunt. Secundum ergo quod est essentiale, est commune tribus, sed appropriatur Spiritui sancto; ut cum dicitur, *Deus caritas est*, 1 Ioan. 4, 16; secundum autem quod est personale, est proprium Spiritus sancti; et dicitur, quod Spiritus sanctus procedit ut amor. Secundum autem quod est notionale, est quaedam relatio vel notio communis Patri et Filio, quae etiam dicitur communis spiratio; et hoc modo significatur amor in hoc verbo 'diligunt': cum dicitur, Pater et Filius diligunt se Spiritu sancto."

141 Cf. H. Mühlen, "Person und Appropriation. Zum Verständniss des Axioms: In Deo sunt unum, ubi non obviat relationis oppositio", in *Münchener theologische Zeitschrift* 16, 1965, pp.37-57. Mühlen wants to see a parallel between the incarnation of the Son and the "uniting function" of the Spirit in the church. Since *Lumen Gentium*, the church is no longer understood simply as the continuation of the incarnation. Rather, the constitution speaks about an analogy between the mystery of the incarnation and the mystery of the church. With

The question is motivated by the desire to clarify the relevance of the Holy Trinity, and in particular the Holy Spirit, in reflections on salvation history. Rahner has criticized most current theologies for their incapacity to state the relevance of the Trinity in salvation history.[142] And Sträter has dismissed speaking of the role of the Holy Spirit in salvation history only in terms of appropriation, as a 'theology as if'.[143]

The point, however, is that the question itself of a proper role of the Holy Spirit in salvation history parallel to the proper role of the Son (incarnation) is badly put. To make this clear, I will look once more at *quaestio* 43 on the missions of the divine Persons.

We reflected above on the structure of *quaestio* 43, which is about the missions of the divine Persons. We already suggested there that the *quaestio* was not only structured along the distinction between the Son and the Spirit, but also along the distinction between visible and invisible missions as well. The question is whether the distinction between visible and invisible missions is not more important for the structure of the *quaestio* than the distinction between Son and Spirit.

According to Thomas there are four missions to be distinguished, in order of appearance: the invisible mission of the Spirit, the invisible mission of the Son, the visible mission of the Son and the visible mission of the Spirit. When Thomas speaks about the invisible mission in general, it is clear that he has primarily the invisible mission of the Spirit in mind. Moreover, from the fact that the invisible mission of the Son and the visible mission of the Spirit are explicitly discussed, we can infer, without further notification, that by 'invisible mission' the (invisible) mission of the Spirit is meant, and that by 'visible mission' the (visible) mission of the Son is meant. But we also saw that Thomas takes great pains to make clear that even when this is the case, we must not forget that there is also an invisible mission of the Son and a visible mission of the Spirit. Why would he do that? Why would he make things more complicated than they already are?

The main reason is that Scripture testifies to an invisible mission of the Son (in particular the Wisdom-literature of the Old Testament) and to visible missions of the Spirit, at the baptism of Jesus, at his transfiguration, and the descending of the Spirit on the Apostles in the shape of tongues of fire. But moreover, he is motivated by his Trinitarian concern to safeguard the unity of the three Persons, in particular the unity of Son and Spirit. We encountered this concern explicitly when he discussed the invisible mission of the Son.

The result of his emphasis on an invisible mission of the Son and a visible mission of the Spirit is that the whole treatise about the missions is no longer

---

respect to this analogy, Mühlen asks: "Sollte diese Analogie nicht auch darin bestehen, dass die einigende Funktion des Hl. Geistes in der Kirche in ähnlicher Weise ein *Proprium* dieses Geistes ist (als Eine Person in den vielen Personen, nämlich in Christus und den Christen), wie die sich mit seiner Menschheit einigende Funktion des Logos *sein* Proprium ist?" (p.57)

[142] K. Rahner, "Der dreifaltige Gott", pp. 319-320.

[143] C. Sträter "Het begrip 'appropriatie'", p.3: "Lijkt dit niet op een 'Theologie des Alsob'?"

structured mainly along the distinction between Son and Spirit. Rather, the distinction between visible and invisible dominates the distinction of the missions of the divine Persons (cf. the introduction to section 1).

When we return to the question of what the proper role of the Holy Spirit in salvation history could be, parallel to the incarnation of the Son, the distinction between visible and invisible forces us to state the question as follows: is there a visible mission proper to the Spirit which is parallel to the visible mission that is proper to the Son? Put in this way, the answer to this question is: yes! The proper role of the Spirit in salvation history is not that the Spirit is sent invisibly, while the Son is sent visibly. What is proper to the Son is that He is sent visibly as man, while what is proper to the Spirit is that the Spirit is sent visibly in the shape of a dove and of tongues of fire. Proper roles of Son and Spirit in salvation history, in other words, can be found in the visible realm. In the invisible realm, however, the singularity of their roles in salvation history remains limited to what can be appropriated in order to manifest their subsequent *propria*, because with respect to the history of salvation, their respective invisible missions first convene in the root of grace, before distinct gifts of grace can be ascribed to one of the divine Persons *through a certain appropriation*.

Creation

As a final exercise, we will look at the way Thomas deals with the notions of *proprium* and *appropriatum* when he reflects on the roles of Father, Son and Spirit in creation.[144]

As said before, the reason why it is impossible for natural reason (i.e. apart from revelation) to arrive at the distinction of divine Persons, is that our only access is through what we know from creation. And since God's creative power (*virtus creativa Dei*) is shared by the whole Trinity, it belongs to the unity of God's essence, and not the distinction of divine Persons.[145] Consequently, we cannot arrive at knowledge about the trinity of divine Persons apart from what has been revealed to us. And even then, we remain in need of appropriation of essential attributes (about which we can acquire knowledge), in order to manifest what has been revealed regarding the Trinity of divine Persons.

Consequently it would seem that, regarding creation, nothing can be said with respect to singular divine Persons.[146] However, it turns out that, according to Thomas, more can be said, and the resulting reflections form a fine example of the use of the notions of *proprium* and *appropriatum*.

The question is whether the distinct formulations regarding creation, which can be found in the Nicean-Constantinopolitan *Symbolum*, and which refer to the distinct divine Persons, must be understood as *propria* or *appropriata*. The

---

[144] *STh* I q.45, a.6 (cf. the prologue to q.45): "Utrum [creare] commune sit toti Trinitati, aut proprium alicuius personae."

[145] *STh* I q.32, a.1 co.

[146] Which is the intention of the quotation in the argument *Sed contra* taken from *De Divinis Nominibus*, that "communia totius divinitatis sunt omnia causalia" (*STh* I q.45, a.6 Sc).

formulations meant are "being Creator of all things visible and invisible", said of the Father, "through whom all things are made", said of the Son, and "Lord and giver of life", said of the Holy Spirit. Based on the fact that the creative power is shared by the whole Trinity and is not a *proprium* of one divine Person[147], one would expect them to be *appropriata*.

Thomas argues as follows for the position that these three sayings are *propria* and not *appropriata*. Creating fits the essence of God, and consequently is shared by the whole Trinity, for all three are God, and all share equally the divine essence or divine nature. But distinction can be made as to how each divine Person possesses divine nature with respect to the other divine Persons, because the Son receives the divine nature from the Father, and the Holy Spirit receives it from both the Father and the Son. And consequently, the creative power, even though shared by the whole Trinity, fits each divine Person according to a certain ordering, because the Son receives it from the Father and the Spirit from both. For this reason, to call the Father Creator, is to indicate that He does not have the creative power *ab alio*. And calling the Son "through whom all things are made" indicates his being *principium de principio*. The preposition 'through' (*per*), indicates precisely that the Son has the creative power, not of him self, but *ab alio*. And since the Holy Spirit has the creative strength from both the Father and the Son, He is said to guide (*gubernare*) by being Lord, (*dominando* = 'by ruling'; cf. *Dominus* = Lord) and to give life to those who are created by the Father through the Son.[148]

Thomas continues by saying that appropriating essential attributes can subsequently manifest these *propria*. Appropriating 'power' to the Father manifests the Father as Creator (power being what is most manifested in the act of creation), while appropriating wisdom to the Son manifests the Father as creating *per intellectum*. That goodness is appropriated to the Holy Spirit is based on the fact that guidance, which leads all things to their ends, belongs to goodness. Furthermore, since life consists in an interior motion, and that which moves first (*primum movens*) is end and goodness (*finis et bonitas*), therefore to give life also belongs to goodness.

Conclusion

We began this section with the remark that in the *Symbolum*, the distinction between Father, Son and Spirit does not simply correspond with the division between the divine acts of creation, incarnation and indwelling, even though each of these has a special relation with each of the divine Persons. Our prime concern was not to reflect on how incarnation and creation are related respectively to God the Father and God the Son. Our prime concern was to understand how indwelling is specially related to the Holy Spirit, so that we can give an answer (as was the whole purpose of this third chapter) to the question of why it is that Scripture and Tradition (and Thomas along with these two) emphasize the special role the Holy Spirit has with respect to the forgiveness of

---

[147] Repeated by Thomas in the *corpus articuli*.
[148] *STh* I q.45, a.6 ad 2.

sins, i.e. the justification and sanctification which are the principle effects of the sacrament of penance. The only reason why we also reflected on incarnation and creation was because these reflections could add to our understanding of the meaning of saying that the forgiveness of sins is *per Spiritum sanctum*.

Let us summarize the results of our reflections. The most important result is that neither indwelling, nor incarnation, nor creation can simply be said of one of the divine Persons. In all three divine operations, all three divine Persons are involved. A theology of the incarnation, without considering the Father who has sent his Son in the world to become man and without considering the role of the Holy Spirit in the life of Christ, is as deficient as a theology of grace, or of indwelling, which only considers the Holy Spirit. The division in theology between Christology and pneumatology (with attempts to restore the lack of Spirit in Christology by (re-) constructing a Pneuma-christology) should, based on our reflections on Thomas' theology, be dismissed, and be substituted by a division between a theology of the visible missions of the Son and the Spirit, and a theology of the invisible missions of the Son and the Spirit. During my work on this subject I have often wondered whether the 'Geistvergessenheit' of western theology (as it is known since Hegel) is in fact not so much a silence with respect to the Spirit as a silence with respect to indwelling. What our reflections have yielded is that this 'Geistvergessenheit' is not something which belongs to the whole of western theology.[149]

A second result, immediately following the first, is that one cannot claim a proper role for the Spirit with respect to our sanctification with a simple reference to the proper role of the Son in the incarnation. When a difference is made between the visible and the invisible realm, it becomes clear that the singularity of the incarnation of the Son does not correspond with a presumed singularity of the indwelling of the Spirit, but with the singularity of visible appearances of the Spirit. Consequently, the notion of 'the visible missions of Son and Spirit' is better suited than the notion of 'incarnation' to indicate what happens between the virginal conception and the birth of the church at Pentecost.

The third result is a negative answer to our question of what it means when we say that our sins are forgiven *per Spiritum sanctum*: it does not mean that the Spirit is the cause of the forgiveness of sins. Either the whole Trinity is cause of the forgiveness of sins, as it is the whole Trinity who is cause of indwelling, or the Father is cause since it is His privilege to adopt us as His sons, or the Son is cause of our forgiveness since Jesus delivered us from sin by giving His life on the cross. The fact that the Latin reads *per* and not *a* should have warned us from the start that Thomas never intended to say that the Holy Spirit is subject of the act of forgiving.[150]

---

[149] A quick glance at contemporaries of Thomas, like Bonaventure or Albert the Great shows that indwelling is certainly not forgotten in their theological reflections.

[150] Revealing in this sense is *ScG* IV, c.21: "Quum igitur per Spiritum sanctum Dei amici constituamur, consequens est quod <u>per ipsum</u> nobis <u>a Deo</u> remittantur peccata. Et ideo Dominus dicit discipulis: *Accipite Spiritum sanctum; quorum remiseritis peccata, remittuntur eis*; et

The fact that the love and the gifts of grace through which God dwells in our hearts are ascribed to the Holy Spirit by way of appropriation manifests that which revelation teaches us about the Spirit, namely that Love and Gift, and Lord and Giver of life are proper names of the Spirit. These appropriations, as all statements about the history of salvation which are appropriated to the divine Persons, point towards a parallel between our relation with God and the relations in God. Saying that the forgiveness of sins is *per Spiritum sanctum* shows that the love and self giving which is constitutive of our friendship with God (and is consequently decisive with respect to the restoration of that friendship when broken through sin) is not something accidental to God, but is based on a Love and Self-giving that belongs to God's essence.

---

ideo blasphemantibus Spiritum sanctum peccatorum remissio denegatur, quasi non habentibus illud per quod homo remissionem consequitur peccatorum." This does not contradict the fact that Thomas interprets *per Spiritum sanctum* in Rom. 5,5 as *est a Spiritu sancto*, because this must be translated as 'is from the Holy Spirit', and not as 'is *[caused]* by the Holy Spirit'.

Chapter 4 The Sacrament of Penance

Introduction

In this chapter, we will proceed with our examination of the role of the Spirit in the forgiveness of sins. What we have found until now, we will place within the context of sacramental forgiveness.[1]

From the historical overview, and from our first glance at the place of the sacrament of penance in the works of Thomas in Chapter One, we have learned that, according to Thomas, the special character of the sacraments of the new covenant consists in that they "effect what they signify" (*efficiunt quod figurant*). When Thomas defends the enumeration of the sacrament of penance among the sacraments of the new covenant, he aims to safeguard this notion of effectiveness of the sacrament of penance. The notion of cause takes up a great part of both his reflection on the sacraments in general and his reflection on the sacrament of penance in particular.

The examination of the notion of sacramental causality in Thomas' theology of the sacrament of penance will provides us with an answer to our primary question, i.e. how Thomas understands God to be the cause of the forgiveness of sins in the sacrament of penance. However, the question of this dissertation goes further than that, as it asks what role Thomas ascribes to the Holy Spirit in the sacrament of penance. Therefore, the question is whether Thomas' notion of sacramental causality leaves room for a role for the Holy Spirit, and if so, what this role is.

We begin our reflections by examining a question that is dominant in our times, namely the question of the relevance of sacramental forgiveness for salvation. In our times, the reason why one must confess has become unclear. The sacrament of penance is in a crisis and only a few people today (in the western countries) practice it. For many people it is even a surprise to hear that the sacrament of penance 'still exists'. The fact that the sacrament of penance itself has disappeared from the life of most Catholics does not mean that they have not found other ways to deal with notions like guilt and forgiveness. However, for many, the sacrament of penance seems to have become irrelevant. Of those who do reflect on the sacrament of penance, some question its necessity for salvation, or they question the particular form in which the church celebrates the sacramental forgiveness.

So before we examine how Thomas uses causality in his theology of the sacrament of penance, we will deal first with this question of the relevance of the sacrament of penance. What is its place in the economy of salvation, and in

---

1   On the sacrament of penance and reconciliation, cf. Th. Schneider, "Busse", in id., *Zeichen der Nähe Gottes. Grundriss der Sakramententheologie*, 1979, pp.187-219; R. Duffy, "Penance", in F. Schüssler Fiorenza, J. Galvin (eds), *Systematic theology. Roman Catholic perspectives*, vol. 2, 1991, pp.233-249; H. Vorgrimmler, "The sacrament of reconciliation", in id., *Sacramental theology*, 1992, p.200-225; A. Cuschieri, *The sacrament of reconciliation. A theological and canonical treatise*, 1992.

what sense does Thomas think it is necessary? Dealing with these questions will not only help us to see how, according to Thomas, the sacrament of penance is situated in the economic order. In addition, it will provide us with a first idea of how Thomas understands the sacrament of penance to be the cause of the forgiveness of sins.

In the second and third sections, we will examine how Thomas reflects on the nature of the sacrament of penance, and we will see that Thomas understands its effectiveness against the background of sacramental signification. In the second section, we will concentrate on the sacraments in general, while in the third section we will look at the sacrament of penance.

In the fourth section, we will examine how Thomas relates the notion of justifying faith, as we encountered it in Chapter Two, with the way the sacrament of penance 'works'. How are faith and sacrament related in Thomas' theology? We will discover that Thomas ascribes an important role to faith. Furthermore, according to Thomas, sacraments contain a strength (*virtus*), which they derive from the passion of Christ. We will examine how the sacrament of penance derives this strength from Christ's passion and what its nature is.

In the fifth and final section, we will discuss the causality of the sacrament of penance in relation to the Holy Spirit, in order to find out if, and if so how, the *per Spiritum sanctum* of divine forgiveness has received a place in Thomas' theology of the sacrament of penance.

1 The need for sacramental forgiveness

The question about the need for sacramental forgiveness concerns primarily the need to confess sins. This is because the sacramental expression of the forgiveness of actual (mortal) sins mainly takes place in the act of confessing sins and in the reception of the absolution. In our days, the question why confession is necessary is asked in different ways, with different emphases. For instance, in the discussion about the legitimacy of general absolution as the normal way of obtaining sacramental forgiveness[2], the question is asked with the emphasis on 'confessing individually': why should one *confess* one's sins *individually* in order to obtain absolution? Why is it not sufficient to say a general confession of sins in order to obtain absolution?

Others ask the same question, but place the emphasis on the priest: Why should one confess *to a priest*? Why can I not just confess my sins to God in private prayer, or why is it not possible to confess to a saintly person who is not a priest, which, as we saw in Chapter One, was the case in the early church? Moreover, why is it somehow not sufficient to confess my sins to a fellow man,

---

[2] Some see the crisis of the sacrament of penance in our days as the crisis of just one form of celebrating it, namely that of the individual confession and absolution. In contrast to this form, the new form of the communal celebrations with general confession and absolution is propagated as an alternative. Cf. K. Koch, "Die eine Botschaft von der Versöhnung im vielfältigen Wandel des Busssakramentes", in J. Müller (hrsg), *Das ungeliebte Sakrament. Grundriß einer neuen Bußpraxis*, 1995; G. Maloney, *Your sins are forgiven you. Rediscovering the sacrament of penance*, 1996.

for instance when there is no priest available? In particular, the question is asked in our days if it would not be more suitable to turn to the victim of my wrongdoings, instead of to a priest. Confession to a priest seems in that respect an easy way of cleansing oneself of one's sins.[3]

One can also place the emphasis on what sins one must confess. In the introduction, we argued that with respect to the crisis of the sacrament of penance there are two main problems. The first has to do with the loss of understanding of the sacraments, the second with the loss of understanding sins. Since the notion of sin itself is in crisis, many of the problems of the sacrament of penance today are caused by uncertainty as to what it is that must be confessed. Can we, in order to determine what sins we must confess, still make use of lists of sinful deeds, the so-called catalogues of sins?[4] Or is a relational conception of sin required, corresponding to the relational notion of grace of the previous chapters? The question that corresponds to this line of thought would not be: why should one confess one's sins individually to a priest?, but: *what* should one confess? However, this latter question, as we explained in the introduction, is not the subject of this dissertation.

In this section, we will concentrate on the question of why one must confess one's sins to a priest in order to obtain forgiveness of sins. We will examine the texts of Thomas in order to find out what reasons he gives.

First, we need to distinguish between two situations in which the sinner can be, the first being that he has committed a mortal sin, the second being that he has committed a venial sin. The sacrament of penance is only necessary if someone has committed a mortal sin. We will see that according to Thomas the sacrament of penance is necessary for us, not for God. God can forgive our sins without the sacrament of penance. However, because of our condition, status and need for rituals, we need sacraments to bring us into the spiritual realm of God.

Next, we will see that the purpose of the act of confessing is that by doing so the penitent subjects himself to Christ. It is in this act of submission, which is an act of the will, that the relationship of grace is restored. Christ, however, is represented in the sacrament of penance by the minister of the sacrament. In the sacrament, he represents Christ in virtue of the power of the keys of the church. The necessity of sacramental confession is, in Thomas' theology, related to the necessity of Christ for salvation.

---

[3]   Cf. the opening section of Chapter Two, where we mentioned that a shift has occurred from attention for the sinner to attention for the victim.

[4]   An example of such a catalogue is the list with 27 sins which the uneducated young men from the Netherlands received in the 19th century when they went to Rome to fight in the army of the pope (so called "Zouaven"). Being unable to speak a foreign language, they received the list of sins written in Dutch, in Italian and in French, so that with the help of this list they could make confession while abroad. At the top of the list the sinner was instructed to indicate with the number of fingers held up how many times he had committed one of the sins. The list contains sins like "I did not attend mass last Sunday, by my own fault"; "I have sinned with a married woman", "I drank too much, however without losing my senses" and "I have been completely drunk".

Finally, we will see precisely why, according to Thomas, an act of confessing sins is the proper manner in which the submission to Christ should take place.

The sacrament of penance and the justification of the godless

In the first *quaestio* on the sacrament of penance in the *Summa theologiae*, after having established that the sacrament of penance is one of the sacraments of the church and after having established its proper matter and proper form, Thomas deals with the question whether or not it is necessary for salvation. In his answer, Thomas begins with distinguishing between absolute and conditional necessity. According to Thomas, only the grace of Christ and the sacrament of baptism are absolutely necessary for salvation. The sacrament of penance, however, is necessary for those who are subjected to sin.[5]

Necessity, it turns out, applies only to the sacrament of penance, in the case of someone being subjected to sin, i.e. someone who by committing a mortal sin has alienated himself from God, and consequently has broken his friendship with God (cf. Chapter Two).[6] The sacrament of penance, we can say, is the sacramental counterpart of the justification of the godless.[7] Similarly, the sacrament of baptism is the sacramental counterpart of justification.[8] There is, in other words, a parallel between justification and justification of the godless on the one hand, and on the other hand, the forgiveness of original sin and of actual mortal sin in the sacraments of baptism and of penance respectively. The distinction between justification and justification of the godless, which we encountered in Chapter Two, runs parallel to the distinction between the sacraments of baptism and penance. The reason why the sacrament of baptism, in contrast to the sacrament of penance, is necessary in an absolute sense is that all are subjected to original sin, whereas not all necessarily commit mortal sins.

The necessity of sacramental forgiveness in both the sacraments of baptism and penance, however, refers to us, and not to God. According to Thomas, God is not bound to the use of sacraments in order to confer justifying grace. In one

---

[5] *STh* III q.84, a.5 co: "Respondeo dicendum quod aliquid est necessarium ad salutem dupliciter: uno modo absolute; alio modo ex suppositione. Absolute quidem necessarium est ad salutem illud, sine quo nullus salutem consequi potest, sicut gratia Christi, et scramentum baptismi, per quod aliquis in Christo renascitur. Ex suppositione autem est necessarium sacramentum poenitentiae; quod quidem est necessarium non omnibus, sed peccato subjacentibus." In the treatise on the sacraments in general, Thomas names three sacraments as necessary for salvation. Of these, baptism and penance are necessary for the individual person: baptism simpliciter et absolute, and penance under the supposition that one has committed a mortal sin after being baptized. The sacrament of order is necessary for the church as a whole. (*STh* III q.65, a.4 co)

[6] That the sacrament of penance is necessary only for those who have committed mortal sins, does not imply that receiving it cannot be meaningful for who has only committed venial sins. Cf. K. Rahner, "Vom Sinn der häufigen Andachtsbeichte", in *Schriften zur Theologie* III, 1956, pp. 211-225.

[7] The reference to Augustine's adage "who has created you without you will not justify you without you", cited at the end of the *corpus articuli*, confirms that we are dealing with justification.

[8] For the distinction between justification and justification of the godless, see Chapter Two.

of the objections of the *articulus* we referred to above, it is argued that because in the eighth chapter of John, Christ is said to absolve an adulterous women without (the sacrament of) penance, consequently the (sacrament of) penance does not seem to be necessary. In his answer, Thomas says that because Christ (and Christ alone) possessed the power of excellence (*potestas excellentiae*), He brought about the effect of the sacrament of penance, i.e. the forgiveness of sins, without an external sacrament of penance. Thomas adds that nevertheless Christ did not bring forgiveness of sins about without internal penance, which He himself had caused in her through grace.[9] Thomas gives a similar answer when he deals with the opposite question, that of whether sins can be forgiven without (the sacrament of) penance. In his answer Thomas distinguishes between penance as sacrament and penance as virtue.[10] Of these, the virtue of penance is indispensable with respect to the forgiveness of actual mortal sin. The reason for this is that God, in contrast to human persons, does not forgive someone's sins without the change of this person's will.[11] In Chapter Two, we saw that, according to Thomas, forgiveness of sins in fact consists in the reordering of the free will towards God. Consequently, what Thomas says here with respect to the necessity of the virtue of penance will not surprise us, for justification and consequently forgiveness of sins consist in a change of the will, i.e. a virtuous act of repentance.

With respect to the sacrament of penance itself, Thomas refers to the previously mentioned article and the passage from John and says that God can forgive sins without the sacrament of penance, i.e. without the ministry of a

---

[9]   *Idem*, ad 3: "Ad tertium dicendum quod ad potestatem excellentiae, quam solus Christus habuit, ut supra dictum est, pertinuit, quod Christus effectum sacramenti poenitentiae, qui est remissio peccatorum, contulit mulieri adulterae sine exterioris poenitentiae sacramento, licet non sine interiori poenitentia, quam ipse in ea per gratiam est operatus." Christ possesses this 'power of excellence' as man (*secundum quod est homo*): (1) it consists in that the merit and the strength of his passion works in the sacraments; (2) it belongs to the power of excellence that the sacraments sanctify in Christ's name; (3) because the sacraments have strength out of their institution by Christ it belongs to the power of excellence that Christ could institute the sacraments; (4) and since a cause does not depend on its effect, therefore Christ can give the effect of the sacraments without the exterior sacrament. (*STh* III q.64, a.3 co)

[10] This distinction corresponds with the two functions sacraments have, namely being instrument of grace and being expression of faith. In the *Scriptum*, Thomas distinguishes with respect to this between the penitent as recipient and the penitent as actor. In the first case, penance is considered as sacrament, in the latter as virtue. Cf. *In IV Sent* d.14, q.1, a.1, qa.2 co: "Ad secundum quaestionem dicendum quod in poenitentia se habet homo et ut recipiens et ut agens. Recipit quidem a Deo veniam et reconciliationem per Ecclesiae ministros, et secundum hoc habet rationem sacramenti. Sed ex parte actus sunt ipsa diversae opiniones." Subsequently, Thomas reflects on two different opinions, which he rejects. The position he takes is that since the act is caused by choice (*ex electione*), penance is properly speaking a virtue. In his answer to the first objection, Thomas summarizes "Ad primum dicendum quod non secundum idem poenitentia est virtus et sacramentum; sed inquantum per poenitentiam recipit gratiam curantem peccati vulnus poenitens potest esse sacramentum; inquantum autem per habitum infusum ordinatur ad actum rectum, sic est virtus."

[11] *STh* III q.86, a.2 co.

priest who binds and loosens.[12] We will return to the subject of the relationship between internal and external penance later. For now it suffices to emphasize that the necessity of the *sacrament* of penance for those who have committed a mortal sin refers to us and not to God.

What reasons does Thomas give for this necessity? Why do human persons need a sacrament, i.e. something visible or in another way sensible? Why do we need an external expression of the internal penance? For an answer to this question, we will look at the reasons Thomas gives for the necessity of sacraments in general.[13] It is important to notice that the arguments Thomas gives for the necessity of the sacraments (cf. *necessitas sacramentorum* in the opening sentence of the *quaestio*) and the reasons why sacraments are necessary (cf. *sacramenta sunt necessaria* in the opening sentence of *art.* 1) are not coercive, but are intended to explain the fittingness of sacraments (cf. *conveniens, convenienter* mentioned thrice in the *corpus articuli* of art. 1), and how they are part of God's providential plan.

Thomas gives three reasons. The first reason can be understood from the condition of the human nature "for which it is proper that it is led through what is physical and sensible to what is spiritual and intelligible".[14] We have encountered this epistemological argument before, in Chapters One and Three, when we dealt with the distinction and relation between the visible and invisible missions of the divine Persons, where Thomas explains that it is "the connatural way of man, that he is led through what is visible to what is invisible".[15] Both the significance of the visible missions of the divine Persons and the significance of sacraments are based on the same epistemological principle: that because of our human nature our knowledge of God is through sensible things.

The second reason is derived from the fact that after the fall, man has become attached to physical things. According to Thomas, man "by sinning subjects himself through his affection to physical things". Consequently, it is fitting that the medicine against sin is applied through physical signs, i.e. sacraments.

The third reason is derived from how human persons act, for human persons tend to engage in superstitious exercises, like demon worship and other acts of sin. For this reason man is given the healthy exercise of sacraments.

---

12 *Ibidem.* "Sacramentum autem poenitentiae, sicut supra dictum est, perficitur per officium sacerdotis ligantis, et solventis, sine quo potest Deus peccatum remittere, sicut remisit Christus mulieri adulterae, ut legitur Joan. 8, et peccatrice, ut legitur Luc. 7; quibus tamen non remisit peccata sine virtute poenitentiae; nam, sicut Greg. dicit in hom. "per gratiam traxit intus (scilicet ad poenitentiam) quam per misericordiam suscepit foris".

13 *STh* III, q.61. The reasons for the need for sacraments Thomas gives in the first *articulus*. In the second, third and fourth *articuli*, Thomas applies these to different moments in the history of salvation: before the first sin (a.2), before Christ's passion (a.3) and after Christ's passion (a.4).

14 *Idem,* a.1 co: "Prima [ratio] sumenda est ex conditione humanae naturae, cuius proprium est, ut per corporalia, et sensibilia in spiritualia, et intelligibilia deducatur."

15 *STh* I q.43, a.7: "Est autem modus connaturalis hominis, ut per visibilia ad invisibilia manuducatur, ut ex supra dictis patet (*q.12, a.12*)." Cf. Chapter One, Section 3; Chapter Three, Section 1.

So according to Thomas, sacraments are God's providential gift to men, with which men are given instruments of communicating with God, which fit their constitution, their status and how they tend to act. They bridge the gap between the physical and sensible world in which human persons live, and the spiritual realm of God.

We have learned that the sacrament of penance in the case of a mortal sin is the sacramental counterpart of the justification of the godless. Furthermore, we have seen what arguments Thomas presents when he explains why God in His divine wisdom provides for sacraments. Now we will focus on the reasons Thomas gives for the need to confess one's sins.

The purpose of confession (1): submission to God's judgment

From the texts of Thomas, we can infer that confessing one's sins has two purposes. The first is submission to the power of the keys. This is the most important purpose of confession, for it is through submission to the power of the keys that the relationship of grace with God is restored. The second purpose of confession is revealing the nature and number of the sins.[16]

The two purposes of confessing correspond, as we will see, with the double nature of the power of the keys. This is because the power of the keys, which plays such an important role in understanding Thomas' theology of the sacrament of penance, is of a double nature. Thomas speaks of two keys, one being the authority to investigate, the other the power to absolve or condemn.[17] As we will see, the power to absolve corresponds with the fact that, by confessing, the penitent submits himself to God's judgment. The authority to investigate, i.e. to know the sin, corresponds with the fact that, by confessing, the penitent reveals the wound of the heart.

The primary purpose of confession in the sacrament of penance is the submission to the judgment of God. According to Thomas, this submission consists in the expression of the inner penance, i.e. the will of the penitent to be reconciled with God and the church. In order to make clear that the

---

[16] Cf. *In IV Sent* d.17, q.3, a.1, qa.1 co: "Sicut autem aliquis per hoc quod baptismum petit, se ministris Ecclesiae subiicit ad quos pertinet dispensatio sacramenti; ita etiam per hoc quod confitetur peccatum suum, se ministro Ecclesiae subiicit, ut per sacramentum poenitentiae ab eo dispensatum remissionem consequatur. Qui congruum remedium adhibere non potest, nisi peccatum cognoscat: quod fit per confessionem peccantis. Et ideo confessio est de necessitate salutis eius qui in peccatum actuale mortale cecidit."; *ScG* IV c.72: "Ideo (..) peccantibus post baptismum salus esse non potest, nisi clavibus Ecclesiae se subiiciant, vel actu confitendo et iudicium ministrorum Ecclesiae subeundo, vel saltem huius rei propositum habendo, ut impleatur tempore opportuno"; *STh* III, q.90, a.2: "Sic igitur requiritur ex parte poenitentis: primo quidem voluntas recompensandi; quod fit per contritionem; secundo, quod se subjiciat arbitrio sacerdotis loco Dei; quod fit in confessione; tertio, quod recompenset secundum arbitrium ministri Dei; quod fit in satisfactione."

[17] Cf. *ScG* IV c.72: "Ad iudiciariam autem potestatem duo requiruntur, scilicet auctoritas cognoscendi de culpa et potestas absolvendi vel condemnandi. Et haec duo dicuntur duae claves Ecclesiae, scilicet scientia discernendi et potentia ligandi et solvendi, quas Dominus Petro commisit, iuxta illud: *Tibi dabo claves regni caelorum* (Matth. xvi, 19). Non autem sic intelligitur Petro commisisse ut ipse solus haberet, sed ut per eum derivarentur ad alios."

penitent expresses his inner will, particularly in the confession of sins, we first need to reflect on the structure of the sacrament of penance. Next, we will relate our findings concerning confession to the conclusion of Chapter Two that divine forgiveness must, in Thomas' theology, be understood against the background of the restoration of the relationship of grace with God. Finally, we will deal with the question why one must confess one's sins to a *priest*.

a.   The place of confession in the sacrament of penance

According to Thomas in his *Summa theologiae*, the sacraments belong to the *genus* of 'sign'. The sacramental sign refers to something, a signified content distinct from the sacramental sign. With respect to the sacrament of penance, Thomas refers to sign and signified content as (visible) external and (invisible) internal penance.

In the *Scriptum*, Thomas distinguishes between *sacramentum tantum*, *sacramentum et res* and *res tantum*. The exterior penance is *sacramentum tantum*, the interior penance is *res et sacramentum* and the forgiveness of sins is the *res tantum*. Two different relationships can be indicated. First, exterior and interior penance relate to each other as *sacramentum* and *res sacramenti*. The external penance, i.e. the external acts by which the penitent cooperates in his salvation, is the sacramental sign.[18] The internal penance, i.e. the contrition including the intention to confess and to give satisfaction, is the *res sacramenti* of the external penance. Second, the interior penance itself is *sacramentum*, in the sense of sign and immediate cause, of the forgiveness of sins, which is *res tantum*.[19]

Let us focus on the relationship between exterior penance and interior penance. Depending on whether the acts of the minister of the sacrament of penance are included, the exterior penance and interior penance relate to each other respectively as sign/effect and cause, or as sign/cause and effect. Without the absolution, the exterior penance must be understood to be caused by the interior penance. The tears, the verbal expression of remorse and the actual penance show ('signify') that the penitent has remorse for his wrongdoings. They are caused by, in the sense of coming forth from, remorse. However, when the absolution is taken into account, the perspective changes. In conjunction with the acts of the minister of the sacrament, consisting in the absolution, the exterior penance is not only the sign but also the cause of the interior penance.[20]

Similarly, the interior penance can be considered in two ways. As an act of the virtue of penance, the interior penance is cause of the external penance. Take for example the relation between pain and tears. Pain causes tears, and as caused by pain, the tears are sign of the interiorly felt pain. However, when understood as part of the sacrament of penance, including the act of

---

[18]   *In IV Sent* d.22, q.2, a.1, qa.1 co.

[19]   *Idem*, qa.2 and 3.

[20]   *Idem*, qa.2 co: "Exterior poenitentia quae est sacramentum tantum in poenitentia, est sacramentum ut signum tantum ex parte actus poenitentis, sed ut signum et causa simul, si coniungatur actus poenitentis cum actu ministri."

absolution, the interior penance is not cause of the external penance, but its effect and *signatum*[21]

Sacramental causality, or the effectiveness of the sacrament of penance, is crucial to our understanding of why someone must confess his or her mortal sins in order to obtain divine forgiveness. This causality is something of the sacramental sign as including both the acts of the penitent (in particular those that form the exterior penance, namely confession and satisfaction), and the acts of the minister of the sacrament, the absolution.

The acts of the penitent and of the minister of the sacrament relate to each other as (quasi) matter and form. We will examine the meaning of the use of these terms by Thomas below. The matter of the sacrament of penance consists not only in the two acts of confessing and giving satisfaction, but also includes the contrition, which is (part of) the interior penance.

In the *Scriptum*, Thomas seems to teach a doubling of the integral parts of penance. When he distinguishes between the interior penance and the exterior penance, he places all three integral parts in both the interior penance and the exterior penance. In the interior penance, the confession and the satisfaction are present as intentions and premeditations, while contrition can be found in the exterior penance, as visible for others or felt only by the penitent himself.[22]

In the *Summa theologiae*, contrition belongs to the interior penance, and it implies the intentions to confess and give satisfaction (Contrition is not complete, is not true contrition, if it does not include the intention to confess and to compensate for the wrongdoings). The exterior penance, on the other hand, consists of confession and satisfaction alone. Contrition does not belong *realiter* to the exterior penance, as the *Scriptum* appears to suggest, but *virtualiter*, precisely insofar as confession and satisfaction that do belong to the exterior penance are intended in the act of contrition.[23]

---

[21] *Idem*, ad 1: "Ad primum ergo dicendum quod poenitentia interior potest considerari dupliciter. Uno modo prout est quidem actus virtutis. Et sic interior poenitentia est omnino causa exterioris : sicut etiam in aliis virtutibus actus interiores sunt causae exteriorum. Alio modo prout est actus operans ad sanationem peccati. Et sic pertinet ad poenitentiae sacramentum. Et ita interior poenitentia non est causa exterioris, sed effectus vel signatum ipsius. Non enim habet efficaciam operandi contra morbum peccati, nisi ex suppositione propositi exterioris poenitentiae et absolutionis desiderio; quamvis poenitentia interior contra morbum peccati operans praecedat tempore exteriorem poenitentiam; sicut iustificatio a peccato interdum praecedit sacramentum baptismi propter ipsius propositum."

[22] *Idem*, ad 3: "Ad tertium dicendum quod tres partes poenitentiae sunt in poenitentia exteriori et in interiori; quia confessio et satisfactio quae viduntur tantum ad exteriorem poenitentiam pertinere, inveniuntur in interiori poenitentia quantum ad propositum et praemeditationem eorum. Et etiam contritio quae videtur tantum interioris poenitentiae esse, invenitur in poenitentia exteriori secundum quaedam signa quibus sensibiliter manifestatur vel aliis vel saltem ipsi poenitenti qui dolorem sensibilem percipit in seipso."

[23] Cf. *STh* III, q.90, a.2 ob 1: "Videtur quod inconvenienter assignentur partes poenitentiae, contritio, confesio, et satisfactio. Contritio enim est in corde (et sic pertinent ad interiorem poenitentiam); confessio autem in ore, et satisfactio in opere; et sic duo ultima pertinent ad exteriorem poenitentiam. Poenitentia autem interior non est sacramentum, sed sola poenitentia exterior, quae sensui subjcet. Non ergo convenienter assignantur hae partes sacramento poenitentiae." Thomas replies: "Ad primum ergo dicendum, quod contritio

The resulting schema of the structure of the sacrament of penance is as follows:

Structure of the sacrament of penance (*Summa theologiae*)

visible			invisible	
sacramentum tantum			*sacramentum et res*	*res tantum*
	poenitentia exterior		*poenitentia interior*	
forma		*quasi materia*		*remissio peccati*
absolutio	*confessio*	*satisfactio*	*contritio*	

The basic structure of the sacrament of penance consists in the sacrament being a visible (or in any other way sensible) sign that signifies something invisible. In the case of the sacrament of penance, the exterior penance belongs to what is visible, while the interior penance and the forgiveness of sins belong to the invisible realm. The sacramental sign in the sense of sign <u>and</u> cause consists in both what the penitent does, i.e. confessing and giving satisfaction, and what the minister of the sacrament does, i.e. giving absolution. Furthermore, contrition, confession and satisfaction on the one hand, and absolution on the other, relate to each other as matter and form.

As to the causal relationships, the sacrament of penance consisting of form and matter, is sign and cause of the forgiveness of sins. In Chapter Two, we saw that contrition and forgiveness of sins are both requirements of the one *processus iustificationis*. In the case of justification of the godless, the four requirements of the *processus iustificationis* imply each other, in the sense that when one is found, the other three are present as well. The justification of the godless, which happens in an instant, is caused by the infusion of grace, which causes the motion of the will towards God (faith) and, consequently, the motion of the will away from sin (the detestation of sin, or contrition), which in turn causes the forgiveness of sins. In the *Scriptum*, the causal relationship between the latter two can be recognized in an argument *Sed contra*, in which the interior penance is called the 'immediate cause' of the *res sacramenti*, i.e. the forgiveness of sins.[24]

When we look at the schema above, it becomes clear that confession and satisfaction are the external expressions of the internal contrition. Since the sacramental sign, the coming together of the matter and the form, is primarily constituted in the dialogue between the confessing penitent and the absolving

---

secundum essentiam quidem est in corde, et pertinent ad interiorem poenitentiam; virtualiter autem pertinet ad exteriorem poenitentiam, inquantum scilicet implicat propositum confitendi et satisfaciendi." (ad 1) Thomas does not deny that contrition is of the heart, and consequently belongs to the interior penance, and that *confessio oris* and *satisfactio operis* belong to the exterior penance (see also ad 4). However, as the intention to confess and give satisfaction is implied in the contrition, it belongs *virtualiter* to the exterior penance.

[24] *In IV Sent* d.22, q.2, a.1, qa.2 Sc 2: "Illud quod immediate causat effectum sacramenti, est res exterioris sacramenti, sicut patet de charactere. Sed poenitentia interior est quae immediate causat remisionem peccatorum, quae est ultima res huius sacramenti. Ergo, etc." In the next *quaestiuncula* the *res sacramenti* of the sacrament of penance is identified as the forgiveness of sins.

minister, it is clear that in the confession of sins the contrite heart expresses itself, and in this it submits itself to the judgment of God.[25]

According to Thomas, it is fitting that this submission takes place in the form of confession. For in a correct confession what one holds in one's heart is manifested.[26] Confession is a manifestation of sin to a minister in the hope of obtaining mercy, which manifestation results in absolution.[27] It is the expression of the inner penance: contrition, i.e. the will of the penitent to be reconciled with God and the church. This expression of inner penance should happen orally, for this is the most common way in which things of the heart are brought out into the open.[28] Only when this is not possible, for instance because one is a mute or does not speak the same language as the minister of the sacrament, is it possible to work with either a written confession, sign-language or an interpreter.[29]

b. Confession against the background of the relationship of grace

In the previous chapters, we have seen that the divine forgiveness of sins should be seen against the background of the restoration of the relationship of grace, which can best be characterized as a relationship of friendship. The relevance of this insight becomes clear when Thomas distinguishes between the compensation which takes place in the sacrament of penance, and the compensation which takes place in vindictive justice.

In vindictive justice, the compensation takes place according to the judgment of judges, whereas in penance the compensation takes places according to the will of the penitent and of God. In penance, what is at stake is not the mere reintegration of an equality of justice, but rather the reconciliation of a friendship.[30] Therefore, Thomas argues, two things are required for the forgiveness of sins, namely the intention or the act of the will of the penitent

---

25   Cf. *In IV Sent* d.17, q.3, a.5, qa.1 co: "Dicendum ad primam quaestionem quod poenitentia inquantum est sacramentum praecipue in confessione perficitur; quia per eam homo ministris Ecclesiae se subdit, qui sunt sacramentorum dispensatores. Contritio enim votum confessionis annexum habet, et satisfactio pro iudicio sacerdotis cui fit confessio taxatur."

26   *In IV Sent* d.17, q.3, a.2, qa.2 co.

27   *In IV Sent* d.17, q.3, a.2, qa.1 co.

28   *In IV Sent* d.17, q.3, a.4, qa.3 co: "Et sicut in baptismo ad significandam interiorem ablutionem assumitur illud elementum cuius est maximus usus in abluendo; ita in actu sacramentali ad manifestandum ordinate assumitur ille actus quo maxime consuevimus manifestare, scilicet per proprium verbum."

29   *In IV Sent* d.17, q.3, a.4 qa.3 ad 2: "Ad secundum dicendum quod in eo qui usum linguae non habet, sicut nutus, vel qui est alterius linguae, sufficit quod per scriptum aut nutum aut interpretem confiteatur, quia non exigitur ab homine plus quam possit". Thomas adds two more conditions. First, the condition that one should confess to one's own priest. Second, when a priest is absent one can also confess to a layperson (*In IV Sent* d.17, q.3, a.3, qa.2).

30   *STh* III q.90, a.2 co: "Alio modo fit recompensatio offensae in poenitentia, et in vindicativa iustitia. Nam in vindicativa iustitia fit recompensatio secundum arbitrium iudicis, non secundum voluntatem offendentis vel offensi; sed in poenitentia fit recompensatio offensae secundum voluntatem peccantis, et secundum arbitrium Dei, in quem peccatur; quia hic non quaeritur sola reintegratio aequalitatis iustitiae, sicut in iustitia vindicativa, sed magis reconciliatio amicitiae, quod fit dum offendens recompensat secundum voluntatem eius quem offendit".

on the one hand and the judgment of God on the other. With respect to the restoration of justice alone, the will of the penitent does not play such a decisive role. With respect to friendship, however, the will of the penitent is important, even decisive.

As the expression of contrition, confession is characterized by freedom, and not by force. The necessity to confess sins is motivated by what the sacrament of penance aims at, namely the restoration of friendship. It is not conducted by a juridical institution – police officers, interrogators and judges – and it is not aimed at getting the penitent's confession in order to convict him. In that case, a forced confession or other evidence would be as valid for the verdict as a free one. Because a relationship of friendship is at stake, the freedom of the penitent and that he freely wants to be reconciled is eminent. Consequently, the confession itself is more an expression of the free will to be reconciled, than a demand forced by threatening with heavier punishments. The sinner by doing what he does and by saying what he says [in the confession] reveals that his heart is moving away from sin.[31]

c. Why must one confess to a priest?

We will proceed with the question of why one must confess *to a priest*. Thomas understands the causality of the sacrament of penance in immediate relation to the power of the keys. The sacramental power of the sacrament of penance consists, as Thomas explains in the *Scriptum*, completely in the minister of the sacrament. Thomas compares the sacrament of penance with the sacrament of baptism. In the sacrament of baptism, all of the sacramental power (*vis sacramentalis*) resides in the matter, i.e. the water. In the sacrament of penance, however, the sacramental power resides in the minister of the sacrament. Just as in the sacrament of baptism the matter needs to be consecrated or sanctified, so in the sacrament of penance, the minister must be consecrated or sanctified. Consequently, the power of the keys relates to the effect of the sacrament of penance the same way as the water of the baptism relates to the effect of baptism.[32]

This explains why Thomas considers the exterior penance only as sign *and* cause when it is taken in conjunction with the acts of the minister of the sacrament, as we saw above. Since the power of the sacrament of penance

---

[31] *STh* III q.84, a.1 co: "(n)am peccator per ea quae egit et dicit, significit cor suum a peccato recississe."

[32] *In IV Sent* d.18, q.1, a.3, qa.1 co: "Respondeo dicendum ad primam quaestionem, quod sacramenta, secundum Hugonem, ex sanctificatione invisibilem gratiam continent. Sed haec sanctificatio quandoque ad necessitatem sacramenti requiritur tam in materia quam in ministro, sicut patet in confirmatione. Et tunc vis sacramentalis est in utroque coniunctim. Quandoque autem ex necessitate sacramenti non requiritur nisi sanctificatio materiae, sicut est in baptismo, quia non habet ministrum determinatum quantum ad sui necessitatem. Et tunc tota vis sacramentalis consistit in materia. Quandoque vero de necessitate sacramenti requiritur consecratio vel sanctificatio ministri, sine aliqua sanctificatione materiae. Et tunc tota vis sacramentalis consistit in ministro, sicut est in poenitentia. Unde eodem modo se habet potestas clavium quae est in sacerdote, ad effectum sacramenti poenitentiae, sicut se habet virtus quae est in aqua baptismi, ad effectum baptismi."

resides in the minister of the sacrament, who must therefore be consecrated, i.e. must possess the power of the keys, the sacramental sign (i.e. the exterior penance) only becomes 'effective' when it is completed by the absolution.

Consequently, the confession must be made to the one in whom the sacramental power resides, i.e. the one who possesses the power of the keys. For Thomas, the one who possesses the power of the keys is 'by definition' a priest, for "the [priestly] mark and the power to consecrate [bread and wine] and the power of the keys are one and the same in essence, but they differ conceptually".[33]

By virtue of the power of the keys, the priest represents Christ in the sacrament of penance. According to Thomas, Christ as God possesses the power of the keys by authority. As human person He has "opened the gates of heaven" through his passion, and because of that is said to have the power of excellence. The ministers of the Church have the power of ministry.[34] Christ is appointed judge of the living and the dead. The priest, to whom confession is made, represents Christ by virtue of the power of the keys. He takes the place of Christ (vice Christi) in the sacrament of penance.[35]

d. Summary

Summarizing, we can say that particularly in the act of confessing, the penitent expresses his inner remorse. When he does so to a priest, i.e. one who has the power of the keys, in virtue of which he represents Christ in the sacrament of penance, this act of confession obtains the character of a submission to the judgment of God. It is important to notice that this notion of 'submission' may be misleading. Thomas speaks about submission to sin and in that case, 'submission' has the negative ring of being brought under the yoke of sin. In contrast, the submission of the will to God consists not in being brought under a yoke, but in a liberation. The metaphorical justice intended in the divine act of justification consists in the mind becoming oriented towards what is truly and infinitely good, and being freed from unhealthy attachments to temporal and imperfect goods (cf. Ch. 2).

---

[33] *In IV Sent* d.18, q.1, a.1, qa.2 ad 1: "(C)haracter et potestas conficiendi et potestas clavium est unum et idem per essentiam, sed differt ratione." Thomas also makes the connection between being minister of the sacrament of penance and minister of the sacrament of the Eucharist when he explicitly deals with the question of whether or not it is necessary to confess to a priest: "Dicendum ad primam quaestionem quod gratia quae in sacramentis datur, a capite in membra descendit. Et ideo ille solus est minister sacramentorum, in quibus gratia datur, qui habet ministerium super corpus Christi verum; quod solius sacerdotis est qui consecrare eucharistiam potest. Et ideo, cum in sacramento poenitentiae gratia conferatur, solus sacerdos est minister huius sacramenti. Et ideo ei soli facienda est sacramentis confessio quae ministro Ecclesiae fieri debet." (*In IV Sent* d.17, q.3, a.3, qa.1 co)

[34] Cf. *In IV Sent* d.18, q.1, a.1, qa.1 co.

[35] *ScG* IV, c.72: "Oportet igitur ministrum cui fit confessionem iudiciariam potestatem habere vice Christi, qui constitutus est iudex vivorum et mortuorum. Ad iudiciariam autem potestatem duo requiruntur, scilicet auctoritas cognoscendi de culpa et potestas absolvendi vel condemnandi. Et haec duo dicuntur duae claves Ecclesiae, scilicet scientia discernendi et potentia ligandi et solvendi, quas Dominus Petro commisit, iuxta illud : « Tibi dabo claves regni caelorum » (Mt. 18, 19)."

The purpose of confession (2): manifestation of the wound of the heart.

The second purpose of confessing one's sins is the manifestation of the wound of the heart in order for the minister of the sacrament to know which medicine he must apply.

In Chapter Two, we saw that in the *Summa contra gentiles* Thomas distinguishes between different detriments (*detrimenta*) that are to be healed in the sacrament of penance: the disorientation of the will (*deordinatio mentis*), the punishable state (*reatum poenae*) and the weakening of the natural good (*debilitatio naturalis boni*).[36]

The submission of the will to the keys of the Church concerns primarily the disorientation of the will. The reorientation of the will to God is presupposed for the further healing of the remaining detriments. We saw that Thomas acknowledges the possibility that the contrition is expressed in confession so vehemently that there is no need for a further healing of the wounds of the heart (the *debilitatio boni*). Normally, however, there remains an obligation to undergo a temporal punishment.

According to Thomas in the *Summa contra gentiles*, the minister of the sacrament of penance has the authority to investigate the sin and to establish what punishments remain, and he has the power to absolve from further punishment. Some of the temporal punishment is remitted when the penitent receives the absolution. For the rest, there remains the fulfillment of the obligation to undergo punishments, which is called satisfaction.[37]

When Thomas reflects on the definitions of satisfaction in the *Scriptum*, he explains that giving satisfaction has two objectives. First, to compensate for past sins, and second to prevent future sins: "satisfaction [..] is a medicine that cures past sins and preserves against future ones".[38] The three traditional works of satisfaction are prayer, fasting and almsgiving.[39]

---

[36] *Ibidem.*

[37] *Ibidem.* "Quia igitur etiam in ipsa confessione et absolutione plenior effectus gratiae et remissionis confertur ei qui prius propter bonum propositum utrumque obtinuit, manifestum ets quod, virtute clavium, minister Ecclesiae, absolvendo, aliquid de poena temporali dimittit, cuius debitor remansit poenitens post contritionem ; ad residuum vero sua iniunctione obligat poenitentem; cuius quidem obligationis impletio satisfactio dicitur, quae est tertia poenitentiae pars."

[38] Cf. *In IV Sent* d.15, q.1, a.1, qa.3 co: "Ad tertium quaestionem dicendum quod iustitia non ad hoc tendit ut inaequalitem praecedentem auferat puniendo culpam praeteritam, sed ut in futurum aequalitatem custodiat; quia secundum philosophum in II Eth. "poenae medicinae sunt". Unde et satisfactio quae est iustitiae actus poenam inferentis, est medicina, curans peccata praeterita et praeservans a futuris. Et ideo quando homo homini satisfacit, et praeterita recompensat et de futuris cavet."

[39] Cf. *ScG* IV, c.72: "(..) per quam [i.e. per satisfactionem] homo totaliter a reatu poenae liberatur, dum poenam exsolvit quam debuit, et ulterius debilitas naturalis boni curatur, dum homo malis abstinet et bonis assuescit, Deo spiritum subiiciendo per oratorium, carnem vero domando per ieiunium, ut sit subiecta spiritui, et rebus exterioribus per eleemosynarum largitionem proximos sibi adiungendo, a quibus fuit separatus per culpam."

Conclusion

In Chapter Two, we have seen that the metaphorical justice that is intended in justification consists in both the submission of reason to God and the submission of the lower parts of the soul to reason. Our examinations have shown that confession comprises both. First, in the act of confession the penitent submits himself to God, represented by the minister of the sacrament of penance by virtue of the power of the keys. Through this act of submission, which is in fact an act of liberation from being subjected to sin, the reorientation of the will away from sin towards God receives its sacramental expression. Second, confessing one's venial and mortal sins enables the minister of the sacrament to investigate which exercises must be prescribed, in order to bring the lower parts of the soul under the rule of reason.

With respect to the necessity of the sacrament of penance, we have seen that a major role is granted to the power of the keys, the *potestas clavium*. The double nature of the power of the keys corresponds with the twofold purpose of confession. The power of the keys is the 'key-term', which in Thomas' theology links the sacrament of penance to the passion of Christ. Confession of sins is necessary insofar as it refers to Christ. Confession has to be made to a priest because only the priest has, by virtue of the power of the keys, the power to forgive in Christ's name.

We will investigate Thomas' notion of sacramental causality below, and see how Thomas understands the relation between Christ's passion and the sacrament of penance. We will explain that in Thomas' theology the necessity of the sacrament of penance has, in the final analysis, its basis in the necessity of Christ's passion for our salvation.[40]

2　The effective signification of the sacraments

In the remainder of this chapter, we will deal with sacramental causality. One of the reasons for this is that throughout his theology of the sacrament of penance, Thomas emphasizes repeatedly that the sacrament of penance is one of the sacraments of the new covenant. He does so in order to safeguard the teaching that the sacrament of penance effects what it signifies. 'Cause' is the dominant notion in Thomas' theology of the sacraments, with which he describes how the sacraments effect what they signify. Sacraments cause grace, produce grace, contain grace, and confer grace. The sacrament of penance causes grace.[41] Such use of the notion of cause to describe how sacraments

---

[40]　Cf. *In IV Sent* d.17, q.3, a.1, qa.1 co.

[41]　*STh* III q.86, pro: "Deinde considerandum est de effectu poenitentiae: et primo quantum ad remissionem peccatorum mortalium: secundo quantum ad remissionem peccatorum venialium: tertio quantum ad reditum peccatorum dimissorum: quarto quantum ad restitutionem virtutum." *STh* III q.62, a.1 co: "Respondeo dicendum quod necesse est dicere sacramenta novae legis per aliquem modum gratiam causare." Note that in two respects Thomas is careful in how he formulates his answer. He does not simply say "sacramenta novae legis gratiam causant". Instead he draws attention to what we must say (cf. *necesse est dicere*). And with respect to the 'how' of sacramental causality Thomas remains vague (cf. *per aliquem modum*).

effect what they signify risks the danger of reifying grace, of making the sacraments into technical means, manufactories of grace, things in themselves.[42] In the second and third chapter, we have shown the relational and linguistic[43] character of Thomas' theology of the forgiveness of sins, and of the Holy Trinity. In this chapter, we will examine Thomas' notion of sacramental causality, and see whether or not it leads to a reification of grace, and of the sacrament itself.

In this section, we will proceed by examining the linguistic character of Thomas' notion of sacrament.[44] First, we will see how Thomas deals with the question of how signification and causality are related in the sacraments. Next, we will make an analysis of the sacramental sign with the help of the notions of things (*res*) and words (*verba*). Finally, we will see what it means to say that the things and words in the sacraments relate to each other as matter and form.

Sign and cause

How does Thomas define the sacraments? In the *Summa theologiae*[45], Thomas defines sacraments as "signs of something sacred (*res sacrae*) in as far as this *res sacrae* sanctifies men".[46] This definition encompasses both the sacraments of the old and of the new covenant, i.e. both the Old Testament sacraments, such as circumcision, and the seven sacraments of the Church that are recognized in

---

[42] L.-M. Chauvet speaks of a "productionist scheme of representation". He questions the usefulness of the category of causality in thinking theologically about the sacramental relationship, as it tends to reify grace. According to Chauvet, the reason why Scholastics like Thomas chose such an inadequate category is that they "were unable to think otherwise; they were prevented from doing so by the onto-theological presuppositions which structured their entire culture." (*Symbol and sacrament. A sacramental reinterpretation of Christian existence*, 1995, p.8) At the same time, Chauvet acknowledges that great thinkers like Thomas "have continually attempted to overcome these inherent conceptual constraints." "For Thomas, the very notion of *esse* ('being') plays a critical role as a corrective to any reductive portrait of God to the extent that this *esse*, uncircumscribed or without limit, is not included in any 'genus'." But Chauvet holds it against Thomas that he did not take this disparity as a point of departure and as a framework for his thought.
It goes beyond the scope of this dissertation to evaluate Thomas' approach in the light of the symbolic approach Chauvet proposes. But his remarks may serve as a warning, and may help us to critically examine Thomas' theology of the sacraments.
[43] Previous studies by the Thomas Instituut at Utrecht have shown the linguistic character of Thomas' christology (H. Schoot, *Christ the 'name' of God. Thomas Aquinas on naming Christ*, 1993) and of his theology in general (H. Goris et al. *Free creatures of an eternal God. Thomas Aquinas on God's infallible foreknowledge and irresistible will*, 1996).
[44] E. Schillebeeckx in particular has shown how linguistic Thomas' approach to the sacraments is (*De Sacramentele heilseconomie*, 1952; *Christus Sacrament van de Godsontmoeting*, 1959³).
[45] For a general introduction to the Treatise on the Sacraments in the *Summa theologiae*, cf. K. Rahner, "Einleitende Bemerkungen zur allgemeine Sakramentenlehre bei Thomas von Aquin", in *Schriften zur theologie* X, 1972, pp.392-404.
[46] *STh* III q.60, a.2 co: "Respondeo dicendum quod signa dantur hominibus, quorum est per nota ad ignota pervenire. Et ideo proprie dicitur sacramentum quod est signum alicuius rei sacrae ad homines pertinentis, ut scilicet proprie dicatur sacramentum, secundum quod nunc de sacramentis loquimur, quod est signum rei sacrae inquantum est sanctificans homines."

Thomas' times and today, including the sacrament of penance. Moreover, this definition encompasses the natural sacraments as well.[47]

One of the difficulties theologians had to overcome was that of how to reconcile such different categories as sign (*signum*) and cause (*causa*). On the one hand, the sacrament is a sign, while on the other hand it is cause of what it signifies. Above, we saw that the sacrament of penance not only signifies the interior penance but, in combination with the absolution (the exterior penance), is simultaneously the cause of the interior penance as well. Depending on one's point of view, either contrition is the cause of the confession, and consequently the sacramental confession is the sign of its cause, i.e. contrition, or the confession in combination with absolution is the cause of the contrition.

In his earlier work, the *Scriptum*, Thomas places the sacraments in the genera of both sign and cause.[48] Of these genera, Thomas emphasizes the notion of cause. By doing so, Thomas was following the theologians of the twelfth century. Since Peter Lombard, the notion of efficacy had received the main accent: sacraments are primarily means for sanctification. They are, in the first place, means of grace. Consequently, in the *Scriptum* the causality is more important than the *significatio*, which is a *modus sanctificandi*. In the first distinction of the treatise of the sacrament of penance, we see that sacraments are defined in terms of active sanctification.[49]

According to this definition of sacrament in the *Scriptum*, the mystery of Christ is *sacramentum*, since the *passio Christi* is the fundamental cause of salvation.[50] Furthermore, the seven sacraments of the new covenant are called sacraments proper, in that *sacramentum* means both the sanctification and the *modus sanctificandi*, namely *per modum signi*.[51] However, when the sacraments of the old covenant are called *sacramentum*, only the signification of the cause of grace is

---

[47] For this reason, Schillebeeckx calls the definition of sacraments in the *Summa theologiae* a univocal definition (*diffinitio univoca*; cf. *Sacramentele heilseconomie*, p.135). For a list of the principal definitions of *sacramentum* in the Middle Ages see L.-M. Chauvet, *Symbol and sacrament*, footnote 4 on pp.12-14.

[48] *In IV Sent* d.1, q.1, a.1, qa.5 ad 1: "Ad primum ergo dicendum quod sicut formae artificiales sunt accidentales, - in artificialibus tota substantia est materia, et propter hoc praedicatur, ut dicatur *Phiala est aurum* – ita etiam cum sacramenti forma non det esse substantiale, sed accidentiale in genere causae et signi, non est inconveniens ut materia sacramenti de ipso praedicetur et in eius definitione sicut genus ponatur; hoc enim etiam in aliis accidentibus contingit, ut dicitur in VII Meta, ut cum dicitur *Simum est nasus curus*." Cf. E. Schillebeeckx, *Sacramentele heilseconomie*, p.127.

[49] "Sacramentum importat sanctitatem active per modum qui nobis sanctificandis competit, ut scilicet adiungatur significatio sanctificationis invisibilis pervisibilia signa." (*In IV Sent* d.14, q.1, a.1 co)

[50] Cf. *In IV Sent* d.1, q.1, a.1, qa.1 co: "Aliquando enim sacramentum importat rem qua fit consecratio. Et sic passio Christi dicitur sacramentum." Cf. E. Schillebeeckx, *Sacramentele heilseconomie*, p.126.

[51] *Ibidem*. "Aliquando vero includit modum consecrationis qui homini competit secundum quod causae sanctificantes et sua sanctificatio per similitudines sensibilium sibi notificantur. Et sic sacramenta novae legis sacramenta dicitur, quia et consecrant, et sanctitatem significant modo praedicto et etiam primas sanctificationis causas, sicut baptismus sanctificat et puritatem designat, et mortis Christi signum est."

meant.[52] Since *sacramentum* is, in the first place, what causes *sanctitas*, the sacraments of the old covenant, which only signify *sanctitas* (i.e. Christ's passion), are thus only called *sacramentum secundum quid*. *Simpliciter*, a sacrament is what causes sanctity.[53]

Between *Scriptum* and *Summa theologiae*, a shift occurs. Sacrament is no longer placed in both the genus of sign and of cause, but is placed only in the genus of sign.[54] The principle of unity with which the two categories of sign and cause are held together is no longer the notion of cause, but instead the notion of sign.[55]

This shift between *Scriptum* and *Summa* has consequences of considerable importance, as Chauvet notices: "Defined as signs, the sacraments bring about only what they signify, and that according to the manner in which it is signified."[56] The notion of causality is thus completely dependent on the notion of sacramental signification. "The 'sign' (*signum*), as it is presented by the celebrating Church, is the *very mediation* of the gift of grace. The whole problem consisted in *harmonizing two categories as completely foreign to one another as are 'sign' and 'cause'*, and doing so in such a way that the type of sign under examination would have these unique traits: it would *indicate what it is causing* and it would *have no other way of causing except by the mode of signification.*"[57]

The resulting notion of sacramental causality is one completely dependent on sacramental signification. Sacraments not only effect what they signify, but they effect through signifying. What they cause and how they cause it are determined by what they signify and the mode of signification.

---

52 *Ibidem*. "Aliquando autem, includit tantum signifactionem praedictarum consecrationum: sicut signum sanitatis dicitur sanum. Et hoc modo sacramenta veteris legis sacramenta dicuntur, inquantum significant ea quae in Christo sunt gesta, et etiam sacramenta novae legis."

53 Cf. *In IV Sent* d.1, q.1, a.1, qa.3 ad 5: "Sacramentum autem simpliciter est quod causat sanctitatem. Quod autem significat tantum, non est sacramentum nisi secundum quid."

54 *STh* III q.60, a.1: "(S)pecialiter autem nunc loquimur de sacramentis, secundum quod important habitudinem signi, et secundum hoc sacramentum ponitur in genere signi."

55 In both the *Scriptum* and the *Summa* Thomas uses the instrument of analogy to order the different notions of *sacramentum*, however differently. In the *Scriptum*, the distinction between the sacraments of the old and the new covenant is not a distinction between species of a genus, but a distinction between analogates (*In IV Sent* d.1, q.1, a.1, qa.3 ad 5: "Ad quintum dicendum quod sacramentum non dividitur per sacramentum veteris et novae legis sicut genus per species, sed sicut analogum in suas partes, ut sanum in habens sanitatem et significans eam." (Cf. *Sacramentele heilseconomie*, p.129)). In the *Scriptum*, the Jewish sacraments are called *sacramentum secundum quid*, as compared to the sacraments of the new covenant. In the *Summa theologiae*, both Christian and Jewish sacraments are called *sacramentum* properly, and other notions of sacramentum (*sacramentum secretum sacrum*, *sacramentum iuramentum* and *sacramentum causa sanctitatis*) are called *sacramentum* analogically. Thomas wants to reserve the proper sense of the term *sacramentum* for the 'cultual symbols of salvation' ("cultuele heilssymbolen") as distinguished from sacraments in the sense of mysteries of faith (Cf. *STh* III q.60, a.1 co: "Specialiter autem nunc loquimur de sacramentis, secundum quod important habitudinem signi, etc"). The most perfect notion of sacrament is held by the sacraments of the new covenant, which effect what they signify, as they are related to what is sacred both *per modum signi* and *per modum causae* (*STh* III q.62, a.1 ad 1).

56 L.-M. Chauvet, *Symbol and sacrament*, p.15.

57 *Idem*, p.17-18, it. Chauvet.

Res et verba

We proceed by examining the structure of the sacramental sign.[58] Above, we have seen that the sacrament of penance is composed of the acts of the penitent, and of the minister of the sacrament, which relate to each as matter and form.[59] In order to discover the meaning of the pair of concepts of matter and form in the treatise of the sacrament of penance in the *Summa theologiae* we have to turn to the treatise on the sacraments in general.[60]

It is not the framework of form and matter, which dominates the treatise on the sacrament of penance, but instead the framework of '*res et verba*' dominates the treatise on the sacraments in general. It is not until the end of the question on the *quiddity* of the sacraments, when confronted with the objection that adding words would threaten the unity of the sacramental sign, that Thomas introduces the notions of form and matter.[61] Before we deal with form and matter, we will first have to examine how this basic framework of things and words constitutes the sacramental sign in general.

The point of departure of Thomas' reflections on the framework of things and words is a quotation from Augustine, "the word is added to the element, and the sacrament is made".[62] Thomas quotes this remark of Augustine twice in *STh* IIIa q.60. Both times, he quotes it in the *Sed contra* argument.[63] The first time, the emphasis is on *elementum*, while the second time it is on *verbum*.

---

[58] Thomas' reflections on the sacramental sign may seem rather deductive. However, Schillebeeckx emphasizes that Thomas reflects on the liturgical practice of the church of his time, in order to develop some basic insights by reduction: "From the actual, liturgical structure of the sacraments – which most of the time he only mentions briefly in the Sed contra – he wants through reflection to develop a deeper intelligibility, since everything God does wisely and is thus an "opus ordinatum", of which human reflection, illumined by faith and tradition, may moderately recover to some extent the inner structure." (*Sacramentele heilseconomie*, p.375; transl. EL).

[59] Cf. *STh* III q.84, a.2 ad 2: "In illis sacramentis, quae habet effectum correspondentem humanis actibus, ipsi actus humani sensibiles sunt loco materiae"; a.3 co: "Unde oportet, quod ea quae sunt ex parte poenitentis, sive sint verba, sive facta, sint quaedam materia huius sacramenti; ea vero quae sunt ex parte sacerdotis, se habeant per modum formae."

[60] Cf. *STh* III q.60, aa.4.5.6.7.

[61] *STh* III q.60, a.6 ad 2: "Ad secundum dicendum, quod quamvis et verba, et aliae sensibiles sint in diverso genere, quantum pertinet ad naturam rei; conveniunt tamen in ratione significandi, quae perfectius est in verbis, quam in aliis rebus; et ideo ex verbis, et rebus fit quoddammodo unum in sacramentis, sicut ex forma et materia; in quantum scilicet per verba perficitur significatio rerum, ut dictum est. Sub rebus autem comprehenduntur etiam ipsi actus sensibiles; puta ablutio, iniunctio, et alia huiusmodi: quia in his est eadem ratio significandi, et in rebus."

[62] 'Accedit verbum ad elementum, et fit sacramentum'. Augustine says this with respect to (the sacrament of) baptism, when commenting on Jn. 15,3: "Detrahe uerbum, et quid est aqua nisi aqua? Accedit uerbum etc." *Tract. in Ioh* LXXX,3 (*CCL* 36, p.529).

[63] *STh* III q.60, a.4 Sc; a.6 Sc. Most of the time the *Sed contra*-argument shows what is at stake or which *auctoritas* is to be interpreted. From the fact that Augustine's line is quoted here, we can derive that this text forms the point of departure for Thomas when he examines the basic structure of the sacraments. The first time it is quoted when he asks the question why something or some event that is perceptible by the senses is necessary in a sacrament, the second time when he asks the question why there are words required for the sacramental

First, Thomas reflects on the fact that all sacraments are composed of sensible things. He determines that it is connatural for human persons to acquire knowledge of the intelligible and spiritual through sensible things. God, who is wise, chooses to give his grace in a way which corresponds to this human constitution.[64] Therefore, sacramental signs, which are given to lead human persons to the sacred things, consist of something sensible.[65] Furthermore, the sensible signs are not passing means, in the sense that after having used them one reaches a 'moment' in which one is present in the spiritual realm, while the sensible sign is absent: as if they are ladders that can be thrown away once the spiritual realm is reached. Sacraments may cease to have their use *in patria*, but in this life, sensible signs are the mode in which humans dwell in the spiritual realm. "The ontological situation of man as spirit-in-the world is not annulled by grace."[66] The sensible sign is the modus in which humans as spirit-in-the-world relate to the spiritual. And in both directions. The sensible sign is both the way humans express their own inner spiritual beings and the way they are brought into the spiritual being of others, of God.

In the next article, Thomas explicitly distinguishes between these two uses of sacraments. They are first expressions of faith, and as such they belong to the divine cult. However, sacraments are also God's signs given to man, as means for his sanctification. In the latter case, the initiative is God's. This makes it highly congruent that the initiative for the determination of the sign through which the sanctification takes place is placed with God.[67]

Chauvet connects this double functionality of the sacraments with the two places in the *Summa* where Thomas pays attention to the sacraments. In the *Secunda secundae pars* of the *Summa*, in the questions concerning the virtue of religion, Thomas primarily sees the sacraments as part of the movement of exterior worship, ascending through Christ to God. With this movement, a

---

signification. The basis for the answer to both questions is formed by the citation of Augustine.

[64] *STh* III q.60 a.4 co "Respondeo dicendum quod sapientia divina unicuique rei providet secundum suum modum"

[65] Note, that it is nevertheless possible that something not sensible is called 'sacrament'. The act of repentance in the human soul can be called 'sacrament' of the remission given by God. However, this is only the case when the act of repentance itself is signified by something sensible, for instance a visible and audible confession, which for its part is sacrament itself of the internal act of repentance (*STh* III q.60 a.4 ad 1; q.84 a.1 ad 3). In that case we have a doubling of the *sacramentum – res sacramenti* -relationship. The confession is sacrament alone (*sacramentum tantum*) of the repentance, which is *res et sacramentum*. The forgiveness of sins *res tantum*.

[66] *Sacramentele heilseconomie*, p.376.

[67] *STh* III q.60 a.5 co: "quia ergo sanctificatio hominis est in potestate Dei sanctificantis, non pertinet ad hominem suo judicio assumere res, quibus sanctificetur; sed hoc debet esse ex divina institutione determinatum." Cf. *Sacramentele heilseconomie*, p.376-377. Schillebeeckx adds that, because Thomas did not have at his disposal the historical information we possess in our days, he took the view that God himself determines the exterior appearance of the matter of the sacraments.

second movement corresponds, descending from God through Christ toward humankind. This movement is one of justification and sanctification.[68]

Second, the sensible thing or event, which functions as *materia sacramenti*, is not able to signify the sanctification without words that accompany it. For this, Thomas gives three "suggestions for intelligibility", which he finds in the original sacrament (Christ), the human nature and finally the sacramental signification itself.[69]

Thomas finds the first suggestion, Christ, in the incarnate Word, who is the cause of the sanctification. Thomas draws a parallel between the sacraments, in which words are added to sensible things, and the mystery of the incarnation in which the Word of God is united with the sensible flesh.[70] As the divine Word was incarnate in external sensible appearance, so the word of faith is incarnated in the liturgical act of celebrating a sacrament.[71]

The second suggestion, Thomas derives from the structure of the human nature. As man is constituted of body and soul, so the sacramental sign must consist of something physical and something spiritual. As such, the sacrament is, as a medicine, proportioned to the human constitution: the visible element touches the body and its word is believed by the soul. Subsequently, Thomas cites Augustine commenting on John 15,3 "You are clean already, by means of the word that I have spoken to you": "From where is all this power of the water, that it touches the body and washes the heart, if not from the word, not because it is said, but because it is believed."[72] Schillebeeckx concludes: "The words (..) are thus a 'verbum fidei', the verbal expression of faith".[73] We will go

---

[68]   *Symbol and sacrament*, p.10. Chauvet adds: "One may regret that Thomas insufficiently emphasizes, in the treatise contained in the Third Part of the Summa, the ascendant and ethical aspects of the sacraments touched upon in the questions relating to the 'exterior' acts of the virtue of religion. This would have allowed him to achieve a better balance in a presentation which, stressing as it does the role of the sacraments in the sanctification of human beings, is too heavily weighted in favor of the 'Christological-descending' aspect." (p.11).

[69]   *STh* III q.60, a.6. Schillebeeckx remarks "The fact St. Thomas observes in the praxis of the liturgy of the church, i.e. that the liturgical acts are accompanied by words, he attempts to make intelligible by making a connection between this praxis, the original sacrament (Christ), the human nature and finally the sacramental signification itself. Here, no deduction, but reduction through insight in the connection between a fact of tradition with another, or with a dogmatically determined fact of faith." (*Sacramentele heilseconomie*, p.378)

[70]   *STh* III q.60, a.6 co: "(P)rimo considerari ex parte causae sanctificantis, quae est Verbum incarnatum; cui sacramentum quodammodo conformatur in hoc, quod rei sensibili verbum adhibetur; sicut in mysterio incarnationis carni sensibili est Verbum Dei unitum".

[71]   Schillebeeckx identifies sacraments as extensions or prolongations of the Incarnation and calls them 'verba incarnata'. (*Sacramentele heilseconomie*, p.380). Cf. also *Symbol and sacrament*, p.21.

[72]   *STh* III q.60, a.6 co: "Secundo possint considerari ex parte hominis, qui sanctificatur, qui componitur ex anima, et corpore, cui proportionatur sacramentalis medicina, quae per rem visibilem corpus tangit, et per verbum ab anima creditur; unde Augustinus super illud Joan. 15,3 'Iam vos mundi estis propter sermonem etc' dicit 'Unde est ista tanta virtus aquae, ut corpus tangat, et cor abluat, nisi faciente verbo, non quia dicitur, sed quia creditur?'".

[73]   *Sacramentele heilseconomie*, p.379.

deeper into the relationship of sacraments and faith below, but here we already get a first glance of the role faith plays in Thomas' theology of the sacraments. The third suggestion Thomas finds in the sacramental signification itself. He says that the signification of the sensible sign alone, for instance the sacramental sign of baptism, expresses the inner meaning in a meaningful way, though ambiguously. Without words accompanying the pouring of the water, it could be taken to mean a spiritual refreshment as well as a spiritual cleansing. Thus, the words "Ego te baptismo" are added in order to determine the signification of the baptism "ad unum determinatum", because words express what the mind holds more distinctly.[74]

In fact, it is the intention of the minister as expressed in the act and in the words that specifies whether or not the pouring of the water that takes place in the sacrament of baptism is meant as a spiritual cleansing or as a refreshment. This appears from the question about the intention of the minister in Thomas' treatment of the sacraments in general. In this question, the same argument returns that Thomas uses when he speaks about the necessity of words in that sacramental signification. Whether a spiritual cleansing is meant or not is determined by the intention of the one who pours the water. This intention is expressed when he utters the words "I baptize you in the name of the Father, the Son and the Holy Spirit".[75] The verbal and sensible parts of the sacrament together form the sacramental sign, and must be understood accordingly.

Matter and form

In the treatise on the sacrament of penance in the *Summa theologiae*, the pair of concepts of *forma et materia* has replaced the notions *res et verba*. Thomas introduces form and matter at the end of the first *quaestio* on the sacraments in general. Why is that, and what is the meaning of these Aristotelian notions in the context of Thomas' theology of the sacraments?

When Thomas uses form and matter to denote the composing elements of the sacraments, he does not mean to describe the 'physical' constitution of the sacraments. Sacraments are not composed of matter and form in the way things in nature are composed of matter and form. In fact, Thomas nowhere says that sacraments are composed of matter and form. He merely says that the things and words in the sacraments relate to each other as matter and form.

Using matter and form to describe something like the physical constitution of sacraments would imply a reification of the sacraments. As a result, sacraments would no longer be understood to be part of the realm of (symbolic) language, but as part of the realm of physics, and as 'things'. Sacraments would then be understood as medicines in the physical sense of the word. Medicines such as

74 *STh* III q.60, a.6 co: "(P)er verba magis distincte possumus exprimere, quod mente concepimus. Et ideo ad perfectionem significationis sacramentalis necesse fuit, ut significatio rerum sensibilium per aliqua verba determinaretur. Aqua enim significare potest et ablutionem propter suam humiditatem, et refrigerium propter suam frigiditatem. Sed cum dicitur: *Ego te baptismo*, manifestatur quod aqua utimur in baptismo ad significandam emundationem spiritualem."
75 *STh* III q.64, a.8 co.

pills or potions are not part of a communication or dialogue between patient and doctor. Pills and potions do their work regardless of the patient's relationship to the doctor. When sacraments are understood to work in such a way they become part of the world of magic[76], as they seem to be effective regardless of the will of the one receiving the sacrament and regardless of the freedom of God. Instead, sacraments are not part of magic but are part of the language with which God and man communicate, and must be understood accordingly.

Thomas does not use the notions of form and matter to describe the physical structure of the sacraments. Instead, he uses them analogously to explain the unity of the sacramental sign. Thomas introduces the pair of concepts in his treatment of the sacraments in general when he replies to an objection concerning the unity of the sacrament. When sacraments are composed of things and words, which are species of different genera, the unity of the sacrament seems to be threatened.

In his reply, Thomas explains first that words and things may be species of different genera with regard to their nature, but as they both work together in the sacramental signification they convene in the same *ratio significandi*. Subsequently, Thomas determines the relationship between word and thing as a relationship of form and matter. Just as the form is the perfection or completion of the matter, so the words make perfect the signification of the things.[77]

The analogy Thomas sees between sacraments, the incarnation and the human structure of body and soul, implies as it were that the relationship between things and words can be compared with the relationship between matter and form. The notions of matter and form enable Thomas to explain not only the unity of the sacramental signification, but also the different contributions of the sensible thing on the one hand and of the words on the other. Because form has the Aristotelian connotation of "making perfect", it helps to put into words how the words in the sacraments complete the signification, by reducing its original ambiguity to one meaning.[78] Moreover, the words emphasize the fact

---

[76] Magic is used here in the 'modern' sense of what is aimed at *coercing* God or divine forces. Cf. the different definitions of 'magic', esp. the difference between the medieval definition and the 'modern' definition of magic, in R. Kieckhefer, *Magic in the Middle Ages*, 1989, pp.8-17.

[77] *STh* III q.60, a.6 ad 2: "(E)x verbis, et rebus fit quoddammodo unum in sacramentis, sicut ex forma, et materia; inquantum scilicet per verba perficitur significatio rerum, ut dictum est.".

[78] *STh* III q.60, a.7 co: "Respondeo dicendum quod, sicut dictum est, in sacramentis verba se habent per modum formae, res autem sensibiles per modum materiae. In omnibus autem compositis ex materia et forma principium determinationis est ex parte formae, quae est quodammodo finis et terminus materiae. Et ideo principalius requiritur ad esse rei determinata forma quam determinata materia, materia enim determinata quaeritur ut sit proportionata determinatae formae. Cum igitur in sacramentis requirantur determinatae res sensibiles, quae se habent in sacramentis sicut materia, multo magis requiritur in eis determinata forma verborum."

that a sacrament signifies something beyond what it is capable of signifying naturally.[79]

Though Thomas plays an important role in the introduction of the Aristotelian concepts of form and matter in the doctrine of the sacraments, he is not the first theologian to speak about form and matter in the context of the sacraments. At first, however, these concepts were used apart from the Aristotelian hylemorphism. It is only from the second half of the thirteenth century that the use of 'materia' and 'forma verborum' receives its hylemorphistic ring, especially for the *aristotelici* of that age.[80]

Later on in the history of theology, the use of the pair of concepts of matter and form will lead to a metaphysics of the sacraments that Thomas never expressed or intended. He was just looking for a way to make it understandable that the composition of words and things in the signification of the sacraments does not harm the unity of the sacramental signification. For this he used the terms 'form' and 'matter', analogously to the Aristotelian hylemorphism. "Saint Thomas understands the 'verbum' and 'elementum', the word of faith and the liturgical act, more as complementary externalizations of one and the same sacramental intention or meaning. Speaking of form and matter outside of the signification or previous to the constitution of the formally sacramental sign-value, places one outside the Thomistic context. Matter and form make sense only in the context of the signification."[81]

Conclusion

In this section, we set out to show that Thomas understands sacramental causality within the context of signification. Despite the fact that he uses words that have a productionist ring, like 'cause', 'effect', 'produce' etc, it has become clear that this does not result in reification of sacrament or of grace. Nor does the introduction of the terms 'form' and 'matter' intend to describe the physical constitution of the sacraments. A sacrament is a sign, a means of

---

[79] Cf. *Sacramentele heilseconomie*, p.379: "Without the verbal expression of the sacramental intention it would not be sufficiently clear whether we are dealing with a (religious) natural symbol, or with a symbol that refers to something beyond what it is capable of signifying by its own nature." (transl. EL)

[80] *Idem*, pp. 368-373. According to Schillebeeckx, the Fathers of the Church already spoke of 'forma sacramenti', but then it simply meant the external prescribed ritual, as opposite to the 'virtus sacramenti'. As such it consisted of both the scholastic *materia* and *forma*. Both Hugo of St.Victor and Peter Lombard use *forma* in both senses, so that the context will decide whether the *forma sacramenti* of the *forma verborum* is meant. Similarly, the term 'matter' is used in the early Church as well (for instance Tertullian). When Hugo of St.Victor in the sixth Chapter of *De Sacramentis* speaks or 'materia sacramenti', not only the 'res et facta' but also the 'dicta' are meant. (cf. pp. 368-9).

[81] *Sacramentele heilseconomie*, p. 381 (Transl. EL). Cf. M. Brinkman, *Schepping en sacrament. Een oecumenische studie naar de reikwijdte van het sacrament als heilzaam symbool in een weerbarstige werkelijkheid*, 1991, pp.112-113: "Door zo nadrukkelijk het significatio-aspect bij Thomas te beklemtonen haalt Schillebeeckx de discussie omtrent de exacte aard van het sacrament uit de sfeer van de tegenstelling tussen sacramentsobjectivisme en sacramentssubjectivisme en benadrukt het gemeenschapstichtende tekenkarakter, waarin het hemelse en aardse elkaar met het oog op het heil van de mens (propter homines) ontmoeten."

communication between God and man. In this sign, both the things (gestures) and words contribute to the one sacramental signification. With respect to the unity of the sacramental sign, the things and words can be understood to be related to each other as matter and form.

Nevertheless, as signs they are not without effect in the one for whom the sign is meant. When God communicates with man through the sacraments, this communication brings about something; in the case of the sacrament of penance, what the sacrament brings about is the grace of conversion, a change of heart and forgiveness of sins.

3 The sacrament of penance

The penitent's act of confessing and the priest's act of absolving constitute the sign under which the purification of sin in the sacrament of penance takes place. According to Thomas, the acts of the penitent and the acts of the priest are the things and words of the sacrament of penance, which relate to each other as matter and form.[82] In this section, we will proceed by examining the matter and form of the sacrament of penance.

Materia sacramenti poenitentiae

The penitent contributes to the sacramental sign by three acts (contrition, confession and satisfaction), which together form the matter of the sacrament of penance. With respect to this, we will make four remarks.

First, according to Thomas, all three acts together are needed in order to constitute the matter of the sacrament of penance. This is why they are called the 'integral' parts of the sacrament of penance.[83] We have already seen that the act of contrition is decisive with respect to obtaining divine forgiveness. Contrition is the act which links the sacrament of penance with the justification of the godless. However, we have also seen that contrition is not perfect when it does not include the intention to confess and to give satisfaction.[84] So the other two parts of the sacrament of penance are already integrated in the act of contrition. Furthermore, we have seen that the inner contrition receives its sacramental expression primarily in the act of confessing to a priest. Nevertheless, the integrity of what the penitent contributes is not complete if it does not include making compensation for the sin by giving satisfaction.

Second, the fact that the acts of the penitent take the place of the matter in the sacrament of penance[85] forced Thomas to broaden the notion of *materia sacramenti*. The sensible elements in the three exemplary sacraments, baptism, confirmation and Eucharist, consist of something corporeal: water, chrism, bread and wine. However, in the sacrament of penance, there is not something corporeal. So in order to fit the sacrament of penance into the structure he had

---

[82] *STh* III q.84, a.2; a.3.
[83] *STh* III q.90, a.3; cf. *In IV Sent* d.16, q.1, a.1, qa.3.
[84] Cf. *In IV Sent* d.17, q.2, a.1 ob 1 and co; *STh* III q.90, a.2 ad 1 (cf. footnote 23).
[85] Cf. *STh* III q.84, a.1 ad 1: "(I)psi actus humani sensibiles sunt loco materiae", and ad.2: "In sacramento poenitentiae sunt actus humani pro materia, qui proveniunt ex inspiratione interna".

developed for the sacraments in general, Thomas has to broaden the notion of sacramental matter.

In the treatise on the sacraments in general, Thomas had already broadened the notion of *res sacramenti* to sensible actions. Under the *res sacramenti* we not only understand the water or the chrism, but also the act of cleansing or of anointing.[86] The definition of sacrament referred to in the treatise on the sacrament of penance ("a sacrament consists in a certain celebration, where a ritual is executed in such a way that we receive significatively what we should receive in holiness") also yields a broadened notion of *materia sacramenti*.[87]

Third, Thomas distinguishes between the nearest and remote matter (*materia proxima* and *materia remota*). The *materia proxima* are the acts of the penitent, who grieves over the sins committed, who confesses them and who gives satisfaction for them. Since sins are in turn the matter of these acts, Thomas calls them the *materia remota* of the sacrament of penance: they are called matter in as far as they are matter of the acts of the penitent.[88]

Fourth, though human actions are involved in sacraments, they are only fundamental in the sacraments of penance and matrimony. While in other sacraments human actions do not belong essentially to the matter of the sacrament, and are only dispositions thereto, in the sacrament of penance the acts of the penitent belong essentially to the constitution of the sacramental sign.[89] So, more than in the other sacraments, the penitent in the sacrament of penance is actively involved with his free will. This has a negative side as well, because, since the penitent is involved with his will, he can impede the effect of the sacrament. The penitent himself contributes to the constitution of the sacramental sign, whereas in baptism, confirmation or the Eucharist, only the minister of the sacrament constitutes the sacramental sign.[90] The penitent and the priest together signify, by what they do and say, how God forgives the sins by grace, turning the heart of the penitent towards Him and away from sin.

Thomas adds that God interiorly inspires what the penitent adds to the sacrament of penance.[91] However, this does not diminish the fact that, in contrast to the first three sacraments of the new covenant, both penitent and priest work together in the constitution of the sacramental sign. In the last section, we will discuss what role the Holy Spirit plays in Thomas' theology

---

[86] *STh* III q.60, a.6 ad 2: "Sub rebus autem comprehenduntur etiam ipsi actus sensibiles; puta ablutio, inunctio, et alia juiusmodi: quia in his est eadem ratio significandi, et in rebus.".

[87] *STh* III q.84, a.1 co: "'(S)acramentum est in aliqua celebratione, cum res gesta ita sit, ut aliquid significative accipiamus, quod sancte accipiendum est'".

[88] *STh* III q.84, a.2 co: "Dictum est autem, quod materia proxima huius sacramenti sunt actus poenitentis, cuius materia sunt peccata, de quibus dolet, et quae confitetur, et pro quibus satisfacit. Unde relinquitur, quod remota materia poenitentiae sint peccata, non acceptanda, sed detestanda, et destruenda."

[89] *Idem*, a.1 ad 1.

[90] *Idem*, ad 2: "(U)nde materia non adhibitur a ministero, sed a Deo interius operante: sed complementum sacramenti exhibet minister, dum poenitentem absolvit."

[91] *Ibidem*.

with respect to what the minister and the penitent contribute to the sacramental sign.

The development of the absolution formula

The sacramental sign of penance is completed and made perfect, and its signification determined *ad unum determinatum* by the words expressed by the minister of the sacrament: "Ego te absolvo".

In Thomas' works we can see a development in how he reflects on the absolution formula.[92] We will first sketch his position in the *Scriptum*. Next, we will discuss the *opusculum De Forma Absolutionis* and, finally, we will look at the position he takes in the *Summa theologiae*.

a. Scriptum

In the *Scriptum*, the specific formula "Ego te absolvo" is absent. There, Thomas argues that there is no fixed formula necessary because unlike baptism and Eucharist, in which the matter is determined, the matter of the sacrament (i.e. the sins that are mourned over and are confessed) is not determined.[93] Although the acts of the penitent have the same function as that of the water in baptism, they do not constitute a determined matter in the same way as the water does. Nevertheless, Thomas gives some guidelines with respect to the absolution formula. In the very last *quaestiuncula* of the treatise on the sacrament of penance in the *Scriptum*, Thomas argues that the words should be in both the deprecatory and the indicative form and not in the deprecatory form alone.[94] Why is that?

Thomas explains that there are sacraments of which the effect cannot be hindered because of an indisposition of the will of the recipient, for instance the sacraments which imprint a character, like baptism, confirmation and ordination. In these sacraments, the words are either in the indicative (baptism and confirmation) or the imperative form (order). In the sacrament of penance, however, the effect of the absolution can be hindered by an indisposition of the will. Nevertheless, the minister of the sacrament should give the absolution in the indicative form (*per modum indicativum*), though with a preceding prayer, namely "Misereatur". The reason is that the absolution, considered in itself,

---

[92] "Ego te absolvo"; cf. Mt. 16:19: "I will give you the keys of the kingdom of Heaven: whatever you bind on earth will be bound in heaven; whatever you loose on earth will be loosed in heaven." The typical expression (which is full of promise) returns twice, and both times within the context of forgiveness of sins, namely in Mt. 18:18: "In truth I tell you, whatever you bind on earth will be bound in heaven; whatever you loose on earth will be loosed in heaven" and Jn 20:23: "Receive the Holy Spirit. If you forgive anyone's sins, they are forgiven; if you retain anyone's sins, they are retained".

[93] *In IV Sent* d.14, q.1, a.1, qa.1 ad 2: "Sed non requiritur tanta determinatio verborum sicut in baptismo et in Eucharistia; quia non est aliqua materia sanctificanda verbo vita, sicut in illis sacramentis."

[94] *In IV Sent* d.22, q.2, a.2, qa.3 co.

causes its effect sufficiently and with certainty, unless there is some sort of impediment.[95]

Thomas distinguishes between the absolution considered in itself, and considered in its final effect in the penitent who receives it. Thomas motivates the choice for the indicative form by referring to the measure of certainty of the effect of the absolution, even though this effect may never arrive in the recipient. The latter is, for Thomas, the reason why a prayer should precede the actual absolution-formula, as it is directed against a possible impediment thrown up by the will of the recipient of the absolution.[96] In other words, the certainty of the absolution, which justifies its indicative form, refers in the first place to the saving power contained by the absolution, and not the arrival of its effect in the recipient.

In these considerations as to the certainty of the effect of the sacrament of penance, we see a consequence of the fact that the acts of the penitent are the matter of the sacrament of penance. Because of this fact, the sacramental signification comes to depend on the sincerity of these acts. As a result, it is possible that the penitent confesses his sins, receives absolution (and is re-admitted to the table of the Eucharist) and gives satisfaction while his sins remain unforgiven, for instance because he simulates his remorse over his sins.

b. De forma absolutionis

Thomas finished *De forma absolutionis* on 22 February (probably in 1269) in Paris, when he had already been working on the *Summa theologiae* for several years.[97] In this booklet, we find the formula "Ego te absolvo" for the first time. *De forma absolutionis* is the result of a consultation with the magister general of his order, John Vercelli "on a *Libellus* whose author contests the use of the formula indicating sacramental absolution ("Ego te absolvo")."[98]

The discussion on the matter of the indicative versus the deprecatory form of the absolution takes place against the background of the discussion about the place of the sacrament of penance among the sacraments of the new covenant, which are said to effect what they signify.[99] As we saw, Thomas had already

---

95 *Ibidem*: "Et tamen ipsa absolutio, quantum est de se, sufficienter et certitudinaliter inducit effectum suum, nisi sit aliquod impedimentum". Thomas qualifies the necessity of such a preceding prayer: "Tamen non est de esse sacramenti, sed de bene esse ipsius."

96 *Ibidem*: "In poenitentia autem impeditur omnis effectus absolutionis per indispositionem voluntatis. Et tamen ipsa absolutio, quantum est de se, sufficienter et certitudinaliter inducit effectum suum, nisi sit aliquod impedimentum. Et ideo absolutio per modum indicativum fit, sed praemittitur deprecatio, scilicet "Misereatur", ut effectus absolutionis non impediatur."

97 J. Weisheipl, *Friar Thomas Aquinas*, 1974, p.390. In full the title reads *De forma absolutionis sacramentalis ad generalem magistrum Ordinis*. In 1266, Thomas had begun writing his *Summa theologiae* when he was in Rome (Santa Sabina, 1265-1267). In 1269, when he probably wrote *De forma absolutionis*, Thomas was in Paris, working on the *secunda pars* of the *Summa* (p. 361).

98 J.-P. Torrell o.p., *Saint Thomas Aquinas*, p.353.

99 Cf. *De forma absolutionis*: "Non solum autem hoc ['Ego te absolvo', EL] convenienter dicere potest, sed necessarium esse videtur. Sacramenta enim novae legis efficiunt quod figurant; figurant autem sive significant sacramenta et ex materia et ex forma verborum, ut in baptismo apparet." Thomas continues with discussing the *formae verborum* of the sacraments of the new covenant, and from there argues that the absolution formula should be "Ego te absolvo".

taken up a position in the *Scriptum*. His arguments concerning the doctrine of
the instrumentality of the minister in the sacrament of penance reappear in *De
forma absolutionis*.[100] This time, however, he was confronted with a specific
indicative absolution formula. The main argument he gives in *De forma
absolutionis* for the use of the specific words "Ego te absolvo" is derived from a
parallel he makes between baptism and penance. The baptismal formula goes
back on Christ's words "Go, therefore, make disciples of all nations; baptize
them in the name of the Father and of the Son and of the Holy Spirit" (Mt.
28:19). The absolution formula, on the other hand, goes back to Christ handing
over the keys of the Church to Peter saying "I will give you the keys of the
kingdom of Heaven: whatever you bind on earth will be bound in heaven;
whatever you loose on earth will be loosed in heaven." (Mt. 16:19). In the Latin
text of the Vulgate, the latter reads "(..) et quodcumque solveris super terram
etc". Therefore, Thomas argues, since the *forma baptismi* is "Ego te baptizo", it
is fitting (*conveniens*) that the *forma absolutionis* should be "Ego te absolvo".[101]

c. Summa theologiae

The discussion of *De forma absolutionis* returns in the *Summa theologiae*. The third
and fourth *articuli* of the first *quaestio* on the sacrament of penance can be
considered as a condensed reproduction of the two themes discussed in *De
forma absolutionis*, namely the *forma sacramenti* and the necessity of the imposition
of hands. The above-mentioned parallel between the *forma baptismi* and the *forma
absolutionis* in *De forma absolutionis* appears in the *Sed contra* argument of *articulus*
three, and is confronted with five objections. The first four objections (of
which the third is new in comparison with *De forma absolutionis*) argue against
the indicative form. Again, what is at stake is the position of penance as one of
the sacraments of the new covenant. In the *corpus articuli*, Thomas places the
sacrament of penance among the sacraments of baptism, confirmation and the
Eucharist, i.e. as one of the sacraments of the new covenant, which effect what
they signify. Since the thing(s) and words in the sacraments make up the
signification, and since the words as *forma* make perfect the signification of the
thing (considered as matter), the form of the sacrament should therefore signify
what is done in the sacrament in a way that is proportionate to the matter of
the sacrament. And since the things that are said and done by the penitent are
like matter in the sacrament of penance, and since what is done in the
sacrament of penance consists in the removal of the sins that are confessed and

---

100 Cf. J.-P. Torrell, *Saint Thomas Aquinas*, p.168: "Thomas' doctrine of the instrumentality of the
     minister in this sacrament [i.e. penance] makes it easy for him to respond to the difficulties
     raised in the name of the deprecative formula."
101 *De forma*, c.1 (675): "Magis autem ex verbis Domini colligitur hanc esse formam debitam
     absolvendi: Ego te absolvo. Sicut enim Dominus discipulis dixit: *Euntes docete omnes gentes
     baptizantes eos*, Matth. ult., ita dicit: *Quodcumque solveris super terram*. Unde sicut conveniens est
     forma baptismi ut minister dicat: Ego te baptizo, quia Dominus ministris actum baptizandi
     attribuit; ita conveniens forma est ut dicatur: Ego te absolvo, quia Dominus ministro actum
     absolutionis attribuit."

mourned over by the penitent, therefore "Ego te absolvo" is proportionate, as together with the acts of the penitent it signifies the removal of the sins.[102]

The fifth objection and its answer constitute the discussion, which in *De forma* takes up a whole chapter (c.3). It deals with 'some' (*Quidam*) who interpret the formula "I absolve thee" as "I show thee that thou art absolved". Although true in a sense, this interpretation is not sufficient in Thomas' eyes, for the sacraments of the new covenant not only signify but also effect what they signify. "I absolve thee" not only shows in a significative sense but also in an effective sense that a man is absolved. Therefore, interpreting "I absolve thee" as "I give thee the sacrament of the absolution" is more perfect.[103]

Conclusion

In the previous section, we learned that Thomas understands sacramental effectiveness in terms of sacramental signification. The sacraments of the new covenant not only effect what they signify, they also effect what they signify by signifying it. Thomas' use of words like 'cause' and 'effect', though they have indisputably a productionist ring, is to be interpreted against this linguistic background of sacramental signification. The same counts for Thomas' use of the Aristotelian pair of concepts of 'form' and 'matter'. They, as well as the notions of 'cause' and 'effect', can easily be misunderstood. 'Form' and 'matter' do not function within a presumed metaphysics of the sacraments, but are used analogously primarily to explain the unity of the sacramental sign.

In the sacrament of penance, matter and form refer to what the penitent and the priest both contribute to the sacramental sign. In contrast to the other ecclesial sacraments, though in correspondence with the sacrament of matrimony, the acts of the penitent are essential with respect to the sacramental signification. In both Thomas' discussion of the *res sacramenti* and of the *verba sacramenti*, we saw the consequences of the special nature of the (quasi) matter of the sacrament of penance. With respect to the matter itself, we saw that Thomas is reluctant to call the acts of the penitent 'matter' in a straightforward way. With respect to the form, we saw that because the acts of the penitent take such a vital place in the constitution of the sacramental sign, Thomas has to take into account that the will of the penitent works against what is signified. By distinguishing between the absolution *in se* and the arrival of its effect in the penitent, Thomas is able to confirm the certainty of its effectiveness, and thus to safeguard its enumeration among the sacraments of the new covenant. When in the course of his life the discussion shifted to the appropriateness of one specific absolution formula, this enabled him to defend the appropriateness and even necessity of the formula "Ego te absolvo" by referring to its baptismal counterpart "Ego te baptismo".

The prominent place of the acts of the penitent in particular makes clear that notions like cause and effect function within interpersonal relationships, in which human acts receive new meaning in the light of the life and death of

---

[102] *STh* III q.84, a.3 co.
[103] *Idem*, ad 5.

Christ. The reinterpretation of the different types of language in terms of the relationship of friendship between God and man which we encountered in Chapter Two is presupposed when we want to understand how Thomas thinks and speaks about how the sacrament of penance 'causes' the forgiveness of our sins.

4 Justifying faith and the sacrament of penance (*fides et sacramentum*)

As all sacraments of the new covenant, the sacrament of penance derives its effectiveness from the person and life of Christ, his words and works, and especially his passion, his death on the cross and his resurrection.[104] In Thomas' treatise on the sacraments, this life of Christ is summoned up in a term which has an almost technical ring, namely the *passio Christi*. Christ's passion is said to be the special source of the strength of the sacraments of the Church, and thus of the sacrament of penance. The relationship between the sacraments and the passion of Christ, from which they derive their efficient strength, is one of sacramental or figurative representation.[105] In this section, we will examine what Thomas means when he says that the passion of Christ is cause of the effective power of the sacrament of penance. What does he mean when he says we are somehow (*quodammodo*) connected with the power of Christ's passion through the reception of the sacraments?[106]

Since Christ's passion divides the history of salvation into the period before and the period after Christ, and since medieval theologians consequently distinguish between the sacraments of the old and new covenants, we will first examine how Thomas compares both. We shall see that faith plays an important role in this comparison.

---

[104] Cf. *STh* III q.60 pro: "Post considerandum eorum, quae pertinent ad mysteria Verbi incarnati, considerandum est de Ecclesiae sacramentis, quae ab ipso Verbo incarnato efficaciam habent". All aspects of the person of Christ are treated in the *quaestiones* 1 to 59, , in particular the mystery of the incarnation (qq.1 to 26), and his *acta et passa* (qq. 27 to 59). Cf. q.27 pro: "Post praedicta, in quibus de unione Dei, et hominis, et de his quae unionem consequuntur, tractatum est, restat considerandum de his quae Filius Dei incarnatus in natura humana sibi unita gessit, vel passus est; quae quidem consideratio quadripartita erit; nam primo considerabimus de his, quae pertinent ad ingressum eius in mundum: secundo, de his quae pertinent ad progressum vitae ipsius in hoc mundo; tertio, de exitu ipsius ab hoc mundo; quarto, de his quae pertinent ad exaltationem ipsius post hanc vitam."

[105] Cf. *In IV Sent* d.4, q.3, a.3, qa.3 co: "Ad tertium quaestionem dicendum quod baptismus aquae efficaciam habet ex passione Christi, inquantum eam sacramentaliter repraesentat."; *STh* III q.66, a.12 co: "(P)assio Christi operatur quidem in baptismo aquae, per quandam figuralem repraesentationem".

[106] *STh* III q.62, a.5: "(S)acramenta Ecclesiae specialiter habent virtutem ex passione Christi, cuius virtus quodammodo nobis copulatur per susceptionem sacramentorum." Also q.84, a.10 ad 5: "Ad quintem dicendum quod baptismus habet virtutem ex passione Christi, sicut quaedam spiritualis generatio cum spirituali morte praecedentis vitae; statutum autem est hominibus semel mori (Hebr. 8), et semel nasci, et ideo semel tantum debet homo baptizari. Sed poenitentia habet virtutem ex passione Christi, sicut spiritualis medicatio, quae frequenter iterari potest."

Next, we will examine the institution of the sacrament of penance. We shall see that it plays an important role in Thomas' theology regarding the relation between Christ's passion and the efficacy of the sacrament of penance.

Finally, we will examine the relationship between sacraments and faith. As we learned in Chapter Two, faith is one of the four requirements of justification of the godless that is signified in the sacrament of penance. As men are justified by faith, so the sacrament of penance, being the sacramental expression of this justification, must be the sacramental expression of this justifying faith, both in the sense of sign and of cause.

The old and the new covenant

The passion of Christ divides the history of salvation into two parts, namely the period before and the period thereafter. The latter is the period of the church and of the sacraments of the church, and is the period we live in. This period is called the period of the new covenant (the new law or *lex nova*, as the medieval theologians call it) as opposed to the period of the old covenant (*lex vetus*).[107]

In medieval theology, the distinction between the sacraments of the old and those of the new covenant was part and parcel of the treatise on the sacraments. This is also the case in the theology of Thomas.[108] This distinction has scriptural roots, for Paul reflects continuously on the relationship of the new law to the old law with which he was brought up. The medieval theologians found the scriptural roots of the distinction between the sacraments of the old and the new covenant in the epistle of Paul to the Galatians (Gal. 4, 8-9):

> "But formerly when you did not know God, you were kept in slavery to things which are not really gods at all, whereas now that you have come to recognize God – or rather, be recognized by God – how can you now turn back again to those powerless and bankrupt elements whose slaves you now want to be all over again?"

By associating 'powerless and bankrupt elements' (*infirma et egena elementa*) with the sacraments of the old covenant, Thomas joins in with the common interpretation of this text in his time. The text is the *locus* of what was considered to be the main distinction between old and new testament sacraments, namely that the former in contrast to the latter do not confer grace.[109] Reflecting on this distinction will add to our understanding of how

---

[107] Medieval theologians divide the salvation history, which is the period between the status of innocence before the fall and the status of glory after the end of days, in (1) the period after the fall and before the Law of Moses was given (*in statu legis naturae*), (2) the period of the Law of Moses, and (3) the period of the Church until the end of days. These three periods correspond to the natural sacraments (cf. *In IV Sent* d.1, q.1, a.2, qa.3), the sacraments of the old law and the sacraments of the new law.

[108] Cf. *STh* III q.62, a.6 and *passim.*

[109] *Idem* Sc: "Sed contra est, quod Gal.4 dicitur: *Convertimini iterum ad infirma et egena elementa:* Gloss. (ord) idest 'ad legem, quae dicitur infirma, quia perfecte non iustificat'. Sed gratia perfecte iustificat; ergo sacramenta veteris legis gratiam non conferebant."

Thomas sees the causal relationships between the sacraments and Christ's passion.

In Thomas' *Summa theologiae*, the reflection on the difference between old and new law is found particularly in the *Prima secundae*, in the *quaestiones* on the old and the new law (I-II qq. 98-108). The new law, being the law that justifies, is principally the grace of the Holy Spirit, which is given to the faithful. The grace of the Spirit, given through faith in Christ, is what is highest in the law of the New Testament. The power of the new law consists totally in this grace.[110] According to Thomas, to belong to the New Testament, in the sense of the new covenant, is to believe in Christ.[111]

What consequences does this have for those who lived before Christ? Thomas' answer is that they belong to the new covenant on the grounds of faith as long as God accepted them through faith.[112] In order to make this intelligible, Thomas distinguishes between what the new law is principally and what it is secondarily. Principally the new law is the grace of the Spirit, which is written in the hearts of the faithful, and which is the law of faith. Secondarily, the new law consists in the written instructions for the faithful on how to live, what to do and what to believe (*facta, moralia et sacramentalia*).[113] There is a difference between the old and the new law in that the new law does not principally consist in these prescriptions, as did the old law.

Consequently, Thomas can count the faithful who lived under the old law among those who belong to the New Testament. So even though they lived before Christ, who is the cause of the justification, they are justified like those who live after Christ. Moreover, they are not only justified by the same cause, namely Christ's passion, but are also justified in the same manner, namely through faith. For the justifying faith of those who lived under the old law is also the faith in Christ's passion.

Hence, even though the passion of Christ seems to divide salvation history into two parts, a before and an after, there is no difference with respect to justification, the cause of justification or the manner in which one is justified between those who lived before and those who live(d) after Christ.

---

110 *STh* I-II q.106, a.1 co: "[I]d autem, quod est potissimum, in lege novi testamenti, et in quo virtus eius consistit, est gratia Spiritus Sancti, quae datur per fidem Christi; et ideo principaliter lex nova est gratia Spiritus Sancti, quae datur Christifidelibus."

111 Cf. *STh* I-II q.106, a.1 ad 3: "[P]er fidem autem Chisti pertinet homo ad novum testamentum; unde quibuscumque fuit lex gratiae indita, secundum hoc ad novum testamentum pertinebant."

112 *STh* I-II q.107, a.1 ad 3: "[I]lli autem, qui in veteri testamento Deo fuerunt accepti per fidem, secundum hoc ad novum testamentum pertinebant: non enim justificabantur, nisi per fidem Christi, qui est auctor novi testamenti."

113 *STh* I-II q.106, a.1 co: "Habet tamen lex nova quaedam sicut dispositiva ad gratiam Spiritus Sancti, et ad usum huius gratiae pertinentia, quae sunt quasi secundaria in lege nova; de quibus oportuit instrui fideles Christi et verbis, et scriptis, tam circa credenda quam circa agenda." and *STh* I-II q.107, a.1 ad 3: "lex nova dicitur lex fidei, inquantum eius principalitas consistit in ipsa gratia, quae interius datur credentibus; unde dicitur gratia fidei: habet autem secundario aliqua facta, moralia et sacramentialia: sed in his non consistit principalitas legis novae, sicut principalitas veteris legis in eis consistebat."

This point returns in so many words in the treatise on the sacraments in general, when Thomas asks the question of whether the sacraments of the old covenant (which are part of the *praecepta ceremonialia* of the old law[114]) cause grace.[115] In this *quaestio*, he states that 'the Fathers from ancient times' (*antiqui Patres*) are justified through faith in the passion of Christ just as we are. Nevertheless, there is a difference. We believe in the preceding passion of Christ, but the Fathers believed in the future passion of Christ. According to Thomas, the passion of Christ could justify the Fathers in so far they apprehended it in their souls.

According to Thomas, the passion of Christ is cause of the justification of the Fathers being earlier in time. To understand this, we must adapt our notion of causality. Following Aristotle, the medieval theologians distinguish more notions of causality than the sole notion of efficient causality we are accustomed to from the (material) world of exact sciences. One of these notions of causality is the notion of final cause, and it explains how some idea of the future can - insofar as it is apprehended by the mind - become motivator of actions in the present. Thomas applies this notion of causality when he explains how the passion of Christ can be cause of the justification of those who lived before Christ. "An end or goal (*finis*) that is later in time moves the agent in as far as he or she has an apprehension of and a desire for it."[116] Put in these terms, it turns out not to be an alien notion to the modern mind.

Two elements are of importance to this application of the notion of final cause. First, since the end has to move the mind, one must have a more or less explicit

---

[114] Cf. *STh* I-II qq.101-103, esp. q.101, a.4 co: "caeremonialia praecepta ordinantur ad cultum Dei: in quo quidem cultu considerari possunt et ipse cultus, et colentes, et instrumenta colendi; ipse autem cultus specialiter consistit in sacrificiis, quae in Dei reverentiam offeruntur. Instrumenta autem colendi pertinent ad sacra; sicut est tabernaculum, et vasa, et alia huiusmodi. Ex parte autem colentium duo possunt considerari: scilicet eorum institutio ad cultum divinum, quod fit per quamdam consecrationem vel populi, vel ministrorum: et ad hoc pertinent sacramenta. Et iterum eorum singularis conversatio, per quam distinguuntur ab his, qui in Deum non colunt. Et ad hoc pertinent observantiae, quod sacrificia offerri oportebat et aliis huiusmodi."

[115] For what follows, cf. *STh* III q.62, a.6 co: "Sicut enim ex praedictis patet, virtus passionis Christi copulatur nobis per fidem et sacramenta: differenter tamen. Nam continuatio, quae est per fidem, fit per actum animae, continuatio autem, quae est per sacramenta, fit per usum exteriorum rerum. Nihil autem prohibit, id quod est posterius tempore, antequam sit, movere, secundum quod praecedit in actu animae. Sicut finis, qui est posterior tempore, movet agentem, secundum quod est apprehensus, et desideratus ab ipso. Sed illud quod nondum est in rerum natura, non movet secundum usum exteriorum rerum, unde causa efficiens non potest esse peterior in esse ordine durationis, sicut causa finalis. Sic ergo manifestum est, quod a passione Christi, quae est causa humanae iustificationis, convenienter derivatur virtus iustificativa ad sacramenta novae legis, non autem ad sacramenta veteris legis. Et tamen per fidem passionis Christi iustificabantur antiqui Patres, sicut et nos. Sacramenta autem veteris legis erant quaedam illius fidei protestationes, inquantum significabant passionem Christ, et effectus eius. Sic ergo patet, quod sacramenta veteris legis non habebant in se aliquam virtutem, qua operarentur ad conferandam gratiam iustificantem, sed solum significabant fidem, per quam justificabantur."

[116] *Ibidem.*

intellectual apprehension of the end; otherwise, the end cannot move the mind. Second, the apprehension in itself is not enough, but an affection, a motion of the will, must accompany it. It is not enough when the end is known or understood; it must be understood as *bonum*, as desirable as well. Both intellect and will are decisive with respect to this application of the notion of final causality.

The sacraments of the old covenant are the external expressions, the so-called protestations (*protestationes*), of this faith in the future Savior of those who lived under the old law. They "were certain protestations of this faith, in so far as they signified the passion of Christ, and the effects thereof."[117] In this sense, the sacraments of the old covenant are part of the cult of God, the movement of exterior worship of men, ascending through Christ to God.

Nevertheless, they are not means of justification and sanctification, that is to say: they do not confer grace, as do the sacraments of the new covenant. The reason for this has to do with the nature of sacraments. Constituted of words and something sensible, sacraments remain within the realm of the external (material) things, even though they refer to the realm of the spiritual. What applies for faith, namely that it can concern something in the future, insofar as this is apprehended and desired by the soul, does not apply to sacraments. Faith and sacraments are two different ways of being connected with the strength of Christ's passion. The former is by an act of the soul, which remains within the realm of the spiritual, while the latter is by use of external things. Moreover, in the realm of external things, that which is later in time cannot move that which is earlier in time. Consequently, it is not possible for the sacraments of the old covenant to derive justifying and sanctifying strength from the passion of Christ, as do the sacraments of the new covenant.

The sacraments of the old covenant are mere protestations of the faith by which one is justified. As such, they only refer to the passion of Christ and its effects and are, accordingly, named 'prefigurations' of the sacraments of the new covenant. According to Thomas, not all of the New Testament sacraments are in this sense prefigured by Old Testament sacraments. Prefigured are the sacraments of baptism, the Eucharist, penance and ordination. The sacrament of baptism is prefigured by the Old Testament sacrament of circumcision and the Eucharist by the meal of the paschal lamb, while the sacrament of ordination is prefigured by the consecration of the Old Testament (high) priest. The sacrament of penance is not prefigured by a specific Old Testament sacrament, but instead by all purifications under the old law.[118] Thomas sketches an interrelatedness of these prefiguring cultic deeds, which seems similar to the interrelatedness of the four sacraments mentioned. As baptism is the gate to the divine cult, of which the Eucharist forms the heart and climax, so circumcision means the institution into the status of those who participate in the cult of God (*institutio in statu colendi Deum*). Without it one is not admitted to

117 *Ibidem.*
118 *STh* I-II q.102, a.5 ad 3.

anything belonging to the (old) law, particularly the eating of the paschal meal. The priests have a similar central role with respect to the use of what belongs to the divine cult. Finally, the purifications that prefigure the sacrament of penance are ordered to remove the impurities that hinder the participation in the divine cult, similarly to the way penance is ordered to remove the sin which excludes one from participating in the Eucharistic meal.[119]

We are particularly interested in the removal of the spiritual impediments, i.e. sins, under the old law because it corresponds with the subject of this study: divine forgiveness in its sacramental form. As examples of sins that excluded men from participating in the divine cult, Thomas mentions idolatry, homicide, adultery and incest. Of these impurities, men were purified by certain sacrifices, either offered for the whole community in general, or for single sins. However, Thomas stresses that these carnal sacrifices did not, of themselves, have the power to expiate sin. Instead, they purified because they signified the expiation of sins through Christ. In this expiation, those who lived under the old law took part by expressing their faith in the Redeemer through the offering of sacrifices.[120] In conclusion, Thomas resolves the notion of active purification of spiritual impediments through carnal sacrifices under the old law, into what is in fact the cause of the forgiveness of sins, i.e. faith in the passion of Christ.

The 'institution' of the sacrament of penance

In the previous subsection, we have seen that, according to Thomas, there are two ways in which we are related to Christ's passion as the source of our salvation, namely through faith and – for us who live after Christ – the sacraments of the new covenant. With respect to the latter, Thomas speaks of a relationship of efficient causality. The notion of 'institution' in Thomas' theology of the sacraments adds to our understanding of this relationship of efficient causality. Christ's institution of the sacraments of the new law provides the link of efficient causality between His death and the effectiveness of the sacraments. He who died on the cross is the same one who instituted the sacraments. Let us see what Thomas has to say about the institution of the sacrament of penance.

Thomas connects the effective power of the sacraments with the institution of the sacraments. Sacraments are said to "have their effect *ex institutione*", they "signify *ex institutione*", they "possess power *ex institutione*", they "confer grace *ex*

---

[119] *Idem*, co.

[120] *STh* I-II q.102, a.5 ad 4: "A cultu autem spirituali impediuntur homines per peccata, quibus homines pollui dicebantur: sicut per idololatriam, et homicidium, per adulteria, et incestus; et ab istis pollutionibus purificabantur homines per aliqua sacrificia, vel communiter oblata pro tota multitudine, vel etiam pro peccatis singulorum; non quod sacrificia illa carnalia haberent ex seipsis virtutem expiandi peccatum. Sed quia significabant expiationem peccatorum futuram per Christum, cuius participes erant etiam antiqui protestantes fidem Redemptoris in figuris sacrificiorum."

sui institutione", "the form and power of the sacrament of penance *totaliter est ex institutione Christi*".[121]

According to Thomas, the institution of the sacrament of penance is responsible for the determination of both matter and form, and of the effect and origin of the sacrament of penance.[122] In the treatise on the sacraments in general, Thomas explains that insofar as sacraments are instruments for the sanctification of human persons, they belong to God. Consequently, it is up to God, and not up to us, to determine what *res* is taken to sanctify us through.[123] As in other sacraments, the matter of the sacrament of penance pre-exists in nature before it is taken to function as matter in the sacrament. It is according to natural reason that man is moved to expiate for the evils he has done. But that one grieves over it in this special way is according to divine institution. As the 'moment' in which Christ has determined that we should do penance in this special way, Thomas refers to the beginning of Christ's preaching, where Christ not only proclaims to the people "be sorry" (*poenitere*), but "do penance" (*poenitentiam agere*). Though Thomas does not refer to a particular verse from Scripture, it is clear that he has in mind the first preaching of Jesus that is mentioned at beginning of the gospel according to Matthew (4,17), which (in the Vulgate-text) reads "Poenitentiam agite". The emphasis lies on 'agere': to <u>do</u> penance. Thomas understands this to signify the specific way of doing penance that is required in the sacrament of penance.[124]

In contrast to the matter, the form and the power of the sacrament are completely derived from Christ's institution.[125] With respect to the institution of both form and power of the sacrament of penance, Thomas refers to Mt. 16,19:

> "I will give you the keys of the kingdom of Heaven: whatever you bind on earth will be bound in heaven; whatever you loose on earth will be loosed in heaven."

As we have seen in the previous section, this text is, according to Thomas, responsible for the final phrasing of the absolution formula. However,

---

[121] Cf. *STh* III q.38, a.3 ad 3: "Sacramenta autem ex vi institutionis suum habent effectum."; q.64, a.2 ad 2: Et hoc est quod Hugo de sancto Victore dicit, quod sacramentum ex institutionem significat."; q.64, a.3 co: "Et quia ex institutione sacramenta virtutem obtinent, inde est quod, tertio, ad excellentiam potestatis Christi pertinet quod ipse, qui dedit virtutem sacramentis, potuit instituere sacramenta."; q.66 a.2 co: "Respondeo dicendum quod, sicut dictum est supra, sacramenta ex sui institutione habent quod conferant gratiam."; a.6 co: "Respondeo dicendum quod, sicut supra dictum est, sacramenta habent efficaciam ab institutione Christi."; q.84, a.7 co: "Sed forma sacramenti [poenitentiae], et virtus ipsius, totaliter est ex institutione Christi, ex cuius passione procedit virtus sacramentorum."
[122] *STh* III q.84, a.7 co.
[123] Cf. *STh* III q.60, a.5 co.
[124] *STh* III q.84, a.7 co: "Sic ergo huius sacramenti materia praexistit a natura; ex naturali enim ratione homo movetur ad poenitendum de malis, quae fecit: sed quod hoc, vel illo modo homo poenitentiam agat, est ex institutione divina; unde et Dominus in principio praedicationis suae indixit hominibus, ut non solum poeniterent, sed etiam poenitentiam agerent, significans determinatos modos actuum, qui requiruntur ad hoc sacramentum."
[125] *Idem*: "sed forma sacramenti, et virtus ipsius totaliter ex institutione Christi, ex cuius procedit virtus sacramentorum."

according to Thomas, by saying this Christ does more than just determine the form of the sacrament of penance. Thomas also interprets the text as the communication of the power to absolve, which is the power of the keys, to the ministers of the sacrament.[126] We will return to this below.

Finally, the determination of its effect and the origin of its power, which are respectively the forgiveness of sin and the passion (and resurrection) of Christ, belong to the institution of the sacrament of penance as well. With respect to this, Thomas refers to Lc. 24, 46-47:

> "So it is written that the Christ would suffer and on the third day rise from the death, and that, in his name, repentance for the forgiveness of sins would be preached to all nations, beginning from Jerusalem."

So with respect to the institution of the sacrament of penance, Thomas refers to different moments in the life of Christ: the beginning of his preaching, the handing over of the power of the keys to Peter, his appearance to the eleven after his resurrection. Together with the passion of Christ, these moments form the origin of the power of the sacrament of penance.

According to Thomas, this handing over of the power of the keys not only applies to Peter, but to all who have received this power from him.[127] By these, Thomas means the priests, for he identifies the power to bind and absolve with the priestly mark, and the power to consecrate bread and wine. The two texts from Scripture that Thomas mentions[128] in this respect are Mt. 16, 19:

> "I will give you the keys of the kingdom of Heaven: whatever you bind on earth will be bound in heaven; whatever you loose on earth will be loosed in heaven."

and Jn. 20, 22-23:

> "Receive the Holy Spirit. If you forgive anyone's sins, they are forgiven; if you retain anyone's sins, they are retained."

How do these texts relate? First, from the texts of Thomas it is clear that only the text from the gospel of Matthew is understood to be part of the institution of the sacrament of penance. Mt. 16, 19 is mentioned each time Thomas discusses the institution of the sacrament, while Thomas does not relate the gift of the Holy Spirit to the institution of the sacrament of penance. In his commentary on Jn. 20, 22-23, he speaks about the handing over of the office (officium) to the Apostles, the gift of the Holy Spirit, and the fruit of this gift, i.e.

---

[126] Cf. STh III q.84, a.3 ad 3.

[127] ScG IV, c.72: "Et haec duo dicuntur duae claves Ecclesiae, scilicet scientia discernendi, et potentia ligandi et solvendi, quas Dominus Petro commisit, iuxta illud Matth. 16, 19: "tibi dabo claves regni caelorum". Non autem sic intelligitur Petro commisisse ut ipse solus haberet, sed ut per eum derivarentur ad alios: alias non esset sufficienter fidelium saluti provisum."

[128] Idem.

that of whomever they forgive sins the sins will be forgiven. However, he does not identify these with 'institution'.[129]

Second, the handing over of the power to absolve happens before the passion of Christ, while the gift of the Spirit occurs after Christ's resurrection. We have seen that the keys derive their power from the passion of Christ. Moreover, according to Thomas, the keys are 'made in the passion' (*fabricare in passione*). This is why, according to Thomas, Christ says (in Mt. 16, 19): "I will give you". With respect to the actual gift of the power of the keys, however, Thomas does not refer to Jn 20, 22-23 but to a verse in the next chapter: Jn. 21, 17 ("Look after my sheep").[130]

Third, though Jn 20, 22-23 is not about the institution itself of the sacrament of penance, it must be read in relation to the gift of the power to absolve, the power of the keys. It appears that both Jn 20, 22-23 and Jn. 21, 17, refer to the same 'laying of the office upon the apostles'. According to Thomas, in Jn 20, 22-23 Christ lays the office upon the apostles[131], while in Jn 21, 17, He lays the office on Peter[132]. We may infer from Thomas' commentary on Mt. 16, 19 that he has the same office in mind in both texts.[133] Therefore, Thomas relates the gift of the Spirit in Jn 20, 22-23 to the promise of the keys to Peter in Mt. 16, 19 and the actual gift of the keys in Jn 21, 17.

From this analysis of the institution of the sacrament of penance, we can conclude that according to Thomas it is possible to distinguish different moments at which the sacrament of penance is instituted. Its matter is instituted in Mt.4, 17, its form and power in Mt. 16, 19, its effect and the origin of its power in Lc. 24, 46-47. With respect to the sacramental power, contained in the power of the keys, this is instituted and promised before the passion (in Mt. 16, 19), it is made in the passion and actually given after the passion to the Apostles (Jn 20, 22-23) and to Peter in particular (Jn.21, 17).

Faith and sacrament

We have seen above that, according to Thomas, all who are justified are justified based on a union with Christ's passion through faith, whether they lived before, or after Christ. We are united with Christ's passion through faith and the sacraments.[134] The notion of faith is crucial to understanding the

---

[129] *In Ioan* c.20, lc.4. As far as I can tell, nowhere in his works does Thomas identify this text from John with the institution of the sacrament of penance.

[130] *Idem.* "Sed dicit, *Tibi dabo*, nondum enim [claves] erant fabricatae; res autem non potest dari antequam sit. Fabricandae autem hae erant in passione; unde in passione fuit eorum efficacia. Unde hic promisit, sed post passionem dedit. cum dixit (Ioan 21, 17): *Pasce oves meas.*"

[131] *In Ioan* c.20, lc.4: "Iniungit Apostolis officium: ... ".

[132] *In Ioan* c.21, lc.3: "Hic iam examinato Petro, iniungit ei officium, dicens: *Pasce agnos meos*, idest fideles meos, a me agno agnos vocatos".

[133] *In Matt* c.16, lc.2: "Sed est alia quaestio, quia alibi habetur, Joan XX,23: *Quorum remiseritis peccata, remittentur eis*; hic vero solum hoc dict Petro. Dicendum quod immediate dedit Petro; alii vero a Petro recipiunt; ideo ne credantur ista solum dici Petro, dicit: *Quorum remiseritis* etc."

[134] *STh* III q.62, a.5 ad 2: "(P)er fidem Christus habitat in nobis, ut dicitur Ephes. 3, et ideo virtus Christi copulatur nobis per fidem. Virtus autem remissiva peccatorum speciali quodam

notion of sacramental effectiveness in Thomas' theology. All sacraments, including those of the Old Testament, are sacraments of faith, and in all sacraments, the justification and sanctification happens through faith. The difference between Old and New Testament sacraments is that, while both are expressions of faith, only the latter play a role in arousing this faith.

Sacraments contain power, which they derive from Christ's passion. And we are somehow (*quodammodo*) united with this power when we receive the sacraments.[135] In this subsection, we will examine what Thomas means by this power (*vis*, *virtus*). Thomas calls it the power of the sacraments, the power *ex passione Christi*, and the power of Christ.[136] Moreover, this power is in the sacraments, and somehow we are united with it through the sacraments. It refers to the most crucial confession of faith, namely that Christ has delivered us from sin through his passion, i.e. his death on the cross.[137] Somehow what has happened at the cross is present as a power in the sacraments of the new covenant. In what does this power consist?

---

modo pertinet ad passionem ipsius Christi, et ideo per fidem passionis eius specialiter homines liberantur a peccatis, secundum illud Rom. 3: *Quem proposuit Deus propitiatorum per fidem in sanguine ipsius*. Et ideo virtus sacramentorum, quae ordinatur ad tollenda peccata, praecipue est ex fide passionis Christi.". Cf. *STh* III q.62, a.6 co: "Sicut enim ex praedictis patet (art. praec), virtus passionis Christi copulatur nobis per fidem et sacramenta: differenter tamen."

[135] *STh* III q.62, a.5 co: "Manifestum est autem ex his quae supra dicta sunt quod Christus liberavit nos a peccatis nostris, praecipue per suam passionem, non solum efficienter, et meritorie, sed etiam satisfactorie. Similiter etiam per suam passionem initiavit ritum christianae religionis, offerens seipsum oblationem, et hostiam Deo, ut dicitur Ephes. 5. Unde manifestum est, quod sacramenta Ecclesiae specialiter habent virtutem ex passione Christi, cuius virtus quodammodo nobis copulatur per susceptionem sacramentorum".

[136] *Ibidem.*

[137] For a reflection in general (but with special attention to Thomas' theology) on how the passion of Christ may, in our days, be understood to bring about what is been signified in the sacraments, see J. Wissink, "De Sacramenten geven de kruisgenade die ze betekenen", in A. van Eijk, H. Rikhof (ed.), *De Lengte en de breedte, de hoogte en de diepte. Peilingen in de theologie van de sacramenten*, pp. 234 - 261. In this article, Wissink proposes an interpretation of the classical doctrine (which he finds in Thomas' theology) that Christ has delivered us from sin through his passion *efficienter*, *meritorie* and *satisfactorie*. For his interpretation he formulates the hypothesis that Christ when dying becomes according to his human nature the giver of the Holy Spirit. "[D]e stelling is dat door Jezus' dood een modificatie optreedt in de *missio* van de Geest. Hij krijgt de gestalte van Jezus, wordt Zijn Geest (vgl. Gal. 4,6; Rom. 8,9; Fil. 1,19). Vanuit het kruis van Jezus krijgt het werk van de Geest vooral de kleur van de vergeving (Joh. 20, 22-23; vergelijk ook de driemalige 'vrede'-wens in Joh. 20, 19-28, welke duidelijk 'vergevings-karakter' heeft; Lucas plaatst dit accent al bij de kruiswoorden van Jezus). Bovendien hoort deze Geest na het Pascha van Jezus onherroepelijk, definitief bij de mensen." (p.250) Wissink reinterprets the 'meritorie' in terms of "having earned the Spirit for us" and "earning us because the work of the Spirit incorporates us with him" (p.254). And with respect to satisfaction, Wissink proposes to understand this – even more than Anselm and Thomas did – in terms of what the death of Jesus on the cross has accomplished in us. The death on the cross does not change anything in God, as if God would not be satisfied for the sins men has committed until after Christ's death. It has changed something in us: "God heeft in Christus genoeg gedaan aan ons en voor ons" (pp.255-257).

For an answer to this question, we must first examine briefly what Thomas says about Christ's passion.[138] Thomas argues that it was more fitting that man should be delivered from sin through Christ's passion, than through God's will alone. Thomas gives five arguments for fittingness, the first of which is that through Christ's passion we learn how much God loves man. Because of this, our love for God is aroused in turn.

> "First through this [Christ's passion], man knows how much God loves man. And through this he [man] is aroused to love Him, in whom the perfection of human salvation consists."[139]

This argument returns when Thomas reflects on the first effect of the passion of Christ, i.e. the liberation from sin. According to Thomas, the passion of Christ is the proper cause of the forgiveness of sins in three ways (*tripliciter*), the first of which is by way of arousing charity (*per modum provocantis ad charitatem*). And it is through this love for God that our sins are forgiven us.[140] This effect is not the only effect of Christ's passion, or the only way in which it is the proper cause of the forgiveness of sins, but it seems to be the most prominent, since on both occasions Thomas puts it in the first place. So the power, which the sacraments of the new covenant contain, and which they derive from the passion of Christ, appears in the first place to be the power to arouse our love for God. The sacraments contain this power, because they represent *sacramentaliter*[141] or *figurative*[142] the passion of Christ.

---

[138] The passion of Christ is dealt with in the third part of the *Summa* in qq.46-49. Q.46 deals with the passion of Christ as such; q.47 with the efficient cause of Christ's passion. Q.48 and q.49 deal with the fruits (cf. q.46 pro) or effects (q.48 pro) of the passion of Christ:. Q.48 with the way in which the passion effects (*de modo efficiendi*), while q.49 deals with the effects themselves.

[139] *STh* III q.46, a.3 co: "Respondeo dicendum, quod tanto aliquis modus convention est ad assequendum finem, quanto per ipsum plura concurrunt, quae sunt expedientia fini. Per hoc autem quod homo per Christi passionem est liberatus, multa concurrerunt ad salutem hominis pertinentia praeter liberationem a peccato. Primo enim per hoc homo cognoscit quantum Deus hominem diligat; et per hoc provocatur ad eum diligendum, in quo perfectio humanae salutis consistit. (..) Secundo per hoc dedit nobis exemplum obedientiae, humilitatis, constantiae, justitiae, et caeterarum virtutum in passione Christi ostensarum, quae sunt necessariae ad humanam salutem. (..) Tertio, quia Christus per passionem suam non solum hominem a peccata liberavit, sed etiam gratiam justificantem, et gloriam beatitudinis ei promeruit, ut infra dicitur. Quarto, quia per hoc est homini inducta maior necessitas se immunem a peccata conservandi, qui se sanguine Christi redemptum cogitat a peccato. Quinto, quia hoc ad majorem dignitatem hominis cessit, ut sicut homo vinctus fuerat, et deceptus a diabolo, ita etiam homo esset, qui diabolum vinceret. Et sicut homo mortem meruit, ita homo moriendo mortem superaret. (..) Et ideo convenientius fuit, quod per passionem Christi liberaremur, quam per solam Dei voluntatem."

[140] *STh* III q.49, a.1 co: "Respondeo dicendum quod passio Christi est propria causa remissionis peccatorum tripliciter: primo per modum provocantis ad charitatem: quia, ut Apostolus dicit Rom. 5: *Commendat Deus suam charitatem in nobis, quoniam cum adhuc inimici essemus, Christus pro nobis mortuus est*. Per charitatem autem consequimur veniam peccatorum, secundum illud Luc. 7: *Dimissa sunt ei peccata multa, quoniam dilexit multum.*" The two other ways are *per modum redemptionis*, and *per modum efficientiae*..

[141] Cf. *In IV Sent* d.4, q.3, a.3, qa.3 co.

With respect to the sacrament of penance, this means that contrition, the immediate cause of forgiveness, is itself eventually caused by the passion of Christ. All sacraments represent the passion of Christ, and as such contain the power to arouse the change of will in which the act of contrition consists. The sacrament of penance contains it in particular since it, at the same time, provides the penitent with the way to express his contrition in an act of confessing his sins. According to Thomas, there are other 'motivators' as well, which bring the human will into motion, for instance the new perspective of eternal life.[143]

Thomas' use of the term 'arousing' (*provocare*) gives an idea of how he understands the cause of the reorientation of the will. Not by force, nor by some form of magic, but by confronting the human soul with an act of love, which, in itself, is capable of re-directing the will, and igniting the fire of love. What is meant by 'cause' is part of a schema of interpersonal relationship, or better: a schema of friendship (*amicitia*), in which faith and disbelief, hope and fear, love and aversion are the terms in which this cause must be understood.

Conclusion

In this section, we have examined how, according to Thomas, the sacrament of penance derives its effectiveness, i.e. its sacramental power, from the passion of Christ. We have seen that the sacraments of the new law correspond with those of the old law in that both are protestations of faith in Christ. Through this faith in Christ men are justified, whether they lived before or after Christ. We have also seen that the sacraments of the new covenant differ from those of the old in that the former derive their justifying power from the passion of Christ, which is the cause of justification.[144]

The link between the sacrament of penance and the passion of Christ from which it derives its sacramental power is the institution. One moment in the institution of the sacrament of penance, the institution of its power which consists in the power of the keys, must be understood against the background of the passion itself in which the keys are fashioned, and the actual handing over after the passion.

Finally, we have seen that the notion of sacramental power, which is contained in the sacrament of penance, refers to the power of the passion of Christ. Our brief analysis has shown that, according to Thomas, this power is, in the first place, the power to arouse love. This power of the passion of Christ is present *sacramentaliter* in the sacrament of penance, and is the power to arouse justifying faith.

---

[142] Cf. *STh* III q.66, a.12 co.

[143] Cf. *STh* III q.85, a. 5 ob 2: "Ad poenitentiam homines provocantur per expectationem regni caelestis, secundum illud Matth. IV: *poenitentiam agite, appropinquabit enim regnum caelorum.*"

[144] Cf. *STh* q.62, a.6 co: "(A) passione Christi, quae est causa humanae iustificationis, convenienter derivatur virtus iustificativa ad sacramenta novae legis, non autem ad sacramenta veteris legis."

5 Sacramental causality and The Holy Spirit

The key term in Thomas' understanding of the sacramental causality of the
sacrament of penance is the power of the keys. The sacramental power of the
sacrament of penance consists completely in these keys. In this final section, we
will examine how Thomas understands the power of the keys. First, we will
examine in particular the power of the keys in relation to the Holy Spirit. Christ
has handed over the power of the keys to the apostles, together with the gift of
the Spirit, so there seems to be a special relation between both.
Next, we will examine Thomas' notion of instrumental causality. Our
examination of the power of the keys will show that their significance lies in
making the minister of the sacrament of penance into an instrument.
Finally, we will draw our conclusion with respect to the role the Holy Spirit
plays with respect to the forgiveness of sins in the sacrament of penance.

The power of the keys

The power of the sacrament of penance consists in the sacrament of penance
representing *sacramentaliter*, i.e. by sacramental signification, the justifying power
of the passion of Christ, which we can understand as the power to arouse
justifying faith. In the opening section of this chapter we saw that, according to
Thomas, the minister holds the power of the sacrament of penance in virtue of
the power of the keys. We have also seen that for Thomas the power of the
keys, the priestly character and the power to consecrate bread and wine are the
same in essence, though they differ *ratione*. The priestly mark deputes one to a
certain spiritual role in the liturgy of the church (e.g. the administering of the
sacrament of penance).[145] The priestly mark is a spiritual power (*potestas
spiritualis*), and an instrumental power: the minister of the sacrament has this
spiritual power *per modum instrumenti*.[146] The priestly mark is the mark of Christ,
according to whose priesthood one is configured. This *configuratio Christo*[147] is
necessary in order to be able to act as instrument of Christ.[148]
Since the text from John (20, 22-23) seems to suggest a special relation between
the Holy Spirit and the power to dispense the sacraments, we will examine what
Thomas has to say about the Holy Spirit in relation to the power of the keys.
First, we will examine how Thomas interprets Jn 20, 22-23, in particular the gift

---

[145] Cf. *STh* III, q.63, a.1 co: "(E)t ideo cum homines per sacramenta deputentur ad aliquid
spirituale pertinens as cultum Dei, consequens est, quod per ea fideles aliquo spirituali
charactere insignantur."; a.2 co: "(S)acramenta novae legis characterem imprimunt,
inquantum per ea deputantur homines ad cultum Dei, secundum ritum christianae religionis";
a.6 co: "Sed ad agentes in sacramentis pertinet sacramentum ordinis; quia per hoc
sacramentum deputantur homines ad sacramenta aliis tradenda."

[146] *Idem*, a.2 co: "Habere enim sacramenti characterem competit ministris Dei. Minister autem
habet se per modum instrumenti."

[147] *STh* III, q.63, a.1 ad 2: "(E)t hoc modo illi, qui deputantur ad cultum christianum, cuius
auctor est Christus, characterem accipiunt, quo Christo configurantur."

[148] *ScG* IV, c.72: "Minister autem comparatur ad Dominum sicut instrumentum ad principale
agens. Sicut enim instrumentum movetur ab agente ad aliquid efficiendum, sic minister
movetur imperio Domini ad aliquid exequendum. Oportet autem instrumentum esse
proportionatum agenti. Unde et ministros Christi oportet esse ei conformes."

of the Holy Spirit. According to Thomas, the Spirit "descends in order to designate the propagation of grace in the sacraments, of which the apostles are the ministers"[149], and to show their power "in the dispensation of the sacraments".[150] The Spirit is given "not in general to all" (as is the case at Pentecost), but "with respect to a certain effect, namely to forgive sins."[151] The fruit of the gift of the Spirit is indicated by the verse "If you forgive anyone's sins, they are forgiven". According to Thomas, the forgiveness of sins is a fitting "effect of the Holy Spirit, who himself is love (*caritas*) and through whom love is given to us."[152]

Next, we will examine whether Thomas identifies this power to dispense the sacraments and to forgive sins as a form of grace. When we dealt with the invisible missions of the divine Persons in Chapter Three, we saw that the Holy Spirit can be sent according to sanctifying grace, or according to gratuitous grace (though in the latter case the Holy Spirit is not given *simpliciter*[153]). We also saw, that the notion of actual operating grace which we encountered in Chapter Two, does not fit into the division of grace into sanctifying grace and gratuitous grace.[154] The question here is whether we must infer from the fact that the power of the keys is associated with the gift of the Holy Spirit that the power of the keys is 'a grace' according to which the Holy Spirit is given.

The first candidate is sanctifying grace. When Thomas continues with his commentary on Jn. 20, 22-23, he explains that even an unworthy priest can be minister in the sacraments, so even when a minister does not have the Holy Spirit, nevertheless he can have the power to dispense the sacraments. For Thomas this is due to the fact that they are ministers: they do not forgive sins based on their own authority, but on the authority of God, whose instruments they are.[155] We will return to the topic of instrumentality later. However, the

[149] *In Ioan* c.20, lc.4: "Super Apostolos autem primo descendit [Spiritus sanctus] in flatu, ad designandam propagationem gratiae in sacramentis, cuius ipsi ministri erant".
[150] *STh* I q.43, a.7 ad 5: "Ad Apostolos autem [missio visibilis facta est] sub specie flatus ad ostendendam potestatem ministerii in dispensatione sacramentorum."
[151] *In Ioan*, c.20, lc.4: "Sed tamen ipse Chrysostomus dicit: *Spiritus sanctus datus fuit ad discipulos non communiter ad omnia, sed ad aliquem effectum*, scilicet ad dimittendum peccata."
[152] *Ibidem.* "Tertio ponitur dationis fructus: *Quorum remiseritis peccata, remittuntur eis.* Quod conveniens effectus est Spiritus sancti, scilicet remissio peccatorum; nam ipse caritas est, et per eum nobis datus caritas. Rom. v, 5: *caritas Dei diffusa est in cordibus nostris per Spiritum sanctum, qui datus est nobis.* Remissio autem peccatorum non fit nisi per caritatem. Quia (Prov. x, 12): *universa delicta operit caritas*; I Petr iv, 8: *Caritas operit multitudinem peccatorum.*"
[153] Cf. *STh* I q.43, a.3 ad 4. See Chapter Three, section 2.
[154] *Ibidem.*
[155] *In Ioan* c.22, lc.4: "Item quaeritur de hoc quod dicit: Accipite Spiritum sanctum: quorum remiseritis peccata, remittuntur eis. Videtur ergo quod qui non habet Spiritum sanctum, non possit peccata dimittere. Ad quod dicendum, quod si remissio peccatorum esset proprium opus sacerdotis, idest quod ex sua virtute hoc faceret; non utique posset sanctificare nisi sanctus. Remissio autem peccatorum est proprium opus Dei, qui propria virtute et auctoritate peccata dimittit; sacerdotis autem non nisi est sicut instrumenti. Sicut ergo dominus per servum et ministrum suum, sive sit bonus sive malus, potest facere voluntatem suam ad exequendum aliqua; ita et Dominus per ministros, etiam si mali sint, potest sacramenta conferre, in quibus datur gratia."

fact that an unworthy priest can forgive sins implies that the power of the keys cannot be sanctifying grace, for even without sanctifying grace (personal holiness) a priest can still dispense sacraments.

The next candidate is gratuitous grace. Does the power of the keys belong to the grace of charismatic gifts? The definition of gratuitous grace itself does seem to suggest this, because gratuitous grace is given in order to bring others to justifying faith[156], and this is precisely what the power of the keys is meant for. However, Thomas himself appears to think otherwise. In the third chapter of *De forma absolutionis*, Thomas denies that the power of the keys should be numbered among the gratuitous graces. The point is that if the power of the keys were to be a gratuitous grace, this would imply that sacramental power would be something belonging to the minister himself. Instead, Thomas argues, the power of the keys resides principally in Christ, and (only) instrumentally or ministerially in the priests who have the keys.[157]

This notion of instrumentality seems to make it unlikely that the power of the keys is a grace at all, for instrumentality refers to the point that it is not the minister himself who forgives, but Christ using the minister as an instrument. How then must we understand the association of the Holy Spirit with the power of the keys, as suggested in Jn. 20, 22-23? I come to three possible explanations based on Thomas' commentary.

(1) There seems to be no reason not to interpret the gift of the Holy Spirit to the apostles in Jn. 20, 22-23 to be according to sanctifying grace. The gift of sanctifying grace in Jn. 20, 22-23 can accompany the handing over of the power to absolve. The only thing we have shown above is that the power of the keys is not the same as sanctifying grace, and that having the power of the keys does not necessarily mean that one has the Holy Spirit. However, the fact that Thomas emphasizes that unworthy priests can forgive sins must not be taken to deny that every priest, as minister of the sacraments, has the moral obligation to be holy, and live a life in the Spirit. Elsewhere, Thomas says that the priestly mark (*character*), in which the power of the keys consists, is given together with grace (which is not necessarily sanctifying grace), so that they who receive the mark "accomplish worthily what they are deputed to".[158] Moreover, as with all sacraments, the sacrament of order confers grace, because it is fitting that the administering of the sacraments is helped by divine grace.[159] Consequently,

---

[156] Cf. *STh* I-II q.111, a.1.

[157] *De forma*, c.3 (699) : "(P)otestas autem clavium non computatur inter gratias gratis data, sed virtus sacramentalis quae principaliter residet in Christo, instrumentaliter autem sive ministerialiter in sacerdotibus habentibus claves."

[158] *STh* III q.63, a.4 ad 1: "(D)ivina largitas recipientibus characterem largitur gratiam, per quam digne impleant ea, ad quae deputantur."

[159] *ScG* IV, c.74: "Administratio autem sacramentorum, ad quae ordinatur spiritualis potestas, convenienter non fit nisi aliquis ad hoc a divina gratia adiuvetur. Et ideo in hoc sacramenti [ordinis] confertur gratia, sicut et in aliis sacramentis."

even though the power of the keys is not a form of grace itself, its handing over can very well be accompanied by a gift of grace.[160]

(2) A second explanation is that the Spirit is given in order for the apostles, and us, to recognize and acknowledge the apostles (and their successors) as ministers of the sacraments, as having the power and authority to forgive in Christ's name, and to be His instrument. In both the *Summa theologiae* and in his commentary on John, Thomas says that the Holy Spirit is given in the form of breathing in order to designate, (*designare*) or show, (*manifestare*) that these are the ministers of the sacraments in which grace is given. The Holy Spirit is not only the one who is given to us to have and enjoy, nor only the one who gives us graces so that we can help others to find God. The Spirit is also the one who is sent in order to make us see and understand the things of God.[161]

(3) A third explanation is that the Spirit is given to the apostles and their successors with respect to those whose sins they will forgive. It is revealing to read what Thomas says with respect to the invisible mission of the Holy Spirit to the sacraments:

"Grace is in the sacraments of the new law *instrumentaliter*, (..) The mission is only said to be with respect to its end term. Hence, the mission of the divine Persons is not to the sacraments, but to those who receive grace through the sacraments."[162]

The end term of the invisible mission is not the minister of the sacraments, but those who receive grace through the sacraments. Consequently, when Thomas speaks of the fruit of the gift of the Holy Spirit to the apostles, he does not mention what fruit this gift will bear for the apostles, but the fruit for those who receive forgiveness.

With respect to the power of the keys, we must conclude that its nature does not lie in being a grace, but in being instrumental. The power of the keys is not a grace making the one who holds it holy, though the fact that it is given together with the gift of the Holy Spirit may refer to the point that whomever has the power of the keys is under a special obligation to live a holy life. Nor is it a charisma, which would mean that it was something of the minister himself. However, the fact that it is given with the Holy Spirit may refer to the point

---

[160] In *STh* III q.63, a.1 ad 1, Thomas deals with the objection that Eph 4, 30 ("do not grieve the Holy Spirit of God who has marked you with his seal") gives grounds for ascribing the sacramental mark to the Spirit. Thomas replies: "Ad primum dicendum quod, Apostolus ibi loquitur de consignatione secundum quam aliquis deputatur ad futuram gloriam, quae fit per gratiam et Spirtui sancto attribuitur, etc." However, 'deputare aliquis ad futuram gloriam' seems to refer to the 'character baptismale', and not the the 'character sacerdotale'. The first refers to the reception of grace, while the latter refers to the handing over (*tradere*) of grace (cf. a.2 co).

[161] Cf. Chapter Two, Section 3, where we discussed the *instinctus Spiritus sancti*, in the context of dealing with the preparation for justification, as that which causes one "to recognize and appreciate in the multitude of articulated points of doctrine the self-revealing First Truth as the highest good."

[162] *STh* I, q.43, a.6 ad 4.

that we need the assistance of the Spirit in order to see the ministers of the sacraments as instruments in the hand of Christ.

Instead, it is a power which makes the one who holds it into an instrument. In the light of the instrumental character of the keys, the gift of the Spirit accompanying it may refer to the point that it is an instrument with which the Spirit is sent to the receiver of the sacrament. Insofar as tradition says that sacraments contain grace, what is meant according to Thomas is that this grace is in the sacraments *instrumentaliter*. In the next subsection, we will examine this notion of instrumentality further.

Instrumentality

In Thomas' theology, we must understand the instrumentality of the sacraments against the background of the instrumentality of Christ's humanity. According to Thomas, Christ's humanity is the instrument of His divinity.[163] Thomas derived this idea from John of Damascene, who says that "the flesh is instrument of the divinity"[164], and that "in Christ, human nature was like the instrument of the divinity".[165]

According to Thomas, "an instrument is said to do something because it is moved by a principal agent, but besides this it can nevertheless have its own operation according to its own form"[166] Therefore, an instrument has two operations: it is moved by the principal agent using the instrument and it acts according to its own form. For instance, a carpenter can make a bed by using a saw as instrument. The saw is the instrument, while the carpenter is the principal agent. However, the saw can only be used to 'cause' the bed, when it is used in accordance with its own form, which is cutting.[167] In other words, the carpenter is not free to choose any instrument, but rather needs an instrument

---

[163] Cf. *STh* III q.13, a.2.3; q.19, a.1 ad 2; q.62, a.5 co; q.64, a.3.

[164] Cf. *In III Sent* d.18, a.1 ob. 4: "Instrumenti et principalis agentis est tantum una actio. Sed, sicut dicit Damascenus (lib. III, c.19): *caro est instrumentum Divinitatis*. Ergo ... "

[165] Cf. *De ver* II, q.27, a.4 co: "Dicendum est ergo, quod nec sacramentum nec aliqua creatura potest gratiam dare per modum per se agentis, quia hoc solius virtutis divinae est, ut ex praecedenti art. patet. Sed sacramenta ad gratiam operantur instrumentaliter; quod sic patet. Damascenus in libro III dicit quod humana natura in Christo erat velut quoddam organum divinitatis; et ideo humana natura aliquid communicabat in operatione virtutis divinae, sicut quod Christus tangendo leprosum mundavit; sic enim ipse tactus Christi causabat instrumentaliter salutem leprosi." Cf. T. Schoof, "Jezus, Gods werktuig voor ons heil. Peilingen naar de theologische procedure van Thomas van Aquino", in *TvT* 14 (1974), pp.217-244 (with a summary in English). Also L.-M. Chauvet, *Symbol and sacrament*, p.20.

[166] *STh* III q.19, a.1 ad 2: "Ad secundum dicendum, quod instrumentum dicitur aliquid agere ex eo, quod movetur a principali agente, quod tamen praeter hoc potest habere propriam operationem secundum suam formam, ut de igne dictum est. Sic igitur actio instrumenti, inquantum est instrumentum, non est alia ab actione principalis agentis, potest tamen habere aliam operationem, prout est res quaedam. Sic igitur operatio, quae est humanae naturae in Christo, inquantum est instrumentum divinitatis, non est alia ab operationem divinitatis, non enim est alia salvatio, qua salvat humanitas Christi, et divinitas eius. Habet tamen humana natura in Christo, inquantum est natura quaedam, quamdam propriam operationem praeter divinam, ut dictum est."

[167] Cf. *De ver* q.27, a.4 co.

that can cut, like an ax or a saw, in order to make the bed. In the end, however, the effect is not assimilated to the instrument, but to the principal agent: the bed is not made in likeness to the saw, but to the design of the bed in the carpenter's mind.[168]

When Thomas applies this notion of instrumental causality to the sacraments, he makes two distinctions. First, he distinguishes between separate and conjoined instruments, and then he distinguishes between animate and inanimate instruments. An example of a separate instrument is the ax, while an example of a conjoined instrument is a hand. Thomas adds that the separate instrument is moved through the conjoined instrument. When applied to the sacraments, this yields the following. The principal agent of grace is God, and God alone.[169] In comparison to God, Christ's humanity is like a conjoined instrument, while the sacraments are like separate instruments.[170]

The second distinction is between animate and inanimate. Christ's humanity is both the conjoined and animate instrument of his divinity in the propagation of grace. The minister of the sacraments, however, is also an animate instrument, though not conjoined but separate. The fact that he is an animate instrument means that he is not only moved by a principal agent, but also somehow (*quodammodo*[171]) moves himself, insofar as his will moves his limbs to act. Accordingly, the minister of the sacraments must have the intention to let himself be used by the principal agent, Christ. It is precisely for this reason that the intention of the minister to do what Christ and the church do (*facit quod facit Ecclesia*[172]) plays a decisive role in making perfect the sacramental sign, as we saw above (section 2).[173]

---

[168] *STh* III, q.62, a.1 co: "Causa vero instrumentum non agit per virtutem suae formae, sed solum per motum, quo movetur a principali agente. Unde, effectus non assimilatur instrumento, sed principali agenti. Sicut lectus non assimilatur securi, sed arti, quae est in mente articifis."

[169] *Ibidem.* "(N)ec sacramentum nec aliqua creatura potest gratiam dare per modum per se agentis, quia hoc solius virtutis divinae est."

[170] *STh* III, q.62, a.5 co: "Respondeo dicendum, quod, sicut dictum est, sacramentum operatur ad gratiam causandam per modum instrumenti. Est autem duplex instrumentum: unum quidem separatum, ut baculus, aliud autem coniunctum, ut manus. Per instrumentum autem coniunctum movetur instrumentum separatum, sicut baculus per manum. Principalis autem causa efficiens gratiae est ipse Deus, ad quem comparatur humanitas Christi, sicut instrumentum coniunctum, sacramentum autem, sicut instrumentum separatum. Et ideo oportet, quod virtus salutifera a divinitate Christi per eius humanitatem in ipsa sacramenta derivetur." Cf. T. Schoof, "Jezus, Gods werktuig", pp.228-229.

[171] According to Schoof, the frequently inserted qualification *quodammodo* (also *quoddam, sicut, veluti, quasi*) is meant to place things in perspective: "Daarmee geef je aan dat het gebruikte woord een sleutel is die niet geheel past en die alleen bij gebrek aan beter en met wat wringen dienst kan doen." (T. Schoof, "Jezus, Gods werktuig", p.241.)

[172] Cf. *De art fid* II (614): "Requiritur etiam in quolibet sacramento persona ministri conferentis sacramentum cum intentione conferendi et faciendi quod facit Ecclesia."

[173] *STh* III q.64, a.8 ad 1: "Ad primum dicendum, quod instrumentum inanimatum non habet aliquam intentionem respectu effectus. Sed loco intentionis est motus, quo movetur a principali agente. Sed instrumentum animatum, sicut est minister, non solum movetur, sed etiam quodammodo movet seipsum, inquantum sua voluntate movet membra ad operandum."

That the sacramental power of the sacrament of penance is in the minister by virtue of the keys of the church means that the minister of the sacrament of penance can act as animate instrument in the hands of Christ who, according to his divinity, acts in the sacrament of penance as principal agent. The power of the keys itself consists in 'being configured' to be used as animate instrument.

The Holy Spirit and the sacrament of penance

In summarizing, what can we say about the role of the Holy Spirit with respect to the causality of the sacrament of penance? Our examinations have shown that the power of the keys is a spiritual power, which in Thomas' theology is only obliquely associated with the Holy Spirit. The testimony of John that the power to forgive or retain sins is given together with the gift of the Holy Spirit gives reason to expect this spiritual power to be a form of grace. Nevertheless, on closer examination, Thomas appears to deny such identification. The main reason for this is that the sacramental power is not something belonging to the priest, but resides principally in Christ himself. The notion of instrumental cause is intended to emphasize that the one who actually forgives the sins is Christ according to his divinity, while at the same time it opens up the possibility to ascribe efficient causality to the sacraments. The priest absolving the penitent is the separate instrument handled by Christ, who is conjoined instrument according to his humanity and principal agent according to his divinity. In Thomas' theology, the personal involvement of the minister of the sacrament of penance remains limited to his intention to do what the church and, in particular, what Christ does, i.e. the intention to let himself be used as instrument of salvation.

The Holy Spirit plays only a secondary role. Though Christ can use unworthy priests as instruments of salvation, nevertheless they are morally obliged to be holy. Furthermore, in the sacrament of ordination grace is given, so that the priest can administer the sacraments worthily. Furthermore, Christ handed over the power to forgive and retain sins together with the Holy Spirit in order to designate that they are ministers in the sacraments. Insofar as the gift of the Holy Spirit refers to the grace of forgiveness, the minister of the sacrament of penance holds it only instrumentally.

In contrast, the penitent is involved in the sacrament of penance as person, even more than in other sacraments. Forgiveness of sins, as we have seen in Chapter Two, consists primarily in a reorientation of the will, towards God and away from sin. Even though Christ can forgive without the sacrament of penance, he does not do so without the virtue of repentance, i.e. without a personal act of the penitent. The forgiveness of sins is something involving the penitent in the deepest sense, and refers to the penitent as a person: mind and body, as well as to his relationships to others.

The connection between the causality of the sacrament of penance and the Holy Spirit turns out to lie primarily in the preparation for justification and the

---

Et ideo requiritur intentio, qua subiiciat principali agenti, ut scilicet intendat facere, quod facit Christus et Ecclesia."

justification itself. In Chapter Two, we saw that, according to Thomas, one is brought to faith in a twofold way, namely externally by what one sees and hears in liturgy and preaching, and internally by the instinct of the Holy Spirit. Walgrave's emphasis on a twofold way points out that the effectiveness of the sacrament is not without the internal help of divine inspiration. This divine inspiration is needed in order "to recognize and appreciate in the multitude of articulated points of doctrine the self-revealing First Truth as the highest good" (cf. Chapter Two). If one understands the sacrament of penance to be part of doctrine, as seems to be reasonable, it appears that the Holy Spirit plays an important role in aiding the penitent in his or her approach of the sacrament of penance: examination of conscience, understanding the meaning of the rite itself, in particular the instrumentality of the priest (i.e. that in the priest he encounters Christ), reception of the absolution, and the new life 'in the Spirit'.

Chapter 5 The Church

Introduction

In this fifth and final chapter, we will examine the role of the Church in Thomas' theology of the sacrament of penance.

The ecclesial dimension of the sacrament of penance has received new attention in the recent liturgical reforms initiated at the Second Vatican Council.[1] On two occasions, the Council proclaimed that in the sacrament of penance the penitent not only receives forgiveness for offending God, but also reconciliation with the Church.[2] These liturgical reforms were, for a great part, prepared by what is known as the liturgical movement, which had arisen through a growing interest in the patristic penitential practice in the second half of the nineteenth and first half of the twentieth century.[3]

The reorientation with respect to the patristic sources resulted in a new understanding of the sacraments: less individualistic, and more in the sense of communal liturgical activities. Sacraments are primarily 'mysteries', representations of the mystery of Christ in worship (cf. the 'Mysterientheologie' of O. Casel[4]). The 'Mysterientheologie' was related to the theme of the Church as mystical body of Christ, confirmed by Pope Pius XII in his encyclical *Mystici*

---

[1]   On the theme of the ecclesial dimension of the sacrament of penance, see K. Rahner, "Vergessene Wahrheiten über das Busssakrament", in *Schriften zur Theologie* II, 1955, pp.143-185; *Kirche und Sakramente*, 1960; "Das Sakrament der Busse als Wiederversöhnung mit der Kirche", in *Schriften zur Theologie* VIII, 1967, pp.447-471; Th. Schneider, *Zeichen der Nähe Gottes*, 1979, pp.208-210.

[2]   *Lumen gentium*, No.11: "Qui vero ad sacramentum poenitentiae accedunt, veniam offensionis Deo illatae ab eius misericordia obtinent et simul reconciliantur cum Ecclesiae." *Presbyterorum ordinis*, No.5: "sacramento poenitentiae peccatores cum Deo et Ecclesia reconciliant."

[3]   According to O.H. Pesch, the reforming attempts go back as early as the 17th and 18th century. Their theological fundamentals were enhanced by the renewed interest in the Church Fathers, the study of the Bible, and the history of the early Christendom: "Dies alles führte schon in den 80er Jahren des 19. Jahrhunderts zu einer liturgischen Erneuerung, die zunächst den Bestrebungen vom Anfang des Jahrhundert zuwiderlief: Sie erneuerte die ursprüngliche Form der *lateinischen* Liturgie, vor allem den Gesang des gregorianischen Chorals – erschloß sie aber eben dadurch eigentlich nur den Gebildeten, einschließlich der ersten Versuche zweisprachiger Volksmeßbücher. Zudem war diese Erneuerung vor allem in Klöstern des Benediktiner-Ordens beheimatet: Solesmes in Frankreich (Père Guèranger), Bueron in Deutschland (Anselm Schott), seit 1913 auch besonders Maria Laach (Ildefons Herwegen). Pius X. nahm 1903 diese Bestrebungen auf, gab ihnen gesamtkirchliche Bedeutung – Neuausgabe der Choralbücher, Reform der Rubriken und des Breviers – und zugleich eine seelsorgliche Ausrichtung. Daran anknüpfend geschah der eigentliche Durchbruch mit der berühmt gewordenen Rede des Benediktiners Lambert Beaudin auf dem Katholikentag in Mecheln 1909 ("Mechelner Ereignis"). Von da an erfaßte die Liturgische Bewegung weite kircheneifriche Kreise in Belgien, Holland, Frankreich und im deutschen Sprachraum." O.H. Pesch, *Das zweite vatikanische Konzil. Vorgeschichte Verlauf-Ergebnisse Nachgeschichte*, 1994, pp.112-3.

[4]   Cf. O. Casel, *Das christliche Kultmysterium*, 1932 (1960⁴). Odo Casel was a monk of the Benedictine monastery of Maria Laach (see footnote 3). On Casel's 'Mysterientheologie', see: E. Schillebeeckx, *De sacramentele heilseconomie*, 1952, pp. 215-222.

Corporis of June 29, 1943. The rediscovery of the theme of the Church as sacrament was also related to this. These rediscoveries: the communal character of the sacraments, sacraments as mysteries, and the Church as sacrament, were adopted by theologians like O. Semmelroth[5], E. Schillebeeckx[6] and K. Rahner[7], and received expression in the Vatican II Constitution on the Church, *Lumen gentium*[8]

The rediscovery of the ecclesial dimensions of the sacraments, and, in particular, the ecclesial dimensions of sin and reconciliation are relevant to our studies. In *Sacrosanctum concilium* No.72, the second Vatican Council called for a revision of the rite and form of the sacrament of penance, so that they would express the nature and effect of the sacrament more clearly.[9] From the Council's acts, it appears that the intention was to clarify the ecclesial respect of (the sacrament of) penance.[10] In *Lumen gentium* No.11, the ecclesial dimensions of both sin and reconciliation receive explicit expression: by sinning, the sinner has hurt the Church, and the Church labors for the conversion of sinners by love, example and prayers.[11]

With respect to the ecclesial dimension of sin: Sin is, in the first and last place, an offense against God. But sin is also an offense against the community that is the Church. As member of the Church, the sinner shares in the holiness of the Church, and by sinning, he offends against her holiness, her mission and task, making, for his part, the Church herself sinful.[12]

With respect to the ecclesial dimension of forgiveness: Penance, in the early Church, had an intercessory character. The sinner was freed from the burden of his sin by the prayer of the Church (understood as body *and* head). In the Church, Christ prays for the penitent. The inner conversion that makes the penitent come to the sacrament of the Church must be understood to be the result of the praying Church as well. With respect to this 'forgotten truth', Rahner points out that we, when we speak of the sacrament of penance, are inclined to focus on the nature of the sacrament in a narrow sense, thus isolating the sacrament from the whole of human and ecclesial life. Hence, we forget that the sacrament of penance is embedded in the wider penitential

---

5   O. Semmelroth, *Die Kirche als Urskrament*, 1953; "Die Kirche als Sakrament des Heils", in *Mysterium salutis* IV,1, pp.309-356.

6   E. Schillebeeckx, *Christus Sacrament van de Godsontmoeting*, 1959³.

7   Cf. K. Rahner, "Vergessene Wahrheiten über das Busssakrament", in *Schriften zur Theologie* II, 1955, pp.143-185; *Kirche und Sakramente*, 1960; "Das Sakrament der Busse als Wiederversöhnung mit der Kirche", in *Schriften zur Theologie* VIII, 1967, pp.447-471.

8   Cf. P. Smulders, "De kerk als sacrament van het heil", in G. Baraúna, *De kerk van Vaticanum II. Commentaren op de Concilieconstitutie Over de kerk*, 1966, pp.372-395; L.J. Koffeman, *Kerk als sacramentum. De rol van de sacramentele ecclesiologie tijdens Vaticanum II*, 1986.

9   *SC*, No.72: "Ritus et formulae paenitentiae ita recognoscantur, ut naturam et effectum sacramenti clarius exprimant."

10 Cf. R. Messner, *Feiern der Umkehr*, p.210.

11 *LG* No.11: "Qui vero ad sacramentum poenitentiae accedunt, veniam offensionis Deo illatae ab eius misericordia obtinent et simul reconciliantur cum Ecclesiae, quam peccando vulneraverunt, et quae eorum conversione caritate, exemplo, precibus adlaborat."

12 Cf. K. Rahner, "Vergessene Wahrheiten", p.145.

context of the Church. In this context, Christ's grace is present through the preaching of the Word, and through the example and word of other Christians. The preceding prayers to the absolution are a remnant of the penitential practice of the early Church in which the Church prayed for the salvation of the sinner. The *Ego te absolvo* is supported by the intercessory prayers of the Church.[13]

Both aspects received their place in the new *Ordo paenitentiae*, promulgated on December 2, 1973 and published in February 1974. With respect to the ecclesial dimension of sin, the *Ordo* speaks about how the sin of one hurts others, just as the holiness of one benefits others (No.5). With respect to the ecclesial dimension of forgiveness, the *Ordo* emphasizes that the Church gives shape to continuous repentance in life and in liturgy (No.4). We can refer to No. 5 as well, insofar as it implies that the holiness of one benefits the sinner, motivating him to do penance. Furthermore, just as people help each other in doing injustice, so they help each other in doing penance (No.5). Moreover, the *Ordo* stresses the fact that that the whole Church, as a priestly people, cooperates with the work of reconciliation in different ways: by preaching the word of God, by intercessory prayers, by helping the penitent with maternal care and aid (No.8).

According to R. Messner, the new *Ordo* has not brought the expected break with the scholastic-Tridentine theology of penance. The private confession in front of a priest sacramentally representing Christ remains the normal way for the reconciliation of the sinner with God and the Church, and the absolution formula is accordingly centered on the words "Ego te absolvo".[14] The cooperation of the (priestly) community of the faithful with the reconciliation of the penitent remains limited. With respect to the celebration of the sacrament of penance, only the priest is truly essential.[15]

In the prescriptions for the celebration of the sacrament of penance for one penitent, the ecclesial dimension receives expression in the invocation of the Holy Spirit (No.15) and in the imposition of hands accompanying the absolution (No.19). The latter must be understood analogously with the imposition of hands in the sacrament of baptism, signifying the initiation, and the admission, or re-admission, into the Church as community of the Holy Spirit.[16]

The ecclesial dimensions of sin and forgiveness receive their best expression in the communal celebration of penance with individual confession and absolution (No.22), and also in the communal celebration of penance with

---

[13] *Idem*, p.174.

[14] R. Messner, *Feiern der Umkehr und Versöhnung*, p.217

[15] Idem, p.218: "(D)ementsprechend kann zwar von der Mitwirkung der Gemeinde als priesterliches Volk beim Werk der Versöhnung durch die Verkündigung des Wortes Gottes, durch Fürbitte und mütterliche Sorge und Aufmerksamkeit für die Sünder gesprochen werden; beim Vollzug des Busssakramentes ist allem Anschein nach allein der Dienst der als Apostelnachfolger verstandenen Priester wesentlich (*OP* No.8)."

[16] *Feiern*, p. 224.

general absolution, though the latter cannot be considered as the normal way of celebrating the sacrament of penance.

The Second Vatican Council 'consciously' (according to: K. Rahner, Th. Schneider[17]) left the question about the relation between reconciliation with God and reconciliation with the Church, and in particular the question whether reconciliation with the Church is the *modus reconciliandi Dei*, undecided.[18] With respect to the theme of reconciliation with the Church as the immediate effect of the sacrament of penance and *modus reconciliandi Deo*, new ground was broken by the dissertation of B. Xiberta, *Clavis Ecclesiae*.[19] He argued that reconciliation with the Church was the *res et sacramentum* of the sacrament of penance, and thus the medium and mode of the *res sacramenti*, the reconciliation with God. K. Rahner adopted this view: the *pax cum Ecclesia* is the sacrament (the *sacramentum et res* of the sacrament of penance) of the *pax cum Deo* (the *res sacramenti*).[20]

In this final chapter, we will investigate whether Thomas acknowledges such a role for the Church with respect to the forgiveness of sins in the sacrament of penance. Does the insight that the sacrament of penance is also a communal celebration of the Church, or that the sinner is a member of the Church, play a role in Thomas' reflections on penance? In the previous chapter, we saw that the Holy Spirit has been given a major role both with respect to the sacrament of penance and its minister, and with respect to the sinner himself. What is the Spirit's relation to the Church, and do Church and Spirit together function within Thomas' theology of the forgiveness of sins in the sacrament of penance?

Posing these questions about the relation between reconciliation with the Church and reconciliation with God enables us to place what we have found with respect to Thomas' theology of the sacrament of penance in the wider context of his ecclesiology.[21] Before we can deal with this question in Thomas' theology, we first have to obtain insight into Thomas' vision of the Church in general.

---

17 Th. Schneider, *Zeichen der Nähe Gottes*, p.210: "Das Konzil lässt bewust die Frage offen, wie genau das Verhältnis zwischen der Schuldvergebung und der Gnadenmitteilung von seiten Gottes einerseits und der Wiederversöhnung mit der Kirche andererseits zu denken ist."

18 Cf. *Feiern*, p. 210: "Die Wiederentdeckung der Versöhnung mit der Kirche als Modus der Versöhnung mit Gott stellt die Grundlage der vom Konzil gewünschten Reform der Riten des Busssakramentes dar. (..) In diesem Sinn stellt LG 11 (ähnlich PO 5) als Wirkungen des Busssakramentes die Verzeihung von Gott und die Versöhnung mit der Gemeinde nebeneinander (simul), ohne allerdingst deren gegenseitiges Verhältnis näher zu bestimmen, und betont die Mitwirkung der Kirche (Gemeinde) an der Bekehrung der Sünder durch Liebe, Beispiel und Gebet."

19 B. Xiberta, *Clavis ecclesiae. De ordine absolutionis sacramentalis ad reconciliationem cum ecclesia*, Romae, 1922.

20 K. Rahner, "Das Sakrament der Busse als Wiederversöhnung mit der Kirche".

21 Cf. K. Rahner's remark that we tend to speak about the sacrament of penance in the narrow sense, thus isolating the sacrament from the whole of human and ecclesial life, in which the sacrament is embedded. ("Vergessene Wahrheiten", p.172)

1 Thomas' notion of the Church

There have been many articles and various monographs written on specific ecclesiological topics in Thomas' theology, as well as many 'Thomistic' ecclesiological works, but only a few works deal with his ecclesiology in a systematic and comprehensive way. Grabmann's *Die Lehre des heiligen Thomas von Aquin von der Kirche als Gotteswerk* of 1903 is, in many ways, outdated and too harmonious. Cuéllar's *La Naturaleza de Iglesia segun Santo Tomas* only deals with Thomas' commentaries on the Pauline corpus. As he says himself, G. Sabra's *Thomas Aquinas' Vision of the Church* "fills a gap in as much as it offers a systematic and comprehensive account of the fundamentals of Thomas' ecclesiology."[22]

According to Sabra, Thomas' notion of the Church is itself partly responsible for the absence of an explicit treatise on the Church in his theology. As we will see, ' Church', in Thomas' theology, is not a simple concept. It is manifold and comprehensive, and it misses the formal clarity which must have been presupposed were it to have been the object of a separate treatise. At the same time, the Church is a dominant concept in Thomas' theology. Therefore, Sabra speaks of an implicit ecclesiology in Thomas' theology.

As a first step towards an understanding of Thomas' notion of the Church, we will deal with the question of why there is no separate treatise 'On the Church' in Thomas' theology.[23] Next, we will discuss two dominant designations of the Church in Thomas' theology: the Church as *congregatio fidelium* and the Church as *corpus mysticum*. These two designations dominate Thomas' implicit ecclesiology. The discussion of these designations will contribute to our understanding of Thomas' notion of the Church. Then, in Sections Three and Four, we will discuss the role of the Holy Spirit and of the sacraments in Thomas' implicit ecclesiology. Finally, we will deal with the topic of membership of the Church.

Why is there no separate treatise De Ecclesia *in Thomas' theology?*

Scholars have given both historical and theological explanations for the absence of an explicit treatise on the Church in Thomas' theology.

Those who favor a historical explanation argue that in Thomas' times the Church was not a problem. However, this argument does not seem to hold, for there were, according to Sabra, many developments "which could have prompted reflection on the Church". He mentions five. (1) The challenge to the Church's political power represented in the struggle between the Church

---

22 G. Sabra, *Thomas Aquinas' Vision of the Church. Fundamentals of an ecumenical Ecclesiology*, 1987, p.17.

23 The absence of such a treatise has immediate relevance for the role the Church plays in Thomas' theology regarding sacramental causality. Cf. K. Rahner, "Einleitende Bemerkungen zur allgemeine Sakramentenlehre bei Thomas von Aquin", in *Schriften zur theologie* X, 1972, p.394: "Da in der theologischen Summe des Thomas von Aquin eine ausgeführte Ekklesiologie fehlt und da auf die Christologie, die dort selber erst verhältnismässig spät behandelt wird, gleich die Sakramentenlehre folgt, kann natürlich auch die Kirche als "Grundsakrament" nicht wirklich thematisch werden."

and the Hohenstaufen dynasty. (2) The challenge to the Church by heretical groups. (3) The new ecclesiological dimension that came into existence through the rise of the mendicant orders. (4) The consequences which the teachings of Joachim of Fiore had for the nature of the Church. (5) The ecclesiological problems regarding the union with the Greek Church.

In fact, these problems did provoke written reactions on topics related to the Church, though not treatises on the nature of the Church as such.[24] From this, it appears that the notion of the Church was not unproblematic in Thomas' times. The assumption that the Church was not a problem, and was taken for granted and therefore was not in the theological consciousness of Thomas and his contemporaries, must consequently be refuted. Besides, the assumption itself that a subject must be a problem in order for it to receive a separate treatise is questionable. For a treatise *De Ecclesiae* could very well arise from the inner logic of a systematic work, especially in those systematic works that aimed to be comprehensive, such as, for instance, Thomas' *Summa theologiae*. Consequently, we have to look for a different reason why a separate treatise on the Church, in particular in the *Summa theologiae*, is missing.

Regarding the theological explanations, these primarily aim at explaining why Thomas, in his systematic works (of which the purpose is to provide a comprehensive summary of theology), and in particular in his *Summa theologiae*, has no section on the Church. With respect to the *Summa theologiae*, being Thomas' most systematic and comprehensive work, the question of why there is no treatise *De ecclesiae* is the most pressing.

One of the reasons which scholars like Grabmann, Congar and Seckler have given for this absence is that the Church functions as a kind of architectonic law, which governs and underlies the whole: everything in Thomas' thought is ecclesiological. Well, this may be true, but it does not explain why Thomas does dedicate explicit and separate treatises to God and Christ, who also undeniably underlie the whole of Thomas' *Summa*, and not to the Church. Is it because the Church, being a historical reality, does not belong *per se* to *sacra doctrina*? If this were true, then this reason would also count for the sacraments; their being historical realities and structures in time. The sacraments, as we have seen, have a separate treatise in the *Summa*.

The explanation that Sabra gives is that the reason why such a separate treatise is missing is that Thomas operated with a manifold, non-univocal and primarily theological notion of the Church, as opposed to the predominantly juridical,

---

[24] *Idem*, pp.24-5. In particular, the teachings of heretical groups accused the Church of being an 'evil church', and, according to Sabra, presented different ecclesiologies. In reaction to these, Moneta of Cremona in the fifth and last book of his *Summa adversus Catharos et Valdensis* (ca. 1244) defends the Roman Church against the claims of heretical movements. "This is one of the earliest works – possibly the first ever – to include a whole treatise on the Church. Nevertheless, it is not a summa of theology, but an apologetic work devoted to the refutation of non-orthodox teachings. It is not a systematic treatise on the Church for it revolves around the claims of heretics and is structured accordingly." (p.25, footnote 30).

political and sociological notion of the Church which operated in the treatises *De Ecclesia* written some thirty years after Thomas' death.

Here we chance upon Thomas' notion of the Church. According to Sabra, Thomas' notion of the Church is, on the level of the constituted and historical reality, inherently twofold. 'Church' can refer to the congregation of the believers, the communion of grace, which is united and ordered to God by hope, faith and love. On the other hand, 'Church' can also refer to the visible institution, the means of grace, and all that relates to its functions in that respect. Both aspects are present in Thomas' theology, though they are nowhere formally and systematically distinguished and elaborated.

> "The Church as *communio* and as effect of grace is located under its sources and constitutive principles, i.e. grace, Christ, Holy Spirit: the Church as means of salvation and institution is located under the functions, structure and properties of the institution, e.g. sacraments, episcopate, papacy, power of keys, worship, etc. This applies foremost in the *Summa theologiae* because of its strictly systematic and scientific character, but also applies in Thomas' other works and in his ecclesiological thought in general, for the twofold conception and the theological outlook are everywhere in Thomas' theology."[25]

Thomas' comprehensive and manifold conception of the Church is the main reason why, according to Sabra, an explicit ecclesiology is missing, because "an explicit reflection on some concept presupposes some degree of formal clarity with respect to that concept, but this is precisely what Thomas did not do in his ecclesiology. He operated with an unclarified, ambivalent, rich and comprehensive notion of the Church that was predominantly theological."[26]

In the next section we will see how theological Thomas' notion of the Church, in fact, is. With respect to the question about the absence of a treatise on the Church, I tend to agree with the explanation Sabra gives. Thomas' notion of the Church is, at the same time, manifold and predominantly theological. The latter means that the focus is on God, and on all things in relation to God. Theologically, the Church is the community of those who are actually or potentially related to God by faith, by love or by glory. I suspect that all other uses of 'Church' relate to this theological notion of Church as many to one (*multa ad unum*), i.e. by way of analogy. The community of those who are actually united with Christ then holds the *ratio propria*. The manifoldness or non-univocality of 'Church' in Thomas' theology seems to be, in some way, the result of the fact that Thomas wants to speak about the Church in the theological sense of the word, before speaking of the Church in the sense of the visible organization or institution.

As a result, the concept of Church in Thomas is hard to define. Had Thomas been primarily interested in the Church as the visible institution, with its bishops, its hierarchical structure, its juridical construction etc., then his use of

---

[25] *Idem*, p.30.
[26] *Idem*, p.25: "This fact, however, does not deny that the concept of the Church which he presupposed and which underlay his theology without being the object of formal reflection is in itself clear and consistent."

the term 'Church' would have been univocal, and consequently his notion of the Church would have been easier to define.

If it is correct that the manifoldness of 'Church' in Thomas' theology is the direct result of his theological interest, provoking distinct uses of 'Church' which relate to each other as analogates, then we have an important key to understanding Thomas' notion of the Church. However, we not only have to deal with the (presumed) fact that Thomas uses 'Church' in different senses, which relate to each other as analogates, we also have to deal with his use of different metaphors, or 'designations', as Sabra calls them, in order to describe the Church. In the next section, we will discuss the two most important designations: *congregatio fidelium* and *corpus mysticum*.

Thomas' notion of the Church

According to Sabra, two designations dominate Thomas' notion of the Church: *congregatio fidelium* and *corpus mysticum*.[27] In his writings, Thomas uses the designation *congregatio fidelium* both with the emphasis on *congregatio*, i.e. the societal part[28], and with the emphasis on *fidelium*, i.e. under the aspect of faith[29].

---

[27] Sabra deals with the different designations of the Church in Thomas' writings under six headings: 1. Occasional symbols and similes; 2. *Civitas*; 3. *Domus*; 4. *Populus*; 5. *congregatio fidelium*, 6. *corpus mysticum*. With respect to the occasional symbols and similes, Sabra remarks that "Thomas' reluctance to use these images and symbols and his lack of interest in developing any of them indicate the direction in which his views about the Church are not to be found." The reason for this are "his Aristotelean insistence on clarity, precision and logical coherence and his dislike for symbolical and allegorical language in scientific theology." (*Thomas Aquinas' Vision of the Church*, pp. 34-36.) The designation *Civitas* is only elaborated on in three main texts, all three being scriptural commentaries. According to Sabra, Thomas' understanding of the Church as city is profoundly scriptural and characteristically theological. "It is not the institutional aspect of the Church but the *communio* one that dominates in the texts discussed above [i.e. Thomas' commentaries on Ephesians 2,19-22, on Ephesians 4,5-6 and on Psalm 45 (46)]." Furthermore, "it [*Civitas*] cannot be described as characteristic of his ecclesiological terminology, though it remains to be seen whether its content is characteristic of Thomas' ecclesiological thought." (p.39) With respect to his use of *Domus*, two themes dominate, namely whether it means the Church militant or the Church triumphant, and its foundation. Again, this designation "is a predominantly theological one, be it in the reference to the nature of the house, the conditions for dwelling in it – the *theological* virtues, or its firmness and strong foundation." The designation *Domus*, however, "cannot be said to be decisive for Thomas' ecclesiology." (pp.42-43) With respect to the fourth designation, *Populus*, Sabra groups the majority of instances to their occurrence in three main contexts: the Christian political context, being identical with the Church as a whole and designating the non-religious lay community. Especially the latter context shows Thomas' conception of *populus* to be predominantly juridical. "*Populus* itself does not denote the institution, but it evokes, nay demands it. Its use by Thomas does not stress the 'human and communal' aspect of the Church, but only one, as it were, passive component, the laity which is the field of work for the institution." (p.49)

[28] For instance *In IV Sent* d.20, q.1, a.4, qa.1 co: "Sed cum Ecclesia sit congregatio fidelium; congregatio autem hominum sit duplex; scilicet oeconomica, ut illi qui sunt de una familia; et politica, sicut illi qui sunt de uno populo; Ecclesia similatur congregationi politicae, quia ipse populus Ecclesia dicitur; sed conventus diversi vel parochiae in una diocesi similantur congregationi in diversis familiis vel in diversis officiis."

[29] For instance *STh* III q.8, a.4 ad 2: "Ecclesia secundum statum viae est congregatio fidelium; sed secundum statum patriae est congregatio comprehedentium."

When the emphasis lies on *congregatio*, the point is that the Church is a union made up of many different elements. "Unity is not conceived of in terms of unity of faith, but of the one artificer, the one gatherer, God."[30] *Congregatio* has to do with movement, with moving together.[31]

When the second part of this designation, the aspect of faith is stressed, *congregatio fidelium* is contrasted to *congregatio comprehendentium*, which contrast is paralleled by the contrast between the Church militant and the Church triumphant.[32] The designation *congregatio fidelium* is then used to stress its imperfection, its *status in via* as opposed to the *status in patria* of the Church triumphant.[33]

Sabra emphasizes the theological character of the designation *congregatio fidelium*, even in those places where the emphasis lies on *congregatio*. The central notion of unity "is not a political or juridical conception of unity, but a theological one, either in terms of unity in faith or, more fundamentally, union in God. (..) What distinguishes this congregation – the Church – from other congregations is not conceived in terms of a different juridical or sociological structure, but rather in terms of its relationship to the Triune God, and, consequently, in terms of the moral conduct that must issue from that relationship."[34]

The origins of the second designation, *corpus mysticum*, lie in the eucharistic controversies of the early Middle Ages.[35] In Thomas' writings, we find the designation in the eucharistic context, i.e. when 'mystical body' is the

---

30 Sabra, *Thomas Aquinas'*, p.54; Cf. *In ad Heb* c.3, lc.1 (163): "Aggregatio autem fidelium, quae est Ecclesia et domus Dei, ex diversis collecta est, scilicet Iudaeis et Gentibus, servis et liberis. Et ideo Ecclesia sicut et omnis domus ab aliquo uniente fabricatur."

31 Cf. *STh* I q.69, a.1 ob 1: "Congregatio ad motum localum pertinet."

32 Cf. *In Ioan*, c.14, lc.1: "Duplex est ergo domus Dei. Una est militans Ecclesia, scilicet congregatio fidelium. (..) Alia est triumphans, scilicet sanctorum collectio in gloria Patris."

33 Sabra adds that the Church as *congregatio fidelium* also discloses an ethical dimension: it ought to be a holy congregation, "because the faithful have been washed and purified by the blood of Christ, because they have been anointed with the grace of the Holy Spirit, because the Trinity dwells in them, and finally because they invoke God." (*Thomas Aquinas' Vision*, p.56). Cf. *In Symb*, a.9 (977-980): ""Ecclesia vero Christi est sancta. (..) Sanctificantur autem fideles huius congregationis ex tribus. Primo, quia sicut Ecclesia cum consecratur, materialiter lavatur, ita et fideles luti sunt sanguine Christi. (..) Secundo ex inunctione: quia sicut Ecclesia inungitur, sic et fideles spirituali inunctione unguntur, ut sanctificentur. (..) Tertio ex inhabitatione Trinitatis: nam ubicomque Deus inhabitat, locus ille sanctus est. (..) Quarto propter invocationem Dei."

34 Cf. G. Sabra, *Thomas Aquinas'* Vision, p.57. Only in one place does Thomas compare the Church as congregation to a political congregation (to a people): *In IV Sent* d.20, q.1, a.4, qa.1 co (See footnote 28)

35 *Idem*, p.61. According to Sabra, "H. de Lubac has convincingly shown how the term *corpus mysticum* was originally applied to the Eucharist. (..) As a result of the eucharistic controversies of the early Middle Ages, the Eucharist is more and more referred to as *corpus Christi verum*. Gradually, and beginning with the twelfth century, the word *mysticum* is added to *corpus (Christi)* to mean the Church in distinction from the Eucharist. A decisive stage begins with William of Auxerre, the first to use *corpus mysticum* in a non-eucharistic context and to make clear the distinction between *corpus Christi naturale*, *corpus verum* and *corpus mysticum*. So, by the mid-thirteenth century and especially with the great scholastics, *corpus mysticum* begins to stabilize as *the* designation for the Church." (p.60)

designation of the Church signified by, or configured in, the sacrament of the Eucharist.[36]

Beyond the eucharistic context, the designation *corpus mysticum* as designation of the Church is used in the christological context. The designation *corpus mysticum* designates, in the first place, the unity of Christ and his Church, and next the unity of the body, the Church itself.

The unity of Christ and the Church is understood in terms of the unity of head and body.[37] Christ is understood as the giver of grace, and the Church as its receiver. Christ and the Church are one person: what Christ merited for himself, he merited for his members.[38]

The unity of the body itself is a unity of a multitude, as opposed to a unity in the sense of simplicity, or indivisibility, or unity in the sense of continuity or connection. Unity is here used in the sense of association, combination, joining, just as a house is constituted of bricks and beams. Similarly, the Church as 'body' is understood as a unity of members, the multitude of which does not remove the unity of the body.[39] The unity of the Church consists in its members having one 'nature' (including both humans and angels), being kept together by faith, kept alive by grace and love, and animated by the Holy Spirit, who is the 'soul' of the Church.[40]

---

[36] For instance *ScG* IV, c.69: "Congruit tamen magis puritati corporis mystici, id est Ecclesiae, quae in hoc sacramento configuratur, usus azymi panis, secundum illud Apostoli: 'Pascha nostrum immolatus est Christus. Itaque epulemur .. in azymis sinceritatis et veritatis' (I Cor. v, 7,8)"; also *De art fid* II (620): "Sic igitur in hoc sacramento est aliquid quod est sacramentum tantum, scilicet ipsa species panis et vini; et aliquid quod est res et sacramentum, scilicet corpus Christi verum; et aliquid quod est res tantum, scilicet unitas corporis mystici, idest Ecclesiae, quam hoc sacramentum et significant et causat."

[37] Everywhere Christ is designated as "head", the Church is implied as "body'. For example *STh* III, q.8 *De gratia Christi, secundum quod est caput Ecclesiae*.

[38] Cf. *STh* III, q.19, a.4 co: "Respondeo dicendum, quod, sicut supra dictum est, in Christo non solum fuit gratia, sicut in quodam homine singulari, sed sicut in capite totius Ecclesiae, cui omnes uniuntur sicut capiti membra, ex quibus constituitur mystice una persona; et exinde est, quod meritum Christi se extendit ad alios, inquantum sunt membra eius."

[39] Cf. *In I ad Cor* c.12, lc.3 (732).

[40] *In III Sent* d.13, q.2, a.2, qa.2 co: "Ad secundam quaestionem dicendum, quod in corpore naturali invenitur quadruplex unio membrorum ad invicem. Prima est secundum conformitatem naturae, quia omnia membra constant ex eisdem similibus partibus, et sunt unius rationis, sicut manus et pes ex carne et osse; et sic dicuntur membra unum genere vel specie. Secunda est per colligationem eorum ad invicem per nervos et juncturas, et sic dicuntur unum continuatione. Tertia est, secundum quod diffunditur vitalis spiritus et vires animae per totum corpus. Quarta est, secundum quod omnia membra perficiuntur per animam, quae est una numero in omnibus membris.

Et hae quatuor uniones inveniuntur in corpore mystico. Prima est, inquantum omnia membra ejus sunt unius naturae vel specie vel genere. Secunda est, inquantum colligata sunt ad invicem per fidem, quia sic continuantur in uno credito. Tertia est, secundum quod vivificantur per gratiam et caritatem. Quarta est, secundum quod in eis est Spiritus Sanctus, qui est ultima perfectio et principalis totius corporis mystici, quasi anima in corpore naturali." Cf. H. Rikhof, "*Corpus Christi Mysticum*. An inquiry into Thomas Aquinas' use of a term", in *Bijdragen* 37, 1976, p.157-159.

The interrelatedness of the 'members' depends on, or has its source in the head: as in the natural body, "the members can only relate to each other in so far as they receive power and influx from the head."[41] Similarly, the members of the Church can only relate to each other insofar as they participate in the theological virtues of hope, faith and love, which cause the unity of the Church.[42] Love is the cause of the unity of the Church, because the members of the Church are connected in love for God and with each other in mutual love, which manifests itself when the members are solicitous about and compassionate toward each other.[43]

'Body' also refers to the variety of gifts and offices. As in the natural body the different members have different functions and abilities, so too, in the Church, the different members have different offices and gifts, all of which flow from Christ to his body.[44]

The idea of unity is essential in Thomas' use of this designation. In fact, Thomas defines *corpus* in terms of unity: body is a *"multitudo ordinata in unum"* (*STh* III q.8, a.4 co). Thomas uses the designation to prove that while being a multitude the Church is still one. Furthermore, the designation is predominantly theological and not juridical or sociological. In the Eucharistic context, the Church as *corpus mysticum* means that "she is the body of Christ which is designated by the sacrament."[45] In the Christological context, the analogy is with a natural body, and not with a socio-political one.[46] The theological nature of this designation appears also from the fact that Thomas never considers the body in itself apart from the head, and always proceeds from the head to the body. As 'body', the Church refers to the 'head', Christ. The designated notion of unity is conceived in terms of being related to the head, of receiving the grace from the head, of participating in the theological virtues of faith, hope and love. The variety of gifts and offices are understood as flowing forth from the one source of all graces, Christ. Membership of the Church is understood not in legal but in theological categories, namely "in the potential or actual participation in faith, love and the enjoyment of heaven."[47]

With respect to the two most characteristic designations, the Church as *congregatio fidelium* and the Church as *corpus mysticum*, Sabra concludes that both are central for Thomas, both are predominantly theological and both share the insistence on the theme of unity. "But each designation is used in different

---

[41] G. Sabra, *Thomas Aquinas' Vision*, p.63.
[42] *In symb* a.9 (973-976).
[43] *Ibidem* "Tertio ex unitate caritatis, quia omnes connectuntur in amore Dei, et ad invicem in amore mutuo."
[44] Cf. *In I ad Cor* c.12, lc.1 (721) : "Sicut enim in corpore naturali caput habet omnes sensus, non autem alia membra, ita in Ecclesia solus Christus habet omnes gratias, quae in aliis membris dividuntur, quod significatur Gen. II, 12, ubi dicitur quod fluvius, scilicet gratiarum, egrediebatur ad irrigandum paradisum, qui inde dividitur in quatuor capita. Et Matth XXV, v.15 dicitur et quod *uni dedit quinque talenta, alii duo, alii unum.*"
[45] G. Sabra, *Thomas Aquinas' Vision*, p.65.
[46] Cf. Rikhof's refutation of Darquenne in H. Rikhof, "Corpus Christi Mysticum", pp.155-156.
[47] G. Sabra, *Thomas Aquinas' Vision*, p.68; see below.

contexts, and each emphasizes a different aspect of the Church." The Church as *corpus mysticum* is a wider concept than the Church as *congregatio fidelium*. *Corpus* is also more explicitly Christological in that "it reflects the Church as something of and in Christ." "*Congregatio fidelium*, on the other hand, reflects the Church under a twofold aspect: that of a human community and that of faith." When regarded more closely, both turn out to "designate a relationship to Christ: one is a relationship of faith in Christ and the other is an incorporation into Christ."[48]

The Holy Spirit as constitutive principle of the Church

In his *De articulis fidei et ecclesiae sacramentis*, Thomas begins by stating that "the whole of Christian faith revolves around Christ's humanity and divinity". Consequently, the twelve (or fourteen, depending on how they are counted) articles of faith can be divided into those which belong to Christ's divinity, and those which belong to his humanity. Thomas classifies the Church under the articles belonging to Christ's divinity. The unity of the Church is treated, together with the sacraments, the gifts of the Holy Spirit, and the justification of man, as an effect of grace, through which the Church is vivified by God.[49]

The Church is primarily and fundamentally an effect of grace, and consequently, in Thomas' thought, the Church will be located where grace is present.[50] And since grace is brought about, manifested and communicated by Christ and the Holy Spirit, we must understand the Church as being constituted by Christ and the Holy Spirit.

In Chapter Three, we saw that the missions of the Son and the Spirit must be kept together: that a distinction can be made between the invisible missions of the Son and the Spirit, but that Thomas takes great pains to avoid the two missions being played off against each other. Besides, we saw that a proper (as opposed to appropriated) role of the Spirit in salvation history can be indicated in the visible realm alone; in the invisible realm of grace, distinct effects in salvation history can be ascribed to either Son or Spirit on the grounds of an appropriation alone. These analyses are the consequence of Thomas' principle that all works of the Trinity *ad extra* are of the Father, the Son and the Holy Spirit together. Furthermore, in Thomas' theology of the Trinity, the Holy Spirit is always the Spirit of the Son: the Holy Spirit does not operate in salvation history except as proceeding from the Son. The Holy Spirit is given

48 *Idem*, p.71.
49 *De art fid* I (598): "In primis igitur vos scire oportet, quod tota fides christiana circa divinitatem en humanitatem Christi versatur. (..) Primo igitur sex articulos sic distinguunt circa fidem divinitatis. Sunt enim circa divinitatem tria consideranda, scilicet unitas divinae essentiae, trinitas personarum, et effectus divinae virtutis. (..) Quartus articulus pertinet ad effectum gratiae, per quam vivificatur Ecclesia a Deo, secundum illud Roman. III, 24: *Iustificati gratis per gratiam ipsius*, scilicet Dei: et sub articulo isto comprehenduntur omnia sacramenta Ecclesiae, et quaecumque pertinent ad Ecclesiae unitatem, et dona Spiritus sancti, et iustitia hominis."
50 According to Sabra, "in the *Summa theologiae*, Thomas' ecclesiology may be viewed as beginning with the treatise on the New Law (Ia IIa, qq.106ff.)." (*Thomas Aquinas' Vision*, p.77)

immediately after Christ's resurrection and ascension, so his coming was a function of Christ's glorification. Moreover, the work of the Spirit refers to teaching, deepening and enlightening the believers about those matters which relate to the work of Christ.

> "Both Christ and the Holy Spirit are (..) operative in the same age: "whatever takes place through the Holy Spirit," says Thomas, "takes place also through Christ." Both have missions in the realm of grace, and though they differ in the effect of grace, "they commune in the root of grace." But since Christ is the "source of grace" and the "author of sanctification", the work of the Holy Spirit is always bound to, and directed towards, that of Christ."[51]

Sabra remarks that that which Thomas imputes to the Holy Spirit is overwhelming. In Thomas' theology, the Holy Spirit is the principle of both the *exitus* and the *reditus*, of creation and re-creation. The Spirit, proceeding *per modum amoris*, as love, is the principle of creation[52], of government and propagation[53], and of vivification, i.e. of life[54].

This brings Sabra to the conclusion that "one could say that Christ is the objective constituent of the Church as the source and the means of grace, but it is the Spirit who enables men to receive and appropriate grace, and He is thus the subjective constituent of the Church."[55] I tend to agree with this conclusion, though, referring to Chapter Three, I prefer not simply to identify the Spirit with what Sabra calls 'the subjective constituent'. First, as far as I can tell, Thomas does not use the modern concepts of objective and subjective. Instead, as we pointed out, the dominating terms are visible and invisible, which are more neutral.[56] Furthermore, I prefer to keep to the careful

---

[51]   *Idem*, p.83. The citations are taken from *In Eph* c.2, lc.3; *STh* I q.43, a.5 ad 3 , a.7 co .

[52]   Cf. *ScG* IV c.20: "Ostensum est enim in superioribus quod bonitas Dei est ratio volendi quod alia sint, et per suam voluntatem res in esse producit. Amor igitur quo suam bonitatem amat est causa creationis rerum. (..) Habitum est autem ex praemissis quod Spiritum sanctus procedit per modum amoris quod Deus amat seipsum. Igitur Spiritus sanctus est principium creationis rerum; et hoc significatur: *Emittes Spiritum tuum, et creabuntur* (Ps. CIII, 30)."

[53]   *Ibidem* "Rerum gubernatio a Deo secundum quamdam motionem esse intelligitur, secundum quod Deus omnia dirigit et movet in proprios fines. Si igitur impulses et motio ad Spiritum sanctum, ratio amoris, pertinet, convenienter rerum gubernatio et propagatio Spiritui sancto attribuitur. Unde dicitur: *Spiritus Dei fecit me* (Job XXXIII, 4); *et Spiritus tuus bonus deducet me in terram rectam* (Ps. CXLII, 10)."

[54]   *Ibidem* "Vita maxime in motu manifestatur; moventia enim seipsa vivere dicimus; et universaliter quaecumque a seipsis aguntur ad operandum. Si igitur, ratione amoris, Spiritui sancto impulsio et motio competit, convenienter etiam sibi attribuitur vita; dicitur enim: *Spiritus est qui vivificat* (Joan. VI, 64); et: *Dabo vobis spiritum, et vivetis* (Ez. 37, 6); et in symbolo fidei nos in Spiritum sanctum vivificantem credere profitemur."

[55]   G. Sabra, *Thomas Aquinas' vision of the Church*, p.96.

[56]   Cf. Johannes-Paulus II, *Over de heilige Geest in het leven van de Kerk en de wereld*, 1986, No.63: "De Kerk is de zichtbare uitdeelster van de gewijde tekenen, terwijl de Heilige Geest hierin werkt als de onzichtbare uitdeler van het leven dat zij betekenen." (Cf. K. Vanhoutte, "Kome over ons uw Geest. De aanroeping van de Geest in de sacramenten", in *Tijdschrift voor liturgie* 82, 1998, p.62.)

formulations of Thomas in terms of ascribing and appropriating, instead of identifying.[57]
But apart from these reservations, it is clear, as we have also seen in the previous chapters that, in Thomas' theology, the Spirit plays an important role in bringing and keeping all men and women together around Christ. We have seen that the instinct which is responsible for the first motion in the preparation to justification, as well as for the growth to perfection, once we have entered life in the Holy Spirit, is ascribed to the Spirit.[58] Furthermore, sanctifying grace, through which the Trinity inhabits man is ascribed to the Holy Spirit. This implies that all that is involved in becoming a member of the body of Christ, and belonging to the congregation of the faithful is ascribed to the Holy Spirit. Being the principle of all motion, the Holy Spirit moves the human will through the inner power of grace; He " – by operating through grace to engender faith – provides the fundamental condition without which there can be no faithful, and, hence, no congregation of the faithful."[59]
As we have seen in the previous chapters, the Holy Spirit is not only the principle of sanctifying grace, but also of gratuitous grace (*gratia gratis data*), which is the grace that is given in order to bring others to justifying faith.[60] Sabra points out that gratuitous grace has important ecclesiological dimensions.[61] Gratuitous grace is given for the common good of the Church.[62] Each member of the Church participates more or less in the graces of the Holy Spirit.[63] Gratuitous grace manifests the fact that the Holy Spirit inhabits the Church, and instructs and sanctifies her, even through sinners and unworthy ministers.[64] In Chapter Three, we saw that whenever the Holy Spirit was sent visibly, this was for the good of the Church.[65] In conclusion, the Holy Spirit is not only responsible for bringing man to justification directly, but also

---

[57] Cf. Chapter Three.
[58] Cf. Chapter Two.
[59] G. Sabra, *Thomas Aquinas' vision of the Church*, p.98.
[60] *STh* I-II q.111, a.1 co: "(D)uplex est gratia: una quidem, per quam ipse homo Deo coniungitur, quae vocatur gratia gratum faciens; alia vero, per quam unus homo cooperatur alteri ad hoc, quod ad Deum reducatur. Huiusmodi autem donum vocatur gratia gratis data; quia supra facultatem naturae, et supra meritum personae homini conceditur."
[61] G. Sabra, *Thomas*, p.99.
[62] *STh* I-II q.111, a.5 ad 1: "(G)ratia autem gratis data ordinatur ad bonum commune Ecclesiae, quod est ordo ecclesiasticus"
[63] *In I ad Cor* c.12, lc. 2 (725): "Sicut enum nullum membrum est in corpore quod non participet aliquo modo sensum vel motum a capite, ita nullus est in Ecclesia qui non aliquid de gratis Spiritus Sancti participet, secundum illud Matth. XXV, 15L *Dedit unicuique secundum propriam virtutem*, et, Eph. IV, 7: *Unicuique nostrum data est gratia*."
[64] *Ibidem* "Manifestatur autem, per huiusmodi gratias, Spiritus Sanctus dupliciter. Uno modo ut inhabitans Ecclesiam et docens en sanctificans eam, puta cum aliquid peccator, quem non inhabitat Spiritus Sanctus, faciat miracula ad ostendendum, quod fides Ecclesiae quam ipse praedicat, sit vera."
[65] Cf. *STh* I q.43, a.7 ad 6: "*Manifestatio spiritus datur alicui ad utilitatem*, scilicet Ecclesiae. (..) Et ideo specialiter debuit fieri missio visibilis Spiritus Sancti ad Christum, ad Apostolos, et ad aliquos primitivos Sanctos, in quibus quodammodo Ecclesia fundabatur."

indirectly through other persons, even through those who are themselves sinful and unworthy.

We distinguished above between, on the one hand, the unity between the body and the head, and on the other, the unity between the members of the body. The Holy Spirit is constitutive with respect to both. The Holy Spirit is the principle of unity.[66] The unity of the Church is conceived in terms of faith, hope and love.[67] And unity is conceived in terms of the one and the same Spirit dwelling in the head and the members.[68] Which notion of unity Thomas uses: unity in terms of either indwelling or in terms of the theological virtues, depends, according to Sabra, on the context:

> "Unity as a result of indwelling seems to occur mainly in those contexts where the theme of Christ's headship is discussed, and is thus more concerned with the unity of the head with the body. Here he [Thomas] cannot use the theological virtues, for Christ is not united to his members in terms of believing, hoping and loving one thing, for *He* is the object of faith, hope and love. Hence, the unity of Christ with the Church as his body is in terms of the one Spirit which dwells in both."[69]

The ministry of the sacraments

Now that we have an idea about Thomas' notion of the Church, we can turn to the Church's functions. In Thomas' theology, three functions of the Church can be distinguished: the ministry of the sacraments, the ministry of the Word, and moral instruction.[70] In other areas of his work, only the first two are mentioned[71], but in those cases, the moral instruction is subsumed under the general category of teaching or doctrine.[72]

As we have seen in Chapter Four, in Thomas' theology the sacraments of the Church must be understood against the background of Christ's redemptive work. Christ is head of the Church according to his human nature. This means

---

[66] *In I ad Cor*, c.12, lc.3 (734) : "Una quidem ratio unitatis est Spiritus Sanctus, secundum illud Eph. IV, 4: *Unum corpus, unus spiritus*. (..) (P)er virtutem unius Spiritus Sancti, omnes nos, qui sumus membra Christi, sumus baptizati in unum corpus, id est in unitatem Ecclesiae, quae est corpus Christi, secundum illud Eph. I, 22: *Ipsum dedit caput super omnem Ecclesiam, quae est corpus eius*; et Gal. III, 27: *Omnes qui Christo baptizati estis, Christum induistis*."

[67] *In symb* a.9 (973-976).

[68] *In III Sent* d.13, q.2, a.1 ad 2: "... quantum ad Spiritum sanctum increatum, qui idem numero est in capite et in membris, et aliquo modo a capite ad membra descendit, non divisus, sed unus." Cf. G. Sabra, *Thomas Aquinas' Vision*, p.101.

[69] G. Sabra, *Thomas Aquinas' Vision*, pp.102-103.

[70] For instance *In I decr* (1138): "Salvator noster discipulos ad praedicandum mittens, tria eis ininuxit. Primo quidem ut docerent fidem; secundo ut credentes imbuerent sacramentis; tertio ut credentes sacramentis imbutos ad observandum divina mandata inducerent. Dicitur enim Matth. ult, 19: *Euntes, docete omnes gentes*, quantum ad primum; *baptizantes eos in nomine Patris et Filii et Spiritus Sancti*, quantum ad secundum; *docentes eos servare omnia quaecumque mandavi vobis*, quantum ad tertium."

[71] For instance *STh* III q.67, a.2 ad 1: "Ad primum ergo dicendum, quod utrumque officium, scilicet docendi et baptizandi, Dominus apostolis iniunxit; quorum vicem gerunt episcopi"

[72] G. Sabra, *Thomas Aquinas*, p.143.

that he is head in terms of what he effects, not just of what he is. "The Church-forming grace which flows from him comes to us via his human nature, i.e. via the redemptive work which he accomplishes as man."[73] Consequently, not only can we say that Christ, as such, is the constitutive principle, we can also say, and must say, that the life and work of Christ, - what he has done and suffered (his *actiones et passiones*) - are, as such, constitutive principles of the Church.

How do the sacraments and the Church relate? According to Sabra, the sacraments take a prominent place in Thomas' ecclesiology, and, in more than one sense, are even ranked above the Church.[74] The Church, understood not primarily as an institution, but as a community of believers, as a community of grace and as the body of Christ, is built up and sustained by the sacraments.[75] The Church is built on faith and sacraments.[76] The sacraments are the causes of grace[77], of which the Church – as we saw above – is the effect.

Furthermore, as far as their number, constitution and necessity is concerned, the sacraments are beyond the competence of the institutional Church and the hierarchy. The power to institute (new) sacraments, to remove already established ones, to change anything in them or to exempt anyone from partaking of them, is Christ's alone.[78] "The Church's function is simply to administer them, and it should understand itself as bound to what the Lord himself instituted."[79]

---

[73] *Idem*, p.88.

[74] *Idem*, p.144.

[75] Cf. *STh* I q.92, a.3 co: "(D)e latere Christi dormientis in cruce fluxerunt sacramenta; idest sanguis, et aqua, quibus est Ecclesia instituta."; *STh* III q.64, a.2 ad 3: "(P)er sacramenta, quae de latere Christi pendentis in cruce fluxerunt, dicitur esse fabricata Ecclesi Christi." (cf. *In I ad Cor* c.11, lc.2 (605)); *In Rom* c.5, lc.4 (429): "Et sicut de latere Adae dormientis sumpta est mulier, ita ex latere Christi dormientis in cruce fluxit sanguis et aqua, ut dicitur Ioan. XIX, 34, quae significant sacramenta quibus est formata Ecclesia." *In Ioan* c.19, lc.5: "(S)icut ex latere Christi dormientis in cruce fluxit sanguis et aqua, quibus consecratur Ecclesia; ita de latere Adae dormientis formata est mulier, quae ipsam Ecclesiam praefigurabat."

[76] Cf. *In IV Sent* d.17, q.3, a.1, qa.5 co: "Ecclesia fundatur in fide et sacramentis".

[77] Cf. Chapter Four.

[78] Cf. *In IV Sent* d.17, q.3, a.1, qa.5 co: "Ad quintam quaestionem dicendum quod ministri Ecclesiae instituuntur in Ecclesia divinitus fundata. Et ideo institutio Ecclesiae praesupponitur ad operationem ministrorum: sicut opus creationis praesupponitur ad opus naturae. Et quia Ecclesia fundatur in fide et sacramentis, ideo ad ministros Ecclesiae nec novos articulos fidei edere, aut editos removere, aut nova sacramenta instituere, aut instituta removere pertinet; sed hoc est potestatis excellentiae quae soli debetur Christo, qui est Ecclesiae *fundamentum* (I Cor. 3, 11)." *ScG* IV c.72: "Per hoc autem excluditur quorumdam error, qui dixerunt hominem posse peccatorum veniam consequi sine confessione et proposito confitendi, vel quod per praelatos Ecclesiae dispensari potest quod ad confessionem aliquis non teneatur. Non enim hoc possunt praelati Ecclesiae ut claves frustrentur Ecclesiae, in quibus tota eorum potestas consistit, neque ut sine sacramento, a passione Christi virtutem habente, aliquis remissionem peccatorum consequatur; hoc enim est solius Christi, qui est sacramentorum institutor et auctor. Sicut igitur dispensari non potest per praelatos Ecclesiae ut aliquis sine baptismo salvetur, ita nec quod aliquis remissionem sine confessione et absolutione consequatur."

[79] G. Sabra, *Thomas*, p.146.

How do the administering of the sacraments and the ministry of the Word relate? Comparing the two, Sabra argues that Thomas assigns greater importance and higher status to the ministry of the word than to that of the sacraments (though this must not be taken to diminish the necessity of sacraments for salvation[80]). "(T)eaching sacred doctrine is more universal, more comprehensive and more excellent than the ministry of the sacraments."[81] Nevertheless, Sabra prefers not to call Thomas' notion of the constituted Church *ecclesia verbi*. "Yet, the centrality of the word and its ministry should serve as a corrective to an over-sacramentalized interpretation of Thomas' notion of the Church."[82]

Are sinners members of the Church?

What does this notion of the Church, as *congregatio fidelium* and *corpus mysticum*, constituted by and united through the Holy Spirit, imply with respect to sinners who approach the sacrament of penance in the hope of receiving forgiveness for their sins? Does Thomas regards them as members of the Church, and if so, in what sense?

Thomas' most fundamental exposition of membership is found in his reflections on Christ's headship of all human beings in his *Summa theologiae*.[83] Thomas begins by pointing out that, in contrast to the members of a natural body, the members of the mystical body are not simultaneous, neither as regards nature nor grace. With respect to nature, the members differ from each other because the mystical body includes not only the actual members of the present time, but all members from the beginning of the world until its end.[84] With respect to grace, Thomas employs the Aristotelian distinction of act and potential, which enables him to distinguish the different grades of membership in terms of union with Christ. These different grades of membership enclose all human beings. Consequently, Thomas can confirm that Christ is head of all

---

[80] *Idem*, p.154: "The distinction Thomas makes between the two functions is not in terms of their necessity for salvation, but in terms of excellence only."

[81] *Ibidem*. Cf. *Quodl* I, q.7, a.2: "In aedificio autem spirituali sunt quasi manuales operarii, qui particulariter insistunt curae animarum, puta sacramenta ministrando, vel aliquod huiusmodi particulariter agendo; sed quasi principales artifices sunt episcopi, qui imperant, et disponunt qualiter praedicti suum officium exequi debeant; propter quod et episcopi, id est superintendentes, dicuntur; et similiter theologiae doctores sunt quasi principales artifices, qui inquirunt et docent qualiter alii debeant salutem animarum procurare. simpliciter ergo melius est docere sacram doctrinam, et magis meritorium, si bona intentione agatur, quam impendere particularem curam saluti huius et illius; unde Apostolus de se dicit, I ad Corinth. I, 17: *non enim misit me Christus baptizare, sed evangelizare*; quamvis baptizare sit opus maxime conferens saluti animarum; et II ad Timoth., II, 2, idem Apostolus: *commenda fidelibus hominibus qui idonei erunt et alios docere.*" Note, that Thomas places the bishops and teachers of theology almost on the same level.

[82] *Idem*, p.155.

[83] *STh* III q.8, a.3. For a comparison between Thomas' treatment of Christ's headship of all human beings in the *Summa theologiae* and in the *Scriptum*, see G. Sabra, *Thomas Aquinas' Vision*, pp. 172-175:

[84] *Ibidem*. "(C)orpus Ecclesiae constituitur ex hominibus, qui fuerunt a principio mundi usque ad finem ipsius"

human beings, though according to different grades: (1) Actual union through glory; (2) Actual union through love; (3) Actual union through faith; (4) Potential, yet-to-be-actualized union; (5) Potential, never-to-be-actualized union.[85]

The notion of Church used here is thought through to its most fundamental (and accordingly theological) level, namely in terms of union with Christ. All other uses of 'Church' in Thomas' theology should be understood analogously to this use of 'Church', which denotes what 'Church' is in its deepest sense.

In the light of this theological notion of Church and of membership in terms of union with Christ, we can evaluate the question about the ecclesiological status of sinners. I treat sinners here as those for whom the sacrament of penance is meant. They are those Christians who, after having been baptized, have fallen into severe or mortal sin, and consequently have lost the grace of being united with Christ through love. Thomas distinguishes between two categories of those guilty of mortal sin, i.e. those who have lost grace (indicated by the term 'macula'; cf. Chapter Two): those who are not members of Christ *actualiter*, but *potentialiter*, and those who still remain united with Christ, though imperfectly, through an uninformed faith. Sinners of the first category are not united with Christ actually, but only potentially, and consequently belong to the grades four and five. Sinners of the second category are actually united with Christ, though not *simpliciter*, but *secundum quid*.[86] These sinners belong to the third grade of membership, and are actual members of the Church, both in the sense of congregation of the faithful and in the sense of mystical body. Even though they lack the grace of the indwelling of the Holy Spirit, they do participate in the grace of the faith of the Church:

"(T)he Church is, properly speaking, *congregatio fidelium* and not *congregatio amantium* or *sperantium*. This does not in any way mean that the faith of the Church excludes hope and love, for faith can (and ought to be) formed by love, and, in a sense, the fullness and perfection of the Church consists in believers whose faith is formed by love. Nevertheless, those whose faith is imperfect (unformed) also have grace and are of the Church."[87]

---

[85] *STh* III, q.8, a.3 co: "Sic ergo dicendum, quod accipiendo generaliter secundum totum tempus mundi, Christus est caput omnium hominum; sed secundum diversos gradus: primo enim, et principaliter est caput eorum, qui actu uniuntur ei per gloriam; secundo eorum, qui actu uniuntur ei per charitatem; tertio eorum, qui actu uniuntur ei per fidem; quarto vero eorum, qui ei uniuntur solum in potentia nondum reducta ad actum, quae tamen est ad actum reducenda secundum divinam predestinationem; quinto vero eorum, qui in potentia sunt ei uniti, quae nunquam reducetur ad actum: sicut homines in hoc mundo viventes, qui non sunt praedestinati: qui tamen ex hoc saeculo recedentes, totaliter desinunt esse membra Christi; quia iam nec sunt in potentia, ut Christi uniantur." According to Sabra, "(t)he significance of the act/potency distinction was that it enabled Thomas to preserve the unity of this all-embracing notion of the Church, for he was not compelled to distinguish between the Church and the body of the Church." (G. Sabra, *Thomas Aquinas' Vision*, p.181).

[86] *STh* III q.8, a.3 ad 2: "qui vero his subduntur peccatis, non sunt membra Christi actualiter, sed potentialiter; nisi forte imperfecte per fidem informem, quae unit Christo secundum quid, et non simpliciter."

[87] G. Sabra, *Thomas Aquinas*, p. 98.

The Church does not only consist of those who are united with Christ through the grace of charity. The Church consists of both good (*fideles et sancti*) and bad (*infideles et peccatores*).[88] This makes the sinner who approaches and receives the sacrament of penance part of the community of the Church. Consequently, we can ask what role the Church plays, as mystical body of Christ in which the Holy Spirit dwells, in Thomas' theology with respect the forgiveness of this sinner.

2 The Church in Thomas' theology of the sacrament of penance

We will deal with the ecclesial or social dimension in Thomas' theology of penance in three steps. First we will see what he has to say about sin in this respect, and next what he has to say about forgiveness. Finally, we will deal with the question of whether there is room in Thomas' theology for reconciliation with the Church as *modus reconciliandi Deo*.

The ecclesial ('social') dimension of sin

Thomas is aware of a social dimension of sin. When he deals with sin he makes several distinctions, one of which is the distinction between the sin against God, the sin against oneself (*in seipsum*) and the sin against a neighbor (*in proximum*).[89] Thomas defines sin as an *actus inordinatus*, and subsequently distinguishes between a threefold *ordo*: one with respect to the rule of reason, one with respect to the rule of divine law, and, since man is by nature a political and social being (*animal politicum, et sociale*), a third *ordo* must be distinguished as well, ordering man to other human beings with whom he has to live together.

The three orders do not stand next to each other, but relate to each other in a hierarchical way. The first *ordo*, which is the *ordo ipsius Dei*, contains the second, the *ordo rationis*, and exceeds it, Thomas says. In a similar way, the second order includes and exceeds the third order.

All sins are, because of these hierarchical relations, in one way or the other 'against God'. Similarly, all sins against other human beings are in one way or another against oneself, namely insofar as they are against reason. However, only those acts are called 'sins against God' that are against what is beyond reason and what belongs to God alone. Only those acts are called 'sins against oneself' that are against what is directive with respect to us alone. Finally, those acts are called 'sins against one's neighbor' that are against what is directive with respect to our neighbors. So Thomas knows about a social dimension of sin, because he acknowledges the fact that a sin can be *in proximum*.

---

[88] Cf. *In Ps* 17, 16: "In Ecclesia sunt multi lucentes, sicut fideles et sancti: Philip. 2: *inter quos lucetis sicut luminaria in mundo, verbum vitae continentes.* Item multi tenebrosi, sicut infideles et peccatores: Ephes. 5: *eratis aliquando tenebrae etc.*" See also *STh* II-II q.108, a.1 ad 3: "Ad tertium dicendum, quod lex Evangelii est lex amoris. Et ideo illis, qui ex amore bonum operantur, qui soli proprie ad Evangelium pertinent, non est timor incutiendus per poenas, sed solum illis, qui ex amore non moventur ad bonum, qui etsi numero sint de Ecclesia, non tamen merito."

[89] *STh* I-II q.72, a.4.

However, the perspective from which he addresses it is exclusively the perspective of the sinner. What comes first is the relationship of the sinner to God, and second the relationship of the sinner to himself. The social dimension of sin in Thomas' theology seems to be secondary with respect to what sin means for the sinner himself and his or her relationship with God.[90]

Moreover, what we, in our days, mean by the social dimension of sin concerns more than the mere possibility of sinning against somebody else. When we speak about the social dimension of sin today, we refer to the fact that sin, by nature, has the power to damage not only the relationship of the sinner to God, but also the social structures and the relationship of its victims to God.

In the opening section of Chapter Two, we mentioned that in our days attention has shifted from our relationship with God to interpersonal relationships, and from the sinner to the victim. It is not the possibility of (divine or interpersonal) forgiveness for the sinner, but the possibility for the victim to forgive, and thus be liberated from the hurts of the past, which is placed in the foreground. The social dimension of sin refers to the fact that it belongs to the nature of sin to tend to corrupt all who come into contact with it, including the victim(s). The sin of one person not only results in the loss of grace of the sinner, but can also result in the loss of grace of the victim. One sin causes new sins, not only in the sinner, but also in all who are affected by the sin. In the end, sins can affect a whole community.[91]

More can be said with respect to new insights into the social dimension of sin, but that would be beyond the scope of this dissertation. What we have aimed to do here is show that the ecclesial or social dimension of sin is only in a very limited sense present in Thomas' theology of penance. His focus is primarily on the individual sinner and his relationship to God, whereas we in our days are more aware of how the sinner, as sinner, is part of a society or community, which on the one hand is hurt by the sin, and on the other is partly responsible for it as well.

The ecclesial ('social') dimension of forgiveness

Next, we will deal with the question of the role of the Church in Thomas theology of penance with respect to the forgiveness of sins. Sacraments are communal celebrations, and the sacrament of penance as such should be considered part of the wider penitential context of the Church, and not as something isolated from the community of the Church. As we saw in the

---

[90] This corresponds with what we found out in Chapter Two regarding interpersonal forgiveness. Justification of the godless refers primarily to the first two relationships, the relationship with God and the inner relationship of man with himself. The relationship with other human persons is not part of justification. Thomas deals with interpersonal forgiveness in the context of satisfaction, and it is secondary with respect to divine forgiveness.

[91] Cf. J. Sobrino, "Latijns-Amerika: plaats van zonde, plaats van vergiffenis", in *Concilium*, 1986/2. Referring to the situation in Latin-America (Medellín, Puebla), he speaks about this aspect of sin "that sin often and in its most severe and massive form is passed on via structures 'on which the sin of those who have produced them has imprinted its destructive seal'". (p.42)

Introduction, the ecclesial dimension of forgiveness was expressed in two ways. First, it was said that through the sacrament of penance one is not only reconciled with God, but also with the Church.[92] Next, it is proclaimed in *Lumen gentium* (No. 11), that the Church labors for the conversion of sinners by love, example and prayers.[93] We will first look at the role the Church can play in bringing the sinner to conversion.

In Thomas' theology, the community of the faithful can play a positive role in bringing the sinner to repentance. The notion of gratuitous grace, which plays an important role in Thomas' theology, refers precisely to this ecclesiological dimension, as we saw above. It is a gift of the Holy Spirit "by which one man might aid another to be led to God." It is always oriented towards others; it is ordained "for the common good of the Church."[94] In the gift of gratuitous grace we can recognize the ecclesial dimension of a community, encouraged by the Holy Spirit, aiding the sinner to conversion. The notion of gratuitous grace in Thomas' theology comes closest to what *Lumen gentium* says with respect to the Church, that she labors for the conversion of sinners by love, example and prayers (*LG*, No.11)

The reconciliation with the Church and the reconciliation with God

Is it possible, in Thomas' theology, to distinguish between a reconciliation with God and a reconciliation with the Church, both being the fruit of one sacrament of penance? And if so, in what way can the second be modus of the first?

Thomas mentions different 'effects' of the sacrament of penance. In the *Summa theologiae*, he mentions the forgiveness of mortal sins (of guilt), of venial sins, and the restitution of virtues, but he does not mention a reconciliation with the Church.[95] Thomas does not mention anywhere explicitly the 'Reconciliation with the Church', which *Lumen gentium* places side by side with forgiveness by God ('veniam offensionis Deo illatae ab eius misericordia obtinent et simul reconciliantur cum Ecclesia', *LG*, No.11). The question, however, is whether he implies it in his theology or not. We will first address this question regarding the Church in the sense of the visible community, and next regarding the Church in the sense of the invisible community. However, let us first see what Thomas means when he calls the sacraments of the new covenant sacraments 'of the Church' (*Ecclesiae sacramenta*).

Here, 'of the Church' means that they are administered by the ministers *of the Church* and transmitted to the members *of the Church*.[96] The sacraments of the Church are called 'of the Church' because they are for members of the Church

---

[92] *LG*, nr.11; *PO*, nr.5.

[93] *LG*, nr.11: "…, et quae [=Ecclesia] eorum conversione caritate, exemplo, precibus adlaborat."

[94] G. Sabra *Thomas Aquinas' vision of the Church*, p.90.

[95] Cf. *STh* III, qq.86-89.

[96] Cf. *In IV Sent* d.2, q.1, a.2 co: "Dicendum quod sacramenta ex hoc quod sunt sacramenta, habent quod sint in remedium contra defectum aliquem; ex hoc autem quod sunt sacramenta Ecclesiae, habent per ministros Ecclesiae dispensari et in membra Ecclesiae transfundi."

only, i.e. for those who are baptized.[97] Consequently, excommunication excludes from the sacraments of the Church, precisely because the excommunicate is no longer part of the Church.[98] Excommunication even excludes from the sacrament of penance: the minister may not absolve the excommunicate before the excommunicate is relieved from his or her excommunication.[99] In conclusion, that the sacraments of the new covenant are 'of the Church' refers both to the Church in the sense of the means of grace, and to the Church in the sense of the body, for whose members the sacraments are meant.

In the *Scriptum*, Thomas distinguishes between being forgiven with regard to God (*quoad Deum*) and being readmitted to the Eucharist.[100] At first sight, this distinction seems to indicate a distinction between being forgiven by God and being reconciled with the Church. After all, both in the early Church and in the Middle Ages, being reaccepted at the table of the Eucharist implied being reconciled with the Church.[101] In Thomas' theology, however, this reconciliation implied in the reacceptance to the Eucharist does not seem to have social connotations. In Thomas' theology, the emphasis is on the re-admittance of the individual sinner to the whole of the sacramental life, in particular to the sacrament of the Eucharist. The sacrament of penance, in Thomas' theology, is aimed at the restoration of the relationship of the sinner with God, and the re-introduction of the penitent into the sacramental life of the Church. The latter, however, does not refer to reintegration into a community, but to regaining new access to the means of salvation. Readmittance at the table of the Eucharist is ecclesial, insofar as 'ecclesial' refers to Church in the sense of 'means of grace', and not to Church in the sense of community of the faithful.

According to Sabra, the Church understood as visible institution in Thomas is "that visible organization which is hierarchically structured and which exercises a certain power and authority: it possesses keys, administers sacraments, teaches, determines precepts and statutes and has the right to treat its members in accordance with, or rejection of, its doctrines and laws."[102] Sabra distinguishes three areas in Thomas' theology where the underlying notion of

---

97 Cf. *In IV Sent* d.16, q.1, a.2, qa.1 co: "Et quia Ecclesiae sacramenta non dispensatur nisi illis qui sunt de Ecclesia, ergo ante baptismum sacramentum poenitentia non competit, cum per baptismum homo de Ecclesia fiat."

98 Cf. *In IV Sent* d.18, q.2, a.4, qa.1 co: "Alia est maior excommunicatio. Et haec separate hominem a sacramentis Ecclesiae et a communione fidelium."

99 *In IV Sent* d.18, q.2, a.5, qa.1 ad 2: "Ad secundum dicendum quod cum excommunicatus non sit particeps sacramentorum Ecclesiae, sacerdos non potest absolvere excommunicatum a culpa, nisi sit prius absolutus ab excommunicatione."

100 "Ad tertium dicendum quod dispensatio eucharistiae pertinet ad ministros Ecclesiae. Et ideo ante remissionem peccati per ministros Ecclesiae non debet aliquis ad Eucharistiam accedere quamvis sit sibi culpa quoad Deum remissa." (*In IV Sent* d.17, q.2, a.5, qa.1 ad 3)

101 Cf. Chapter One.

102 G. Sabra *Thomas Aquinas' vision of the Church*, p.108.

the Church is this notion of Church in its institutional and juridical aspect: his theology of the sacraments; his discussion of the gifts, offices, states and organization of the Church; his views on schism, heresy, infidelity, excommunication, etc. Sabra points out that Thomas nowhere reflects on the institution as such, nor speaks about *ecclesia visibilis*. The notion of 'visibility' is however discussed in relation to the sacraments in general and the sacrament of order in particular. "In a very real sense, the sacraments and the ministry are the main constituents of the visible organization of the Church."[103]

Sacraments and the ministry in particular, are, in Thomas' theology, understood in terms of instrumentality. Ministry and instrumentality even seem to be interchangeable in many places. The consequence is that Thomas' conception of the Church as visible institution is predominantly instrumental: "If the sacraments and the ministers of the Church - two major constituents of the whole institution - can be called instruments in this sense, then surely the whole institutional Church may also be conceived of as an *instrumentum*."[104]

Moreover, the opposite appears to be true as well, namely that the instrumentality of the Church in Thomas' theology is found almost completely in the sacraments and the ministry and not in the visible community of men as such. Though the Church, in the sense of the visible institution, is a social organization (as an hierarchical organization, the Church exercises powers and authority, which refer to a social and juridical context), nevertheless, as a social organization, the Church is, in Thomas' theology, structured by the sacraments and in particular by the ministry. The functionality and, in particular, the instrumentality of the Church is not found in the community as such, but in its sacraments and ministers. In Thomas' theology, we can distinguish something like a reconciliation with the Church as distinct from the reconciliation with God. However, such a distinct reconciliation with the Church in Thomas' theology does not refer to a reconciliation with a visible community, but with the hierarchical organization.

Such an ecclesial reconciliation in Thomas' theology cannot be understood as *modus reconciliandi Deo*. Being *modus reconciliandi Deo* presupposes that the reconciliation with the Church precedes the reconciliation with God, maybe not in time, but then at least logically. In Thomas' theology, however, the opposite seems is true: the reconciliation in the sense of being being readmitted to the Eucharist is itself the fruit of one's reunion with Christ, i.e. the reconciliation with God.

Is it possible to distinguish between reconciliation with God and reconciliation with the Church, when the latter is understood as the invisible Church? As far as membership of the Church is concerned, we saw that according to Thomas, one is an actual member of the Church when one is united with Christ, either through faith and love, or through faith alone. In terms of membership, reconciliation refers to the transition from a union with Christ through faith alone to union through faith *and love*. Since one's membership of the Church is defined in terms of union with Christ, the forgiveness of sins (the restoration of the relationship of grace with Christ: justification) and the reconciliation with the Church appear to coincide. One becomes part of the community of those united with Christ precisely by becoming united with Christ. This seems to exclude in advance the notion of a reconciliation with the Church as *modus reconcilandi Deo*.

However, despite the fact that forgiveness of sins and reconciliation with the Church appear to coincide, it nevertheless seems possible to distinguish between them because, though Thomas understands unity in terms of unity in faith, hope and love, in all of which Christ is the object,[105] on some occasions, however, he understands the unity of the Church in terms of mutual love of the members for each other as well.[106] Church members can be viewed from the perspective of their unity with Christ, as well from the perspective of their unity with each other. Consequently, we can distinguish between a reconciliation with Christ and a reconciliation with the Church. Due to the theological character of Thomas' notion of the Church, however, this distinction between the two reconciliations is *ratione* only. In reality, both reconciliations coincide, for there cannot be 'Church' without unity with Christ. In one place, though, Thomas appears to think that the opposite is true as well: there can only be unity with Christ in unity with the other members of the Church:

> The unity of this Mystical Body is a spiritual one, through which by faith and the affectivity of love for each other we are united with God.[107]

This text seems to suggest that we are united with God through a spiritual unity with each other, which itself is based in faith and love. Here, the horizontal and vertical dimensions of faith appear to be interrelated. We are united with each other through our union of faith in, and love for, Christ, and we are united with Christ through affectivity and love for each other. In other words, our union with Christ is the *modus* in which we are united with each other, while, at the same time, our union with each other, as community of faithful, is the *modus* in which we are united with Christ. However, in both cases, the love and affectivity which unites is the love and affectivity we receive from Christ.

---

[105] Cf. *In I decr* (1182): "Unitas autem Ecclesiae est praecipue propter fidei unitatem; nam Eclesia nihil est aliud quam aggregatio fidelium." See also *In Symb* a.9 (973-976).

[106] Cf. *In symb* a.9 (975) : "Tertio ex unitate caritatis, quia omnes connectuntur in amore Dei, et ad invicem in amore mutuo." See also *In II Cor* c.13, lc.3: "Constat enim quod corpora non possunt servari et ordinari, nisi membra ordinentur ad invicem. Similiter nec Ecclesia, nec Ecclesia membra, nisi ordinentur ut uniantur ad invicem."

[107] *In Rom* c.12, lc.2 (974): "Huius autem corporis mystici est unitas spiritualis, per quam fide et affectu charitatis invicem unimur Deo, secundum illud Eph. IV, 4: *Unum corpus, et unus spiritus*."

In conclusion, it appears that the idea of a reconciliation with the Church as *modus reconciliandi Deo* is not completely foreign to Thomas' theology. However, with respect to the 'visible' Church, it also appears that Thomas only ascribes instrumentality to the sacraments and its ministers, i.e. to the hierarchical organization, and not to the visible community as such. It seems that the main reason for this is that Thomas wants to safeguard Christ as the sole source of salvation.

3 Church and Holy Spirit and the sacrament of penance

If we want to discover the role of the Holy Spirit in Thomas' theology of penance, we have to distinguish between his visible and his invisible mission.

With respect to his visible mission, we have seen that the Holy Spirit is sent for the good of the Church, to Christ and the Apostles, and to the first saints of the Church, insofar as the Church is founded upon them.[108] 'Church', we have seen in this chapter, is an ambivalent term in Thomas' theology, because it can stand both for the visible Church, and for the invisible Church, and in both cases, 'Church' means something different. The visible Church, though Thomas nowhere reflects on it as such, is, in Thomas' theology, the visible institution, which he understands primarily in terms of instrument. Sacraments and the ministry are the main constituents of the visible Church, and since both sacraments and their ministers are understood in terms of instrumentality, so is the visible Church. The visible Church refers consequently to the hierarchical Church, the sacraments, their ministers, in the sense of 'separate' instruments in the hands of Christ. Thomas does not ascribe instrumentality to the visible Church in the sense of the visible community of men, the visible body of Christ. Instrumentality as such is a vertical term: it refers to the hierarchy, to the sacraments and their ministers, and it is through the sacraments and the ministers that the visible Church refers to Christ. In other words, the Church in the sense of a visible community of members does not refer to Christ instrumentally, i.e. as instrument of salvation.

Therefore, sacramental causality is not, in Thomas' theology, ascribed to the visible community, but solely to the hierarchical Church, i.e. the sacraments and their ministers. With respect to the sacraments and the ministers, the invisible mission of the Holy Spirit only plays a secondary role. For Thomas, instrumentality refers to Christ. When grace is said to be in the sacraments only instrumentally, Thomas means to say that sacramental power, operative in the sacrament of penance, is not something belonging to the minister, the priest himself. That is why the power of the keys is not a grace, because, were it a grace, then the power of the keys would be something belonging to the minister himself. Instead, insofar as grace is in the minister of the sacrament of penance only instrumentally, this means that the minister of the sacrament of penance is the instrument with which Christ confers grace to the one who receives the sacrament of penance. Grace, and the invisible mission of the Holy

---

[108] Cf. *STh* I, q.43, a.7, ad 1.

Spirit, concerns not the sacrament of penance itself, nor its minister, but the penitent receiving it. However, grace, or the invisible mission of the Holy Spirit, does concern the sacrament insofar as its minister is morally obliged to be holy, or insofar as it enables the minister to administer the sacrament worthily, or insofar as it designates or manifests the minister as minister of the sacrament.

In Thomas' theology, the invisible mission of the Holy Spirit concerns, in other words, not the visible Church, but the invisible Church, and, in particular, it concerns the receiver of the sacrament of penance insofar as he is (an actual) member of the invisible Church. First, the Holy Spirit is sent invisibly in order to inspire the penitent so that he recognizes the First Truth, as it is revealed in liturgy and preaching, as the highest good. As such, the Holy Spirit is responsible for the preparation for justification, the conversion of the sinner preparatory to the reception of the sacrament of penance. Furthermore, the Holy Spirit is responsible for the actual justification, because Thomas ascribes the gift of charity, through which the penitent is made 'acceptable' (*gratus*) to the indwelling of Father, Son and Spirit, to the Holy Spirit. Finally, the Holy Spirit is responsible for the life 'in the Spirit', because the gifts of the Spirit are given in order to adapt man in such a way that he can be moved by the divine instinct.

With respect to the Church, understood as the invisible community of those who are united with Christ, the Holy Spirit is invisibly sent to the Church according to gratuitous grace, so that one is able to help others to be led to God. The Church, then, is the community of the Holy Spirit, not only because the Holy Spirit is the principle of unity of the Church, or because the Holy Spirit dwells in the head and each member of the body of Christ as one and the same, but also because the Holy Spirit directly and indirectly brings all back to Christ.

General conclusion

Our research into the role of the Holy Spirit in Thomas' reflection on the sacrament of penance has yielded a number of insights, which we will briefly recapture here.

The first insight regards appropriation. Our reflections on how appropriation functions in Thomas' theology has shown that, according to Thomas, appropriation is not aimed at distinguishing separate roles of divine Persons in salvation history. Instead it is aimed at manifesting what is proper to the divine Person, i.e. how the divine Person is related to the other divine Persons. Appropriation parallels analogy in that knowledge of created things helps in saying something about God in an essential way. Appropriation is not about the question of which divine Person has done what in salvation history. Instead, it is about making manifest to us what God has revealed about himself, about the inner-trinitarian life, with the help of similarities between what can be found in creation, or in salvation history, and the opposite relationships in God.

Accordingly, when Thomas says that goodness is appropriated to the Holy Spirit, he means that goodness can manifest how the Spirit is related to the Son and the Father, because there is a similitude between goodness and the Spirit proceeding from the Father and the Son *per modum voluntatis*, as love. A similarity between proceeding as love and movement is grounds for appropriating all movement in salvation history to the Holy Spirit: the first movement that is creation, and the movement of all things to their ends, which falls under the government and propagation of all things.[1]

However, we must not understand this as if it is the proper role of the Spirit, as opposed to or distinguished from assumed proper roles of the Father and of the Son, to create, govern and to lead all things to their proper ends, and all human persons back to the Father. Again, the attribution of divine activities in salvation history to divine persons is meant to manifest the inner-Trinitarian dynamism in God. A likeness or similitude between what God operates in salvation history and what is proper to the divine Person functions as a basis for the appropriation.

In conclusion, appropriation is a meta-term. Appropriating helps to explain what Scripture and tradition do naturally, namely associating moments in salvation history with divine Persons. It warns us not to read too much into these associations, especially not to make God into three Gods. Is does so by focusing our attention on the unity and simplicity of God, which is essentially relational.

Related to this first insight is the insight that asking about a proper role of the Holy Spirit, as compared to what incarnation is for the Son, is misleading. First, because speaking of incarnation as something proper to the Son is itself misleading. Both Father and Spirit are involved in the divine act of incarnation,

---

[1]   Cf. *ScG* IV, cc.20-22.

even though only the Son is involved in the term of the assumption, the union itself.[2] Second, because it appears that, in Thomas' theology of the Trinity, the notion 'proper' (*proprium*) is primarily used to indicate the mutual relationships in God. This notion of 'proper' differs from the notion of 'proper' when we say that it is proper to the Son to have taken human nature to himself. When used in the latter sense, a proper role of the Holy Spirit in salvation history can be distinguished, however only with respect to the visible mission of the Spirit. As it is proper to the Son to have been sent visibly as a man, so it is proper to the Holy Spirit to have been sent in the shapes of a dove, a cloud, breath and tongues of fire.

A third insight regards the invisible dimension of the missions of the Son and the Holy Spirit. From Thomas' texts it appears that 'visibility' dominates the mission of the Son, while at the same time 'invisibility' dominates the mission of the Holy Spirit. But this must not lead us into thinking that all that concerns the invisible presence of God in salvation history is something exclusively of the Holy Spirit. Thomas understands the invisible mission of the Holy Spirit primarily in terms of indwelling, i.e. the intimate presence of God in our heart as known and loved. Thomas emphasizes that this presence is not a derivative presence alone, in the sense of grace, which is an effect of the divine presence. God himself becomes present, and in this presence as known and loved we, as it were, reach God. At the same time, he carefully explains that this becoming present does not involve a change in God, but in us. In its deepest sense, we have learned to understand forgiveness of sins in terms of a renewed presence of God as known and, in particular, as loved.
Even though the Holy Spirit is the first Person to be mentioned when dealing with indwelling, nevertheless it is not something exclusive to the Holy Spirit. Indwelling concerns all three divine Persons. But since indwelling refers to the presence of God as known and loved, how we know God is relevant to how God dwells in us. And here the relevance of the Trinity to our salvation becomes apparent, as well as the relevance of appropriation. Appropriation enables us to 'understand' how God is three and one, and consequently helps us to know God insofar as we can know him from creation. Consequently, appropriation enables us to know and love God, to have Him dwell in us in the way He has revealed Himself: as three and one, as inner loving dynamism, as a unity of love.

With respect to the theology of the sacraments, we have indicated the similarity or coherence there appears to be between the way Thomas reflects on the missions of Son and Spirit and the sacraments themselves. Let us recapture the different instances at which this connection is found, implicitly or explicitly. On two occasions Thomas suggests an interrelatedness of sacraments and

---

2   On the theological grammar of *assumere*, and the distinction between the principle and the term of the assumption, see H. Schoot, *Christ, the 'name' of God*, p.121-122.

incarnation, i.e. the visible mission of the Son. First, as we have seen, Thomas understands both the sacraments and the assumed human nature of Christ in terms of instrument. God himself is principal efficient cause. Compared to this, the human nature of Christ is conjoined instrument, while the sacraments are separate instruments. Second, when dealing with the reason why sacraments are constituted of words and things, Thomas argues that this is fitting because, in the mystery of the incarnation, the divine Word is united to the sensible flesh. There is a parallel between Word on the one hand and flesh and the sacramental sign on the other, being composed of word and thing. This parallel regards the visible dimension of both the mission of the Son and the sacraments.

A similar parallel is at least suggested by Thomas when he explains the visible missions of the Holy Spirit. We saw that in Thomas' explanation each of the appearances of the Spirit is accompanied by words, which explain the meaning of the event. Similarly to the sacrament, the visible missions of the Spirit seem to be composed of things (event) and words. The similarity becomes more apparent when we take into account that Thomas describes the relation of the visible mission to the invisible mission of the Spirit in terms of signification (*manifestari, indicare, demonstrare, significare*). The visible and invisible mission of the Spirit relate to each other as sign and *res significata*. Furthermore, the reason why the Spirit is sent visibly is identical with the reason he gives for the necessity of sacraments. Both are given for the same reason, i.e. that human persons are led to what is invisible through what is visible.

The coherence between sacraments and missions suggests a continuity between the missions and the sacraments. With respect to the visible mission of the Son, the incarnation, the idea that there is a continuity with the sacraments is not new. What is new (or forgotten) is that sacraments are understood as continuations of the mission of the Spirit as well.

Furthermore, the continuity between sacraments and missions concerns not only the missions insofar as they are distinguished between being of the Son and of the Spirit, but also insofar as they are distinguished according to their visible and invisible dimensions. Sacraments are continuations of the missions according to their visible dimension, as well as according to their invisible dimension. They are not only continuances of the incarnate Word, but also of the invisible mission of the Holy Spirit.

Understanding sacraments as continuations of both the (visible) mission of the Son (and the Spirit) and the (invisible) mission(s) of the Spirit (and the Son) throws new light on the notion of sacramental causality. In the sacraments, God is not only actively present along the (visible line) of the Son, but also along the (invisible) line of the Holy Spirit.

The sacrament of penance contains and gives the grace of forgiveness. For the meaning of this notion of containing and giving grace, we not only revert to the treatise on the sacraments but to the treatise on the missions as well. With respect to the first, we can say that the sacrament of penance contains the power of the passion of Christ sacramentaliter, i.e. through signification (*sicut in signo*), and through instrumental causation (*sicut in causa*).[3] These notions of signification and causation refer to the fact that Christ, who has instituted the sacraments, has suffered on the cross and has given his life for our salvation, is somehow present in the sacrament of penance, as in all sacraments of the new law. Institution and passion have given the sacraments an instrumental strength to induce the sacramental effect, i.e. to give grace.

In the treatise on the missions, Thomas argues that the divine Persons are not sent to the sacraments themselves, but to those who receive the sacraments. In other words, we do not speak about mission with respect to the sacrament, but with respect to the receiver of the sacraments. With respect to sacraments, we speak about 'instruments'. The grace they are said to contain is in the sacraments insofar as the sacrament is handled as an instrument by the principal efficient cause, God himself. When it comes to God's active presence along the visible line of the Son, we must say, on the one hand, that Christ is principal cause of the grace of forgiveness according to his divine nature, and instrumental cause according to his human nature (as are the sacraments), while we must say, on the other hand, that the Son becomes newly present as known and loved in the heart of the recipient of the sacrament.

When we explore the invisible line of the Holy Spirit (and the Son), we must add to this that, even before the sacrament of penance is actually received, God is actively present as a divine instinct moving the will of the penitent towards the sacrament of penance, and ultimately towards Christ. Moreover, this active presence in the form of a divine instinct moving the will does not end at the moment of the justification, but continues when the justified human person starts to live a life in the Spirit. We have seen that, in Thomas' theology, the gifts of the Holy Spirit are given precisely in order to adapt man so that he can be moved by the instinct of the Holy Spirit.

When both lines are taken into account, it becomes clear why sacraments are at the same time signs and causes, and that they not only effect what they signify, but also do so through signification. It shows that Christ not only works through the sacrament of penance in order to give the penitent the grace of forgiveness, but that at the same time the Spirit works in the penitent to lead him through the sacrament to Christ. In the sacramental sign, Christ is present in a way that corresponds to the human condition, namely in visible, audible and even tangible form, and it is under the guidance of the Spirit that the penitent recognizes this presence as salutary. The missions of both Son and Spirit reach their goal when, together with the Father, they become present in the hearts of man as known and loved, thus bringing him back to the Father.

In the introduction to this dissertation we said that the sacrament of penance is in a crisis, and we stated that we would deal with two of the many factors that are responsible for this crisis. These are the lack of a genuine understanding of

---

[3]   *STh* III, q.62, aa.3.4.

what is under discussion in the sacrament of penance, and the lack of a genuine understanding of sacramentality. At the end of this dissertation, we hope that we have shown that, in Thomas' theology, the sacrament of penance is about a personal relationship with God, which in its deepest sense consists in the intimate presence of Father, Son and Spirit in our hearts as known and loved, and that we have shown that sacramentality is about God's active presence, visible and invisible, in our world, inviting us to join Him in the union of love which He himself is.

Bibliography

ALBERIGO, G. et al -- *Conciliorum Oecumenicorum Decreta*, 1973.

ASHWORTH, E. -- "Logic, Medieval", in: E. Graig, *Routledge Encyclopedia of Philosophy*, vol. 5, 1998, p.746-759.

BEEMER, TH. -- "Thomas on the extinction of guilt", in H. Schoot (ed), *'Tibi soli peccavi'. Thomas Aquinas on guilt and forgiveness*, 1996, pp.47-58.

BOEHNER O.F.M., PH. -- *Medieval Logic. An Outline of its Development from 1250 to c.1400*, 1966 (1952).

BOUILLARD, H. -- *Conversion et grace chez S. Thomas d'Aquin*, 1944.

BOYLE, J. -- "The ordering of trinitarian teaching in Thomas Aquinas' second commentary on Lombard's *Sentences*", in E. Manning (ed), *Thomistica*, (*Recherches de théologie ancienne et médiévale*, Suppl., vol 1), 1995, pp.125-136.

BRINKMAN, M. -- "Penance as an indispensable existential sacramental moment. A Protestant contribution", in H. Schoot (ed), *'Tibi soli peccavi'. Thomas Aquinas on guilt and forgiveness*, 1996, 97-122.

BRINKMAN, M. -- *Schepping en sacrament. Een oecumenische studie naar de reikwijdte van het sacrament als heilzaam symbool in een weerbarstige werkelijkheid*, 1991.

BURRELL, D. -- *Aquinas. God and Action*, 1979.

CASEL, O. -- *Das christliche Kultmysterium*, 1960⁴ (1932).

CHÂTILLON, J. -- "Unitas, aequalitas, concordia vel connexia. Recherches sur les origines de la théorie thomiste des appropriations", in *Thomas Aquinas 1274-1974. Commemorative studies*, 1974, pp. 337-380.

CHAUVET, L.-M, -- "Sacramentologie en Christologie", in J. Lamberts (ed), *Hedendagse accenten in de sacramententheologie*, 1994, pp.87-110.

CHAUVET, L.-M. -- *Symbol and sacrament. A sacramental reinterpretation of Christian existence*, 1995.

CHOLLET, A. -- "Analogie", in *Dictionnaire de théologie catholique*, t.I, col.

CHOLLET, A. -- "Appropriation aux personnes de la sainte Trinité", in *Dictionnaire de théologie catholique* I,2, 1931, pp.1708-1717.

Concilium, 1986/2.

CONGAR, Y. -- *I believe in the Holy Spirit*, 1997 (1983).

CORIDEN, J e.a. (ed) --*The Code of Canon Law A text and commentary*, commissioned by the Canon Law Society of America and edited by J.A. Coriden, T.J. Green, D.E. Heintschel, 1995.

CUNNINGHAM, D. -- *These three are one. The practice of trinitarian theology*, 1998.

CUSCHIERI, A. -- *The sacrament of reconciliation. A theological and canonical treatise*, 1992.

DEFERRARI, R. -- *A Latin-English dictionary of St. Thomas Aquinas*, 1986.

DENZINGER, H. -- *Enchiridion symbolorum definitionum et declarationum de rebus fidei et morum*. Kompendium der Glaubensbekenntnisse und kirchliche Lehrentscheidungen. Lateinisch - Deutsch. Herausgegeben von P. Hünermann, 1999³⁸.

DILLEN, A. -- "Vergeving of 'exoneratie'? Kritische kanttekeningen vanuit en bij de theorie van Ivan-Boszormenyi-Nagy", in *Tijdschrift voor theologie* 41, 2001, pp.61-84.

DUFFY, R. -- "Penance", in F. Schüssler Fiorenza, J. Galvin (eds), *Systematic theology. Roman Catholic perspectives*, vol. 2, 1991, pp.233-249.

DUFFY, S. -- *The dynamics of grace. Perspectives in theological anthropology*, 1993.

EMERY, G. -- "Essentialism or personalism in the treatise on God in Saint Thomas Aquinas", in *The Thomist* 64, 2000, pp.521-563.

EMERY, G. -- "Trinité et création. Le principe trinitaire de la création dans les commentaires d'Albert le Grand, de Bonaventure en de Thomas d'Aquin sur les *Sentences*", in *Revue des Sciences philosophiques et theologiques* 79, 1995, pp.405-430.

GORIS, H. -- *Free Creatures of an Eternal God. Thomas on God's infallible foreknowledge and irresistible will*, 1996.

GRIJS, F. DE -- "Spreken over God en Thomasinterpretatie", in *Jaarboek 1984 van het Thomasinstituut te Utrecht*, pp.7-38.

HAIGHT, R. -- "Sin and grace", in F. Schüssler Fiorenza, J. Galvin (eds), *Systematic theology. Roman Catholic perspectives*, vol. 2, 1991, pp.75-141.

HIBBERT, G. -- "Mystery and metaphysics in the trinitarian theology if Saint Thomas", in *Irish Theological Quarterly* 31, 1964, pp.187-213.

HILL, E. -- "Karl Rahner's remarks on the dogmatic treatise De Trinitate and St. Augustine", in *Augustinian studies*, vol. 2, 1971, pp.67-80.

HILL, E. -- "St. Augustine's *De Trinitate*. The doctrinal significance of its structure", in *Revue des Etudes Augustiniennes* 19, 1973, pp.277-286.

HILL, E. -- *St. Augustine. The Trinity. Introduction, translation, notes*, 1991.

Hill, W. -- *The Three-Personed God. The Trinity as a Mystery of Salvation*, 1982.

JORDAN, M. -- "Error, failure and sin in Thomas's *peccatum*", in *Jaarboek 1996 van het Thomasinstituut te Utrecht*, 1996, pp, 11-36.

KIECKHEFER, R. -- *Magic in the Middle Ages*, 1989.

KOCH. K. -- "Die eine Botschaft von der Versöhnung im vielfältigen Wandel des Busssakramentes", in J. (hrsg), Müller, *Das ungeliebte Sakrament. Grundriss einer neuen Busspraxis*, 1995, pp.93-117.

KOFFEMAN, L.J. -- *Kerk als sacramentum. De rol van de sacramentele ecclesiologie tijdens Vaticanum II*, 1986.

KURTSCHIED, B. -- *Das Biechtsiegel in seiner geschichtliche Entwicklung*, 1912.

LACUGNA, C. "The trinitarian mystery of God", in F. Schüssler Fiorenza, J. Galvin (eds), *Systematic theology. Roman Catholic perspectives*, vol. 1, 1991, pp.149-192.

LASCARIS, A. -- "Kan God vergeven als het slachtoffer niet vergeeft?", in: *Tijdschrift voor Theologie* 1, 39 (1999), pp.48-68 (with a summary in English).

LASH, N. -- *Believing three ways in one God. A reading of the Apostles' creed*, 1994².

LEGET, C. -- *Living with God. Thomas Aquinas on the relation between life on earth and 'life' after death*, 1997.

LEGET, C. -- *Thomas van Aquino. Over het Onzevader en het Weesgegroet*, 2000.

LIES, L. -- "Trinitätsvergessenheit gegenwärtiger Sakramententheologie?", in *Zeitschrift für katholische Theologie* 105, 1983, pp.290-314.

LONERGAN, B. -- *Grace and freedom. Operative grace in the thought of St. Thomas Aquinas*, (Collected works of Bernard Lonergan, vol. 1), 2000.

MAHONEY, J. -- *The making of moral theology. A study of the Roman Catholic tradition*, 1987.

MALONEY, G. -- *Your sins are forgiven you. Rediscovering the sacrament of reconciliation*, 1999.

MANTHEY, F. -- *Die Sprachphilosophie des hl. Thomas von Aquin und ihre Anwendung auf Probleme der Theologie*, 1937.

MCGRATH, A. -- *Iustitia Dei. A history of the Christian doctrine of justification*, Second edition, 1998.

MCINERNY, R. -- "The analogy of names is a logical doctrine", in *Atti del congresso internazionale (Roma-Napoli-17/24 aprile 1974) Tommaso d'Aquino nel suo settimo centenario, VI: l'Essere*, 1978.

MCINERNY, R. -- *The logic of analogy. An interpretation of St. Thomas*, 1961.

MCNEILL, J., GAMER, H. -- *Medieval handbooks of penance. A translation of the principal Libri Poenitentiales*, 1990.

MERZ, R. -- *Die Generalabsolution als ausserordentliche Spendeweise des Busssakramentes: Herkunft, Ortsbestimmung, Grenzen*, 1992.

MESSNER, R. -- *Feiern der Umkehr und Versöhnung (Handbuch der Liturgiewissenschaft 7,2)*, 1992.

MÜHLEN, H. -- "Person und Appropriation. Zum Verständniss des Axioms: In Deo sunt unum, ubi non obviat relationis oppositio", in *Münchener theologische Zeitschrift* 16, 1965, pp.37-57.

MÜLLER, G. -- *Katholische Dogmatik für Studium und Praxis der Theologie*, 2000[4].

NEWMAN, J. -- *An essay in aid of a grammar of assent*, 1992[4] (1979).

O'CARROLL, "Appropriation", in *Trinitas: a theological encyclopedia of the Holy Trinity*, 1987, p.16.

O'NEIL, C. -- *St. Thomas Aquinas. On the truth of the catholic faith. Summa contra gentiles*, book four: Salvation, 1957.

O'ROURKE BOYLE, M. -- "Chaff: Thomas Aquinas's repudiation of his *Opera omnia*", in *New Literary History* 28, 1997, pp.383-399.

PARK, S.-C. -- *Die Rezeption der mittelalterlichen Sprachphilosophie in der Theologie des Thomas von Aquin. Mit besonderer Berücksichtigung der Analogie*, 1999.

PESCH, O.H. -- *Das zweite vatikanische Konzil. Vorgeschichte Verlauf-Ergebnisse Nachgeschichte*, 1994.

PESCH, O.H. -- *Die Theologie der Rechtfertigung vei Martin Luther und Thomas von Aquin: Versuch eines systematisch-theologischen Dialogs*, 1967.

PESCH, O.H. -- *Hinführung zu Luther*, 1993[2] (1982).

PESCH, O.H. -- *Thomas von Aquin. Grenze und Grösse mittelalterlicher Theologie*, 1995[3] (1988).

PESCH, O.H., A. Peters -- *Einführung in die Lehre von Gnade und Rechtfertigung*, 1989.

PIEPER, J. -- *Über den Begriff der Sünde*, 1977.

PINBORG, J. -- *Die Entwicklung der Sprachtheorie im Mittelalter*, 1967.

PINBORG, J. -- *Logik und Semantik im Mittelalter. Ein Überblick*, 1972.

POSCHMANN, B. -- *Busse und Letzte Ölung (Handbuch der Dogmengeschichte* IV, 3), 1951.

RAHNER, K. -- "Beichtprobleme", in *Schriften zur theologie* III, 1956, pp.227-245.

RAHNER, K. -- "Bemerkungen zum dogmatischen Traktat «De Trinitate»", in *Schriften zur Theologie* IV, 1962.

RAHNER, K. -- "Der dreifaltige Gott als transzendenter Urgrund der Heilsgeschichte", in *Mysterium salutis*, Bd. 2, pp.317-401.

RAHNER, K. -- "Einleitende Bemerkungen zur allgemeine Sakramentenlehre bei Thomas von Aquin", in *Schriften zur theologie* X, 1972, pp.392-404.

RAHNER, K. -- "Vergessene Wahrheiten über das Busssakrament", in *Schriften zur Theologie* II, 1955, pp.143-185.

RAHNER, K. -- "Vom Sinn der häufigen Andachtsbeichte", in *Schriften zur Theologie* III, 1956, pp.211-225.

RAHNER, K. -- Das Sakrament der Busse als Wiederversöhnung mit der Kirche", in *Schriften zur Theologie* VIII, 1967, pp.447-471.

RAHNER, K. -- *Kirche und sacrament*, 1960.

RIJK, L. DE -- "The origin of the theory of the properties of terms", in: Kretzmann, Kenny, Pinborg (Ed.), *The Cambridge History of Later Medieval Philosophy*, 1982, pp.161-173.

RIJK, L. DE -- *Logica Modernorum. A Contribution to the History of early terminist logic*, 1962 (2 vols).

RIJK, L. DE -- *Middeleeuwse wijsbegeerte. Traditie en vernieuwing*, 1977.

RIKHOF, H. -- "Trinity in Thomas. Reading the Summa theologiae against the background of modern problems", in *Jaarboek 1999 van het Thomas Instituut*, pp.83-100.

RIKHOF, H. -- *Lumen Cordium*, Catholic Theological University at Utrecht, 1993.

RIKHOF, H. -- *Over God spreken. Een tekst van Thomas van Aquino uit de Summa theologiae. Vertaald, ingeleid en van aantekeningen voorzien door dr. H.W.M. Rikhof*, 1988.

RIKHOF. H. -- "Corpus Christi Mysticum, An inquiry into Tomas Aquinas' use of a term", in *Bijdragen. Tijdschrift voor filosofie en theologie* 37, 1976, pp.149-171.

ROCCA, G. -- "The distinction between *res significata* and *modus significandi* in Aquinas's theological epistemology", in *The Thomist* 55, 1991, pp.173-197.

ROUWHORST, G. -- "De viering van bekering en verzoening", in *Tijdschrift voor liturgie* 81, 1997, pp.29-42.

RUYS, TH. -- "De E-8. Mijmeringen langs de snelweg", in: *Een lange adem. Opstellen over kerk en beleid in het artsbisdom Utrecht*, 1993, pp.37-49.

SABRA, G. -- *Thomas Aquinas' Vision of the Church. Fundamentals of an ecumenical Ecclesiology*, 1987.

SALMANN, E. -- "Appropriation", in *Lexicon für Theologie und Kirche* 1, 1993, pp.891-892.

SCHILLEBEECKX, E. -- "Het niet begrippelijke kenmoment in de geloofsdaad: een probleemstelling", in id., *Openbaring en theologie*, 1964, pp.233-261 (originally published in *Tijdschrift voor theologie* 3, 1963, pp.167-194).

SCHILLEBEECKX, E. -- *Christus Sacrament van de Godsontmoeting*, 1959³.

SCHILLEBEECKX, E. -- *De sacramentele heilseconomie. Theologische bezinning op S. Thomas' sacramentenleer in het licht van de traditie en van de hedendaagse sacramentsproblematiek*, 1952.

SCHMAUS, M. -- "Appropriation", in *Lexicon für Theologie und Kirche* 1, 1957, pp.773-775.

SCHMIDBAUR, H.C. -- *Personarum Trinitas. Die trinitarische Gotteslehre des heiligen Thomas von Aquin*, 1995.

SCHNEIDER, TH. -- *Zeichen der Nähe Gottes. Grundriss der Sakramententheologie*, 1979.

SCHOOF, T. -- "Jezus, Gods werktuig voor ons heil. Peilingen naar de theologische procedure van Thomas van Aquino", in *Tijdschrift voor theologie* 14, 1974, pp.217-244.

SCHOOT, H. -- *Christ the 'name' of God. Thomas Aquinas on naming Christ*, 1993.

SECKLER, M. -- *Instinkt und Glaubenswille nach Thomas von Aquin*, 1962.

SEMMELROTH, O. -- *Die Kirche als Ursakrament*, 1953.

SEMMELROTH, O. -- "Die Kirche als Sakrament des Heils", in *Mysterium salutis* IV,1, 1972, pp.309-356.

SMITH, T. -- "The context and character of Thomas' theory of appropriations", in *The Thomist* 63, 1999, pp. 579-612.

SMULDERS, P. -- "De kerk als sacrament van het heil", in G. Baraúna, *De kerk van Vaticanum II. Commentaren op de Concilieconstitutie Over de kerk*, 1966, pp.372-395.

SOBRINO, J. - "Latijns-Amerika: plaats van zonde, plaats van vergiffenis", in *Concilium*, 1986/2.

SOKOLOWSKI, R. -- *The God of faith and reason. Foundations of Christian theology*, 1982.

STRÄTER, C. -- "Het begrip 'appropriatie' bij S. Thomas", in *Bijdragen. Tijdschrift voor filosofie en theologie* 9, 1948, pp.1-41; 144-186.

STRIJARDS, H. -- *Schuld en pastoraat. Een poimenische studie over schuld als thema voor het pastoraal groepsgesprek*, 1997.

TANNER, N. -- *The decrees of the ecumenical councils*, 1990.

TORRELL, J.-P. -- *Saint Thomas Aquinas. Vol.1. The person and his work*. Transl. by R. Royal, 1996.

VANHOUTTE, K. -- "Kome over ons uw Geest. De aanroeping van de Geest in de sacramenten", in *Tijdschrift voor liturgie* 82, 1998, p.59-81.

VOGEL, C. -- *Le pécheur et la penitence au Moyen-Age*, 1969.

VOGEL, C. -- *Le pécheur et la penitence dans l'église ancienne*, 1966.

VORGRIMMLER, H. -- "The sacrament of reconciliation", in id., *Sacramental theology*, 1992, p.200-225.

VORGRIMMLER, H. -- *Busse und Krankensalbung (Handbuch der Dogmengeschichte IV, 3)*, 1978.

WALGRAVE, J. -- "Instinctus Spritus Sancti. Een proeve tot Thomas-interpretatie", in J. Walgrave, *Selected writings*, 1982, pp.126-140 (originally published in: *Ephimerides theologicae Lovaniensis* 45, 1969, pp.153-167).

WAWRYKOV, J. -- *God's grace and human action. 'Merit' in the theology of Thomas Aquinas*, 1995.

WEISHEIPL, J. -- *Friar Thomas Aquinas: his life, thought, and works*, 1983[2] (1974).

WISSINK, J. -- "De sacramenten geven de kruisgenade die ze betekenen. Over het verband tussen het heilswerk van Christus en de sacramenten", in A. van Eijk, H. Rikhof, *De lengte en de breedte, de hoogte en de diepte. Peilingen in de theologie van de sacramenten*, 1996, pp.234-261.

WISSINK, J. -- "Satisfaction as part of penance. According to Thomas Aquinas." in H. Schoot (ed), *'Tibi soli peccavi'. Thomas Aquinas on guilt and forgiveness*, 1996, pp.75-95.

WISSINK, J. -- *Thomas van Aquino. De actuele betekenis van zijn theologie. Een inleiding*, 1998.

XIBERTA, B. -- *Clavis ecclesiae. De ordine absolutionis sacramentalis ad reconciliationem cum ecclesia*, Romae, 1922.

Index

Index locorum

Index nominum

PRINTED ON PERMANENT PAPER • IMPRIME SUR PAPIER PERMANENT • GEDRUKT OP DUURZAAM PAPIER - ISO 9706

N.V. PEETERS S.A., WAROTSTRAAT 50, B-3020 HERENT